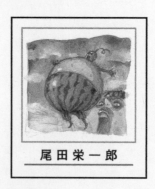

尾田栄一郎

I...I've been lied to*!!!*
Is it possible...that when you swallow watermelon seeds...
They don't grow inside your tummy*?!*
Is it possible that Volume 83 is about to start*?!*

-Eiichiro Oda, 2016

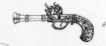

iichiro Oda began his manga career at the age of
17, when his one-shot cowboy manga **Wanted!**
won second place in the coveted Tezuka manga
awards. Oda went on to work as an assistant to
some of the biggest manga artists in the industry,
including Nobuhiro Watsuki, before winning the
Hop Step Award for new artists. His pirate
adventure **One Piece**, which debuted in
Weekly Shonen Jump in 1997, quickly became
one of the most popular manga in Japan.

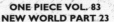

ONE PIECE VOL. 83
NEW WORLD PART 23

SHONEN JUMP Manga Edition

STORY AND ART BY EIICHIRO ODA

Translation/Stephen Paul
Touch-up Art & Lettering/Vanessa Satone
Design/Yukiko Whitley
Editor/Alexis Kirsch

Printed in the U.S.A.

Published by VIZ Media, LLC
P.O. Box 77010
San Francisco, CA 94107

10 9 8 7 6 5 4 3 2 1
First printing, August 2017

www.viz.com

PARENTAL ADVISORY
ONE PIECE is rated T for Teen and is recommended
for ages 13 and up. This volume contains fantasy
violence and tobacco usage.
ratings.viz.com

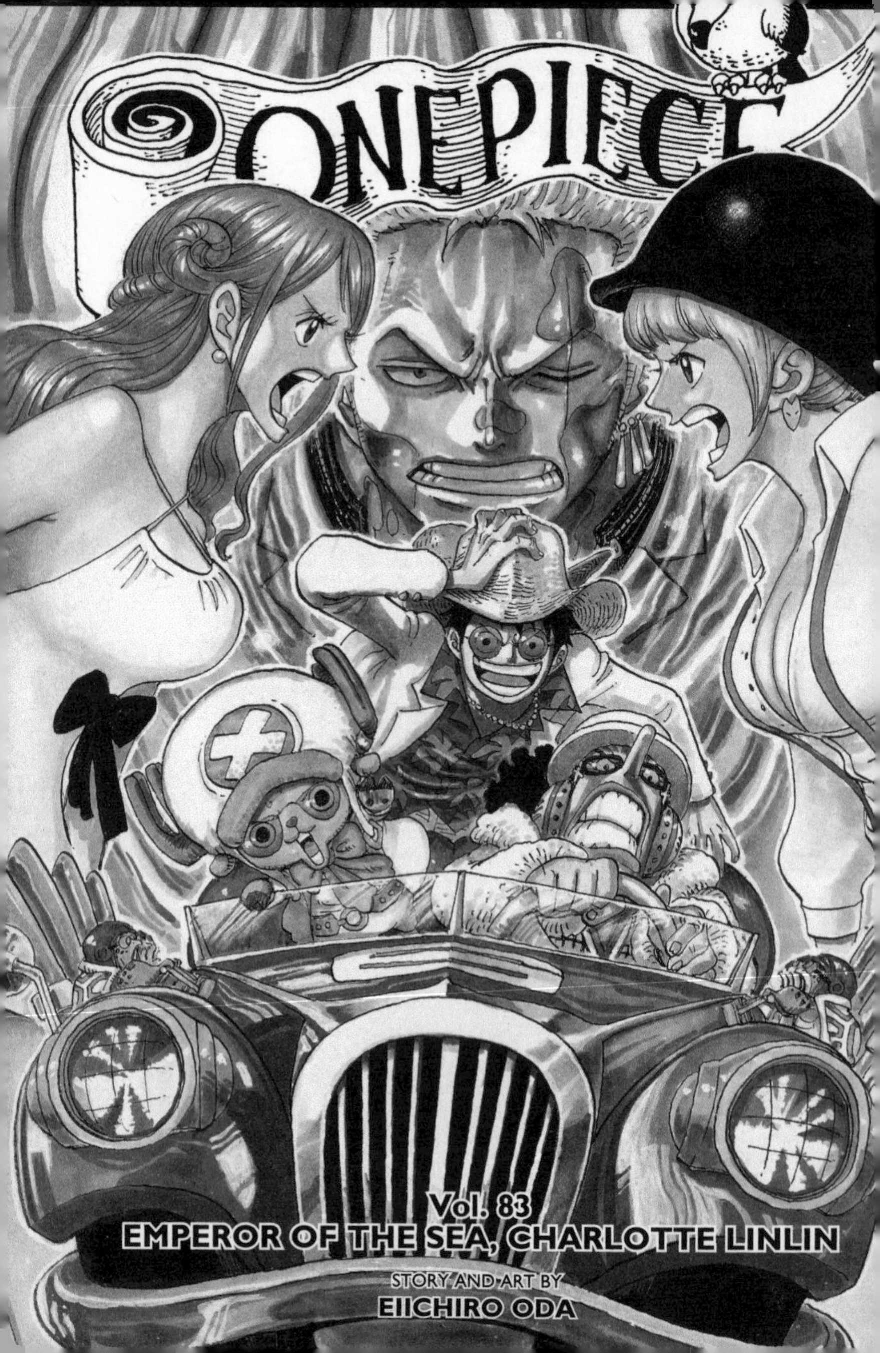
ONE PIECE

Vol. 83

EMPEROR OF THE SEA, CHARLOTTE LINLIN

STORY AND ART BY

EIICHIRO ODA

The Straw Hat Crew

Monkey D. Luffy

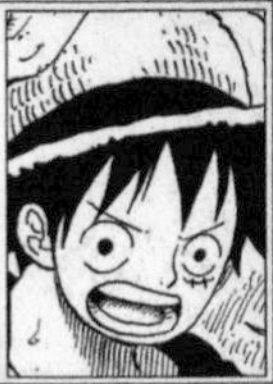

A young man who dreams of becoming the Pirate King. After training with Rayleigh, he and his crew head for the New World!

Captain, Bounty: 500 million berries

Roronoa Zolo

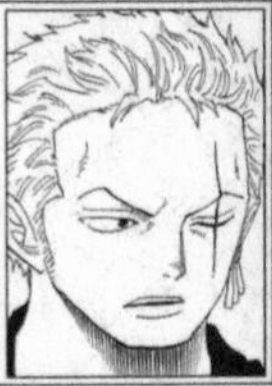

He swallowed his pride and asked to be trained by Mihawk on Gloom Island before reuniting with the rest of the crew.

Fighter, Bounty: 320 million berries

Nami

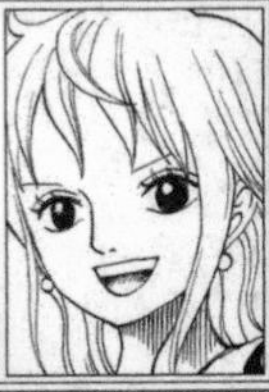

She studied the weather of the New World on the small Sky Island Weatheria, a place where weather is studied as a science.

Navigator, Bounty: 66 million berries

Usopp

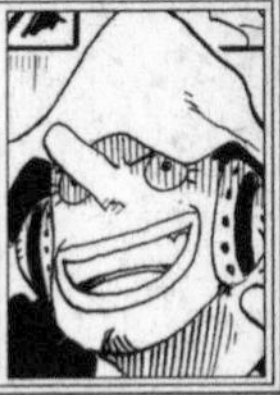

He trained under Heracles at the Bowin Islands to become the King of Snipers.

Sniper, Bounty: 200 million berries

Sanji

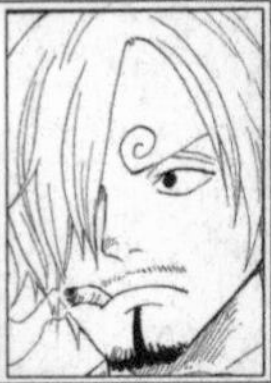

After fighting the New Kama Karate masters in the Kamabakka Kingdom, he returned to the crew.

Cook, Bounty: 177 million berries

Tony Tony Chopper

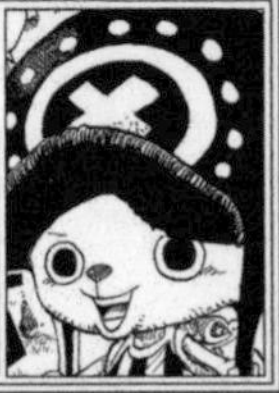

After researching powerful medicine in Birdie Kingdom, he reunited with the rest of the crew.

Ship's Doctor, Bounty: 100 berries

Nico Robin

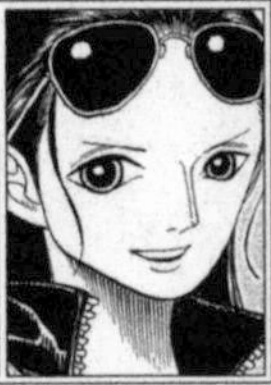

She spent her time in Baltigo with the leader of the Revolutionary Army: Luffy's father, Dragon.

Archeologist, Bounty: 130 million berries

Franky

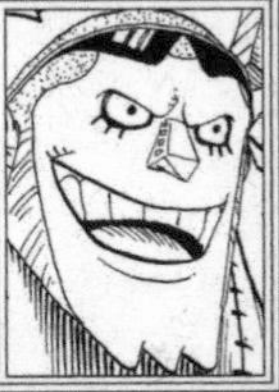

He modified himself in Future Land Baldimore and turned himself into Armored Franky before reuniting with the rest of the crew.

Shipwright, Bounty: 94 million berries

Brook

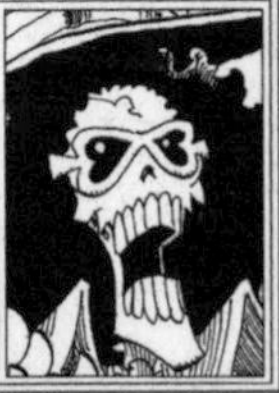

After being captured and used as a freak show by the Longarm Tribe, he became a famous rock star called "Soul King" Brook.

Musician, Bounty: 83 million berries

Shanks

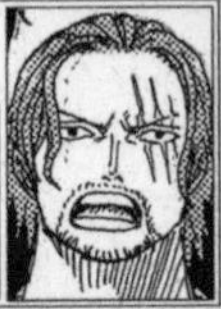

One of the Four Emperors. Waits for Luffy in the "New World," the second half of the Grand Line.

Captain of the Red-Haired Pirates

from his control. Then, in order to topple Kaido, the crew forms an alliance with the samurai and the minks of Zou...but meanwhile, Sanji is in terrible danger. His true father has arranged a political marriage for him with Big Mom's daughter. Sanji heads to Big Mom's island in order to refuse the marriage while the rest of the crew splits up. Half head to Wano, and the rest sail to Big Mom's Whole Cake Island to get their cook back...

The story of ONE PIECE 1»83

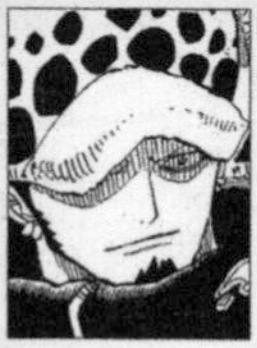

Trafalgar Law

Captain of the Heart Pirates

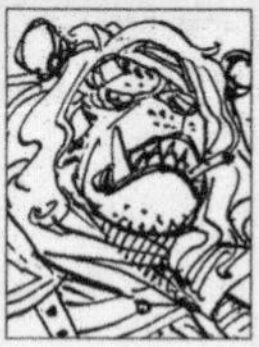

Treetop Pedro (Jaguar Mink)

Leader of the Guardians

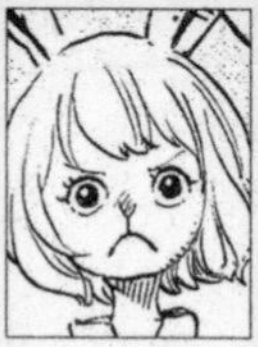

Carrot (Bunny Mink)

Battlebeast Tribe

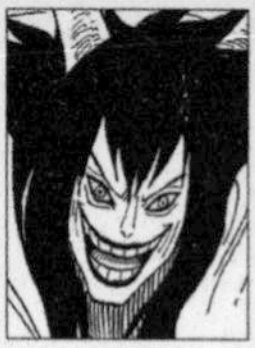

Caesar Clown

Former Govt Scientist

Big Mom Pirates

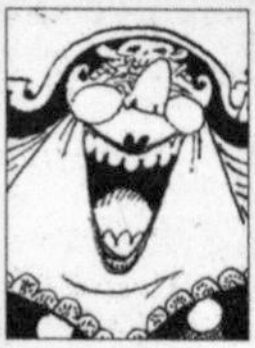

Charlotte Linlin

Captain, Big Mom Pirates

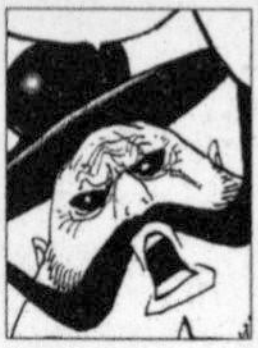

Baron Tamago

Fighter, Big Mom Pirates

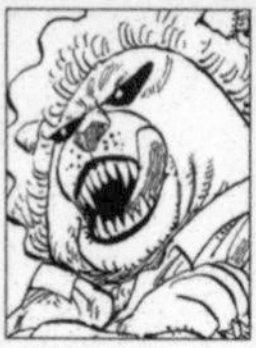

Pekoms

Fighter, Big Mom Pirates

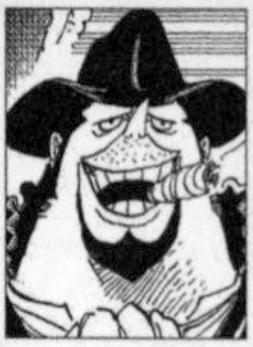

Capone "Gang" Bege

Captain of the Firetank Pirates

Germa 66

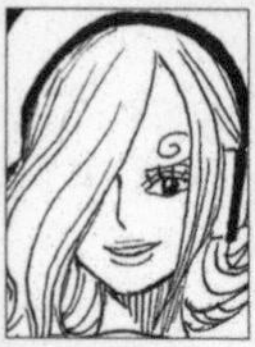

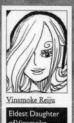

Vinsmoke Reiju

Eldest Daughter of Vinsmoke

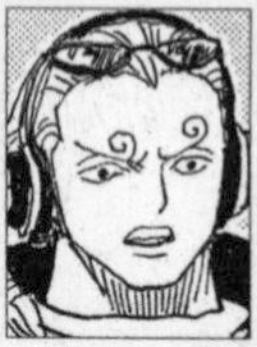

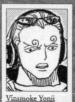

Vinsmoke Yonji

Fourth Son of Vinsmoke

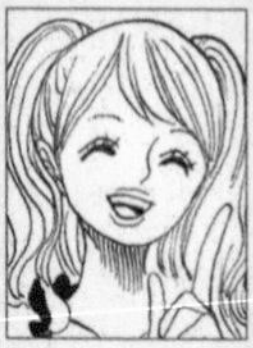

Charlotte Pudding

35th Daughter of Charlotte

Story

After two years of hard training, the Straw Hat pirates are back together, first at the Sabaody Archipelago and then through Fish-Man Island to their next stage: the New World!!

The crew happens across Trafalgar Law on the island of Punk Hazard. At his suggestion, they form a new pirate alliance that seeks to take down one of the Four Emperors. The group infiltrates the kingdom of Dressrosa in an attempt to topple Doflamingo, Kaido's trading partner, and find themselves in a battle to liberate the kingdom

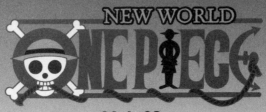

Vol. 83
EMPEROR OF THE SEA, CHARLOTTE LINLIN

CONTENTS

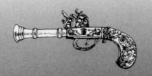

Chapter 828:
1 AND 2

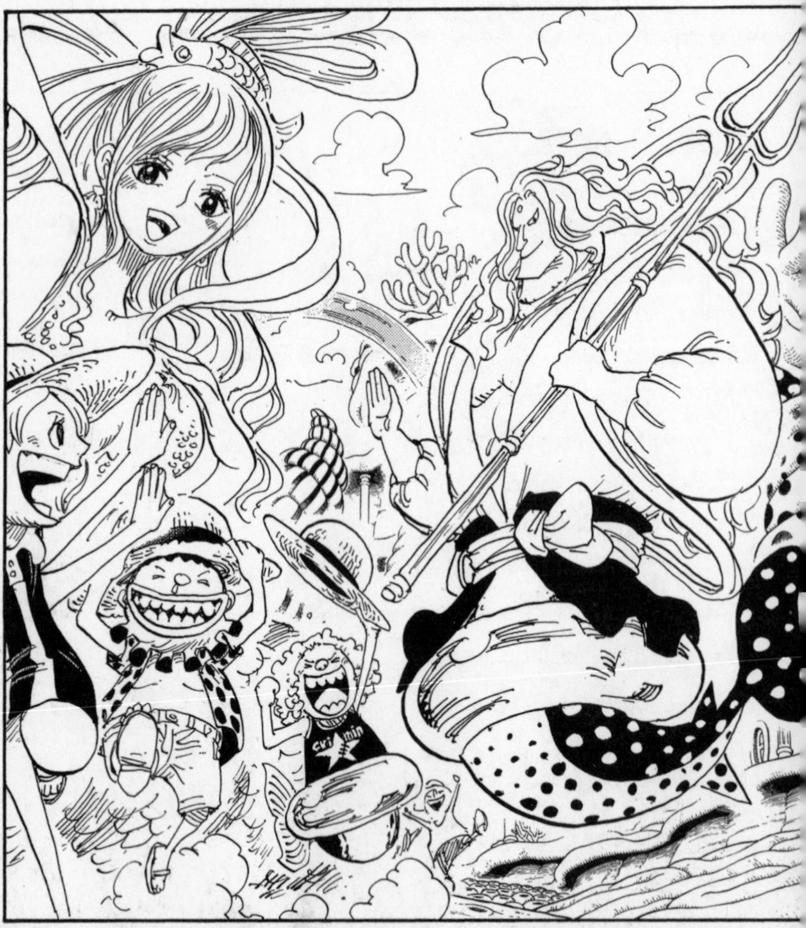

DECKS OF THE WORLD, 500-MILLION-MAN ARC, VOL. 19:
"FISH-MAN ISLAND--THOSE POPULAR HERO HATS"

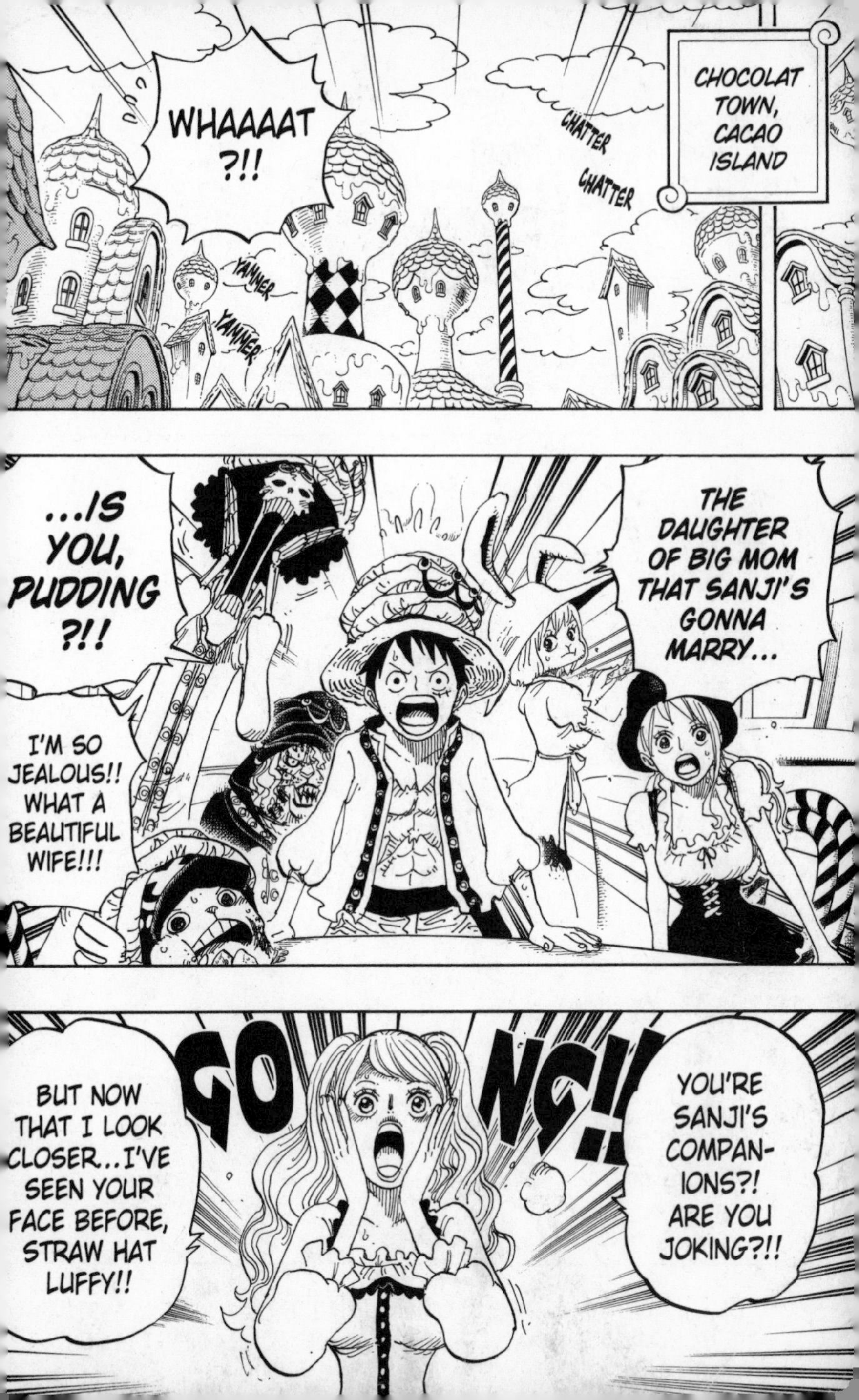
CHOCOLAT TOWN, CACAO ISLAND
CHATTER
CHATTER
WHAAAAT ?!!
YAMMER
YAMMER
THE DAUGHTER OF BIG MOM THAT SANJI'S GONNA MARRY...
...IS YOU, PUDDING ?!!
I'M SO JEALOUS!! WHAT A BEAUTIFUL WIFE!!!
YOU'RE SANJI'S COMPAN-IONS?! ARE YOU JOKING?!!
GONG!!
BUT NOW THAT I LOOK CLOSER...I'VE SEEN YOUR FACE BEFORE, STRAW HAT LUFFY!!

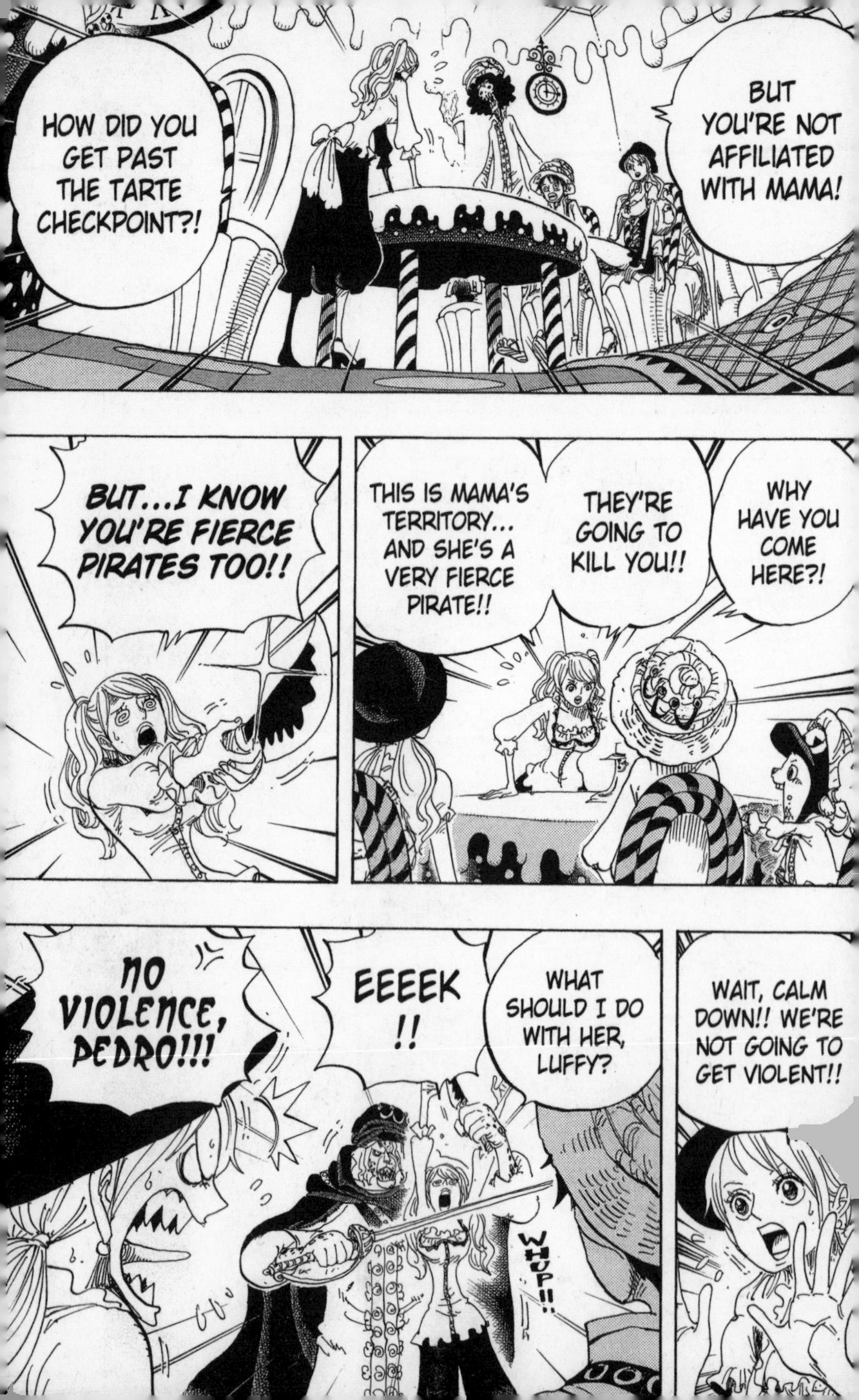
BUT YOU'RE NOT AFFILIATED WITH MAMA!
HOW DID YOU GET PAST THE TARTE CHECKPOINT?!
WHY HAVE YOU COME HERE?!
THEY'RE GOING TO KILL YOU!!
THIS IS MAMA'S TERRITORY... AND SHE'S A VERY FIERCE PIRATE!!
BUT...I KNOW YOU'RE FIERCE PIRATES TOO!!
WAIT, CALM DOWN!! WE'RE NOT GOING TO GET VIOLENT!!
WHAT SHOULD I DO WITH HER, LUFFY?
EEEEK !!
NO VIOLENCE, PEDRO!!!
WHUP!!

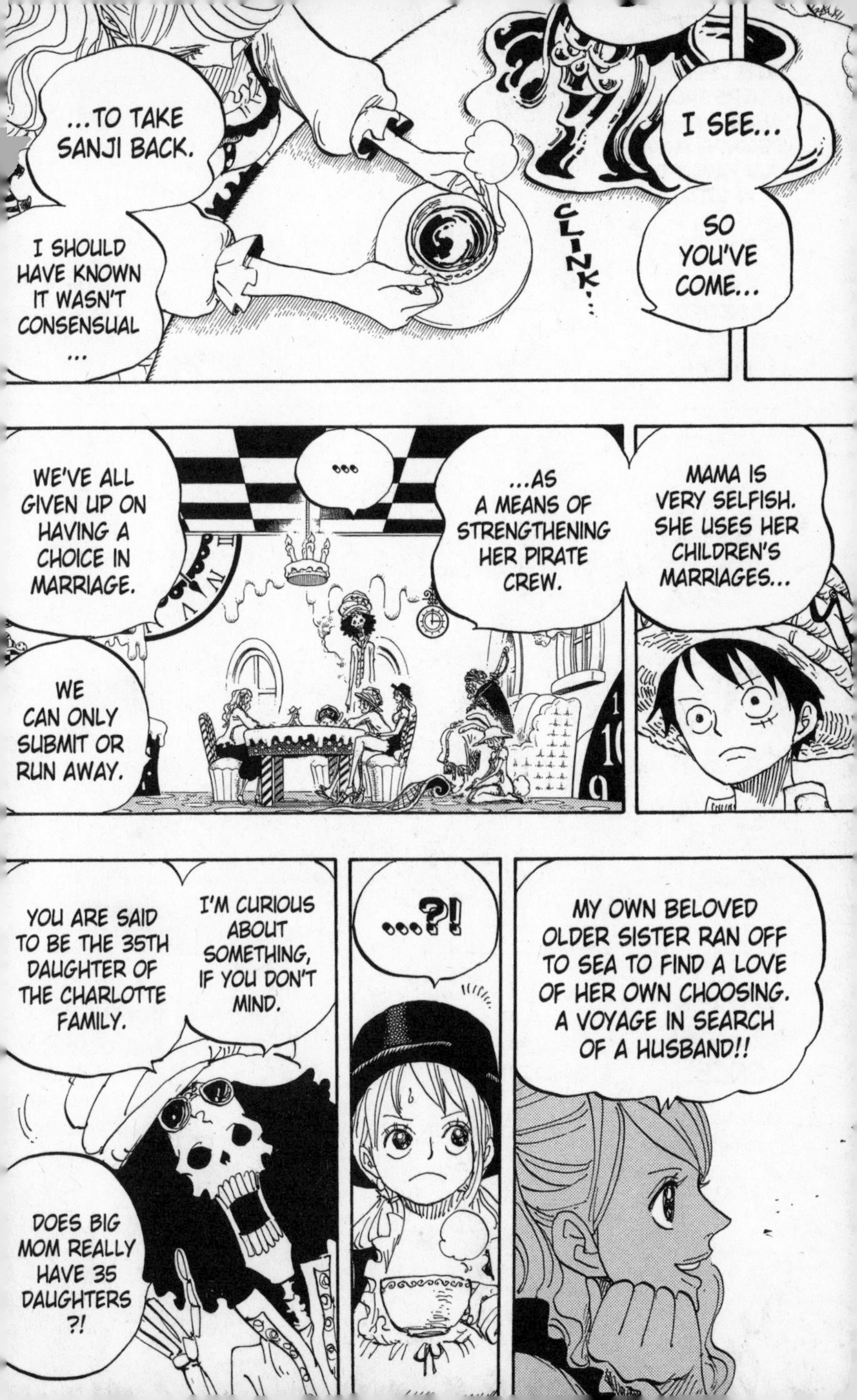
I SEE...
SO YOU'VE COME...
...TO TAKE SANJI BACK.
CLINK...
I SHOULD HAVE KNOWN IT WASN'T CONSENSUAL...
MAMA IS VERY SELFISH. SHE USES HER CHILDREN'S MARRIAGES...
...AS A MEANS OF STRENGTHENING HER PIRATE CREW.
...
WE'VE ALL GIVEN UP ON HAVING A CHOICE IN MARRIAGE.
WE CAN ONLY SUBMIT OR RUN AWAY.
MY OWN BELOVED OLDER SISTER RAN OFF TO SEA TO FIND A LOVE OF HER OWN CHOOSING. A VOYAGE IN SEARCH OF A HUSBAND!!
...?!
I'M CURIOUS ABOUT SOMETHING, IF YOU DON'T MIND.
YOU ARE SAID TO BE THE 35TH DAUGHTER OF THE CHARLOTTE FAMILY.
DOES BIG MOM REALLY HAVE 35 DAUGHTERS?!

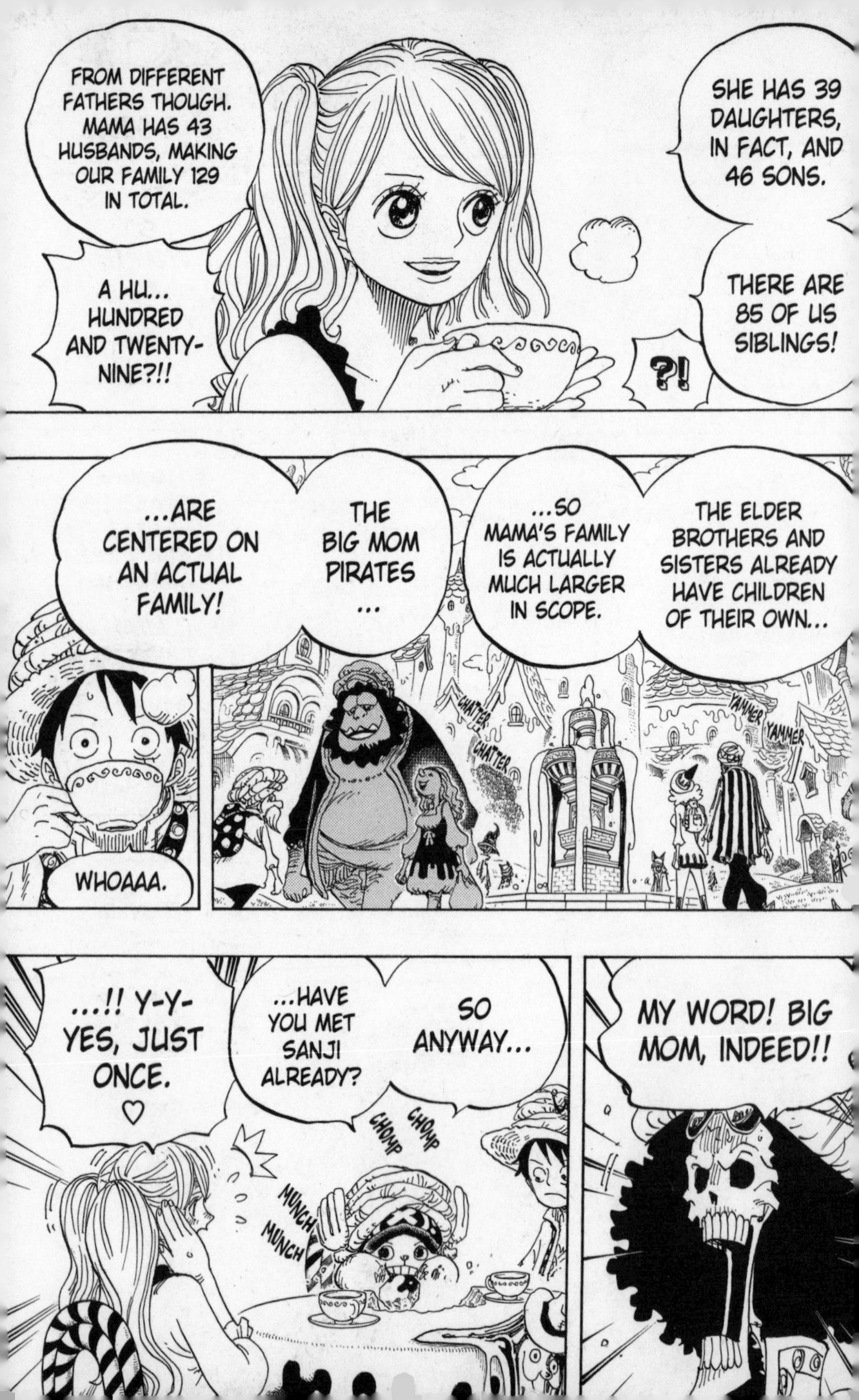
THERE ARE 85 OF US SIBLINGS!
?!
SHE HAS 39 DAUGHTERS, IN FACT, AND 46 SONS.
FROM DIFFERENT FATHERS THOUGH. MAMA HAS 43 HUSBANDS, MAKING OUR FAMILY 129 IN TOTAL.
A HU... HUNDRED AND TWENTY-NINE?!!
THE ELDER BROTHERS AND SISTERS ALREADY HAVE CHILDREN OF THEIR OWN...
...SO MAMA'S FAMILY IS ACTUALLY MUCH LARGER IN SCOPE.
THE BIG MOM PIRATES ...
...ARE CENTERED ON AN ACTUAL FAMILY!
YAMMER
YAMMER
CHATTER
CHATTER
WHOAAA.
MY WORD! BIG MOM, INDEED!!
SO ANYWAY...
...HAVE YOU MET SANJI ALREADY?
CHOMP
CHOMP
MUNCH
MUNCH
...!! Y-Y-YES, JUST ONCE. ♡

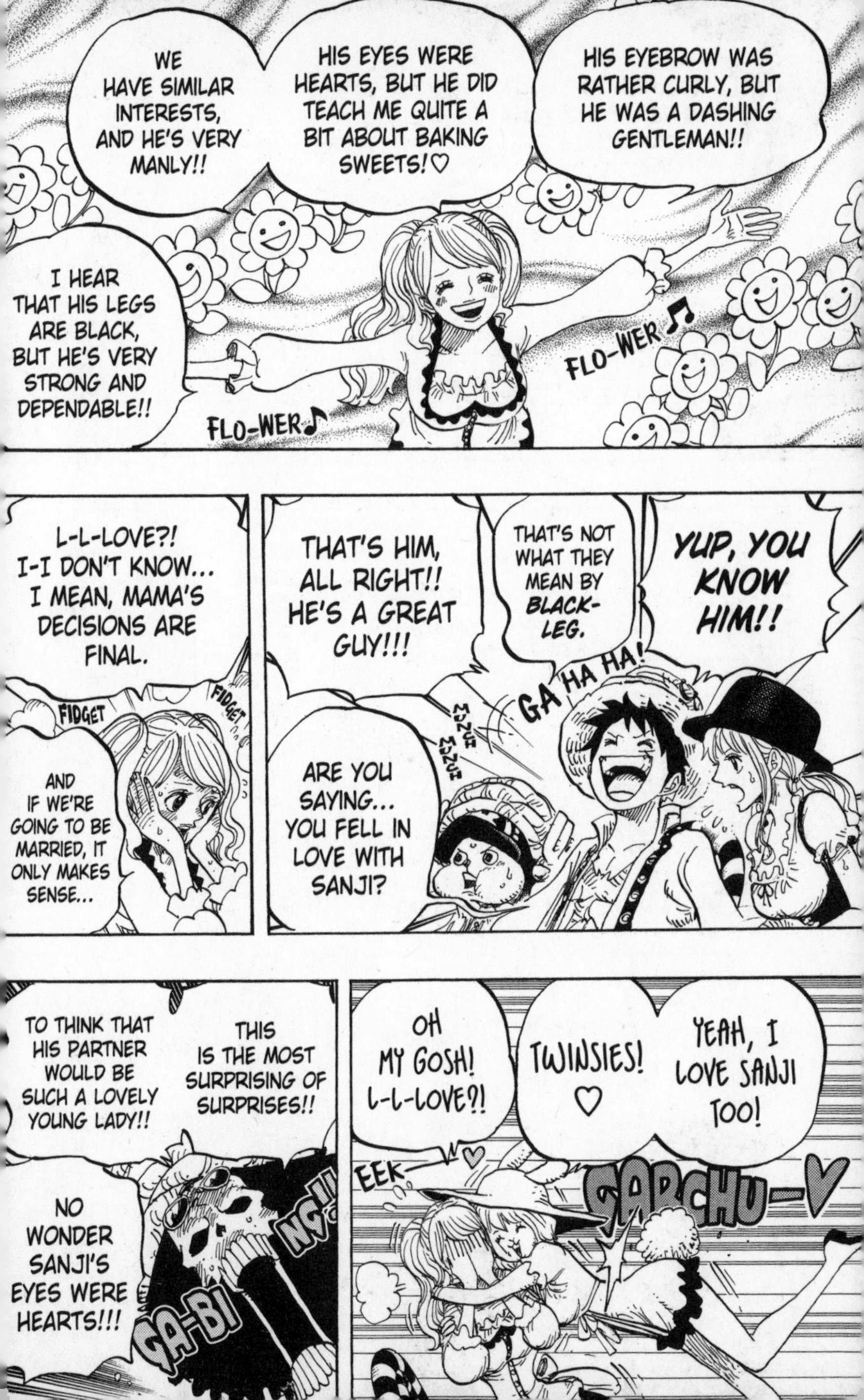
HIS EYEBROW WAS RATHER CURLY, BUT HE WAS A DASHING GENTLEMAN!!
HIS EYES WERE HEARTS, BUT HE DID TEACH ME QUITE A BIT ABOUT BAKING SWEETS! ♡
WE HAVE SIMILAR INTERESTS, AND HE'S VERY MANLY!!
FLO-WER ♫
I HEAR THAT HIS LEGS ARE BLACK, BUT HE'S VERY STRONG AND DEPENDABLE!!
FLO-WER ♪
YUP, YOU KNOW HIM!!
THAT'S NOT WHAT THEY MEAN BY BLACK-LEG.
GA HA HA!
THAT'S HIM, ALL RIGHT!! HE'S A GREAT GUY!!!
MUNCH MUNCH
ARE YOU SAYING... YOU FELL IN LOVE WITH SANJI?
L-L-LOVE?! I-I DON'T KNOW... I MEAN, MAMA'S DECISIONS ARE FINAL.
FIDGET
FIDGET
AND IF WE'RE GOING TO BE MARRIED, IT ONLY MAKES SENSE...
YEAH, I LOVE SANJI TOO!
TWINSIES! ♡
OH MY GOSH! L-L-LOVE?!
GARCHU-♥
EEK ♥
THIS IS THE MOST SURPRISING OF SURPRISES!!
TO THINK THAT HIS PARTNER WOULD BE SUCH A LOVELY YOUNG LADY!!
NG!!
NO WONDER SANJI'S EYES WERE HEARTS!!!
GA-BI

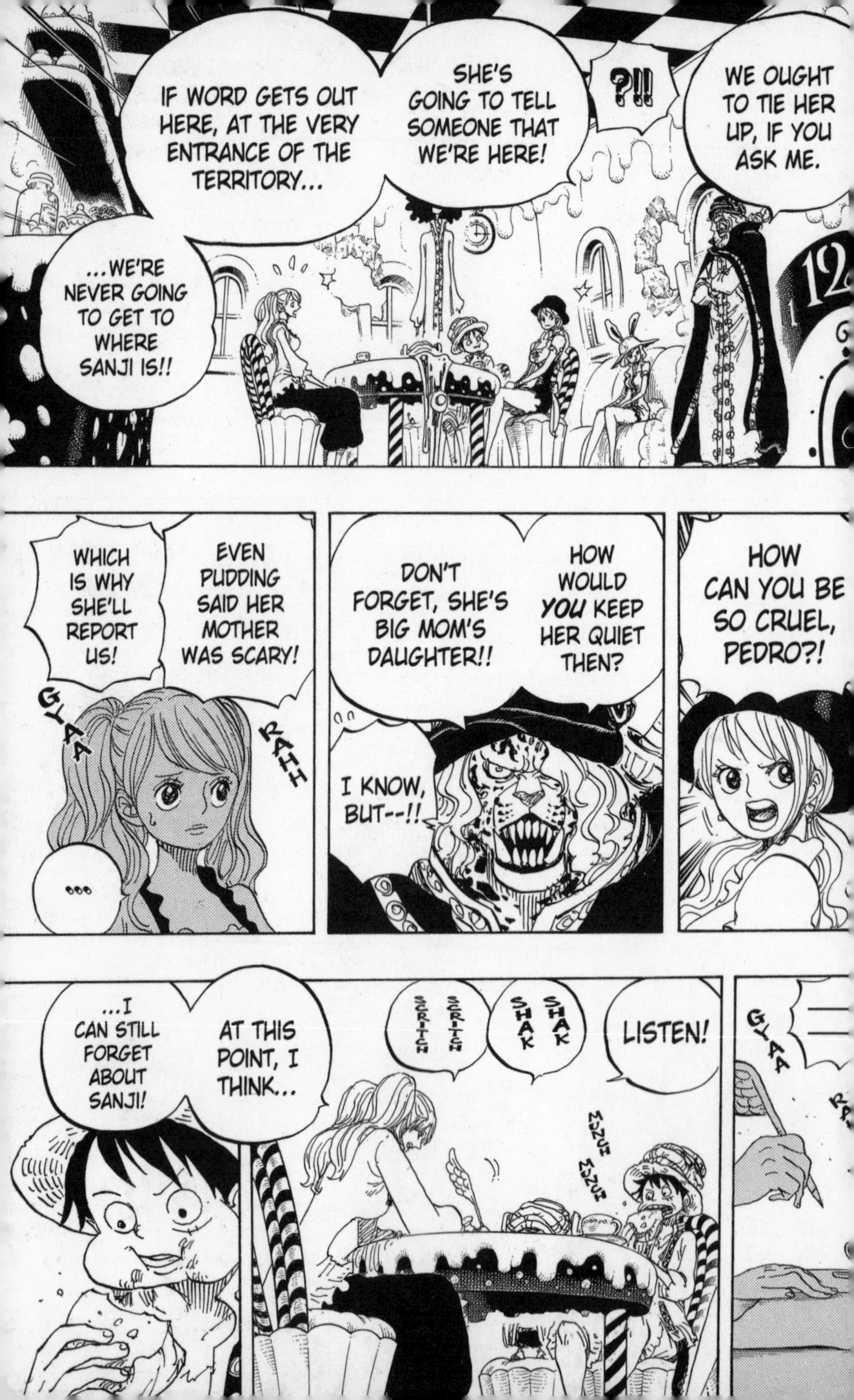
WE OUGHT TO TIE HER UP, IF YOU ASK ME.
?!!
SHE'S GOING TO TELL SOMEONE THAT WE'RE HERE!
IF WORD GETS OUT HERE, AT THE VERY ENTRANCE OF THE TERRITORY...
...WE'RE NEVER GOING TO GET TO WHERE SANJI IS!!
HOW CAN YOU BE SO CRUEL, PEDRO?!
HOW WOULD *YOU* KEEP HER QUIET THEN?
DON'T FORGET, SHE'S BIG MOM'S DAUGHTER!!
I KNOW, BUT--!!
EVEN PUDDING SAID HER MOTHER WAS SCARY!
WHICH IS WHY SHE'LL REPORT US!
RAHH
GYAA
...
GYAA
LISTEN!
SHAK SHAK
SCRITCH SCRITCH
AT THIS POINT, I THINK...
...I CAN STILL FORGET ABOUT SANJI!
MUNCH MUNCH

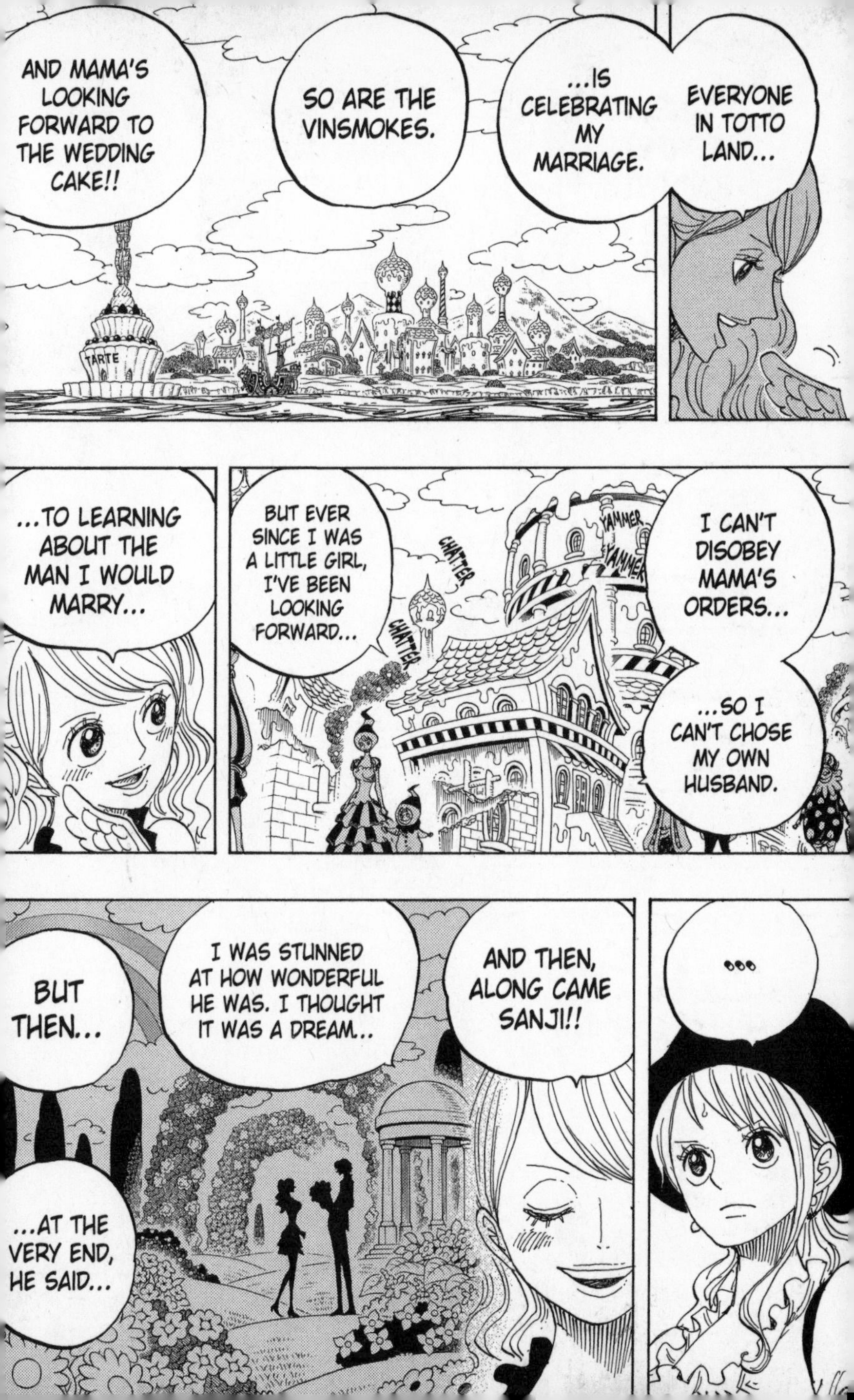
EVERYONE IN TOTTO LAND...
...IS CELEBRATING MY MARRIAGE.
SO ARE THE VINSMOKES.
AND MAMA'S LOOKING FORWARD TO THE WEDDING CAKE!!
TARTE
I CAN'T DISOBEY MAMA'S ORDERS...
...SO I CAN'T CHOSE MY OWN HUSBAND.
YAMMER
YAMMER
CHATTER
CHATTER
BUT EVER SINCE I WAS A LITTLE GIRL, I'VE BEEN LOOKING FORWARD...
...TO LEARNING ABOUT THE MAN I WOULD MARRY...
...
AND THEN, ALONG CAME SANJI!!
I WAS STUNNED AT HOW WONDERFUL HE WAS. I THOUGHT IT WAS A DREAM...
BUT THEN...
...AT THE VERY END, HE SAID...

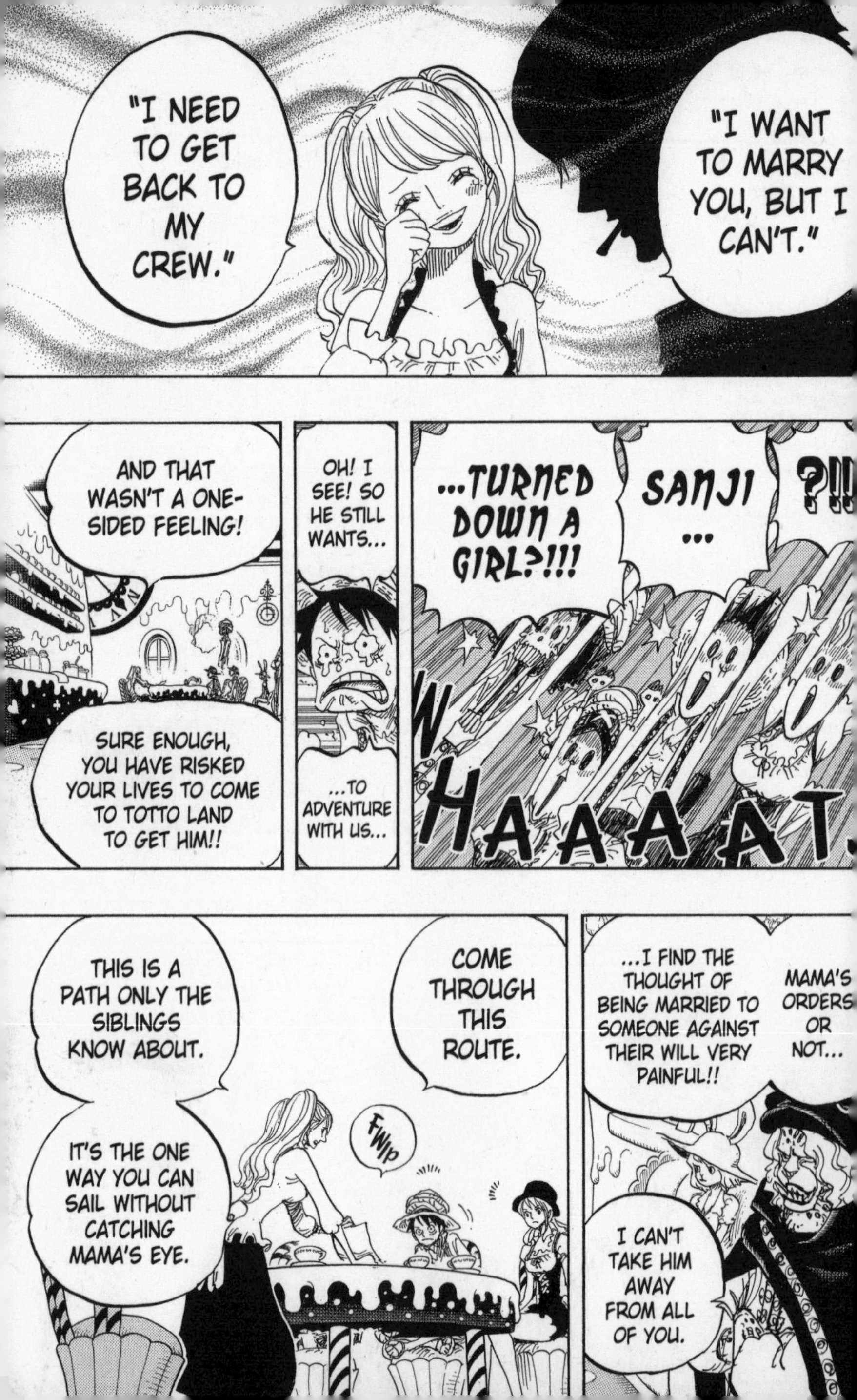
"I WANT TO MARRY YOU, BUT I CAN'T."
"I NEED TO GET BACK TO MY CREW."
?!!
SANJI ...
...TURNED DOWN A GIRL?!!!
WHAAAAT.
OH! I SEE! SO HE STILL WANTS...
...TO ADVENTURE WITH US...
AND THAT WASN'T A ONE-SIDED FEELING!
SURE ENOUGH, YOU HAVE RISKED YOUR LIVES TO COME TO TOTTO LAND TO GET HIM!!
MAMA'S ORDERS OR NOT...
...I FIND THE THOUGHT OF BEING MARRIED TO SOMEONE AGAINST THEIR WILL VERY PAINFUL!!
I CAN'T TAKE HIM AWAY FROM ALL OF YOU.
COME THROUGH THIS ROUTE.
THIS IS A PATH ONLY THE SIBLINGS KNOW ABOUT.
FWIP
IT'S THE ONE WAY YOU CAN SAIL WITHOUT CATCHING MAMA'S EYE.

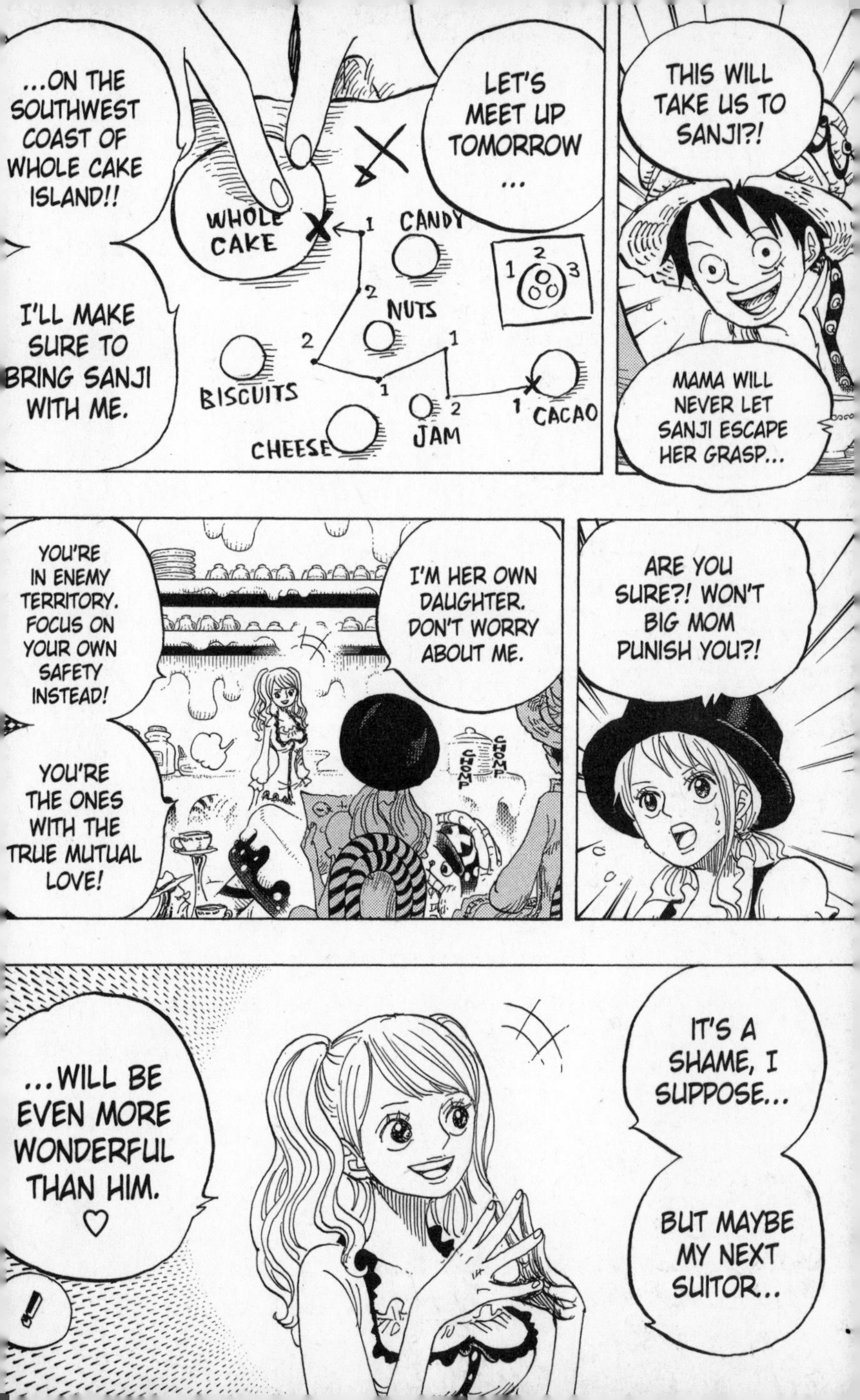
THIS WILL TAKE US TO SANJI?!
MAMA WILL NEVER LET SANJI ESCAPE HER GRASP...
LET'S MEET UP TOMORROW...
...ON THE SOUTHWEST COAST OF WHOLE CAKE ISLAND!!
I'LL MAKE SURE TO BRING SANJI WITH ME.
WHOLE CAKE
CANDY
NUTS
BISCUITS
CHEESE
JAM
CACAO
ARE YOU SURE?! WON'T BIG MOM PUNISH YOU?!
I'M HER OWN DAUGHTER. DON'T WORRY ABOUT ME.
YOU'RE IN ENEMY TERRITORY. FOCUS ON YOUR OWN SAFETY INSTEAD!
YOU'RE THE ONES WITH THE TRUE MUTUAL LOVE!
CHOMP
CHOMP
IT'S A SHAME, I SUPPOSE...
BUT MAYBE MY NEXT SUITOR...
...WILL BE EVEN MORE WONDERFUL THAN HIM. ♡
!

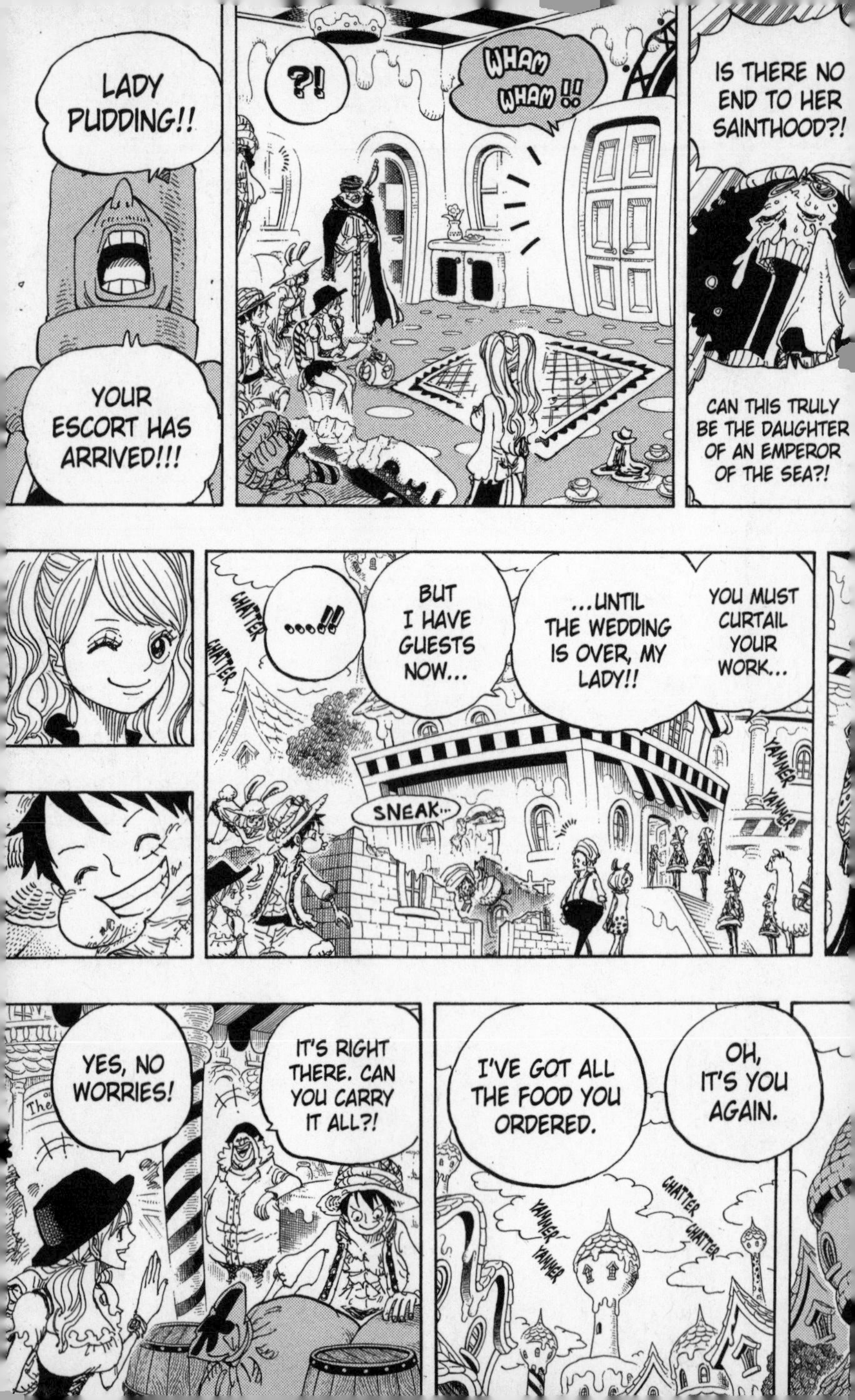
IS THERE NO END TO HER SAINTHOOD?!
CAN THIS TRULY BE THE DAUGHTER OF AN EMPEROR OF THE SEA?!
WHAM WHAM!!
?!
LADY PUDDING!!
YOUR ESCORT HAS ARRIVED!!!
YOU MUST CURTAIL YOUR WORK...
...UNTIL THE WEDDING IS OVER, MY LADY!!
BUT I HAVE GUESTS NOW...
....!!
YAMMER YAMMER
CHATTER CHATTER
SNEAK...
OH, IT'S YOU AGAIN.
I'VE GOT ALL THE FOOD YOU ORDERED.
CHATTER CHATTER
YAMMER YAMMER
IT'S RIGHT THERE. CAN YOU CARRY IT ALL?!
YES, NO WORRIES!

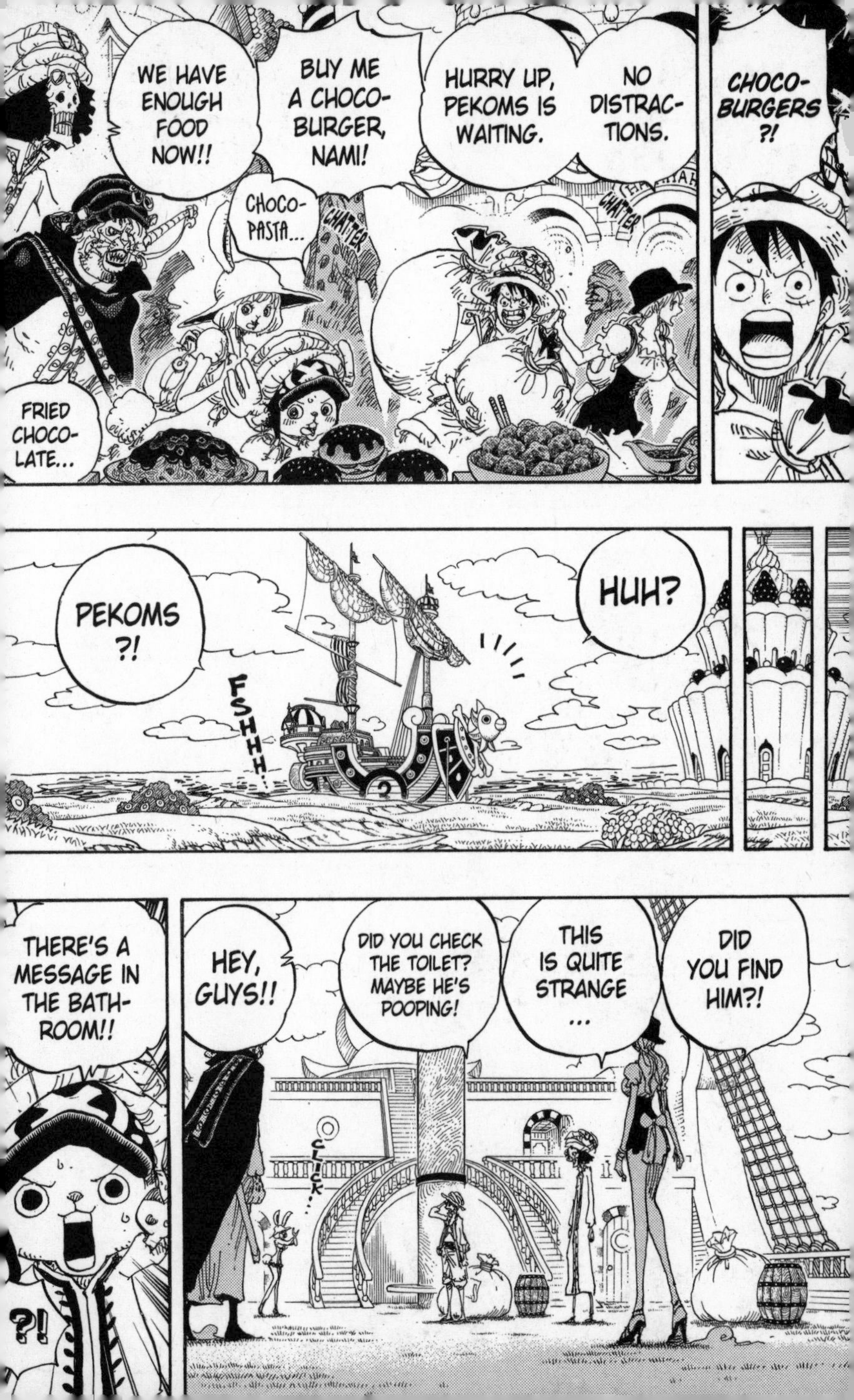
CHOCO-BURGERS ?!
NO DISTRACTIONS.
HURRY UP, PEKOMS IS WAITING.
BUY ME A CHOCO-BURGER, NAMI!
WE HAVE ENOUGH FOOD NOW!!
CHATTER
CHATTER
CHOCO-PASTA...
CHATTER
FRIED CHOCOLATE...
HUH?
PEKOMS ?!
FSHHH...
DID YOU FIND HIM?!
THIS IS QUITE STRANGE ...
DID YOU CHECK THE TOILET? MAYBE HE'S POOPING!
HEY, GUYS!!
CLICK...
THERE'S A MESSAGE IN THE BATHROOM!!
?!

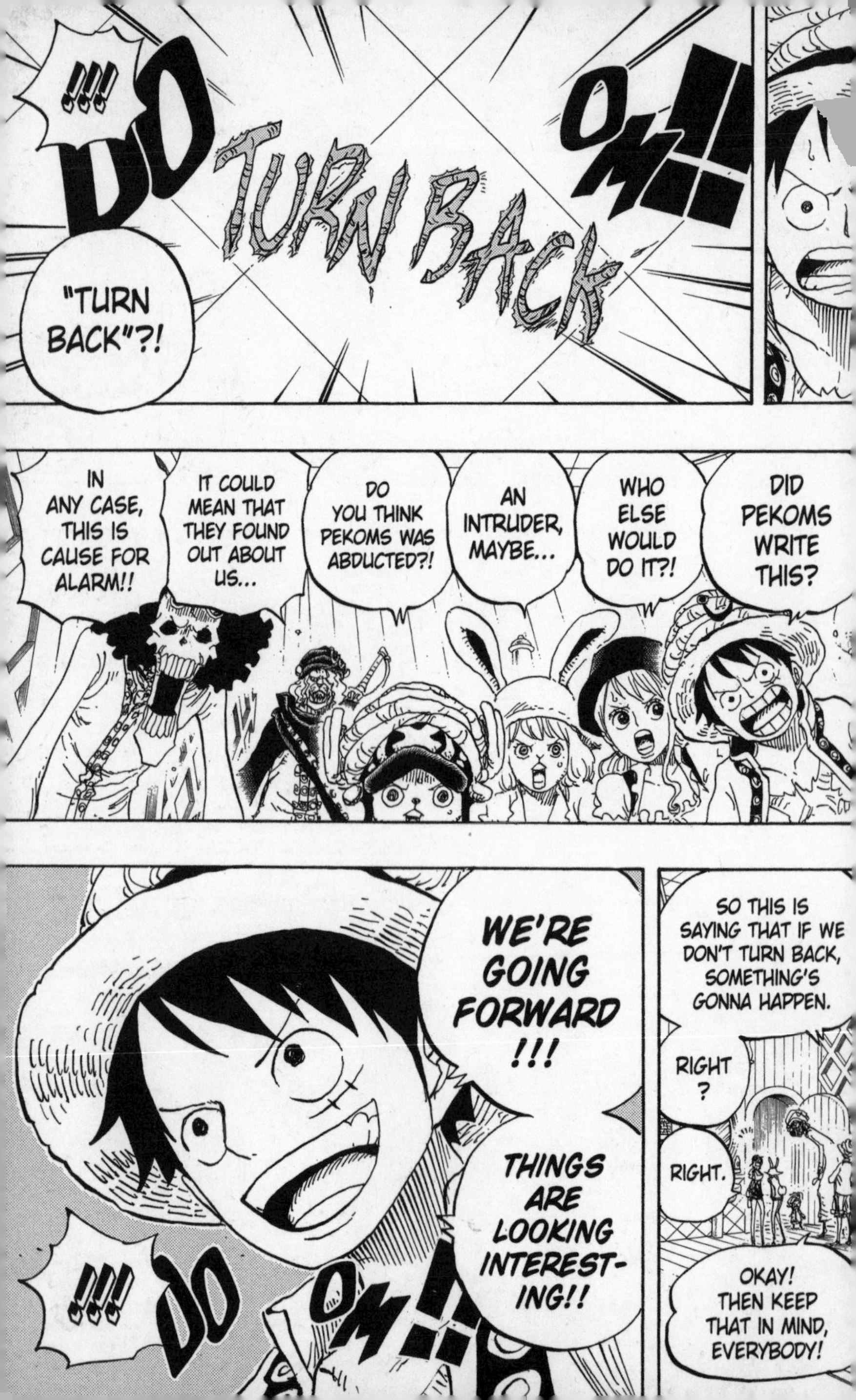
!!!
DO
OM!!
TURN BACK
"TURN BACK"?!
DID PEKOMS WRITE THIS?
WHO ELSE WOULD DO IT?!
AN INTRUDER, MAYBE...
DO YOU THINK PEKOMS WAS ABDUCTED?!
IT COULD MEAN THAT THEY FOUND OUT ABOUT US...
IN ANY CASE, THIS IS CAUSE FOR ALARM!!
SO THIS IS SAYING THAT IF WE DON'T TURN BACK, SOMETHING'S GONNA HAPPEN.
RIGHT?
RIGHT.
OKAY! THEN KEEP THAT IN MIND, EVERYBODY!
WE'RE GOING FORWARD!!!
THINGS ARE LOOKING INTEREST-ING!!
!!!
DO
OM!!

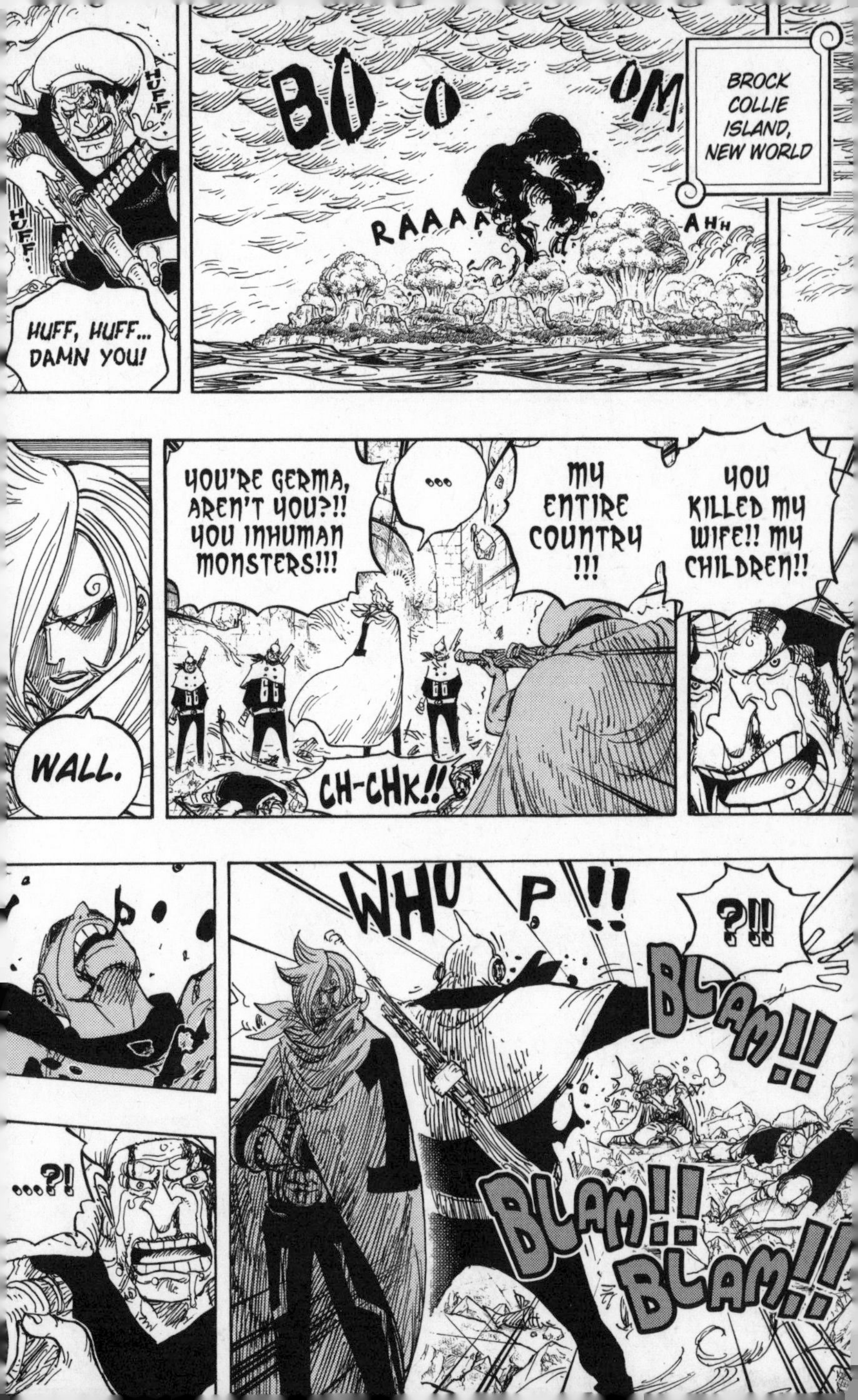
BROCK COLLIE ISLAND, NEW WORLD
BOOOM
RAAAAAHH
HUFF HUFF
HUFF, HUFF... DAMN YOU!
YOU KILLED MY WIFE!! MY CHILDREN!!
MY ENTIRE COUNTRY!!!
...
YOU'RE GERMA, AREN'T YOU?!! YOU INHUMAN MONSTERS!!!
CH-CHK!!
WALL.
?!!
WHUP!!
BLAM!!
BLAM!!
BLAM!!
...?!

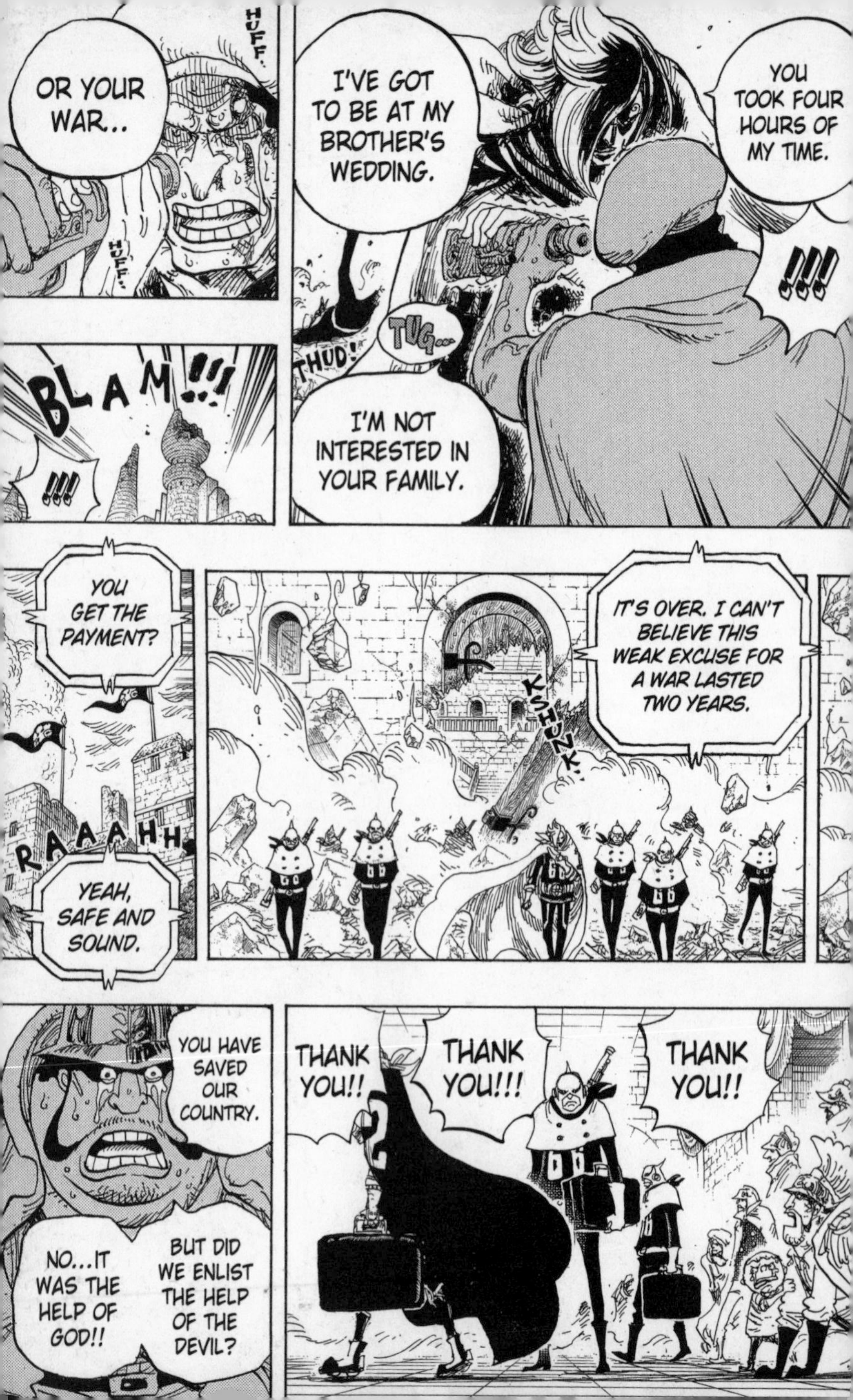
YOU TOOK FOUR HOURS OF MY TIME.
!!!
I'VE GOT TO BE AT MY BROTHER'S WEDDING.
TUG...
THUD!
I'M NOT INTERESTED IN YOUR FAMILY.
HUFF
OR YOUR WAR...
HUFF
BLAM!!!
!!!
IT'S OVER. I CAN'T BELIEVE THIS WEAK EXCUSE FOR A WAR LASTED TWO YEARS.
KSHUNK
YOU GET THE PAYMENT?
RAAAHH
YEAH, SAFE AND SOUND.
THANK YOU!!
THANK YOU!!!
THANK YOU!!
YOU HAVE SAVED OUR COUNTRY.
BUT DID WE ENLIST THE HELP OF THE DEVIL?
NO...IT WAS THE HELP OF GOD!!

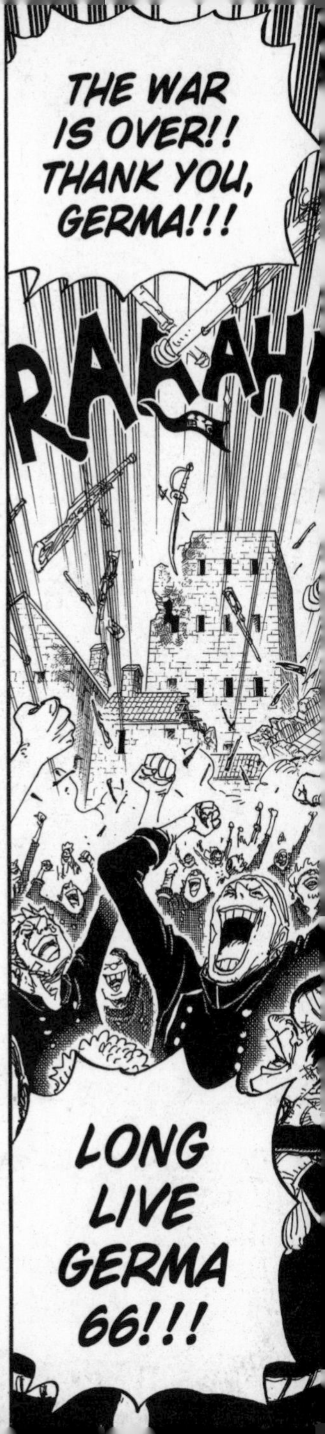
THE WAR IS OVER!! THANK YOU, GERMA!!!
LONG LIVE GERMA 66!!!

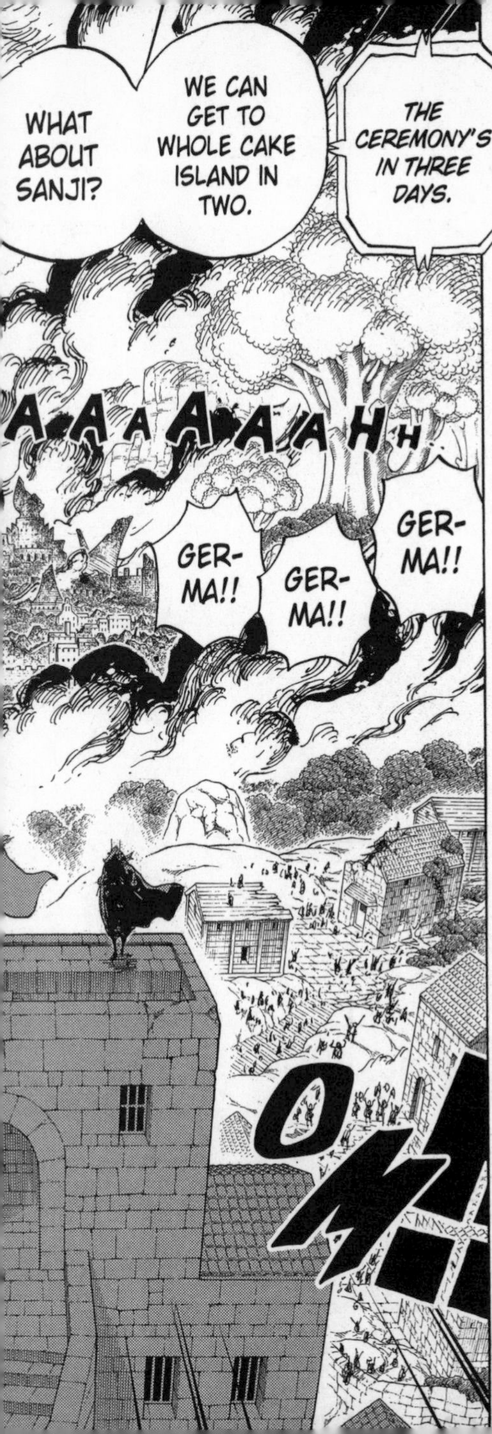
THE CEREMONY'S IN THREE DAYS.
WE CAN GET TO WHOLE CAKE ISLAND IN TWO.
WHAT ABOUT SANJI?
AAAAAAAHH
GER-MA!!
GER-MA!!
GER-MA!!

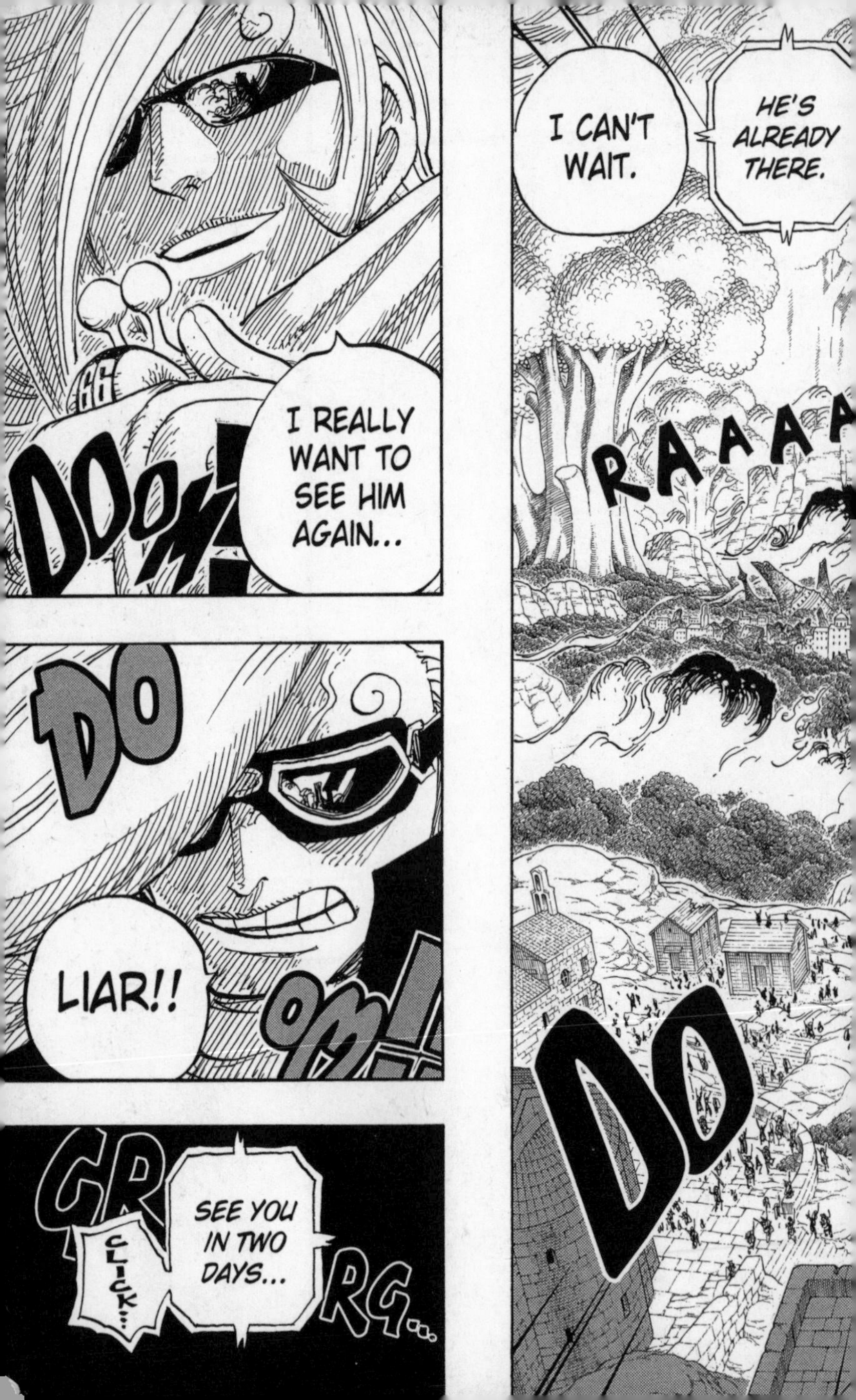
HE'S ALREADY THERE.
I CAN'T WAIT.
RAAAA
DO
I REALLY WANT TO SEE HIM AGAIN...
DOOM!
DO
OM!
LIAR!!
GR
RG...
SEE YOU IN TWO DAYS...
CLICK...

THE SEA, CHARLOTTE LINLIN

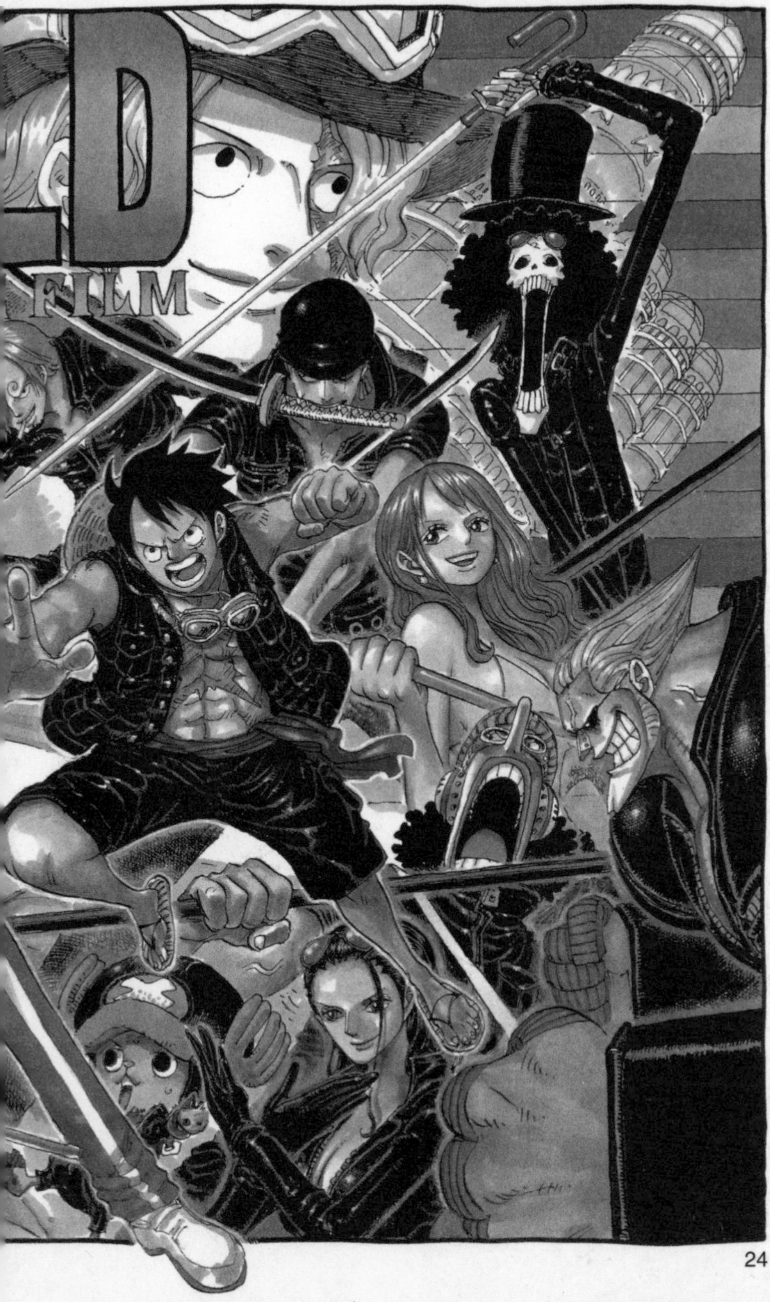
D
FILM

Chapter 829: EMPEROR OF

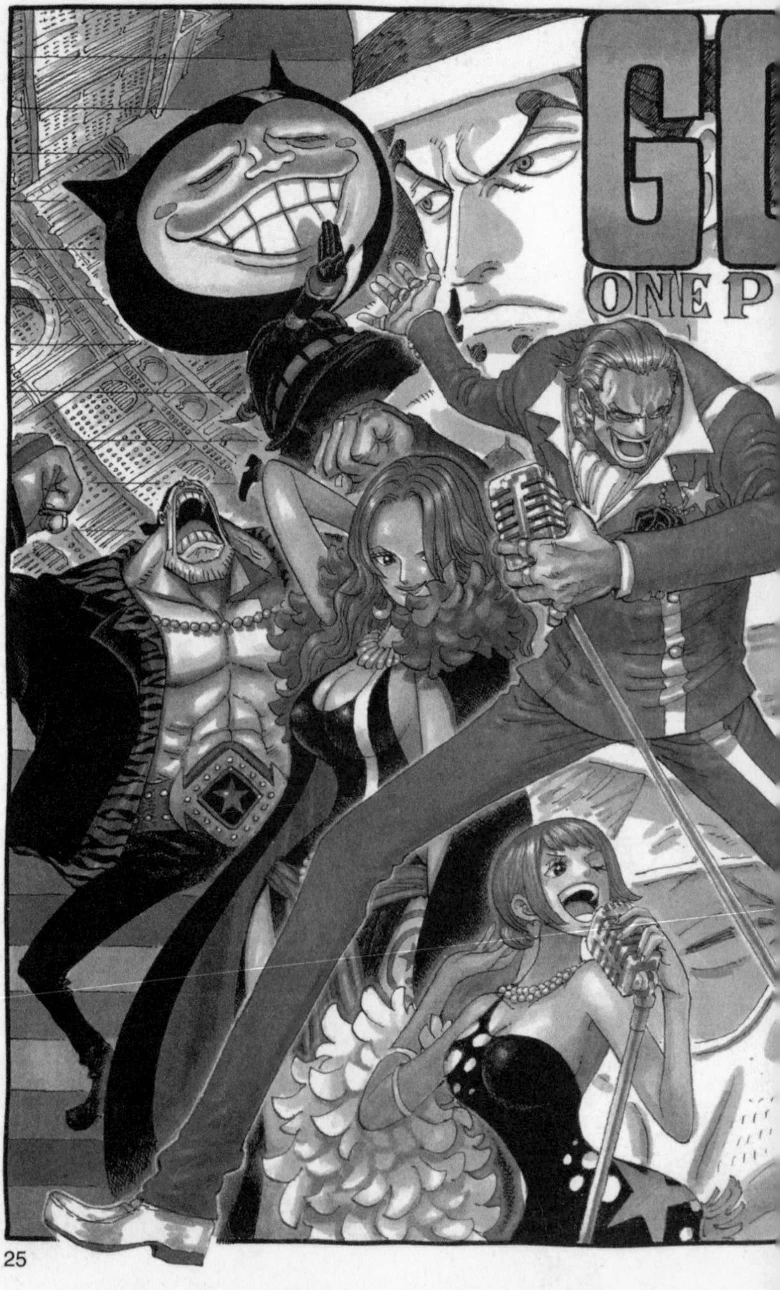
GO
ONE P

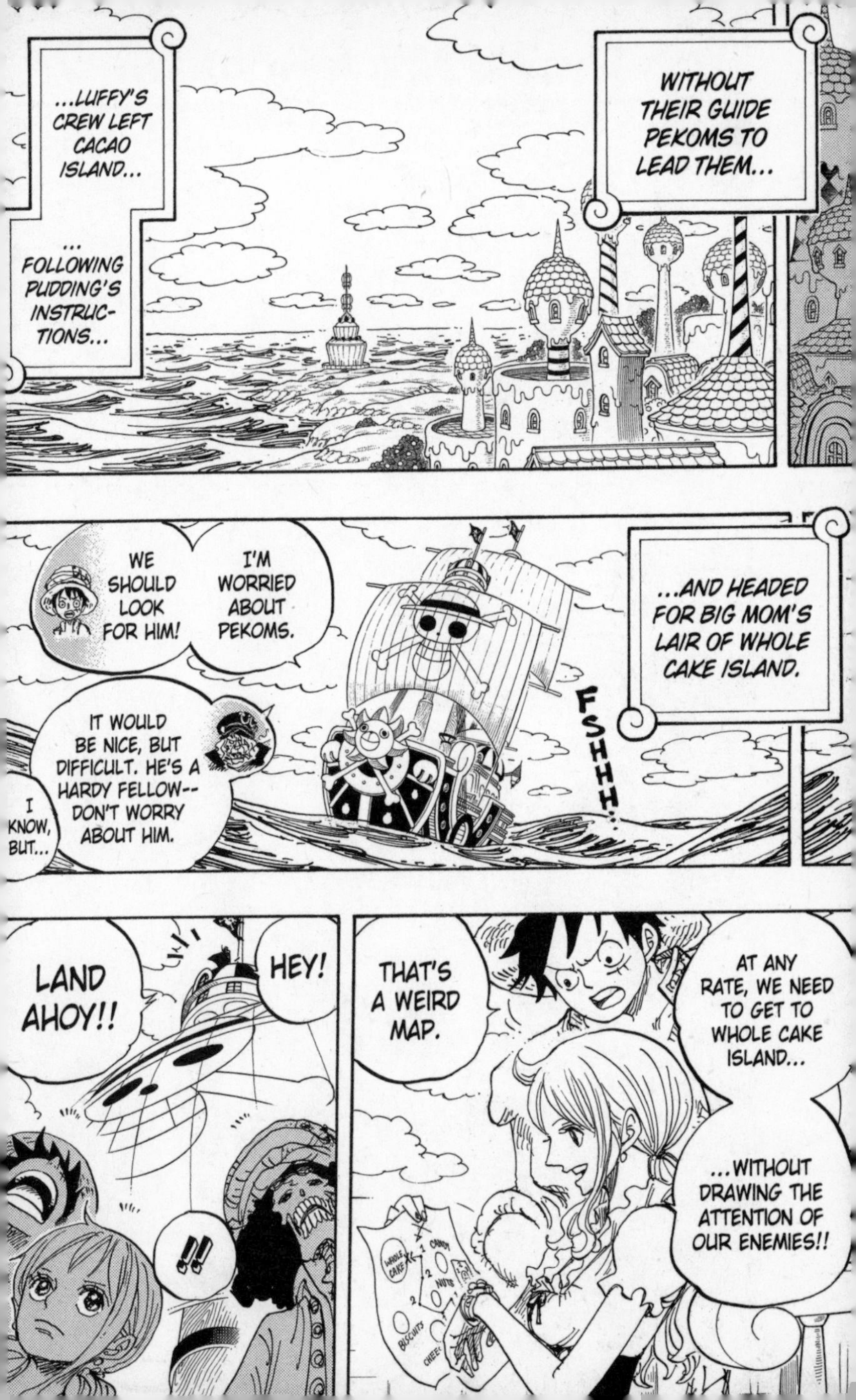
WITHOUT THEIR GUIDE PEKOMS TO LEAD THEM...
...LUFFY'S CREW LEFT CACAO ISLAND...
...FOLLOWING PUDDING'S INSTRUCTIONS...
...AND HEADED FOR BIG MOM'S LAIR OF WHOLE CAKE ISLAND.
FSHHH...
I'M WORRIED ABOUT PEKOMS.
WE SHOULD LOOK FOR HIM!
IT WOULD BE NICE, BUT DIFFICULT. HE'S A HARDY FELLOW-- DON'T WORRY ABOUT HIM.
I KNOW, BUT...
AT ANY RATE, WE NEED TO GET TO WHOLE CAKE ISLAND...
...WITHOUT DRAWING THE ATTENTION OF OUR ENEMIES!!
THAT'S A WEIRD MAP.
WHOLE CAKE
CANDY
NUTS
BISCUITS
HEY!
LAND AHOY!!
!!

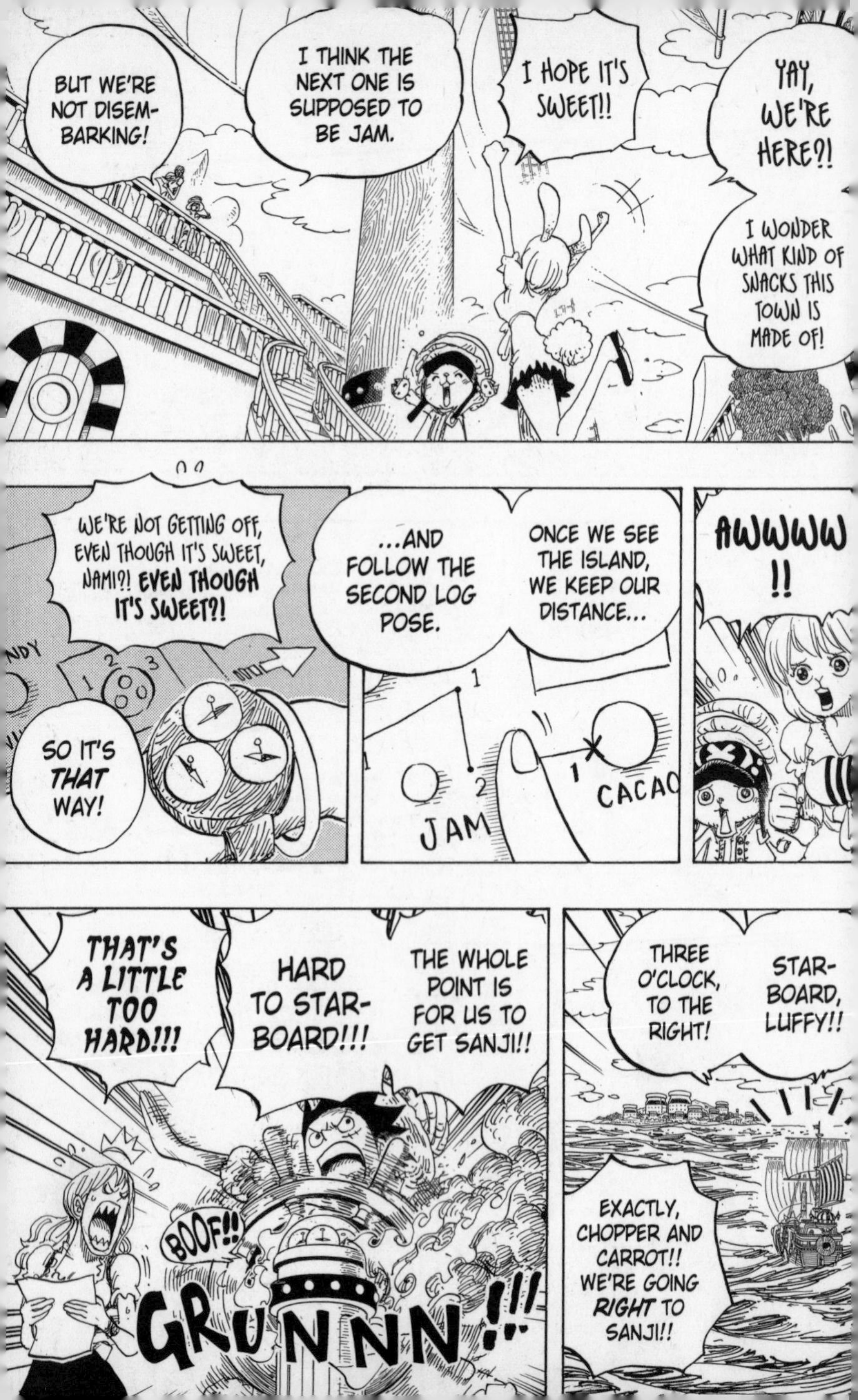
YAY, WE'RE HERE?!
I WONDER WHAT KIND OF SNACKS THIS TOWN IS MADE OF!
I HOPE IT'S SWEET!!
I THINK THE NEXT ONE IS SUPPOSED TO BE JAM.
BUT WE'RE NOT DISEMBARKING!
AWWWW!!
ONCE WE SEE THE ISLAND, WE KEEP OUR DISTANCE...
...AND FOLLOW THE SECOND LOG POSE.
CACAO
JAM
WE'RE NOT GETTING OFF, EVEN THOUGH IT'S SWEET, NAMI?! EVEN THOUGH IT'S SWEET?!
SO IT'S THAT WAY!
STAR-BOARD, LUFFY!!
THREE O'CLOCK, TO THE RIGHT!
EXACTLY, CHOPPER AND CARROT!! WE'RE GOING RIGHT TO SANJI!!
THE WHOLE POINT IS FOR US TO GET SANJI!!
HARD TO STAR-BOARD!!!
THAT'S A LITTLE TOO HARD!!!
BOOF!!
GRUNNN!!!

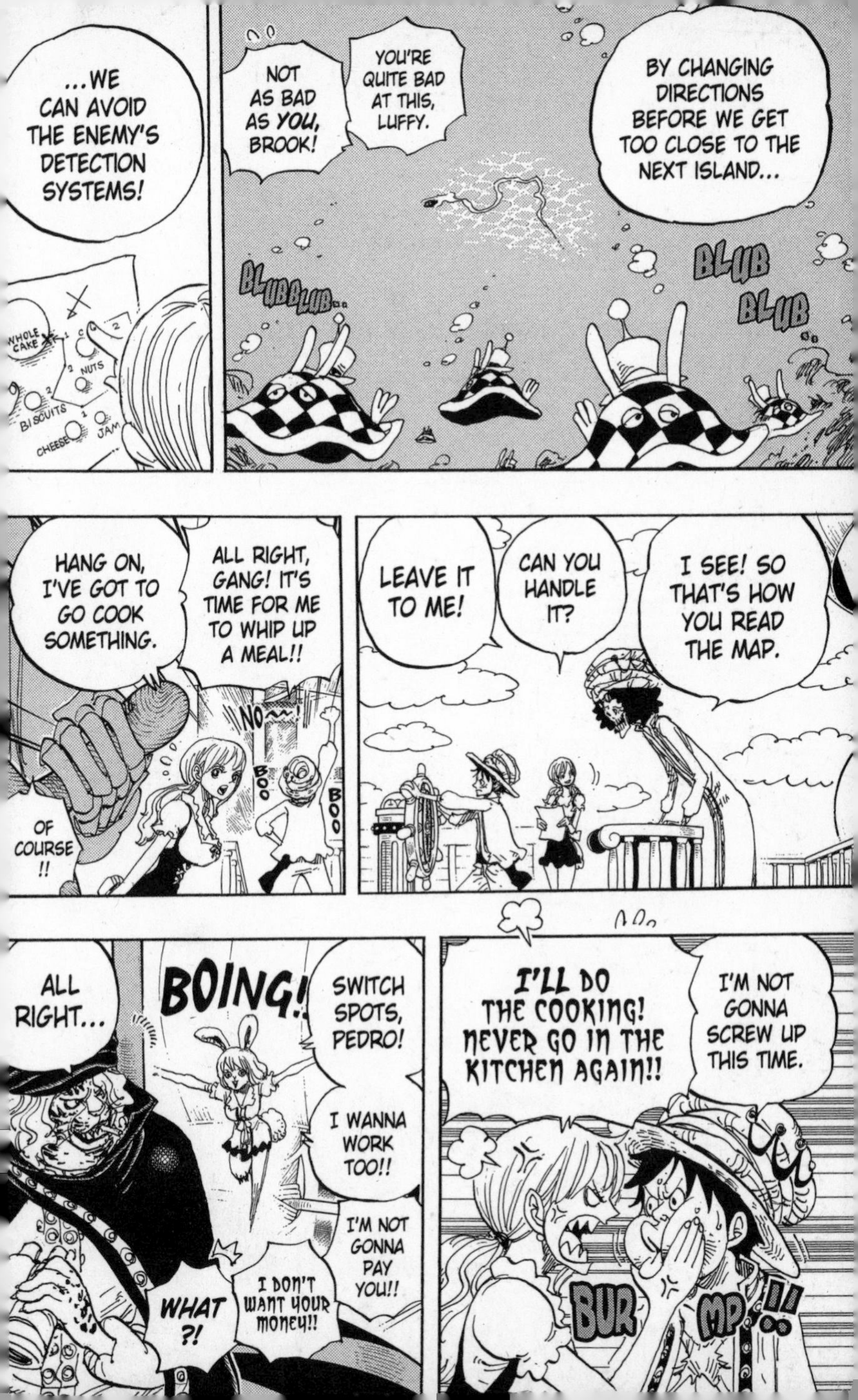
BY CHANGING DIRECTIONS BEFORE WE GET TOO CLOSE TO THE NEXT ISLAND...
YOU'RE QUITE BAD AT THIS, LUFFY.
NOT AS BAD AS YOU, BROOK!
BLUB
BLUB
BLUBBLUB...
...WE CAN AVOID THE ENEMY'S DETECTION SYSTEMS!
WHOLE CAKE
NUTS
BISCUITS
CHEESE
JAM
I SEE! SO THAT'S HOW YOU READ THE MAP.
CAN YOU HANDLE IT?
LEAVE IT TO ME!
ALL RIGHT, GANG! IT'S TIME FOR ME TO WHIP UP A MEAL!!
HANG ON, I'VE GOT TO GO COOK SOMETHING.
NO~~!
BOO
BOO
OF COURSE!!
I'M NOT GONNA SCREW UP THIS TIME.
I'LL DO THE COOKING! NEVER GO IN THE KITCHEN AGAIN!!
BURMP!!
SWITCH SPOTS, PEDRO!
BOING!
ALL RIGHT...
I WANNA WORK TOO!!
I'M NOT GONNA PAY YOU!!
I DON'T WANT YOUR MONEY!!
WHAT?!

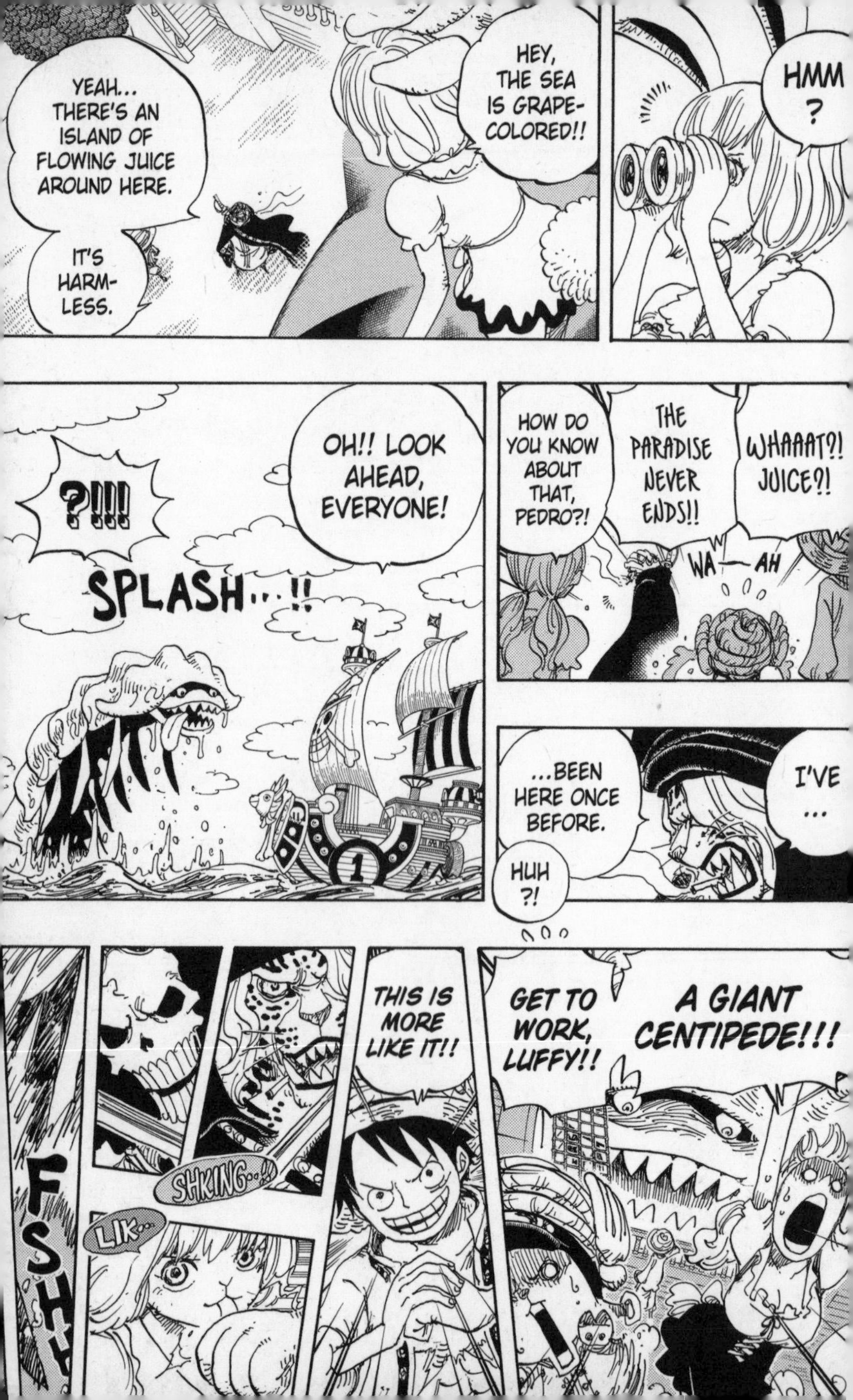
HMM ?
HEY, THE SEA IS GRAPE-COLORED!!
YEAH... THERE'S AN ISLAND OF FLOWING JUICE AROUND HERE.
IT'S HARMLESS.
WHAAAT?! JUICE?!
THE PARADISE NEVER ENDS!!
HOW DO YOU KNOW ABOUT THAT, PEDRO?!
WA—AH
I'VE ...
...BEEN HERE ONCE BEFORE.
HUH ?!
OH!! LOOK AHEAD, EVERYONE!
?!!!
SPLASH...!!
A GIANT CENTIPEDE!!!
GET TO WORK, LUFFY!!
THIS IS MORE LIKE IT!!
SHKING...!!
LIK...
FSHH

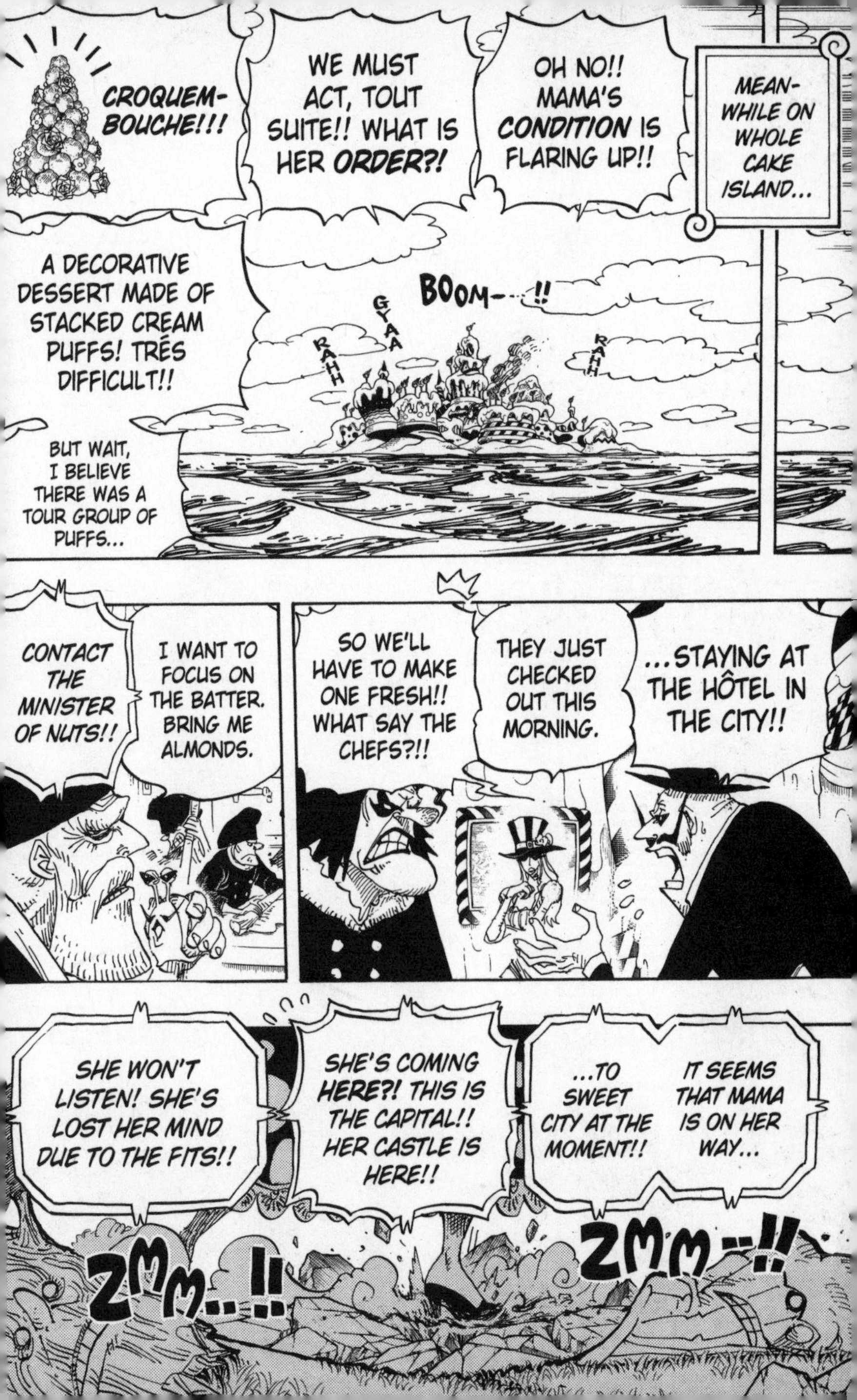
MEANWHILE ON WHOLE CAKE ISLAND...
OH NO!! MAMA'S CONDITION IS FLARING UP!!
WE MUST ACT, TOUT SUITE!! WHAT IS HER ORDER?!
CROQUEMBOUCHE!!!
BOOM--!!
RAHH
GYAA
RAHH
A DECORATIVE DESSERT MADE OF STACKED CREAM PUFFS! TRÉS DIFFICULT!!
BUT WAIT, I BELIEVE THERE WAS A TOUR GROUP OF PUFFS...
...STAYING AT THE HÔTEL IN THE CITY!!
THEY JUST CHECKED OUT THIS MORNING.
SO WE'LL HAVE TO MAKE ONE FRESH!! WHAT SAY THE CHEFS?!!
I WANT TO FOCUS ON THE BATTER. BRING ME ALMONDS.
CONTACT THE MINISTER OF NUTS!!
IT SEEMS THAT MAMA IS ON HER WAY...
...TO SWEET CITY AT THE MOMENT!!
SHE'S COMING HERE?! THIS IS THE CAPITAL!! HER CASTLE IS HERE!!
SHE WON'T LISTEN! SHE'S LOST HER MIND DUE TO THE FITS!!
ZMM--!!
ZMM...!!

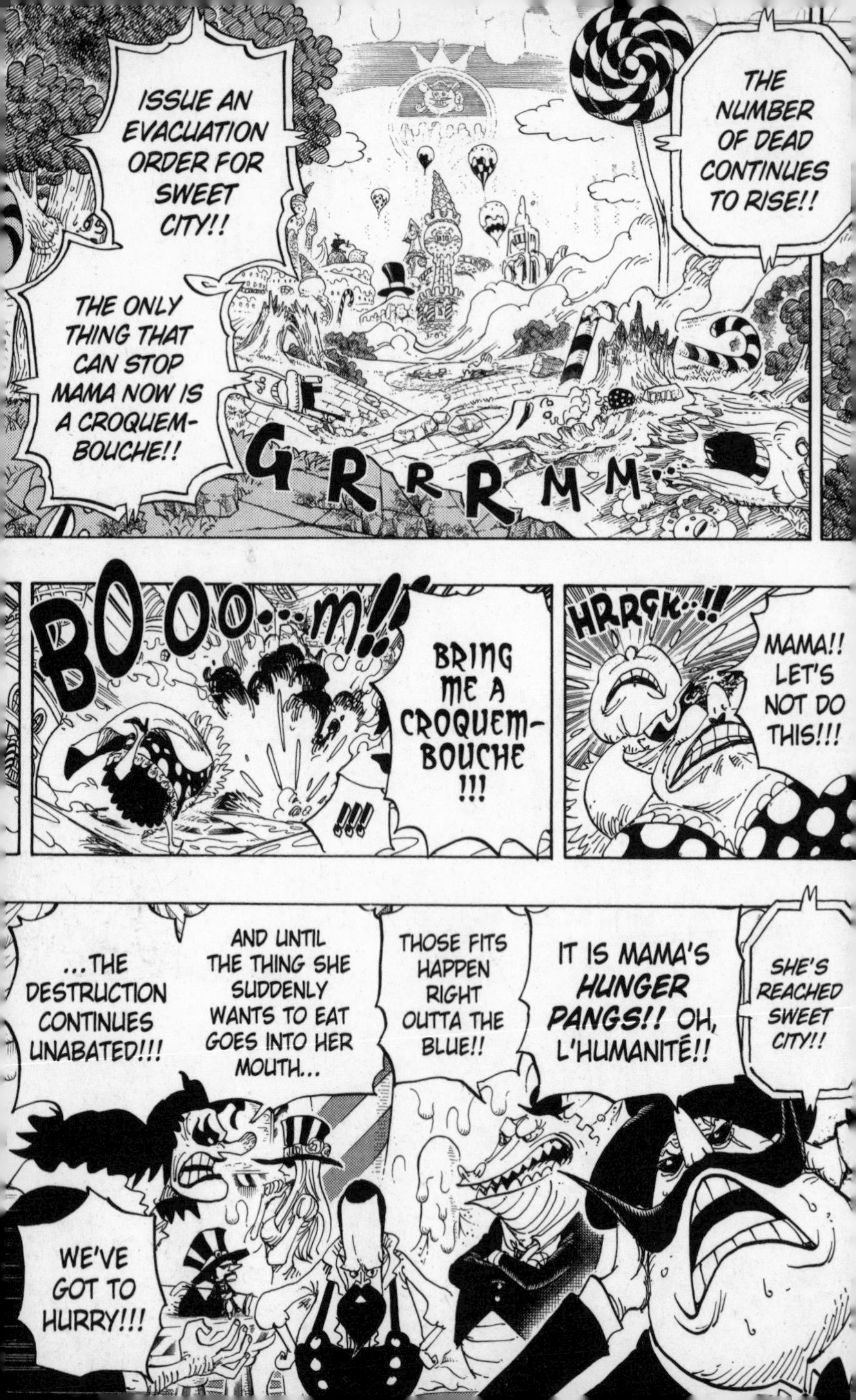
THE NUMBER OF DEAD CONTINUES TO RISE!!
ISSUE AN EVACUATION ORDER FOR SWEET CITY!!
THE ONLY THING THAT CAN STOP MAMA NOW IS A CROQUEMBOUCHE!!
GRRRRMM
HRRGK..!!
MAMA!! LET'S NOT DO THIS!!!
BOOO...M!!
BRING ME A CROQUEMBOUCHE!!!
!!!
SHE'S REACHED SWEET CITY!!
IT IS MAMA'S *HUNGER PANGS!!* OH, L'HUMANITÉ!!
THOSE FITS HAPPEN RIGHT OUTTA THE BLUE!!
AND UNTIL THE THING SHE SUDDENLY WANTS TO EAT GOES INTO HER MOUTH...
...THE DESTRUCTION CONTINUES UNABATED!!!
WE'VE GOT TO HURRY!!!

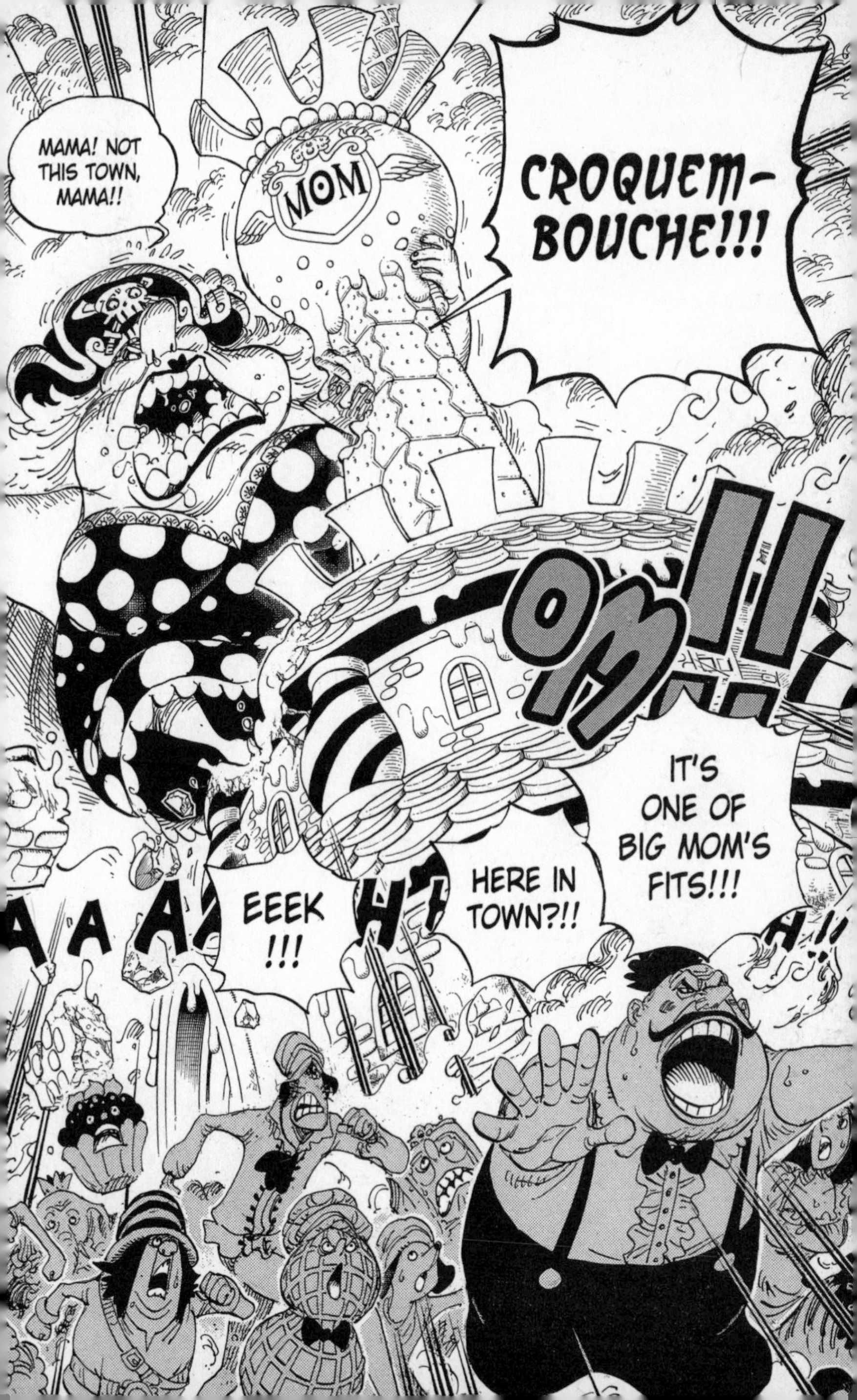
CROQUEM-BOUCHE!!!
MAMA! NOT THIS TOWN, MAMA!!
OM!!
IT'S ONE OF BIG MOM'S FITS!!!
HERE IN TOWN?!!
EEEK !!!

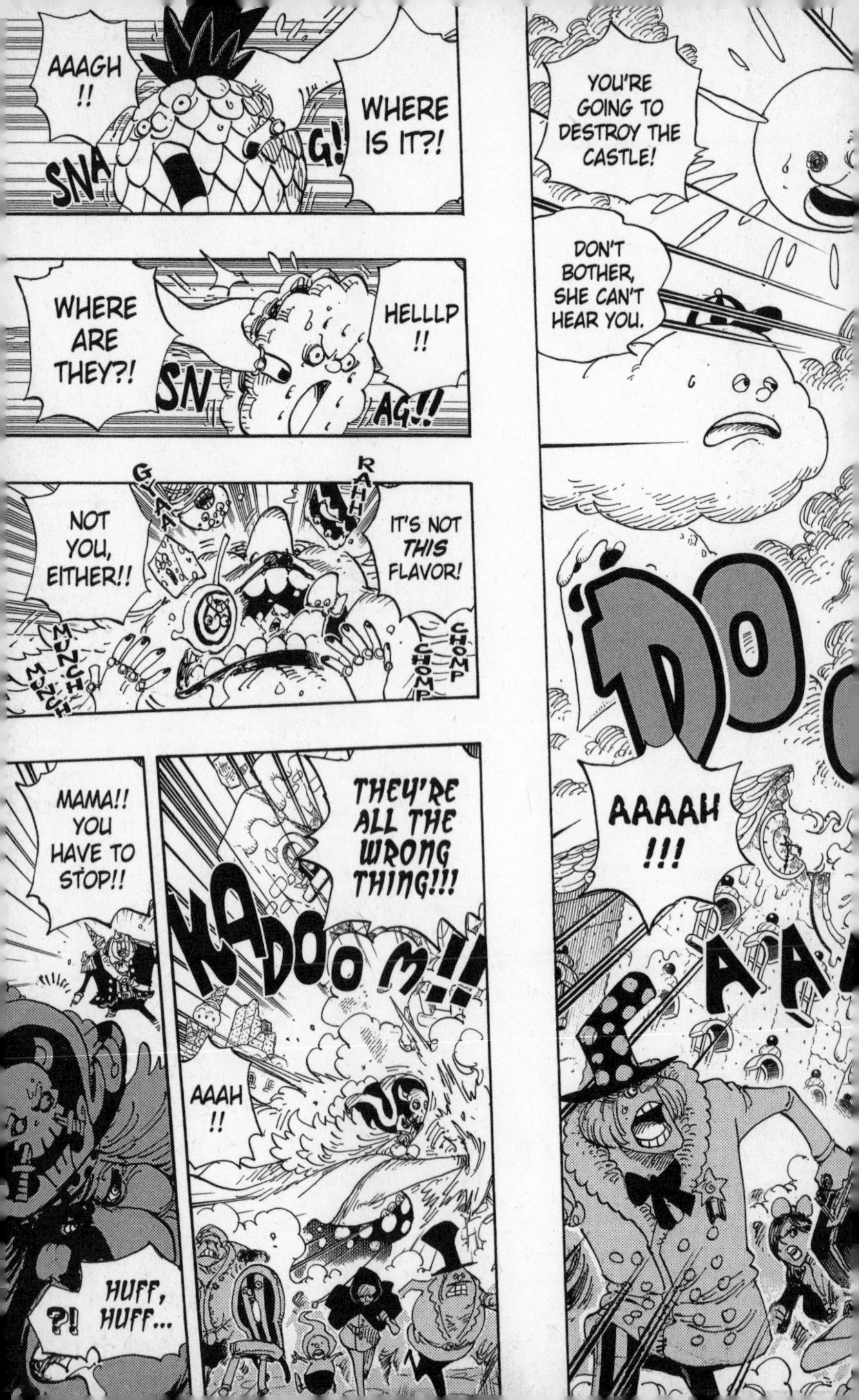
YOU'RE GOING TO DESTROY THE CASTLE!
DON'T BOTHER, SHE CAN'T HEAR YOU.
DO
AAAAH !!!
AA
WHERE IS IT?!
SNAG!
AAAGH !!
HELLLP !!
SNAG!!
WHERE ARE THEY?!
IT'S NOT THIS FLAVOR!
RAHHH
CHOMP
CHOMP
GYAA
NOT YOU, EITHER!!
MUNCH
MUNCH
THEY'RE ALL THE WRONG THING!!!
KADOOOM!!
AAAH !!
MAMA!! YOU HAVE TO STOP!!
HUFF, HUFF...
?!

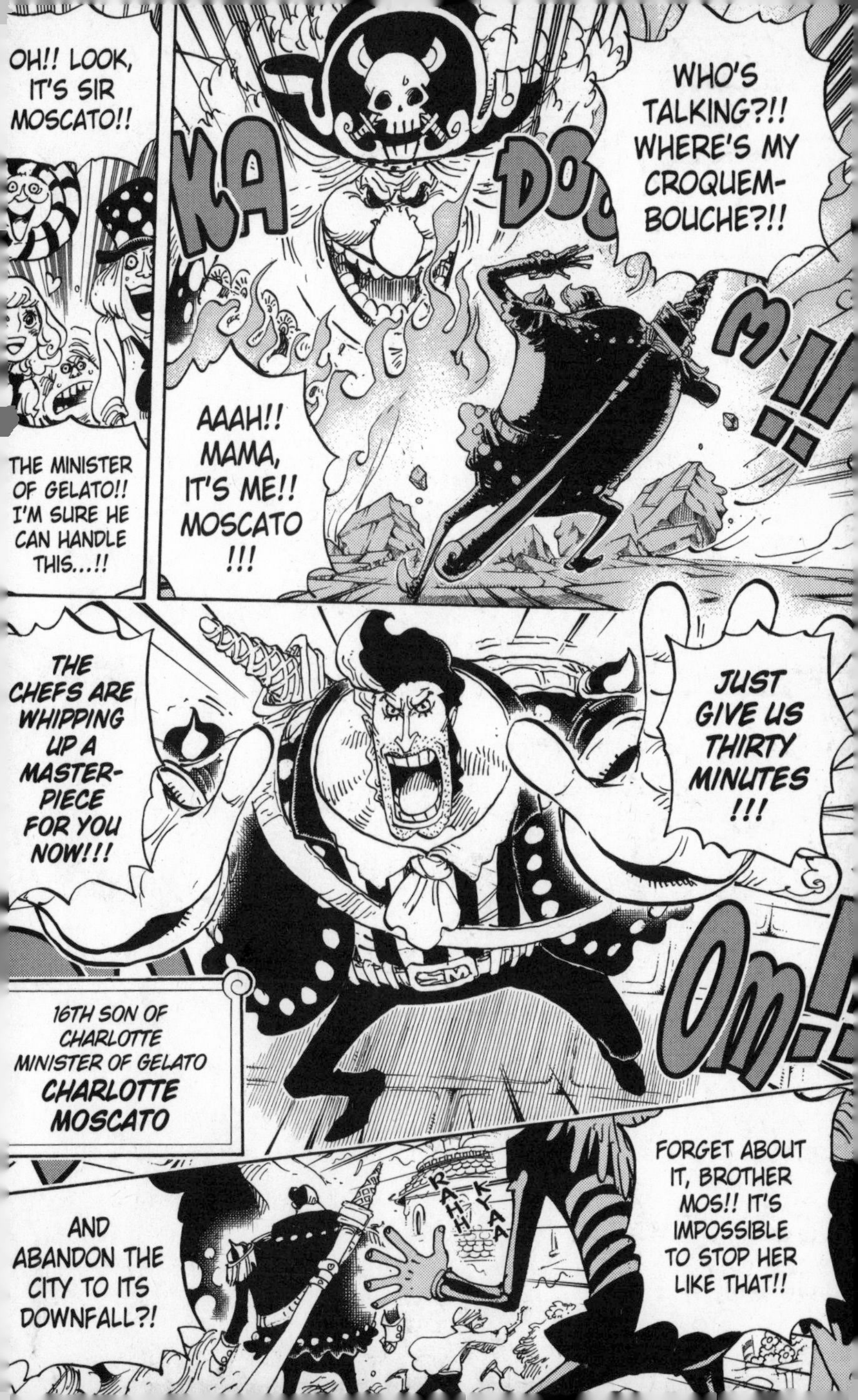
WHO'S TALKING?!! WHERE'S MY CROQUEMBOUCHE?!!
KA DOOM!!
AAAH!! MAMA, IT'S ME!! MOSCATO!!!
OH!! LOOK, IT'S SIR MOSCATO!!
THE MINISTER OF GELATO!! I'M SURE HE CAN HANDLE THIS...!!
JUST GIVE US THIRTY MINUTES!!!
THE CHEFS ARE WHIPPING UP A MASTERPIECE FOR YOU NOW!!!
OM!!
16TH SON OF CHARLOTTE MINISTER OF GELATO
CHARLOTTE MOSCATO
FORGET ABOUT IT, BROTHER MOS!! IT'S IMPOSSIBLE TO STOP HER LIKE THAT!!
KYAA
RAHH
AND ABANDON THE CITY TO ITS DOWNFALL?!

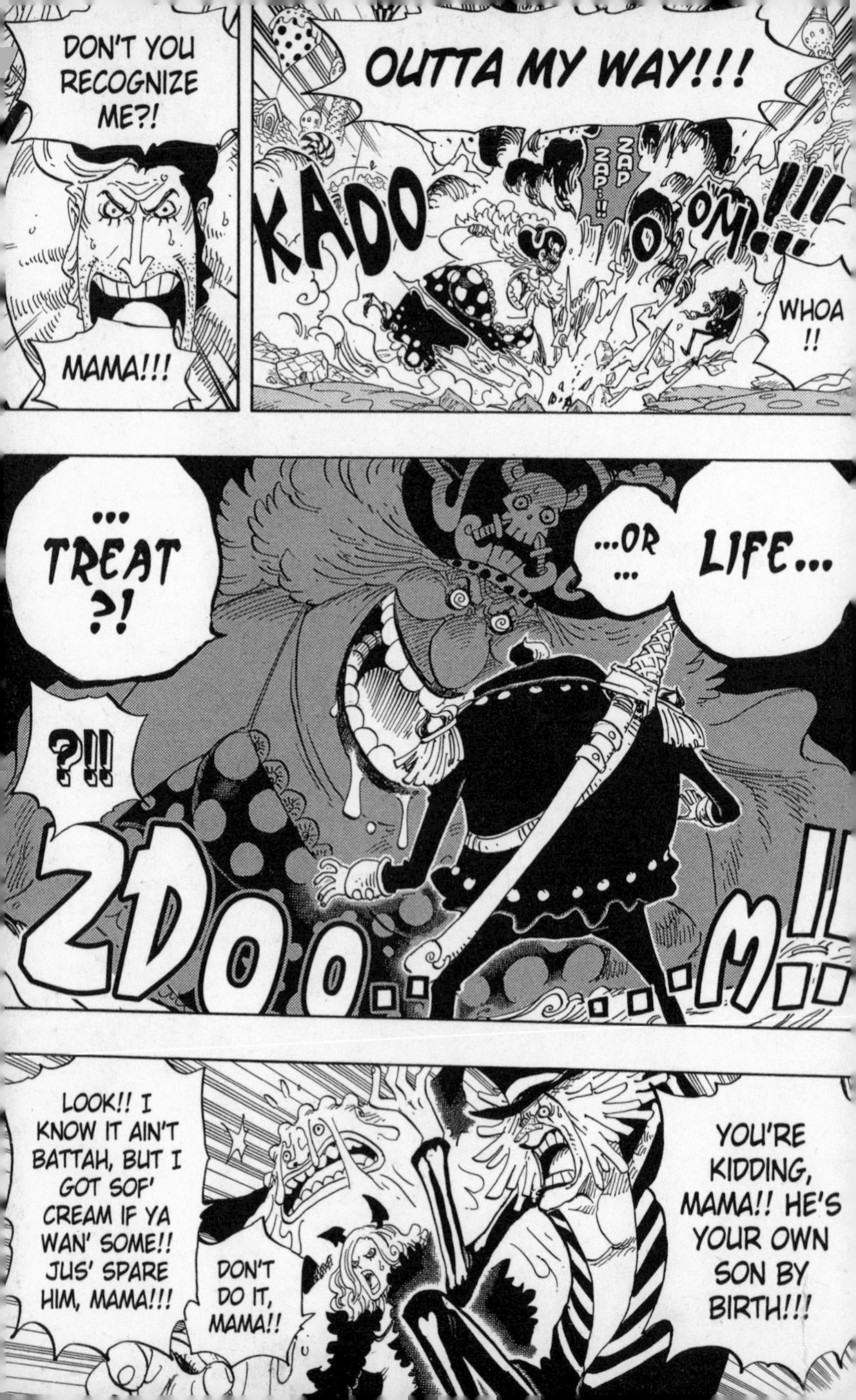
OUTTA MY WAY!!!
ZAP ZAP..!!
KADO OOM!!!
WHOA!!
DON'T YOU RECOGNIZE ME?!
MAMA!!!
...OR ... LIFE...
...TREAT?!
?!!
ZDOO......M!!
YOU'RE KIDDING, MAMA!! HE'S YOUR OWN SON BY BIRTH!!!
DON'T DO IT, MAMA!!
LOOK!! I KNOW IT AIN'T BATTAH, BUT I GOT SOF' CREAM IF YA WAN' SOME!! JUS' SPARE HIM, MAMA!!!

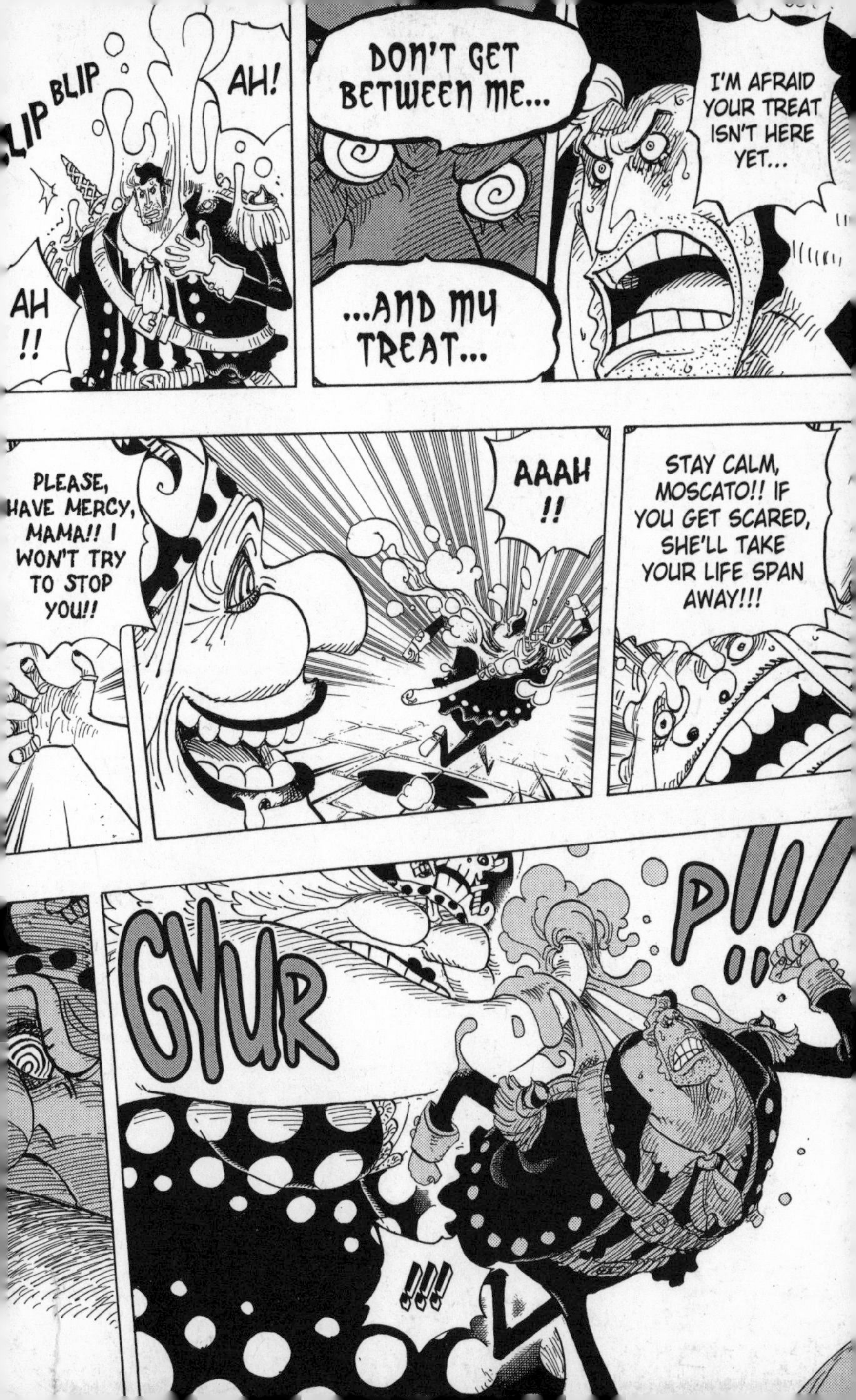
I'M AFRAID YOUR TREAT ISN'T HERE YET...
DON'T GET BETWEEN ME...
...AND MY TREAT...
AH!
BLIP BLIP
AH !!
STAY CALM, MOSCATO!! IF YOU GET SCARED, SHE'LL TAKE YOUR LIFE SPAN AWAY!!!
AAAH !!
PLEASE, HAVE MERCY, MAMA!! I WON'T TRY TO STOP YOU!!
P!!!
GYUR
!!!

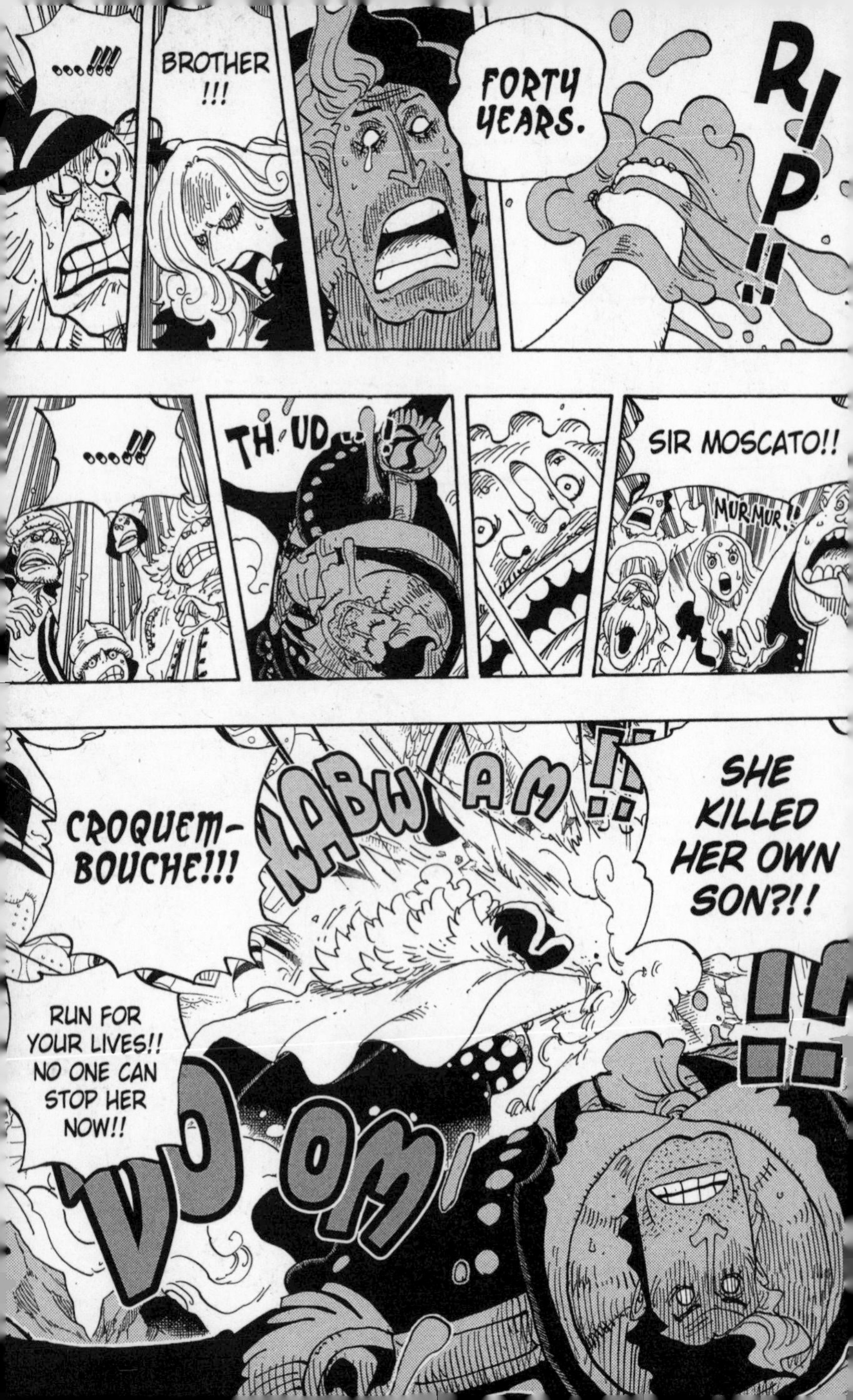
RIP!!
FORTY YEARS.
BROTHER !!!
...!!!
SIR MOSCATO!!
MURMUR!!
THUD..!
...!!
SHE KILLED HER OWN SON?!!
KABWAM!!
CROQUEM-BOUCHE!!!
!!
RUN FOR YOUR LIVES!! NO ONE CAN STOP HER NOW!!
VOOOM

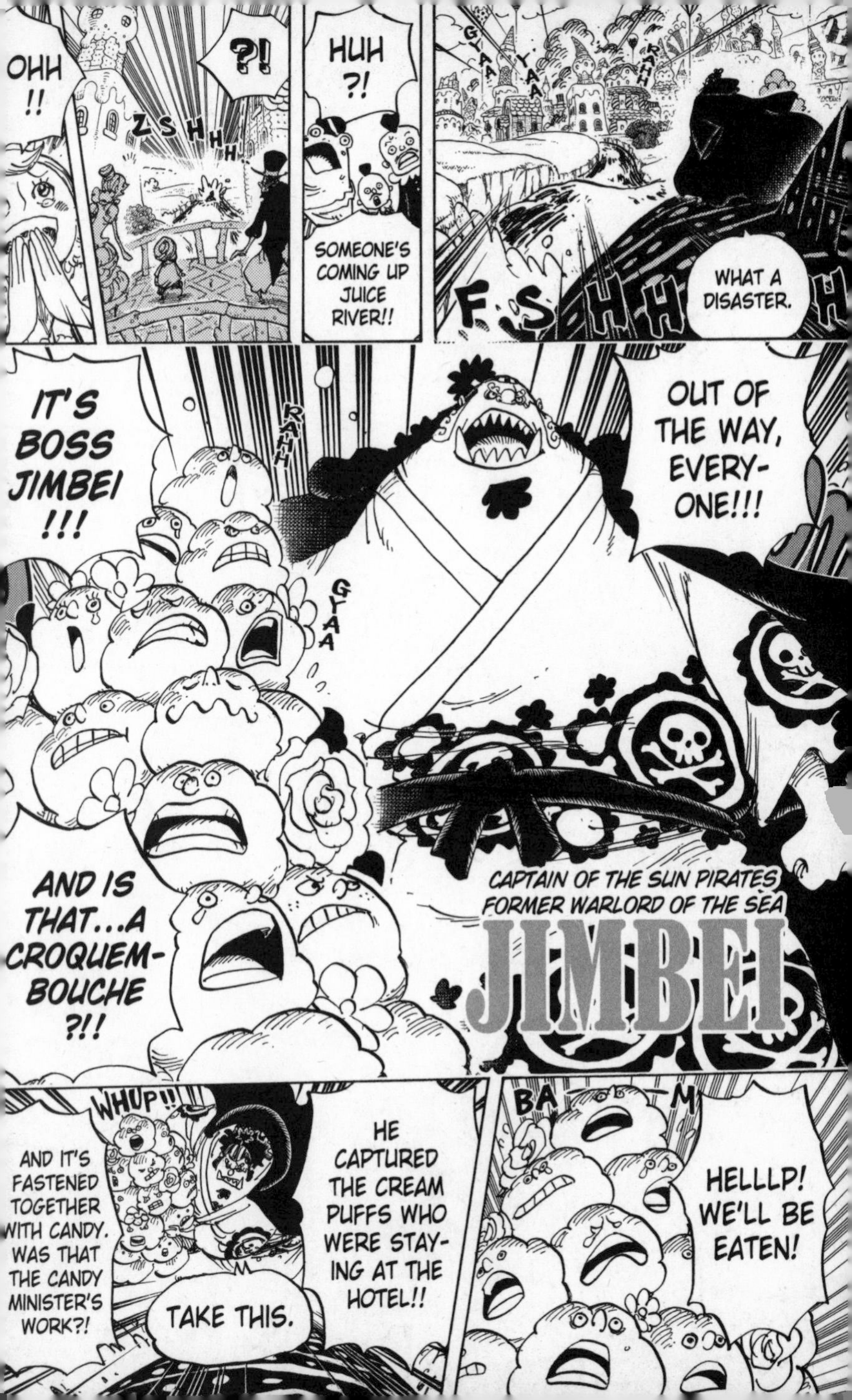
GYAA
YAA
RAHH
WHAT A DISASTER.
FSHHHH
HUH ?!
SOMEONE'S COMING UP JUICE RIVER!!
?!
ZSHHH
OHH !!
OUT OF THE WAY, EVERY-ONE!!!
RAHH
IT'S BOSS JIMBEI !!!
GYAA
CAPTAIN OF THE SUN PIRATES
FORMER WARLORD OF THE SEA
JIMBEI
AND IS THAT...A CROQUEM-BOUCHE ?!!
BA-M
HELLLP! WE'LL BE EATEN!
HE CAPTURED THE CREAM PUFFS WHO WERE STAY-ING AT THE HOTEL!!
WHUP!!
TAKE THIS.
AND IT'S FASTENED TOGETHER WITH CANDY. WAS THAT THE CANDY MINISTER'S WORK?!

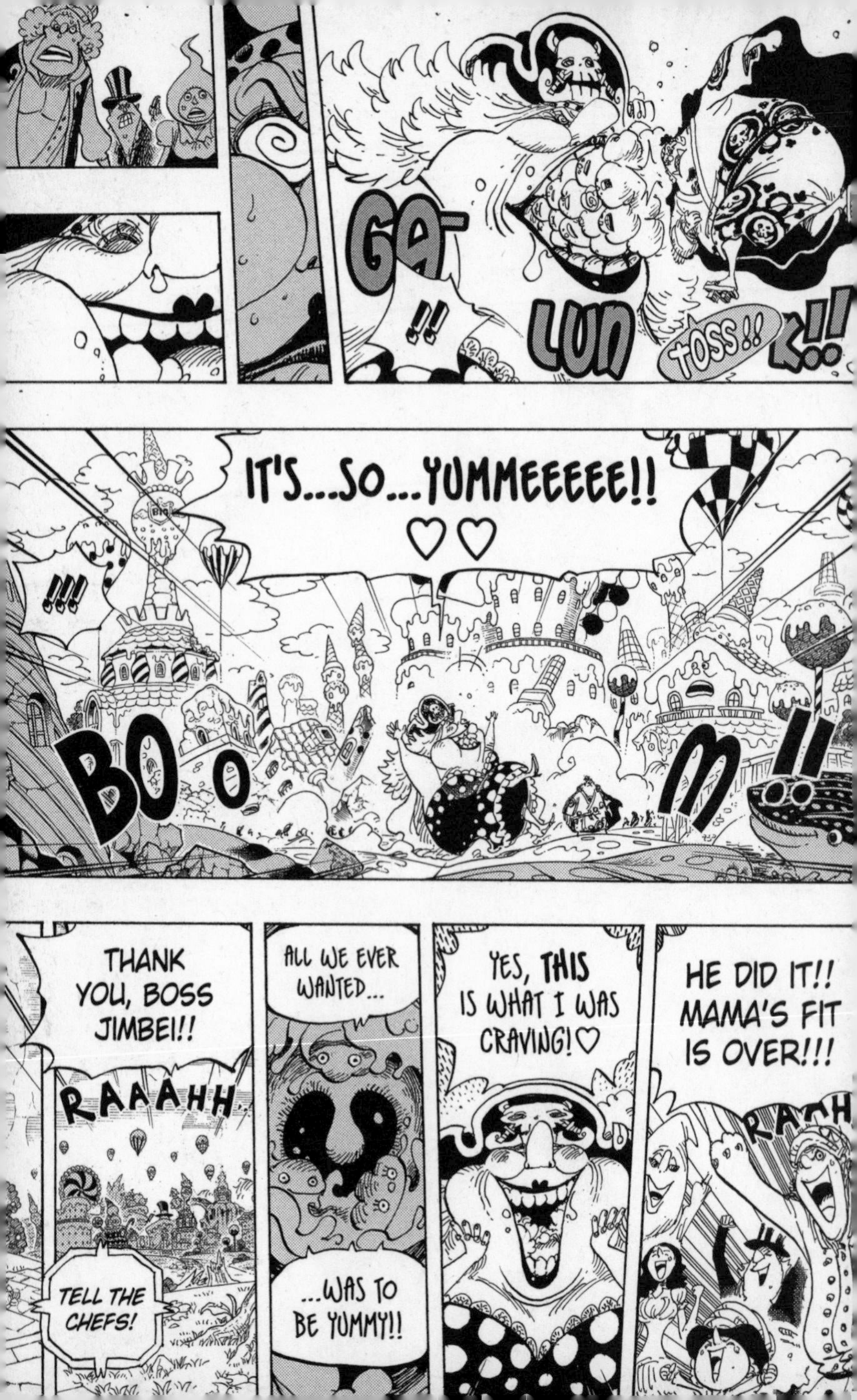

GA-
!!
LUN
TOSS!!
K...!!
IT'S...SO...YUMMEEEEE!! ♡♡
!!!
BOOOM!!
HE DID IT!! MAMA'S FIT IS OVER!!!
RAAH
YES, THIS IS WHAT I WAS CRAVING! ♡
ALL WE EVER WANTED...
...WAS TO BE YUMMY!!
THANK YOU, BOSS JIMBEI!!
RAAAHH
TELL THE CHEFS!

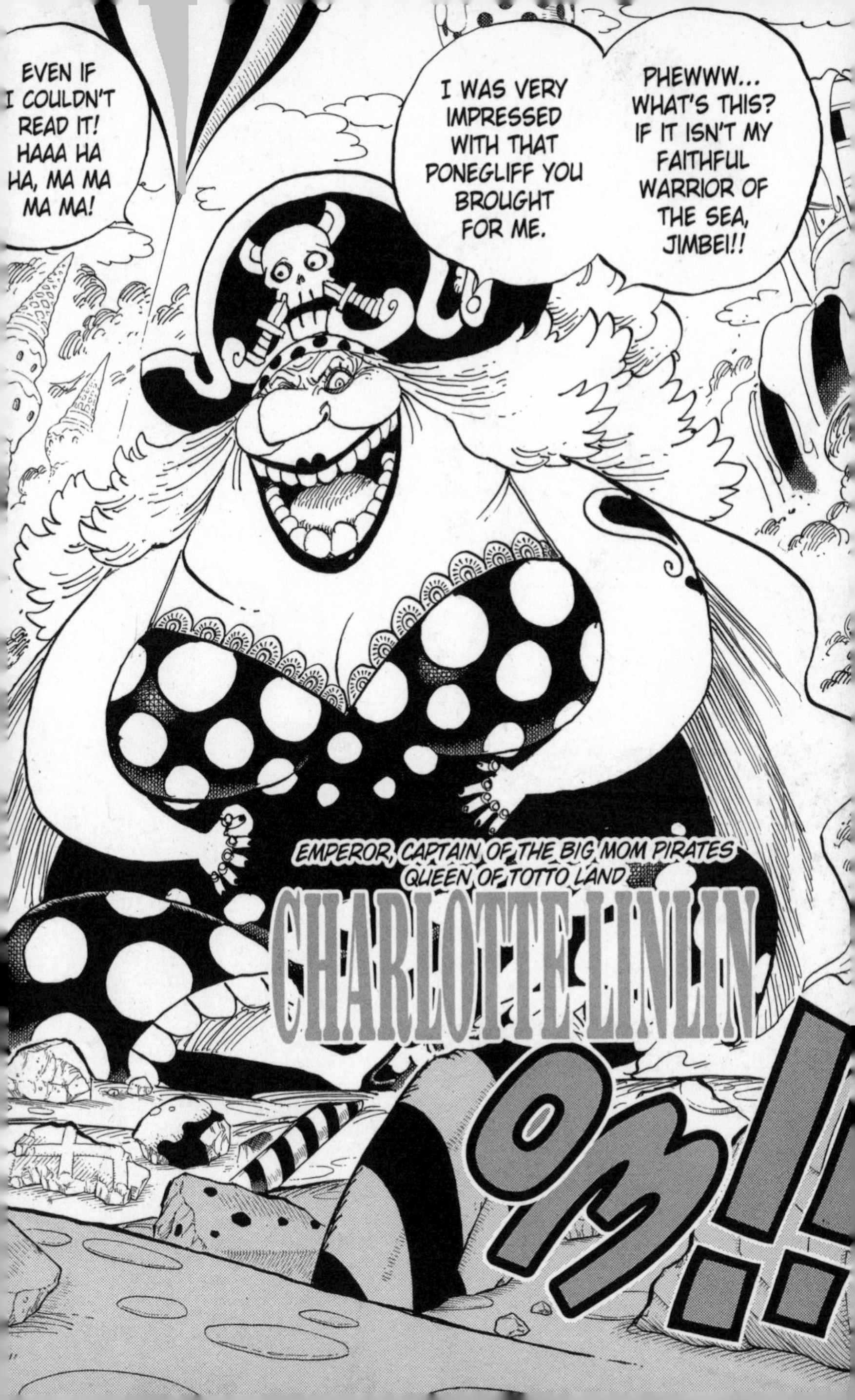
PHEWWW... WHAT'S THIS? IF IT ISN'T MY FAITHFUL WARRIOR OF THE SEA, JIMBEI!!
I WAS VERY IMPRESSED WITH THAT PONEGLIFF YOU BROUGHT FOR ME.
EVEN IF I COULDN'T READ IT! HAAA HA HA, MA MA MA MA!
EMPEROR, CAPTAIN OF THE BIG MOM PIRATES
QUEEN OF TOTTO LAND
CHARLOTTE LINLIN

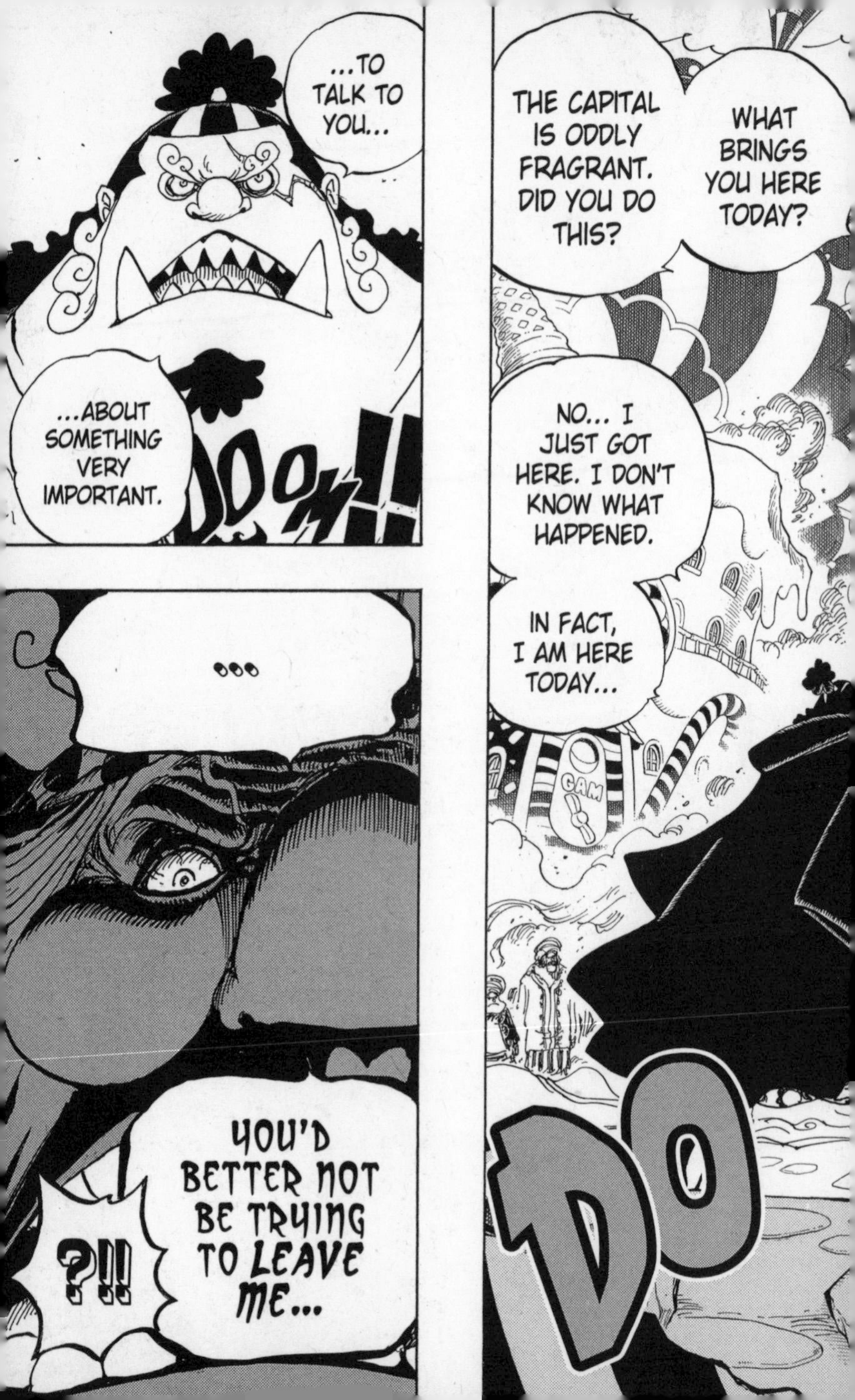
WHAT BRINGS YOU HERE TODAY?
THE CAPITAL IS ODDLY FRAGRANT. DID YOU DO THIS?
NO... I JUST GOT HERE. I DON'T KNOW WHAT HAPPENED.
IN FACT, I AM HERE TODAY...
GAM
DO
...TO TALK TO YOU...
...ABOUT SOMETHING VERY IMPORTANT.
...
YOU'D BETTER NOT BE TRYING TO *LEAVE* ME...
?!!

質問コーナー
Isn't the SBS about to start?
I think it might!
It's not starting yet!
So what if it starts?!
It's already started!!!

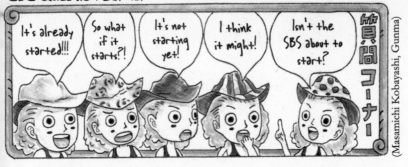

(Masamichi Kobayashi, Gunma)

A: ⬆ Whaaat?! Whaaat...whaaat... The SBS has begun.

Q: Hello, Oda Sensei! ☆ Please give us an introduction to the other twenty members of the Heart Pirates, who were treated with such disrespect in Chapter 815!! I thought they'd be all men, but I spotted a woman too! Right? What a shocker.

--Black-and-White Panda

A: Whaaat?! This is a shocker too! All of them? Why d'you wanna know?! Well, I can at least pick out three of them I meant to be voices of protest against the Straw Hat Alliance, but didn't get to draw for lack of space.

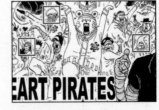

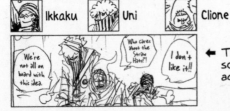

EART PIRATES

Ikkaku

Uni

Clione

I don't like it!!
Who cares about the Straw Hats?!
We're not all on board with this idea.

⬅ This was my idea for the scene. They might still be against the alliance idea.

Q: Oda Sensei, you can't just come up with Whitebeard's son and give us **Weevil!** The only resemblance is the white facial hair!

--Huge Whitebeard Fan

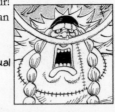

A: Right? So we've got this real weirdo as a new member of the Seven Warlords, and we can't even tell if he's Whitebeard's actual son. Let me just say that your reaction is exactly what I'm hoping for.
Heh heh heh heh heh. Heh heh heh heh heh.

Q: In chapter 792, you introduced the "nearby Applenine Island." Did you come up with that name because nearby (or adjacent) is *ringoku* in Japanese, plus *ringo* is apple and *ku* is the number nine?

--Haru

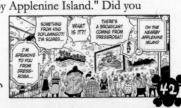

ON THE NEARBY APPLENINE ISLAND
THERE'S A BROADCAST COMING FROM DRESSROSA!!
WHAT IS IT?!
SOMETHING FROM KING DOFLAMINGO?! I'M SCARED...
I'M SPEAKING TO YOU FROM DRESS-ROSA...

A: Heh heh heh Gwahakk koff koff heh heh heh.

Chapter 830:
A MAN YOU CAN BET ON

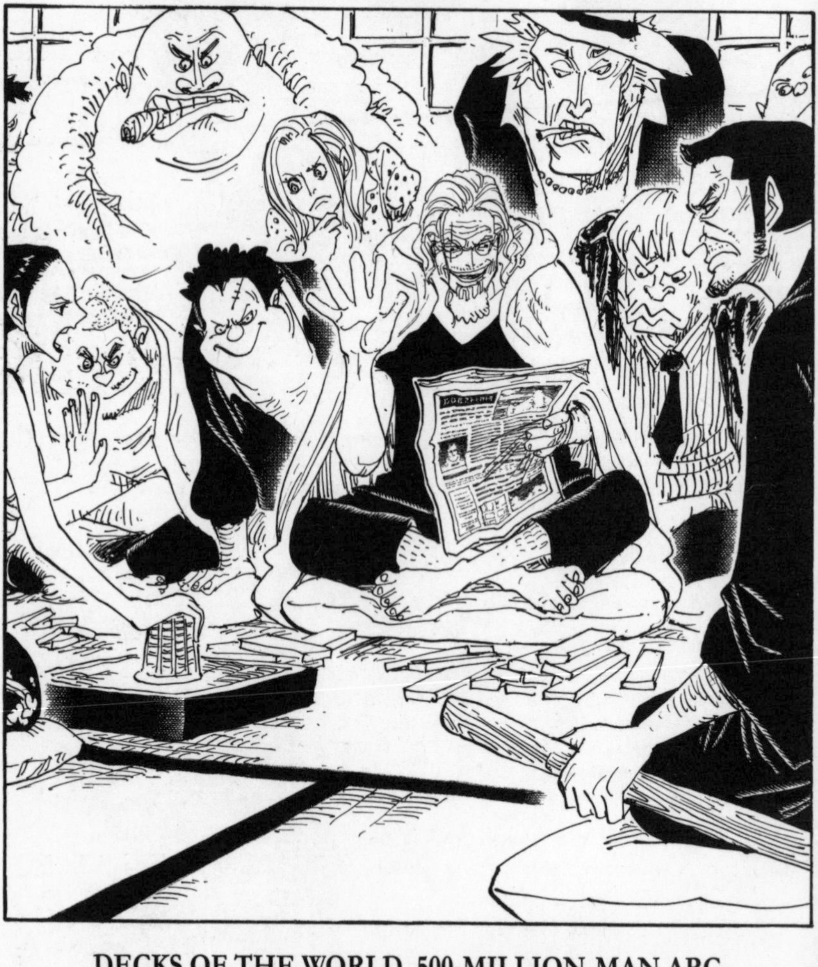

DECKS OF THE WORLD, 500-MILLION-MAN ARC,
VOL. 20: "SABAODY ARCHIPELAGO"

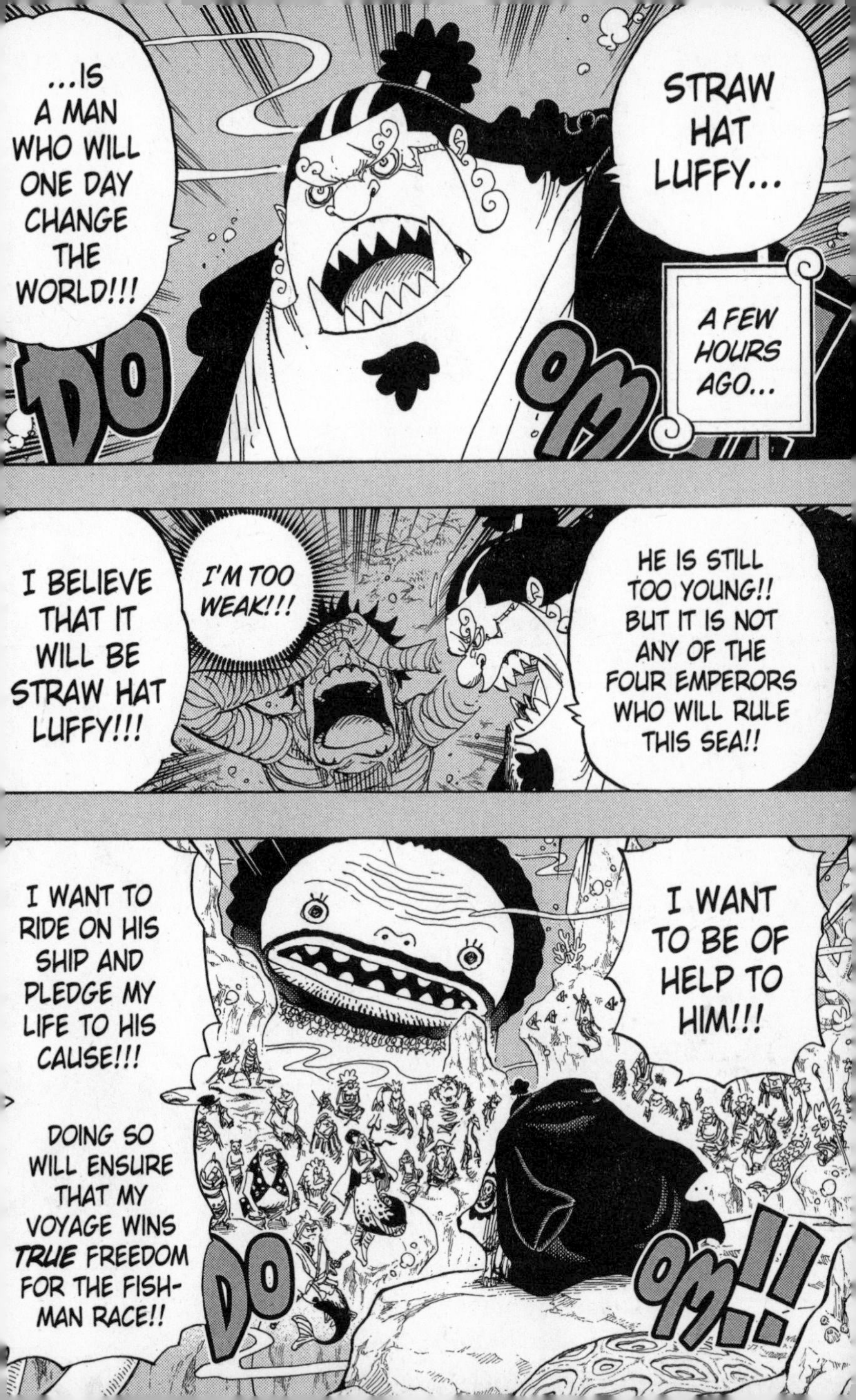
STRAW HAT LUFFY...
A FEW HOURS AGO...
...IS A MAN WHO WILL ONE DAY CHANGE THE WORLD!!!
DOOM
HE IS STILL TOO YOUNG!! BUT IT IS NOT ANY OF THE FOUR EMPERORS WHO WILL RULE THIS SEA!!
I'M TOO WEAK!!!
I BELIEVE THAT IT WILL BE STRAW HAT LUFFY!!!
I WANT TO BE OF HELP TO HIM!!!
I WANT TO RIDE ON HIS SHIP AND PLEDGE MY LIFE TO HIS CAUSE!!!
DOING SO WILL ENSURE THAT MY VOYAGE WINS *TRUE* FREEDOM FOR THE FISH-MAN RACE!!
DOOM!!

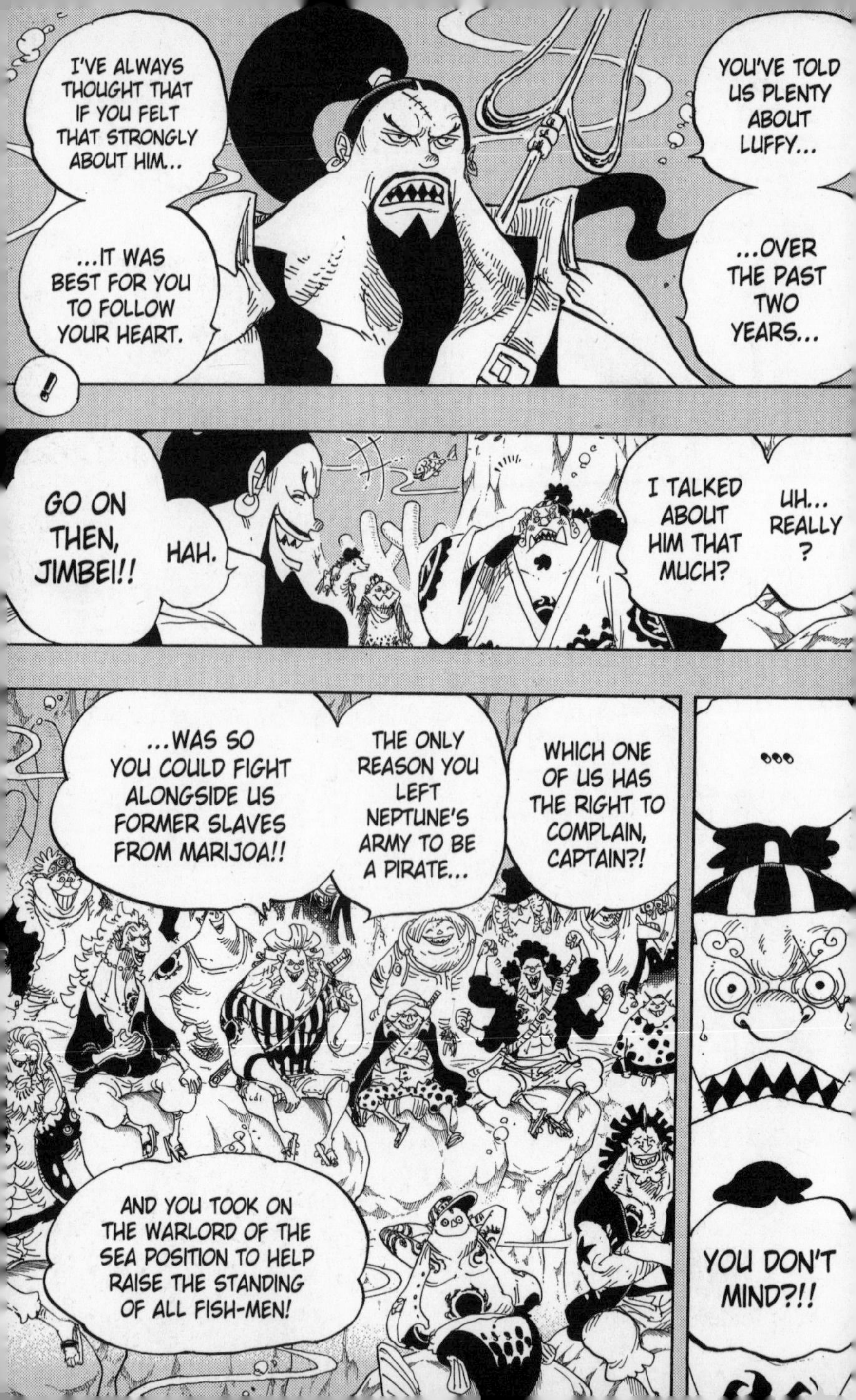
YOU'VE TOLD US PLENTY ABOUT LUFFY...
...OVER THE PAST TWO YEARS...
I'VE ALWAYS THOUGHT THAT IF YOU FELT THAT STRONGLY ABOUT HIM...
...IT WAS BEST FOR YOU TO FOLLOW YOUR HEART.
!
UH... REALLY?
I TALKED ABOUT HIM THAT MUCH?
HAH.
GO ON THEN, JIMBEI!!
...
YOU DON'T MIND?!!
WHICH ONE OF US HAS THE RIGHT TO COMPLAIN, CAPTAIN?!
THE ONLY REASON YOU LEFT NEPTUNE'S ARMY TO BE A PIRATE...
...WAS SO YOU COULD FIGHT ALONGSIDE US FORMER SLAVES FROM MARIJOA!!
AND YOU TOOK ON THE WARLORD OF THE SEA POSITION TO HELP RAISE THE STANDING OF ALL FISH-MEN!

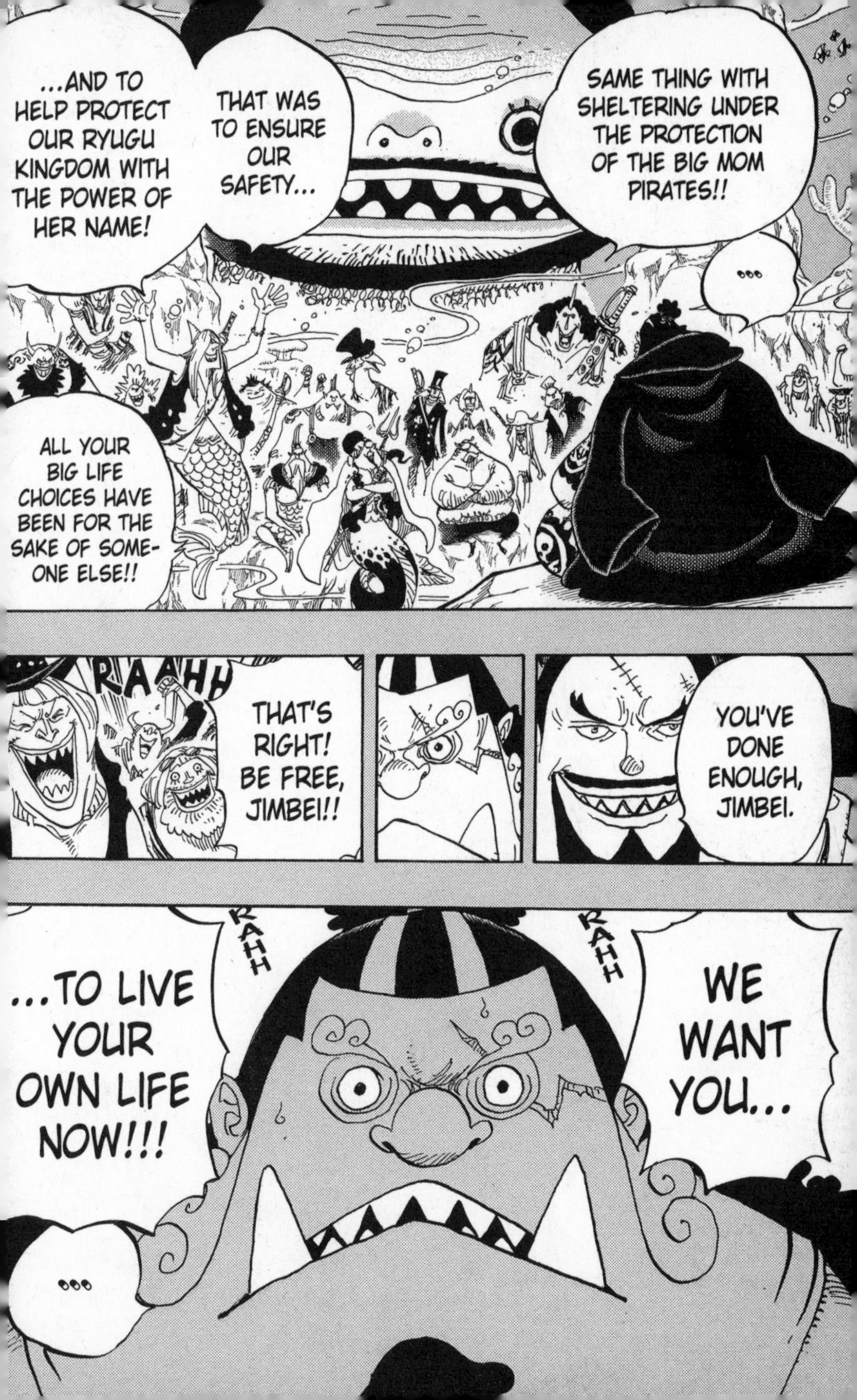
SAME THING WITH SHELTERING UNDER THE PROTECTION OF THE BIG MOM PIRATES!!
THAT WAS TO ENSURE OUR SAFETY...
...AND TO HELP PROTECT OUR RYUGU KINGDOM WITH THE POWER OF HER NAME!
...
ALL YOUR BIG LIFE CHOICES HAVE BEEN FOR THE SAKE OF SOME-ONE ELSE!!
YOU'VE DONE ENOUGH, JIMBEI.
RAAHH
THAT'S RIGHT! BE FREE, JIMBEI!!
RAHH
WE WANT YOU...
RAHH
...TO LIVE YOUR OWN LIFE NOW!!!
...

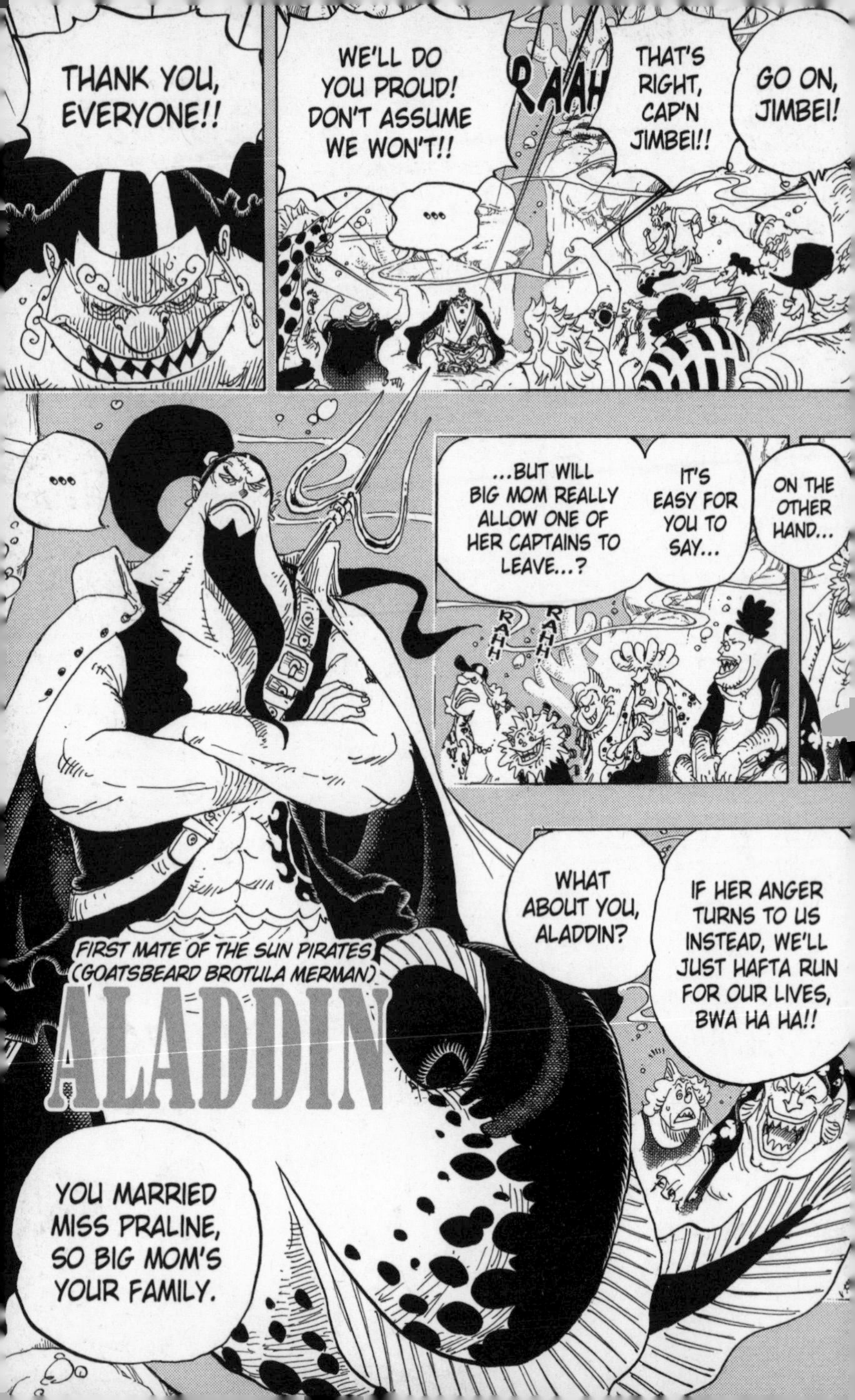
GO ON, JIMBEI!
THAT'S RIGHT, CAP'N JIMBEI!!
RAAH
WE'LL DO YOU PROUD! DON'T ASSUME WE WON'T!!
...
THANK YOU, EVERYONE!!
ON THE OTHER HAND...
IT'S EASY FOR YOU TO SAY...
...BUT WILL BIG MOM REALLY ALLOW ONE OF HER CAPTAINS TO LEAVE...?
RAHH
RAHH
IF HER ANGER TURNS TO US INSTEAD, WE'LL JUST HAFTA RUN FOR OUR LIVES, BWA HA HA!!
WHAT ABOUT YOU, ALADDIN?
...
FIRST MATE OF THE SUN PIRATES (GOATSBEARD BROTULA MERMAN)
ALADDIN
YOU MARRIED MISS PRALINE, SO BIG MOM'S YOUR FAMILY.

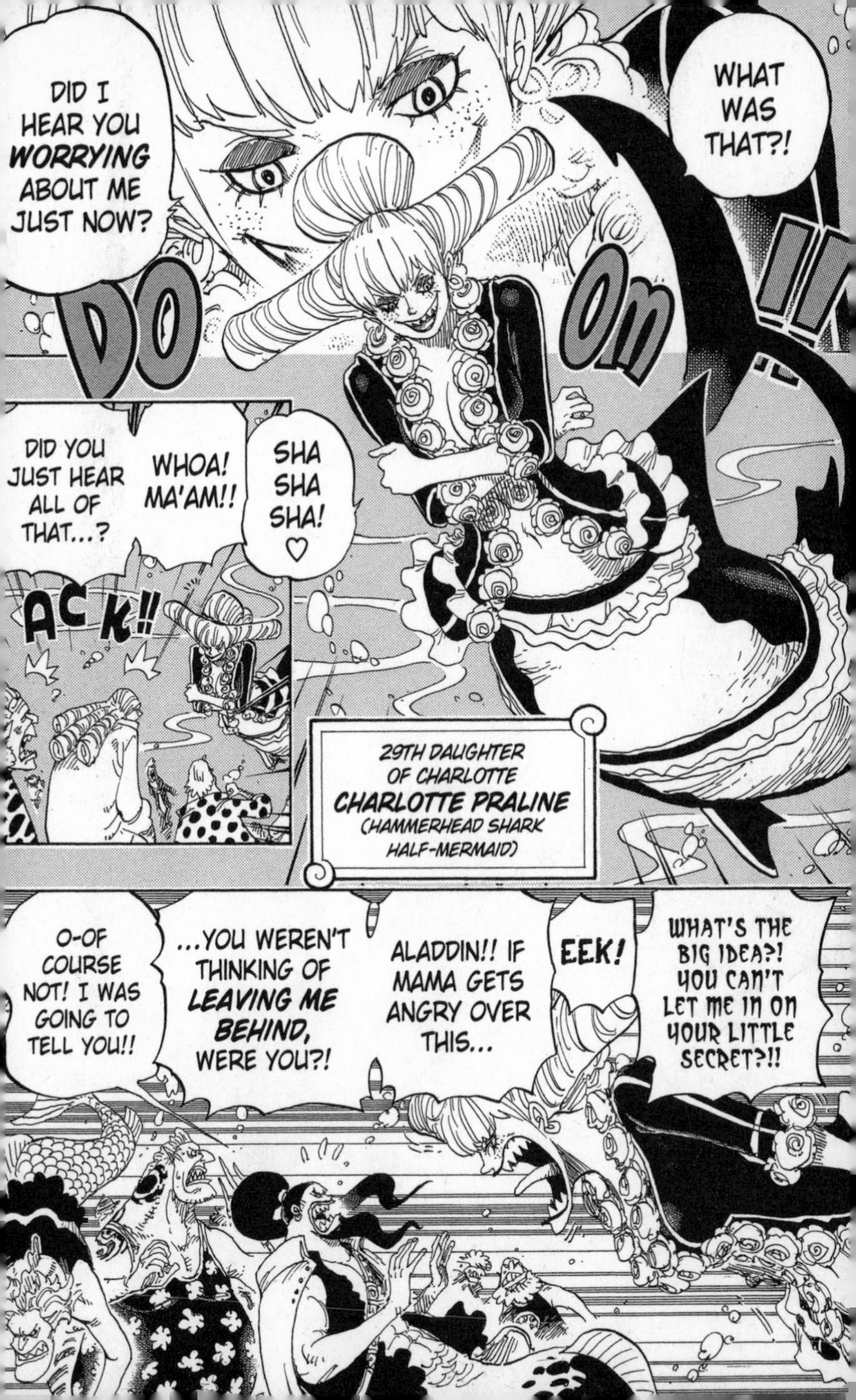
WHAT WAS THAT?!
DID I HEAR YOU ***WORRYING*** ABOUT ME JUST NOW?
DOOM
!!
29TH DAUGHTER OF CHARLOTTE
CHARLOTTE PRALINE
(HAMMERHEAD SHARK HALF-MERMAID)
SHA SHA SHA! ♡
WHOA! MA'AM!!
DID YOU JUST HEAR ALL OF THAT...?
ACK!!
WHAT'S THE BIG IDEA?! YOU CAN'T LET ME IN ON YOUR LITTLE SECRET?!!
EEK!
ALADDIN!! IF MAMA GETS ANGRY OVER THIS...
...YOU WEREN'T THINKING OF ***LEAVING ME BEHIND,*** WERE YOU?!
O-OF COURSE NOT! I WAS GOING TO TELL YOU!!

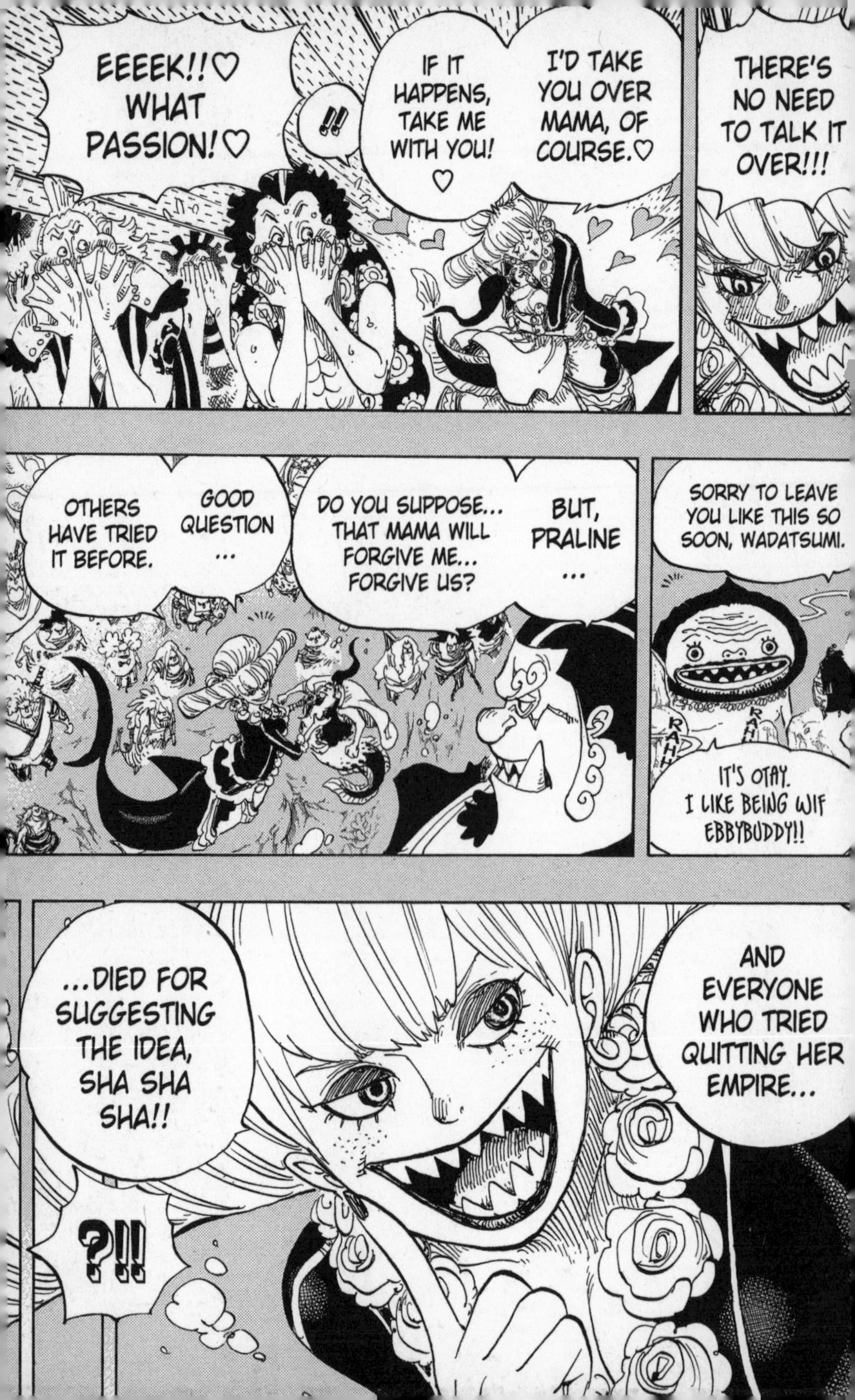
THERE'S NO NEED TO TALK IT OVER!!!
I'D TAKE YOU OVER MAMA, OF COURSE.♡
IF IT HAPPENS, TAKE ME WITH YOU! ♡
!!
EEEEK!!♡ WHAT PASSION!♡
SORRY TO LEAVE YOU LIKE THIS SO SOON, WADATSUMI.
IT'S OTAY. I LIKE BEING WIF EBBYBUDDY!!
BUT, PRALINE...
DO YOU SUPPOSE... THAT MAMA WILL FORGIVE ME... FORGIVE US?
GOOD QUESTION...
OTHERS HAVE TRIED IT BEFORE.
AND EVERYONE WHO TRIED QUITTING HER EMPIRE...
...DIED FOR SUGGESTING THE IDEA, SHA SHA SHA!!
?!!

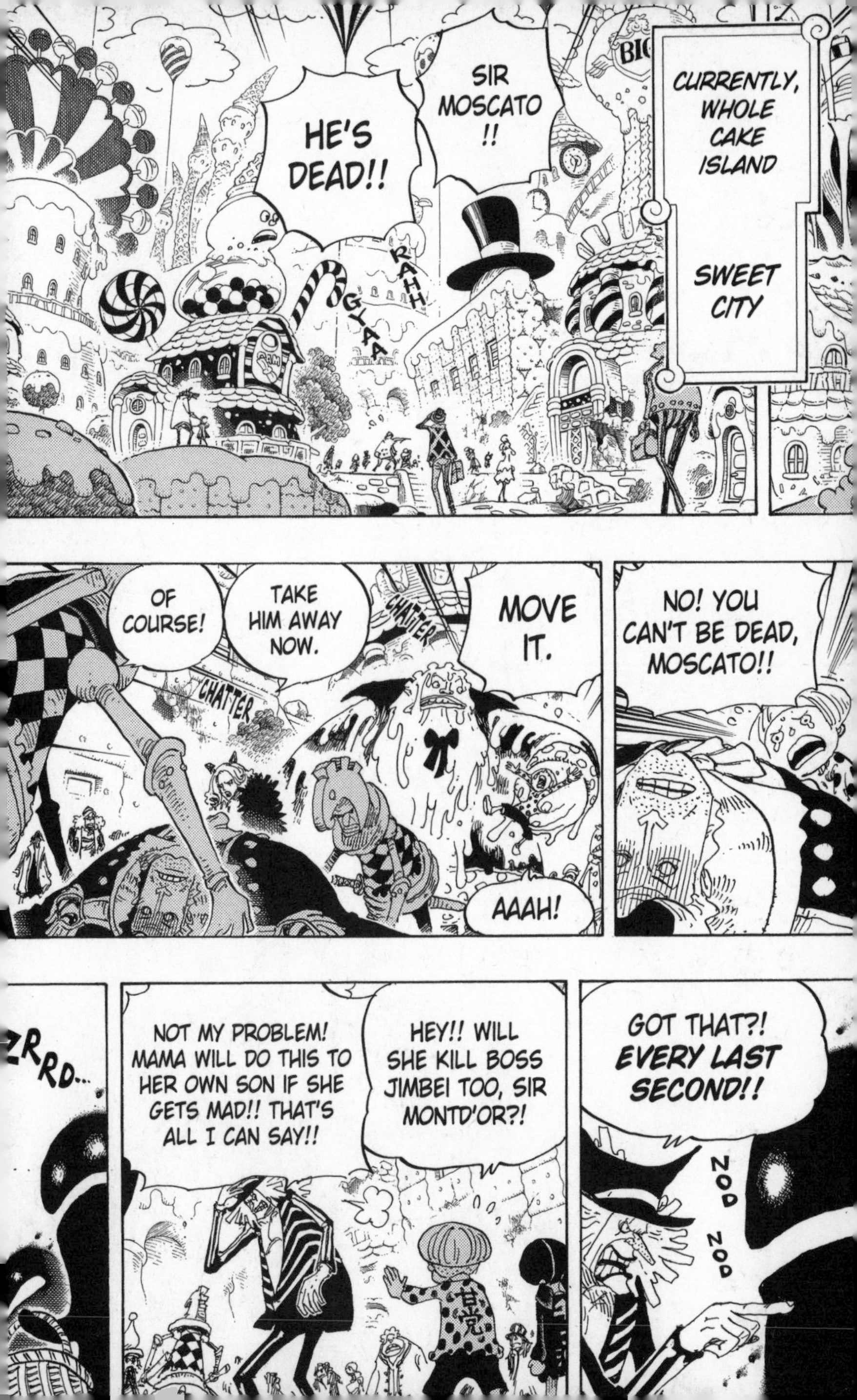
CURRENTLY, WHOLE CAKE ISLAND
SWEET CITY
SIR MOSCATO!!
HE'S DEAD!!
RAHH
GYAA
NO! YOU CAN'T BE DEAD, MOSCATO!!
MOVE IT.
CHATTER
TAKE HIM AWAY NOW.
OF COURSE!
CHATTER
AAAH!
GOT THAT?! EVERY LAST SECOND!!
NOD NOD
HEY!! WILL SHE KILL BOSS JIMBEI TOO, SIR MONTD'OR?!
NOT MY PROBLEM! MAMA WILL DO THIS TO HER OWN SON IF SHE GETS MAD!! THAT'S ALL I CAN SAY!!
ZRRD...

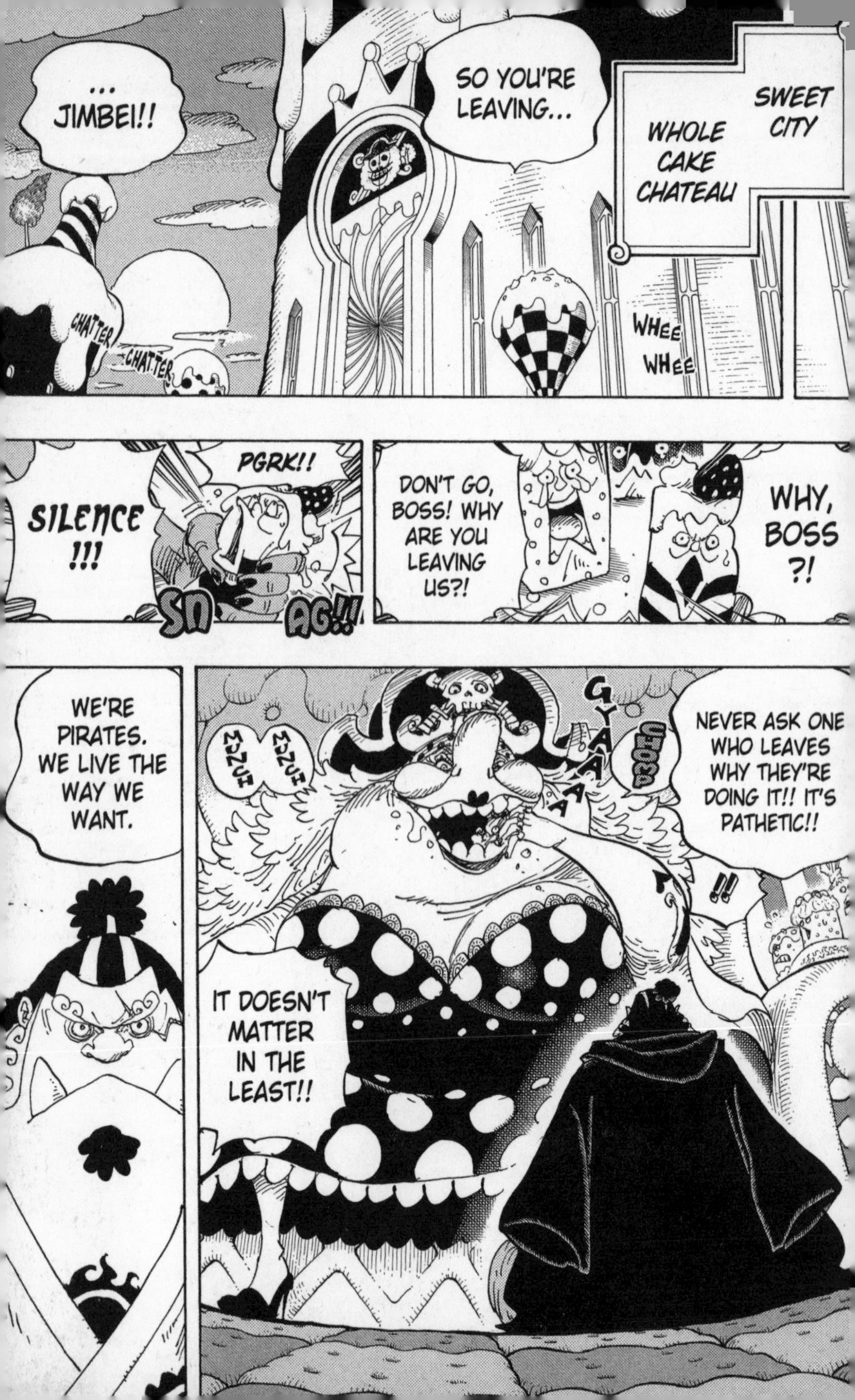
SWEET CITY
WHOLE CAKE CHATEAU
SO YOU'RE LEAVING...
... JIMBEI!!
WHEE WHEE
CHATTER CHATTER
WHY, BOSS ?!
DON'T GO, BOSS! WHY ARE YOU LEAVING US?!
PGRK!!
SILENCE !!!
SNAG!!
NEVER ASK ONE WHO LEAVES WHY THEY'RE DOING IT!! IT'S PATHETIC!!
!!
CHOMP
GYAAAAA
MUNCH
MUNCH
IT DOESN'T MATTER IN THE LEAST!!
WE'RE PIRATES. WE LIVE THE WAY WE WANT.

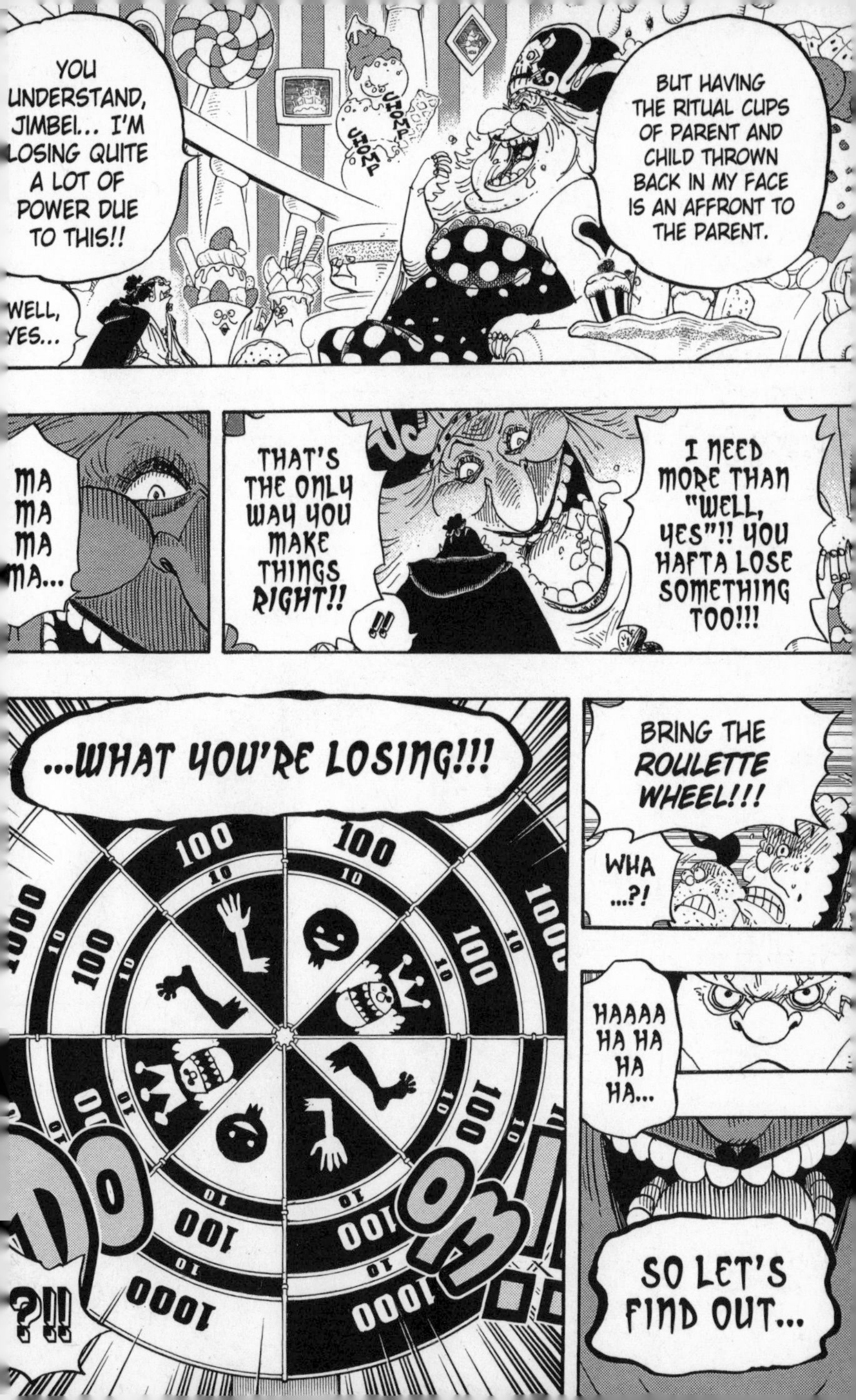
BUT HAVING THE RITUAL CUPS OF PARENT AND CHILD THROWN BACK IN MY FACE IS AN AFFRONT TO THE PARENT.
CHOMP
CHOMP
YOU UNDERSTAND, JIMBEI... I'M LOSING QUITE A LOT OF POWER DUE TO THIS!!
WELL, YES...
I NEED MORE THAN "WELL, YES"!! YOU HAFTA LOSE SOMETHING TOO!!!
THAT'S THE ONLY WAY YOU MAKE THINGS RIGHT!!
!!
MA MA MA MA...
BRING THE ROULETTE WHEEL!!!
WHA ...?!
HAAAA HA HA HA HA...
SO LET'S FIND OUT...
...WHAT YOU'RE LOSING!!!
?!!

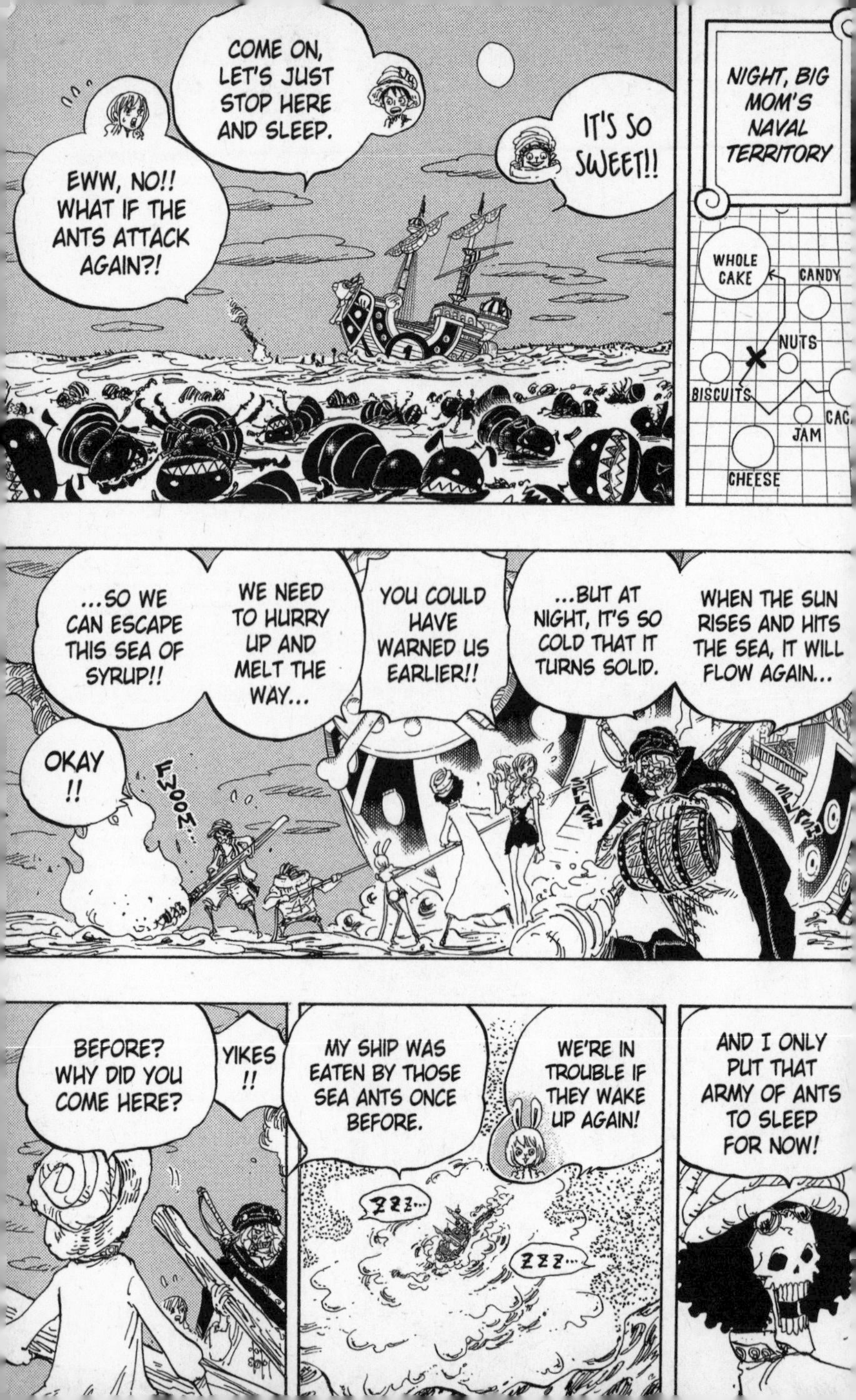
NIGHT, BIG MOM'S NAVAL TERRITORY
WHOLE CAKE
CANDY
NUTS
BISCUITS
CAC
JAM
CHEESE
IT'S SO SWEET!!
COME ON, LET'S JUST STOP HERE AND SLEEP.
EWW, NO!! WHAT IF THE ANTS ATTACK AGAIN?!
WHEN THE SUN RISES AND HITS THE SEA, IT WILL FLOW AGAIN...
...BUT AT NIGHT, IT'S SO COLD THAT IT TURNS SOLID.
YOU COULD HAVE WARNED US EARLIER!!
WE NEED TO HURRY UP AND MELT THE WAY...
...SO WE CAN ESCAPE THIS SEA OF SYRUP!!
SPLASH
OKAY!!
FWOOM
AND I ONLY PUT THAT ARMY OF ANTS TO SLEEP FOR NOW!
WE'RE IN TROUBLE IF THEY WAKE UP AGAIN!
MY SHIP WAS EATEN BY THOSE SEA ANTS ONCE BEFORE.
ZZZ...
ZZZ...
YIKES!!
BEFORE? WHY DID YOU COME HERE?

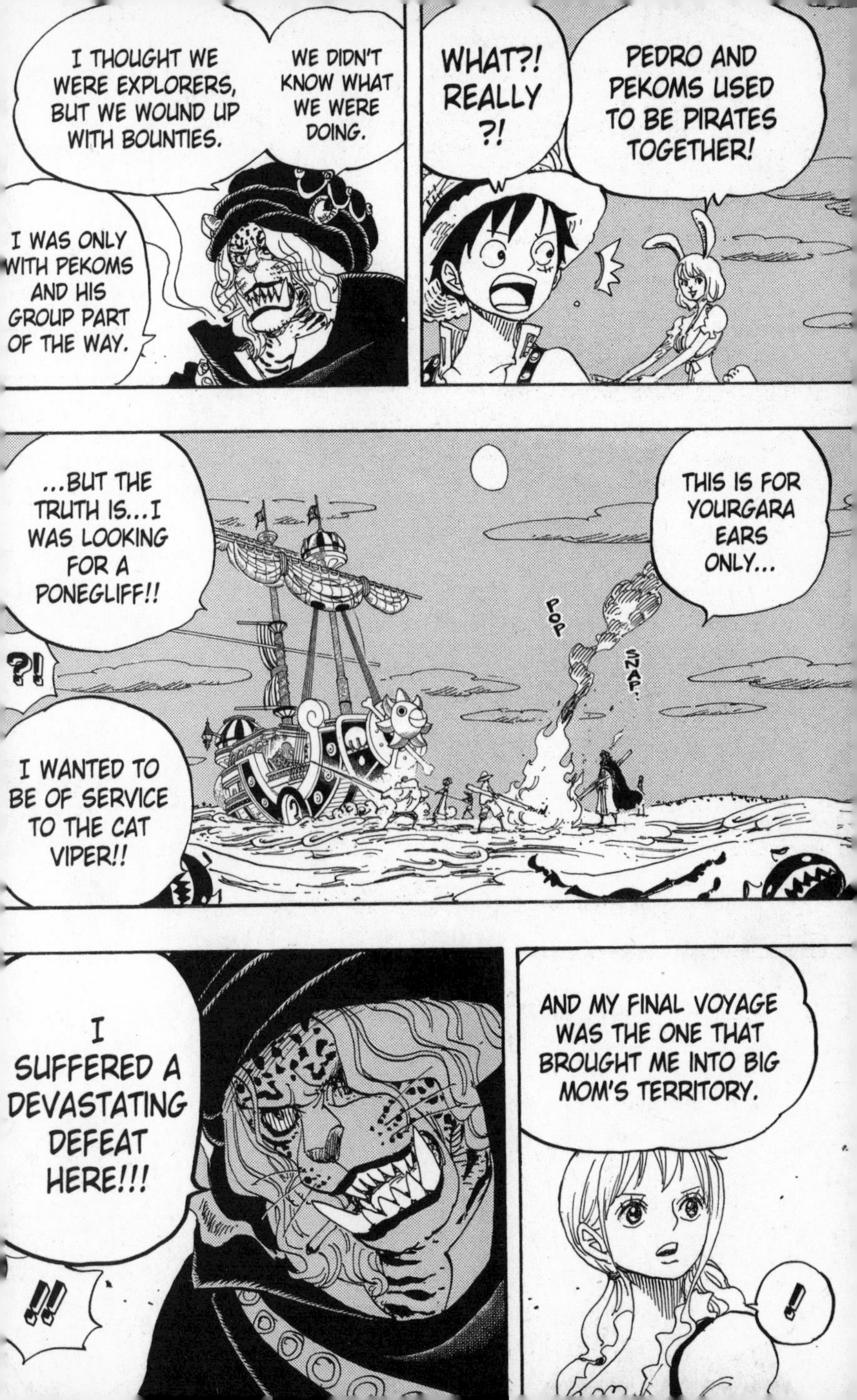
PEDRO AND PEKOMS USED TO BE PIRATES TOGETHER!
WHAT?! REALLY ?!
WE DIDN'T KNOW WHAT WE WERE DOING.
I THOUGHT WE WERE EXPLORERS, BUT WE WOUND UP WITH BOUNTIES.
I WAS ONLY WITH PEKOMS AND HIS GROUP PART OF THE WAY.
THIS IS FOR YOURGARA EARS ONLY...
POP
SNAP
...BUT THE TRUTH IS...I WAS LOOKING FOR A PONEGLIFF!!
?!
I WANTED TO BE OF SERVICE TO THE CAT VIPER!!
AND MY FINAL VOYAGE WAS THE ONE THAT BROUGHT ME INTO BIG MOM'S TERRITORY.
!
I SUFFERED A DEVASTATING DEFEAT HERE!!!
!!

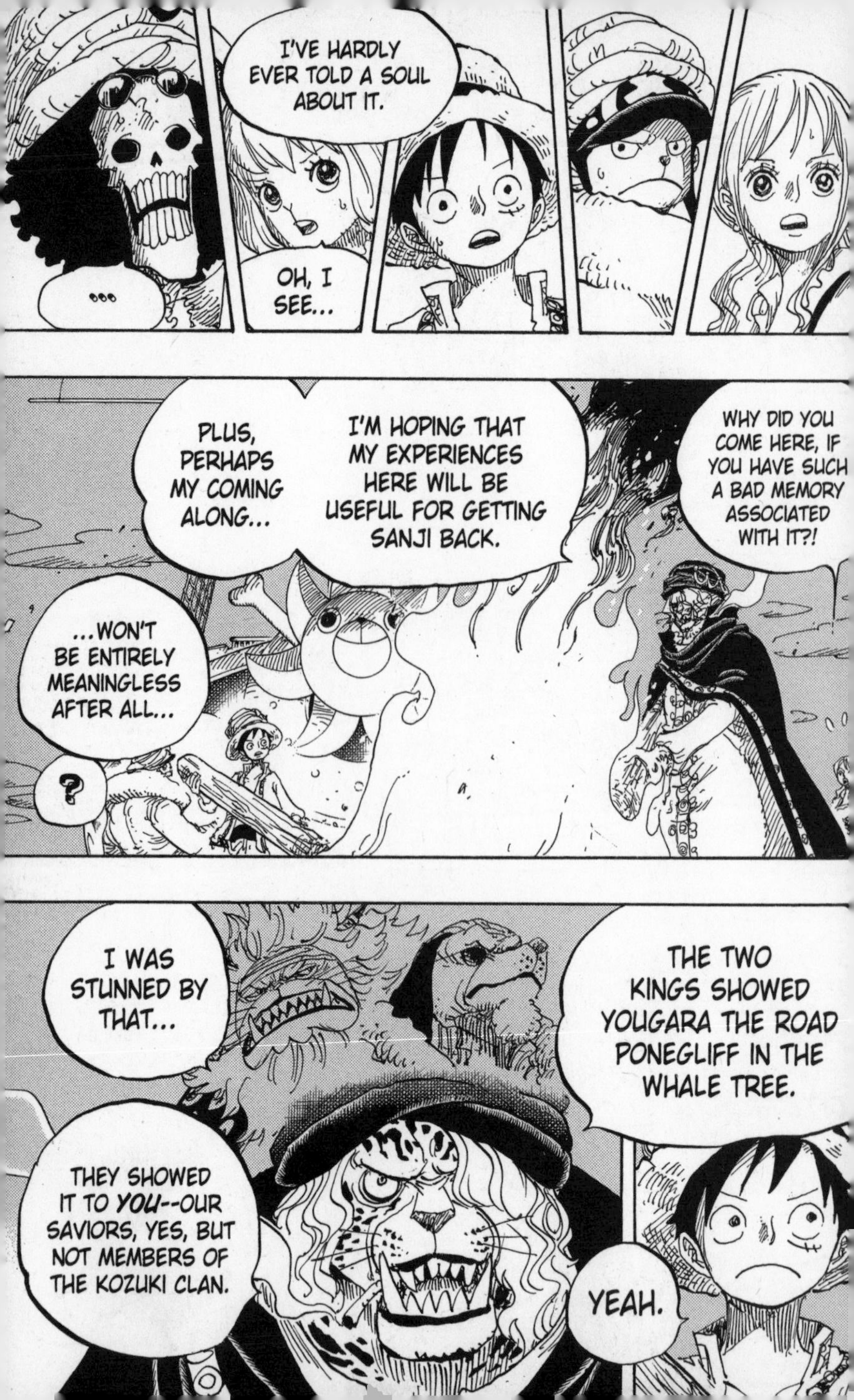
I'VE HARDLY EVER TOLD A SOUL ABOUT IT.
OH, I SEE...
...
WHY DID YOU COME HERE, IF YOU HAVE SUCH A BAD MEMORY ASSOCIATED WITH IT?!
I'M HOPING THAT MY EXPERIENCES HERE WILL BE USEFUL FOR GETTING SANJI BACK.
PLUS, PERHAPS MY COMING ALONG...
...WON'T BE ENTIRELY MEANINGLESS AFTER ALL...
?
THE TWO KINGS SHOWED YOUGARA THE ROAD PONEGLIFF IN THE WHALE TREE.
I WAS STUNNED BY THAT...
THEY SHOWED IT TO *YOU*--OUR SAVIORS, YES, BUT NOT MEMBERS OF THE KOZUKI CLAN.
YEAH.

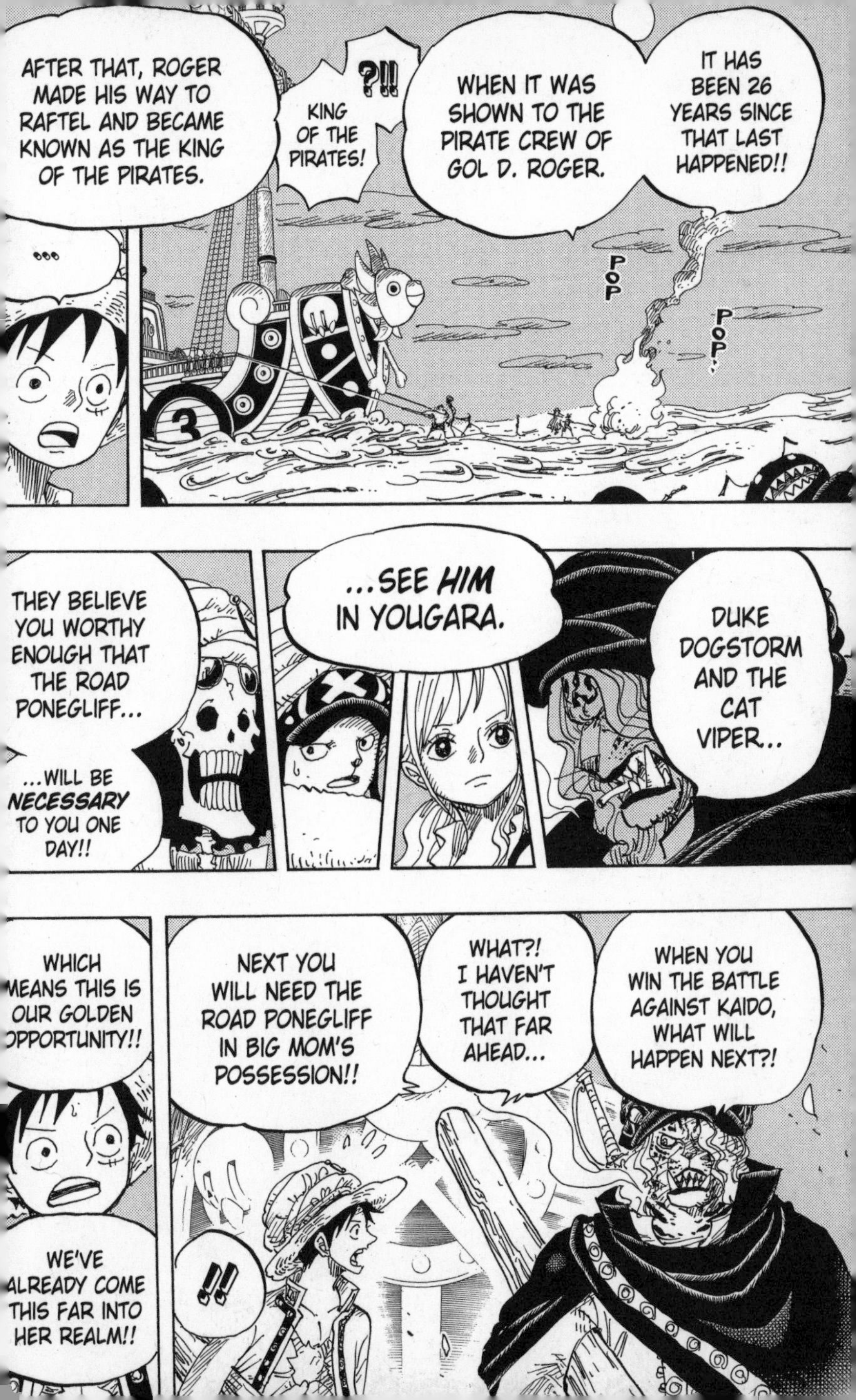
IT HAS BEEN 26 YEARS SINCE THAT LAST HAPPENED!!
WHEN IT WAS SHOWN TO THE PIRATE CREW OF GOL D. ROGER.
?!!
KING OF THE PIRATES!
AFTER THAT, ROGER MADE HIS WAY TO RAFTEL AND BECAME KNOWN AS THE KING OF THE PIRATES.
POP
POP
...
DUKE DOGSTORM AND THE CAT VIPER..
...SEE *HIM* IN YOUGARA.
THEY BELIEVE YOU WORTHY ENOUGH THAT THE ROAD PONEGLIFF...
...WILL BE ***NECESSARY*** TO YOU ONE DAY!!
WHEN YOU WIN THE BATTLE AGAINST KAIDO, WHAT WILL HAPPEN NEXT?!
WHAT?! I HAVEN'T THOUGHT THAT FAR AHEAD...
NEXT YOU WILL NEED THE ROAD PONEGLIFF IN BIG MOM'S POSSESSION!!
!!
WHICH MEANS THIS IS OUR GOLDEN OPPORTUNITY!!
WE'VE ALREADY COME THIS FAR INTO HER REALM!!

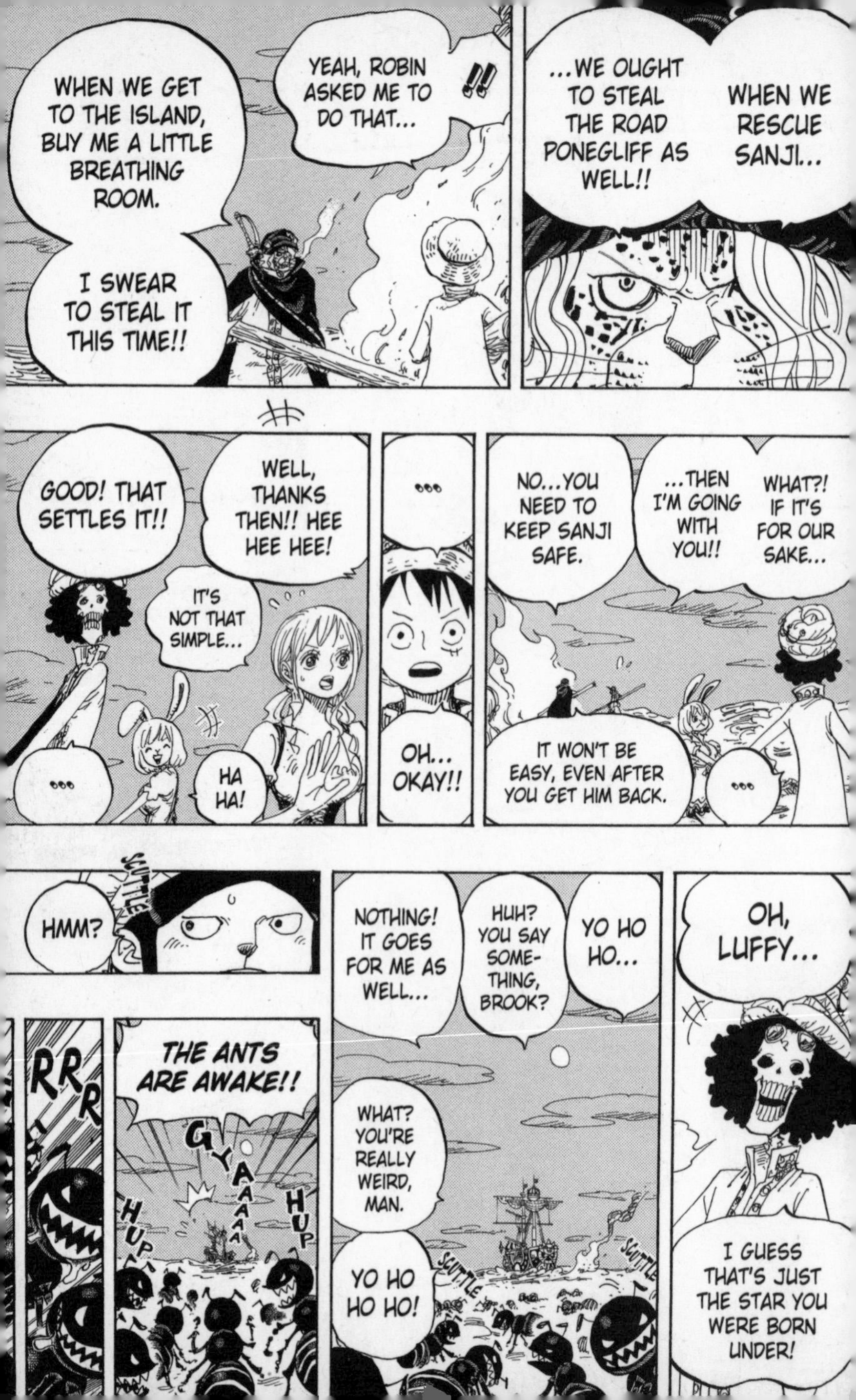
WHEN WE RESCUE SANJI...
...WE OUGHT TO STEAL THE ROAD PONEGLIFF AS WELL!!
!!
YEAH, ROBIN ASKED ME TO DO THAT...
WHEN WE GET TO THE ISLAND, BUY ME A LITTLE BREATHING ROOM.
I SWEAR TO STEAL IT THIS TIME!!
WHAT?! IF IT'S FOR OUR SAKE...
...THEN I'M GOING WITH YOU!!
NO...YOU NEED TO KEEP SANJI SAFE.
IT WON'T BE EASY, EVEN AFTER YOU GET HIM BACK.
...
...
OH... OKAY!!
WELL, THANKS THEN!! HEE HEE HEE!
GOOD! THAT SETTLES IT!!
IT'S NOT THAT SIMPLE...
HA HA!
...
OH, LUFFY...
I GUESS THAT'S JUST THE STAR YOU WERE BORN UNDER!
YO HO HO...
HUH? YOU SAY SOME-THING, BROOK?
NOTHING! IT GOES FOR ME AS WELL...
WHAT? YOU'RE REALLY WEIRD, MAN.
YO HO HO HO!
SCUTTLE
SCUTTLE
SCUTTLE
HMM?
THE ANTS ARE AWAKE!!
GYAAAAA
HUP
HUP
RRR

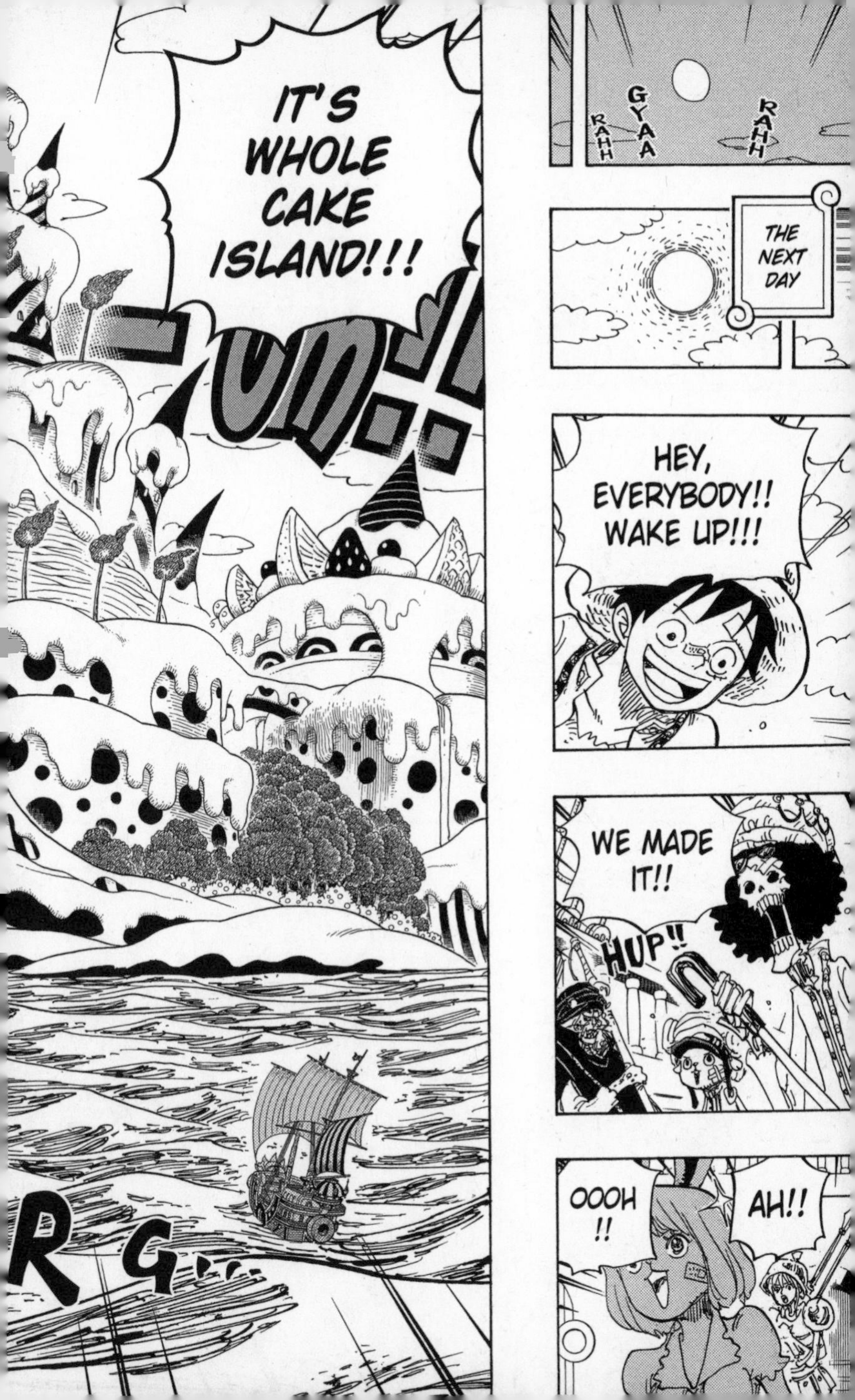
RAHH
GYAA
RAHH
THE NEXT DAY
HEY, EVERYBODY!! WAKE UP!!!
WE MADE IT!!
HUP!!
AH!!
OOOH !!
IT'S WHOLE CAKE ISLAND!!!

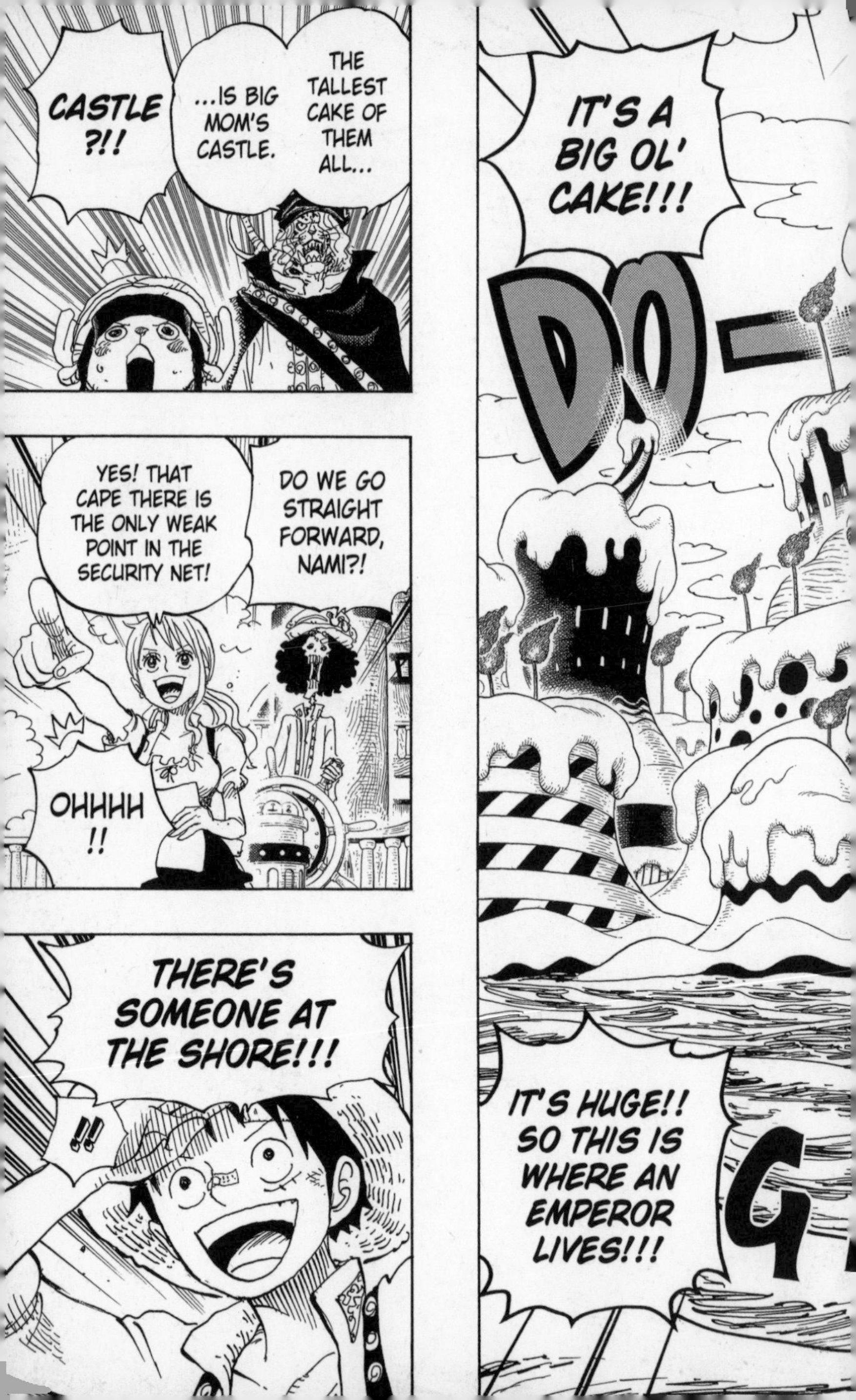
IT'S A BIG OL' CAKE!!!
DO-
IT'S HUGE!! SO THIS IS WHERE AN EMPEROR LIVES!!!
G
THE TALLEST CAKE OF THEM ALL...
...IS BIG MOM'S CASTLE.
CASTLE ?!!
DO WE GO STRAIGHT FORWARD, NAMI?!
YES! THAT CAPE THERE IS THE ONLY WEAK POINT IN THE SECURITY NET!
OHHHH !!
THERE'S SOMEONE AT THE SHORE!!!
!!

SBS Question Corner

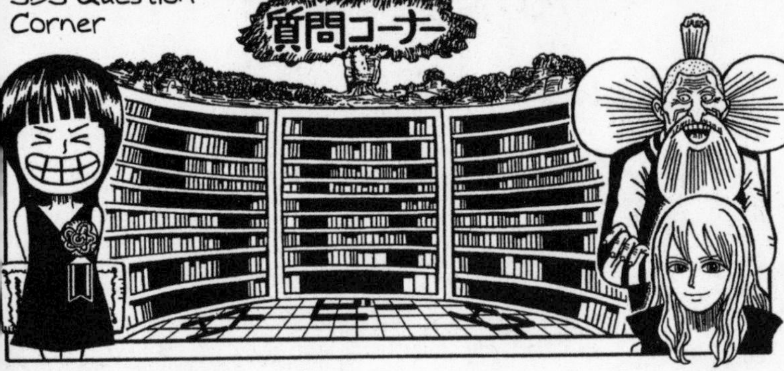

質問コーナー

(Fujima, Fukuoka)

Q: Can you explain how the Longleg people ride a bicycle? I can't figure it out.

--K Jun

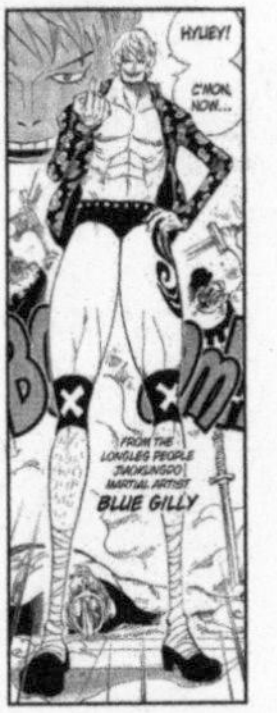

HYUEY!
C'MON, NOW...
FROM THE LONGLEG PEOPLE
MARTIAL ARTIST
BLUE GILLY

A: Well, it would be awkward for them if they tried to ride a normal human bicycle, but back home they have their own bicycle makers that sell special Longleg bikes, so have no fear. They're doing just fine.

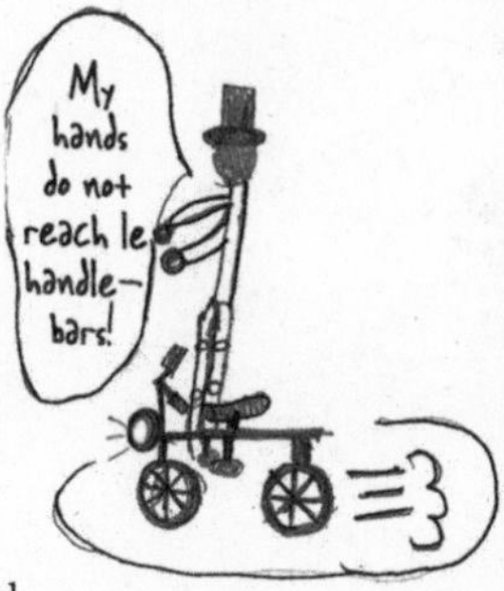

My hands do not reach le handle-bars!

Q: What's with all the "yougara" and "theygara" and "youteia" and all that stuff the minks say? It seems to be part of their non-first-person pronouns, but are there rules to the pattern? Tell me…and let me garchu you! *(laughs)*

--Jimbei's student, Magu

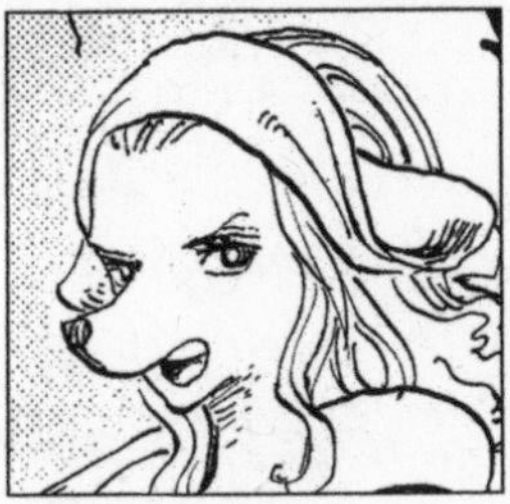

A: Garchuuuuuu!♡♡ There.
I'm pretty sure it was confusing at first, but it's really quite simple. Males say -gara, and females say -teia. So...
You → yougara, youteia
We → wegara, weteia
They → theygara, theyteia
And so on, and so on. There may be a few other instances here and there, but don't think too hard about it. It's just for fun. They're a species that developed its own culture on an isolated island, so it's practically a miracle we can understand each other at all.

Chapter 831:
ADVENTURE IN THE MYSTERIOUS FOREST

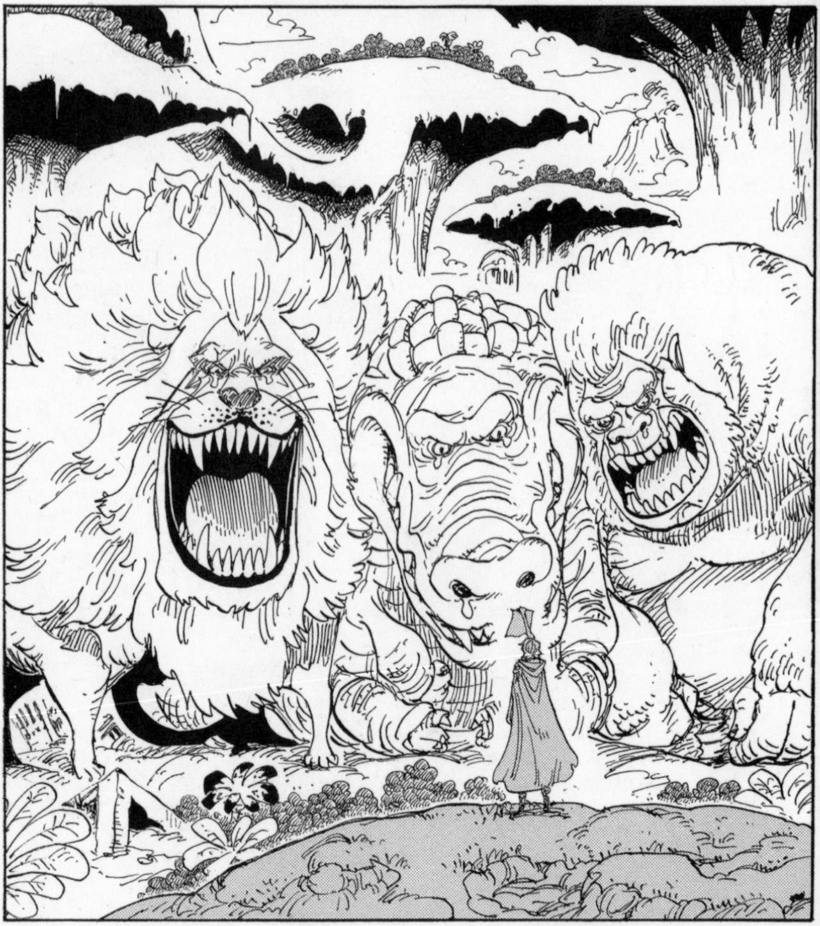

DECKS OF THE WORLD, 500-MILLION-MAN ARC, VOL. 21:
"RUSKAINA--IT'S THE FACE OF OUR BELOVED BOSS"

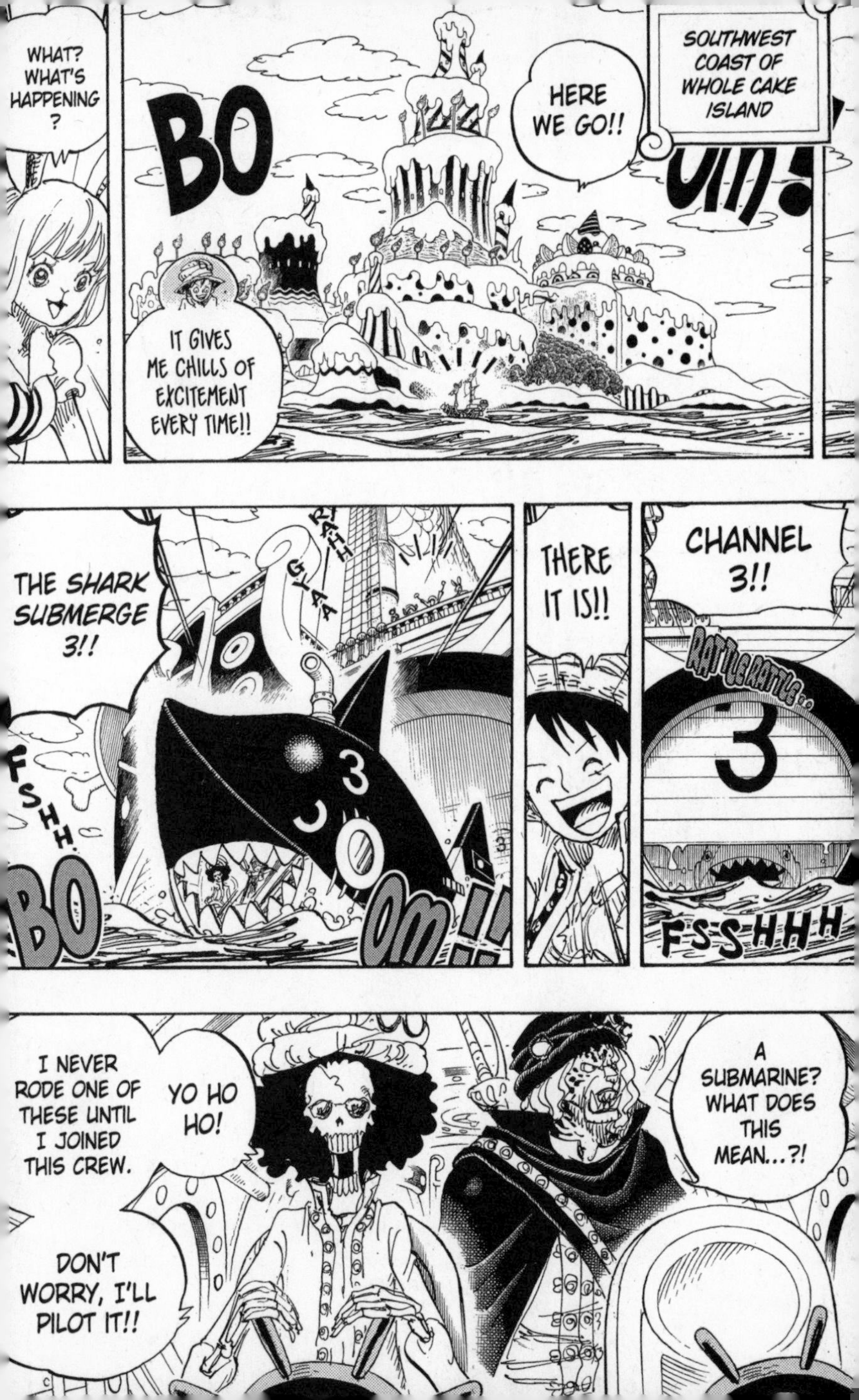
SOUTHWEST COAST OF WHOLE CAKE ISLAND
HERE WE GO!!
BO
UN!
IT GIVES ME CHILLS OF EXCITEMENT EVERY TIME!!
WHAT? WHAT'S HAPPENING ?
CHANNEL 3!!
RATTLE RATTLE...
FSSHHH
THERE IT IS!!
THE SHARK SUBMERGE 3!!
FSHH
BOOM!!
A SUBMARINE? WHAT DOES THIS MEAN...?!
YO HO HO!
I NEVER RODE ONE OF THESE UNTIL I JOINED THIS CREW.
DON'T WORRY, I'LL PILOT IT!!

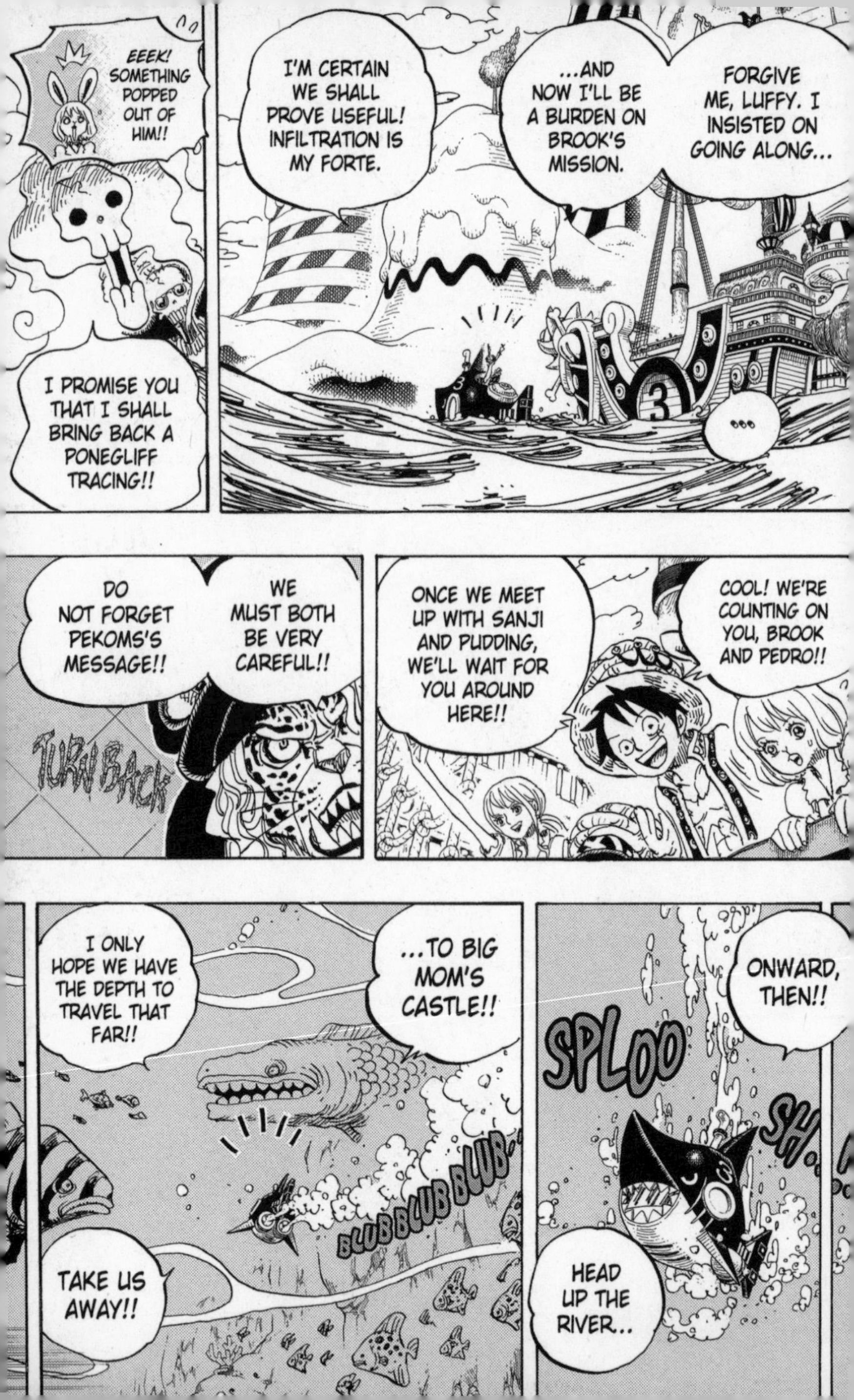
FORGIVE ME, LUFFY. I INSISTED ON GOING ALONG...
...AND NOW I'LL BE A BURDEN ON BROOK'S MISSION.
I'M CERTAIN WE SHALL PROVE USEFUL! INFILTRATION IS MY FORTE.
...
EEEK! SOMETHING POPPED OUT OF HIM!!
I PROMISE YOU THAT I SHALL BRING BACK A PONEGLIFF TRACING!!
COOL! WE'RE COUNTING ON YOU, BROOK AND PEDRO!!
ONCE WE MEET UP WITH SANJI AND PUDDING, WE'LL WAIT FOR YOU AROUND HERE!!
WE MUST BOTH BE VERY CAREFUL!!
DO NOT FORGET PEKOMS'S MESSAGE!!
TURN BACK
ONWARD, THEN!!
SPLOO
SH
HEAD UP THE RIVER...
...TO BIG MOM'S CASTLE!!
I ONLY HOPE WE HAVE THE DEPTH TO TRAVEL THAT FAR!!
BLUB BLUB BLUB
TAKE US AWAY!!

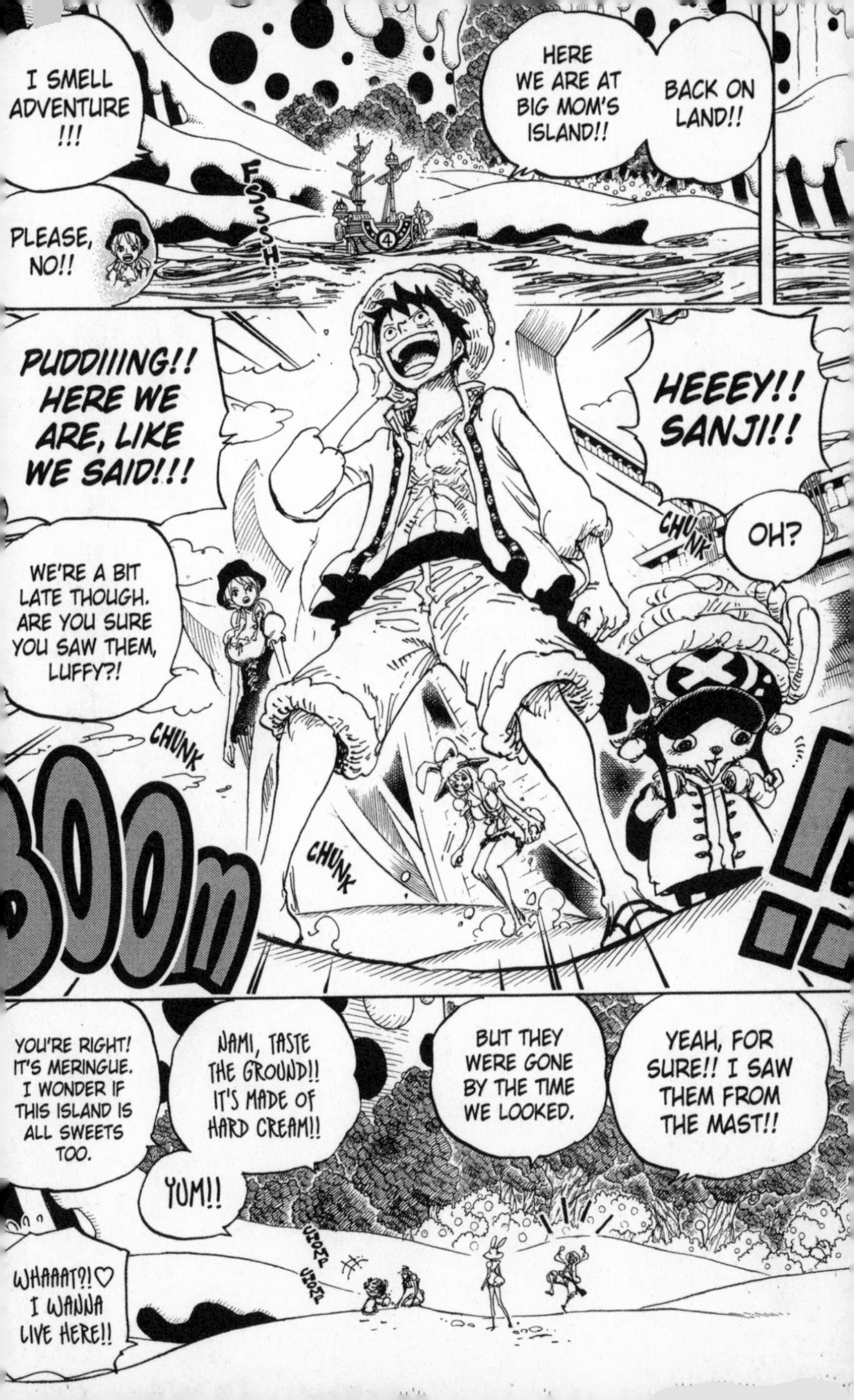

BACK ON LAND!!
HERE WE ARE AT BIG MOM'S ISLAND!!
I SMELL ADVENTURE!!!
FSSSH!!
PLEASE, NO!!
HEEEY!! SANJI!!
PUDDIIING!! HERE WE ARE, LIKE WE SAID!!!
OH?
CHUNK
WE'RE A BIT LATE THOUGH. ARE YOU SURE YOU SAW THEM, LUFFY?!
CHUNK
!!
BOOM
CHUNK
YEAH, FOR SURE!! I SAW THEM FROM THE MAST!!
BUT THEY WERE GONE BY THE TIME WE LOOKED.
NAMI, TASTE THE GROUND!! IT'S MADE OF HARD CREAM!!
YOU'RE RIGHT! IT'S MERINGUE. I WONDER IF THIS ISLAND IS ALL SWEETS TOO.
YUM!!
CHOMP
CHOMP
WHAAAT?!♡ I WANNA LIVE HERE!!

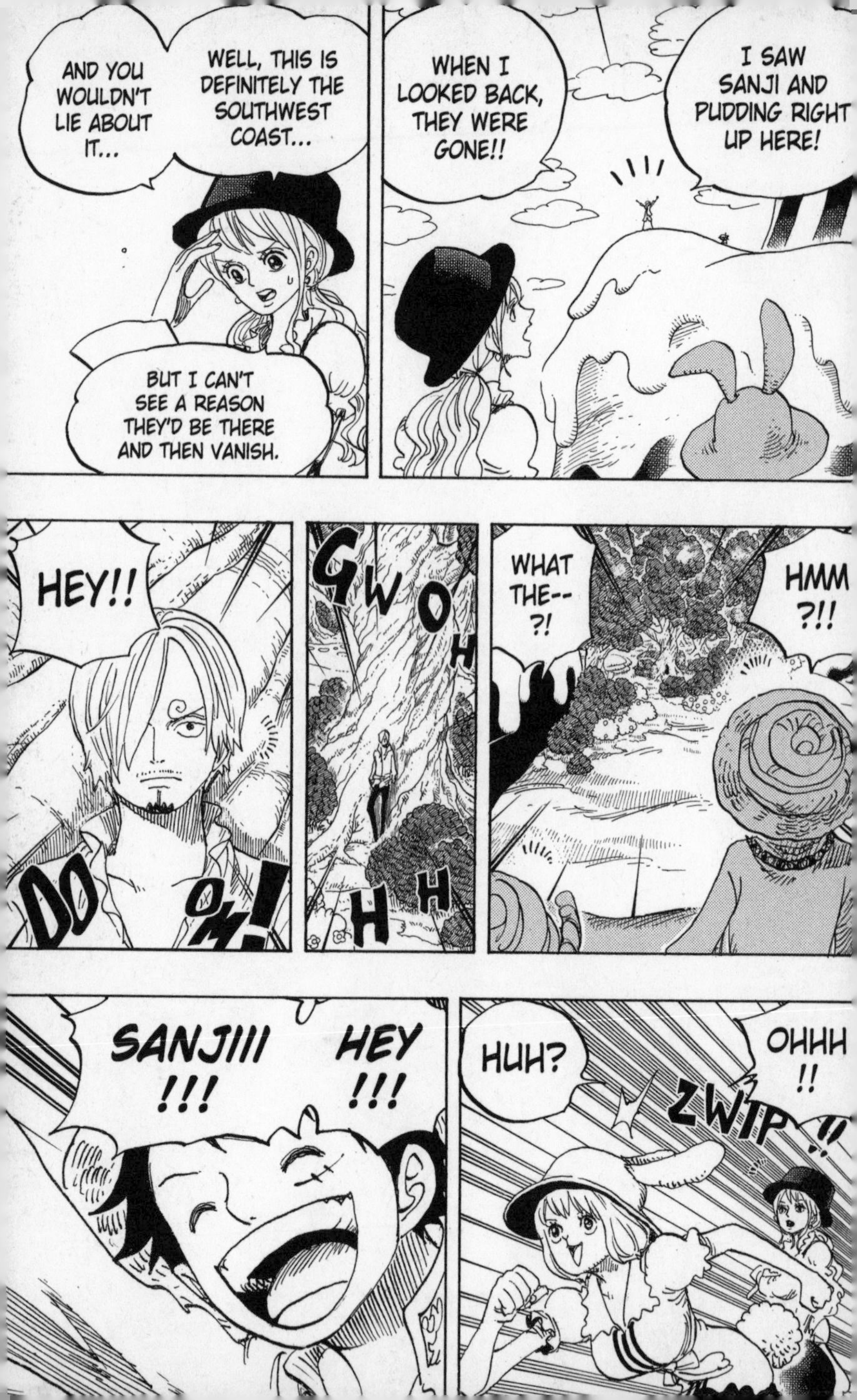
I SAW SANJI AND PUDDING RIGHT UP HERE!
WHEN I LOOKED BACK, THEY WERE GONE!!
WELL, THIS IS DEFINITELY THE SOUTHWEST COAST...
AND YOU WOULDN'T LIE ABOUT IT...
BUT I CAN'T SEE A REASON THEY'D BE THERE AND THEN VANISH.
HMM ?!!
WHAT THE-- ?!
GWOHHH
HEY!!
DOOM!
OHHH !!
HUH?
ZWIP !!
HEY !!!
SANJIII !!!

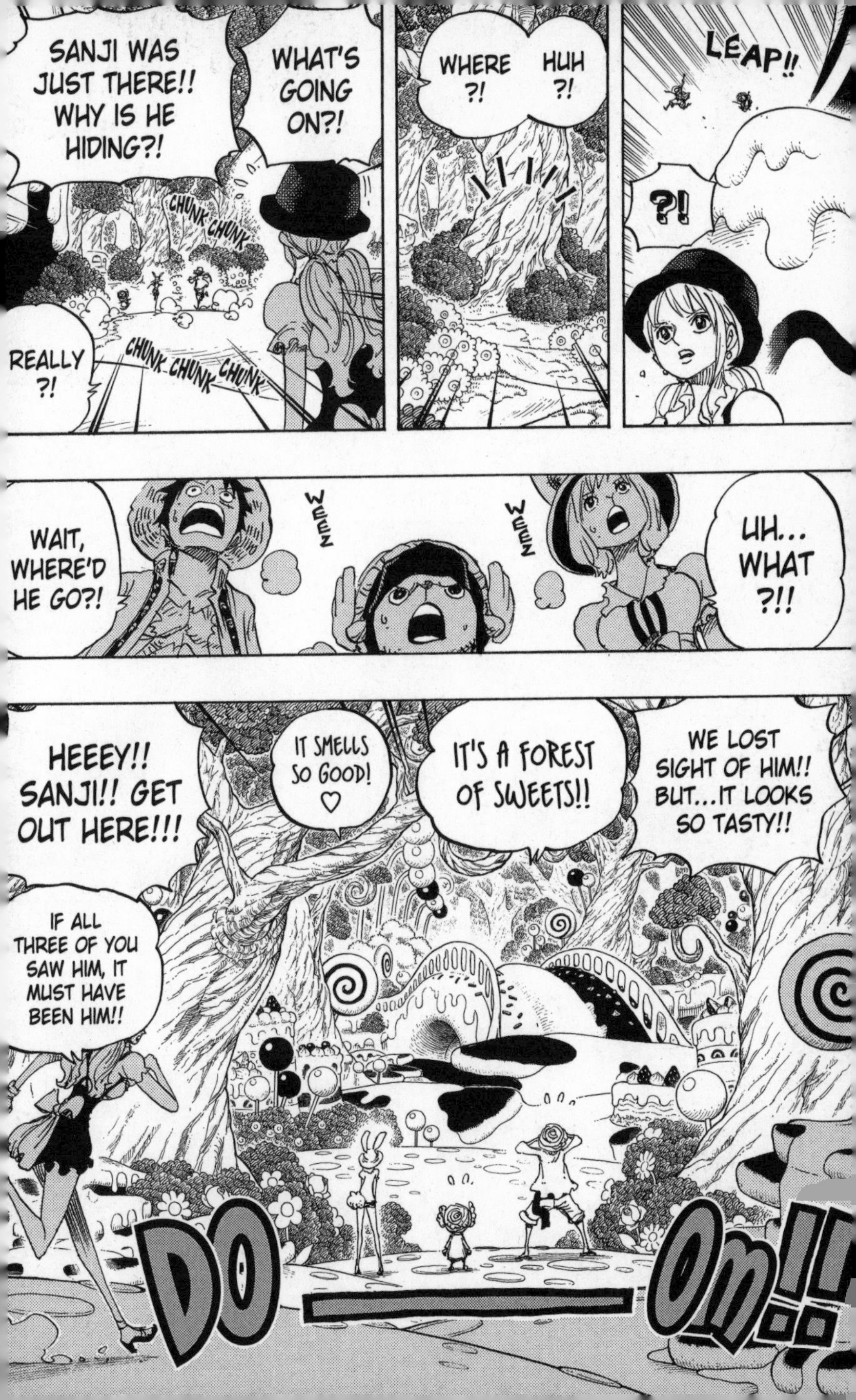
LEAP!!
?!
HUH ?!
WHERE ?!
WHAT'S GOING ON?!
SANJI WAS JUST THERE!! WHY IS HE HIDING?!
CHUNK CHUNK
CHUNK CHUNK CHUNK
REALLY ?!
UH... WHAT ?!!
WEEZ
WEEZ
WAIT, WHERE'D HE GO?!
WE LOST SIGHT OF HIM!! BUT...IT LOOKS SO TASTY!!
IT'S A FOREST OF SWEETS!!
IT SMELLS SO GOOD! ♡
HEEEY!! SANJI!! GET OUT HERE!!!
IF ALL THREE OF YOU SAW HIM, IT MUST HAVE BEEN HIM!!
DOOOM!!

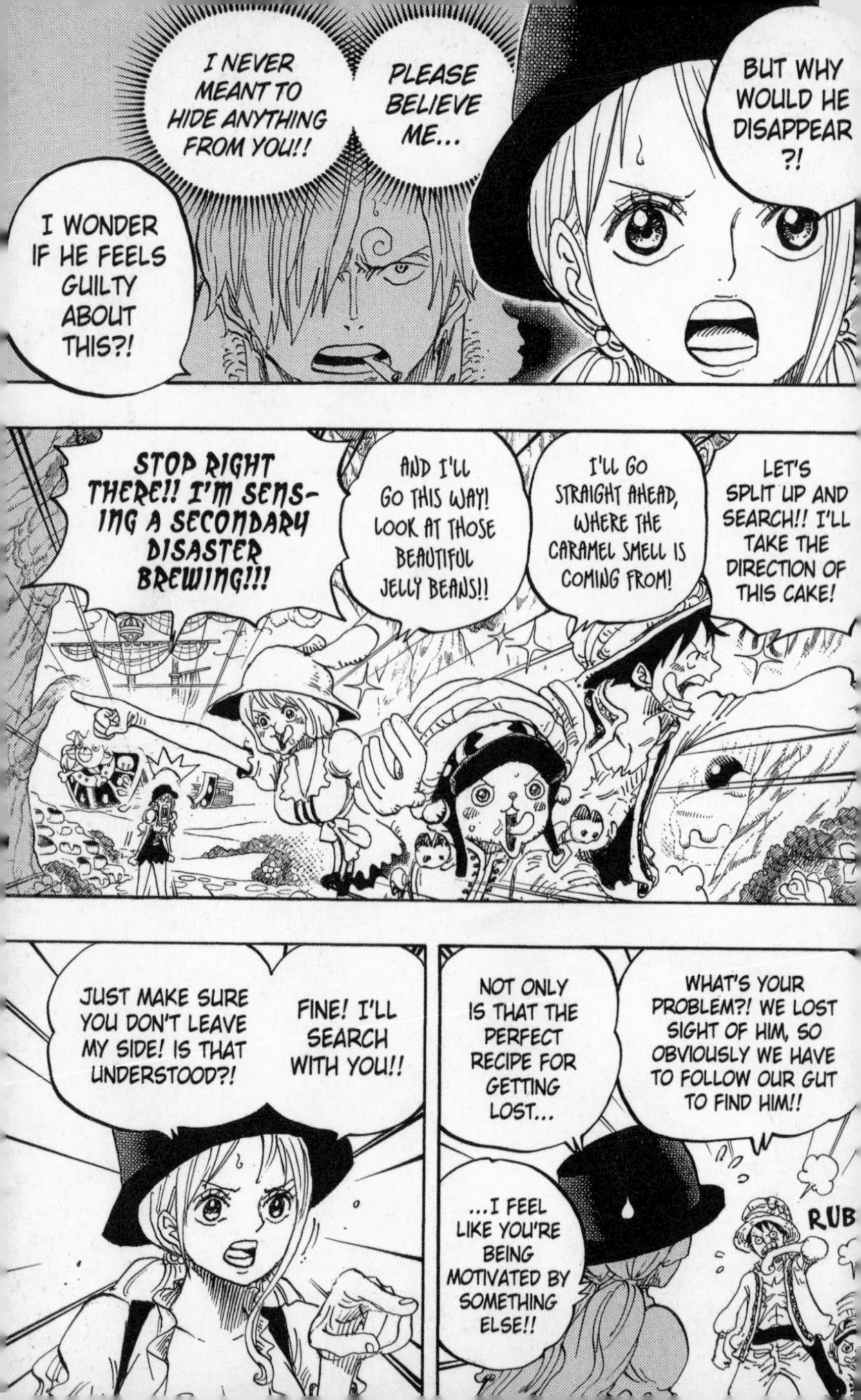
BUT WHY WOULD HE DISAPPEAR ?!
PLEASE BELIEVE ME...
I NEVER MEANT TO HIDE ANYTHING FROM YOU!!
I WONDER IF HE FEELS GUILTY ABOUT THIS?!
LET'S SPLIT UP AND SEARCH!! I'LL TAKE THE DIRECTION OF THIS CAKE!
I'LL GO STRAIGHT AHEAD, WHERE THE CARAMEL SMELL IS COMING FROM!
AND I'LL GO THIS WAY! LOOK AT THOSE BEAUTIFUL JELLY BEANS!!
STOP RIGHT THERE!! I'M SENSING A SECONDARY DISASTER BREWING!!!
WHAT'S YOUR PROBLEM?! WE LOST SIGHT OF HIM, SO OBVIOUSLY WE HAVE TO FOLLOW OUR GUT TO FIND HIM!!
NOT ONLY IS THAT THE PERFECT RECIPE FOR GETTING LOST...
RUB
...I FEEL LIKE YOU'RE BEING MOTIVATED BY SOMETHING ELSE!!
FINE! I'LL SEARCH WITH YOU!!
JUST MAKE SURE YOU DON'T LEAVE MY SIDE! IS THAT UNDERSTOOD?!

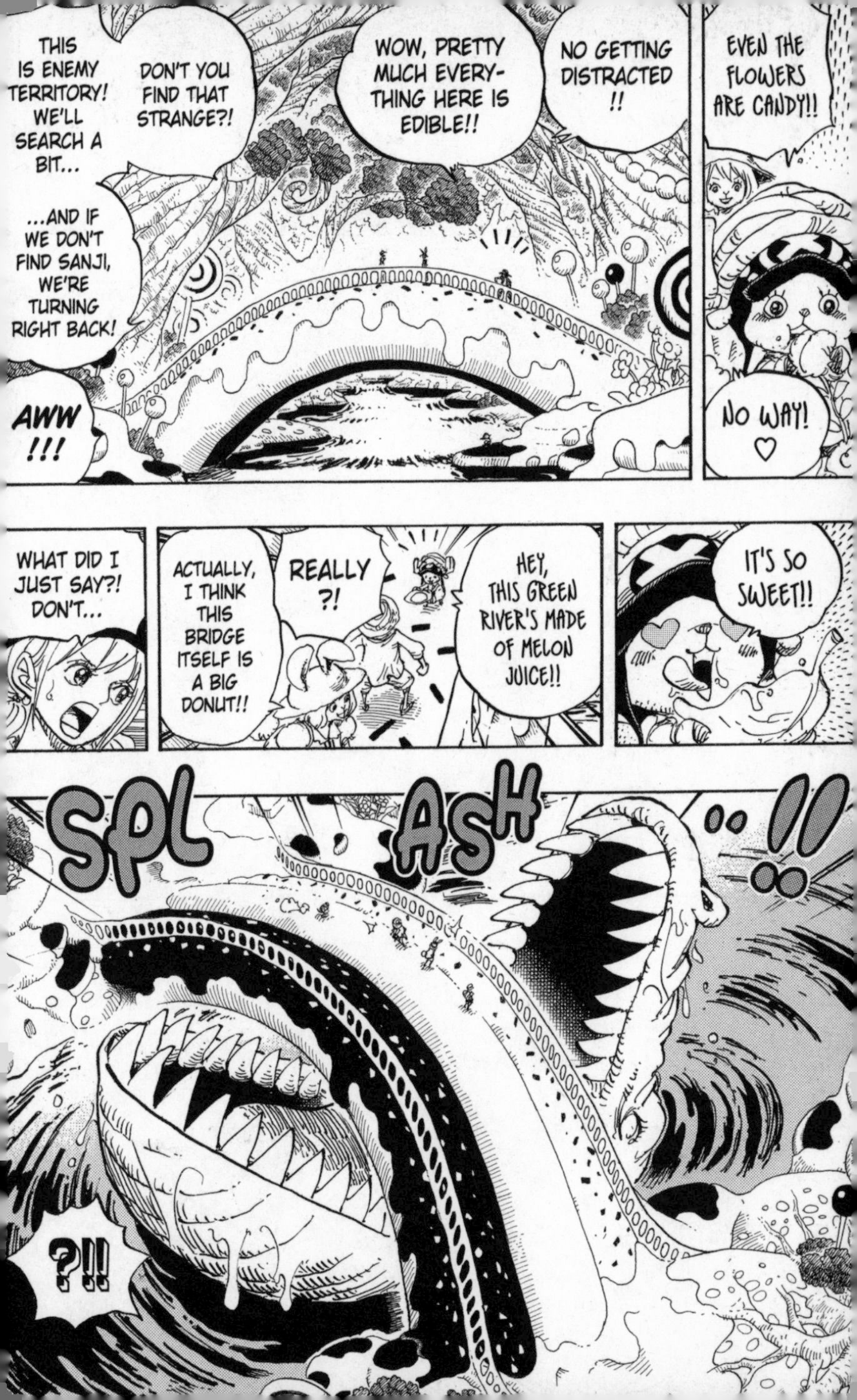
EVEN THE FLOWERS ARE CANDY!!
NO WAY! ♥
NO GETTING DISTRACTED!!
WOW, PRETTY MUCH EVERY-THING HERE IS EDIBLE!!
DON'T YOU FIND THAT STRANGE?!
THIS IS ENEMY TERRITORY! WE'LL SEARCH A BIT...
...AND IF WE DON'T FIND SANJI, WE'RE TURNING RIGHT BACK!
AWW!!!
IT'S SO SWEET!!
HEY, THIS GREEN RIVER'S MADE OF MELON JUICE!!
REALLY?!
ACTUALLY, I THINK THIS BRIDGE ITSELF IS A BIG DONUT!!
WHAT DID I JUST SAY?! DON'T...
SPLASH..!!
?!!

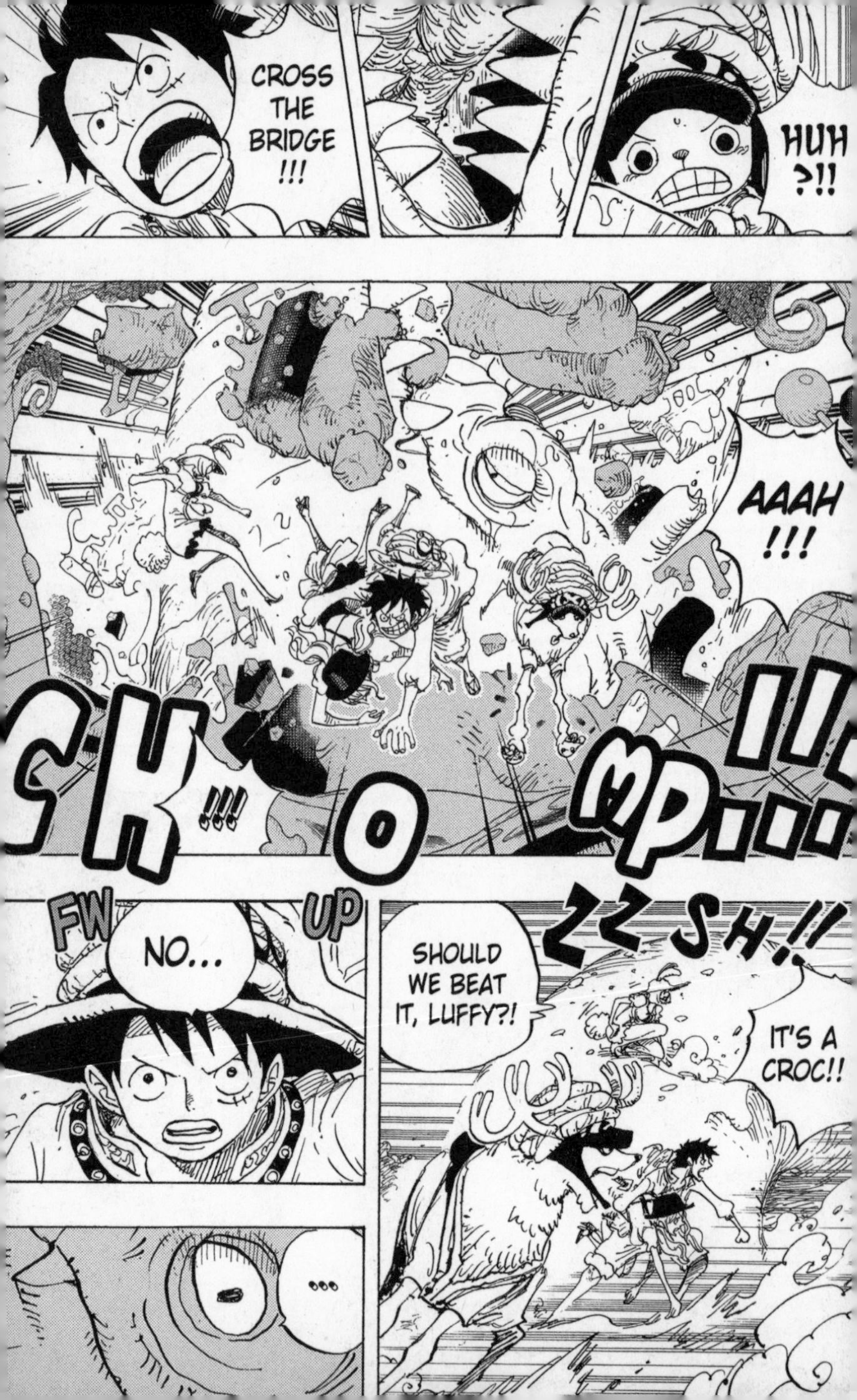
HUH ?!!
CROSS THE BRIDGE !!!
AAAH !!!
CHOMP!!!
ZZSH!!
IT'S A CROC!!
SHOULD WE BEAT IT, LUFFY?!
FWUP
NO...
...

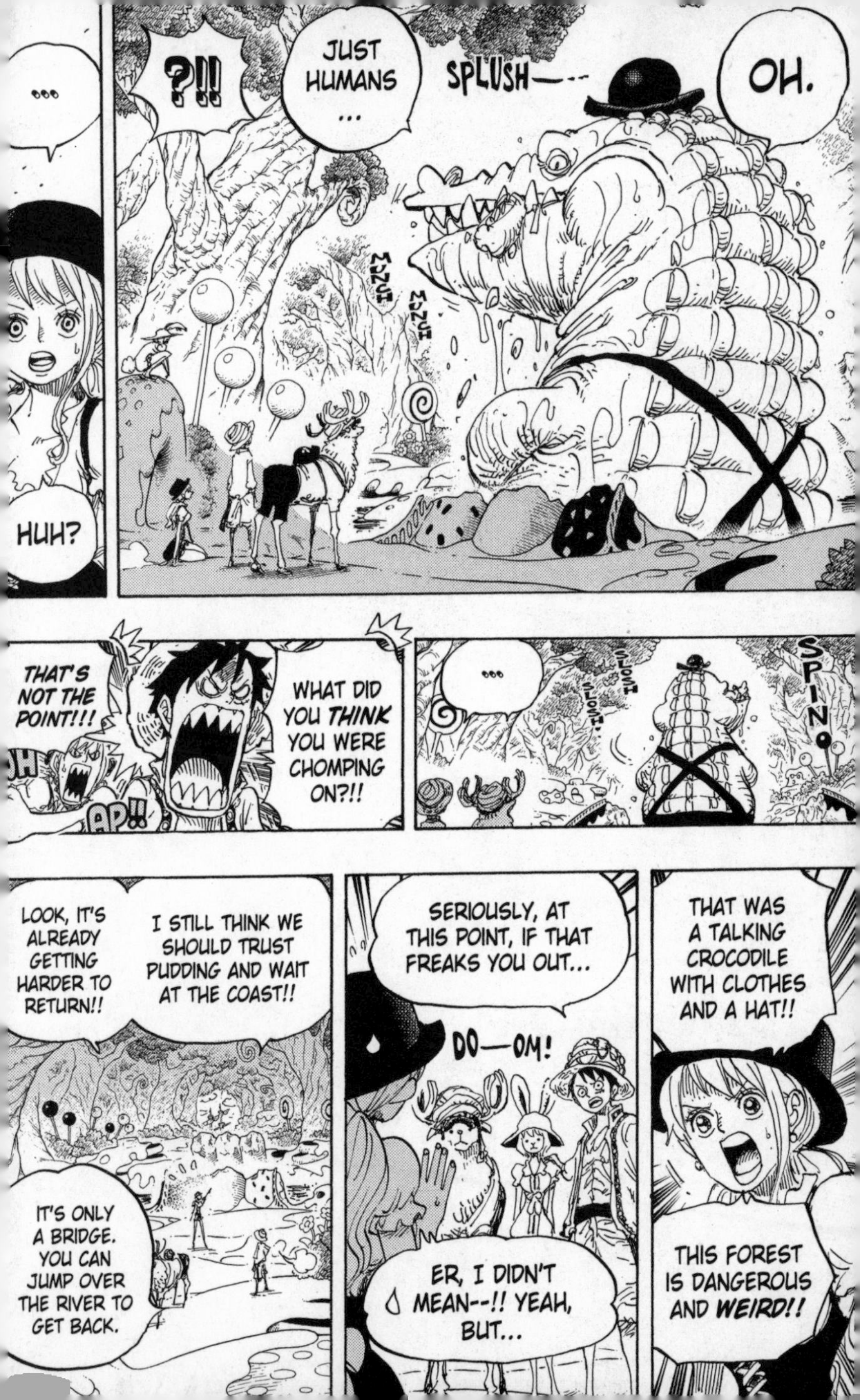
OH.
SPLUSH---
JUST HUMANS ...
?!!
MUNCH
MUNCH
...
HUH?
...
SLOSH
SLOSH
SPIN
WHAT DID YOU THINK YOU WERE CHOMPING ON?!!
THAT'S NOT THE POINT!!!
THAT WAS A TALKING CROCODILE WITH CLOTHES AND A HAT!!
THIS FOREST IS DANGEROUS AND WEIRD!!
SERIOUSLY, AT THIS POINT, IF THAT FREAKS YOU OUT...
DO—OM!
ER, I DIDN'T MEAN--!! YEAH, BUT...
I STILL THINK WE SHOULD TRUST PUDDING AND WAIT AT THE COAST!!
LOOK, IT'S ALREADY GETTING HARDER TO RETURN!!
IT'S ONLY A BRIDGE. YOU CAN JUMP OVER THE RIVER TO GET BACK.

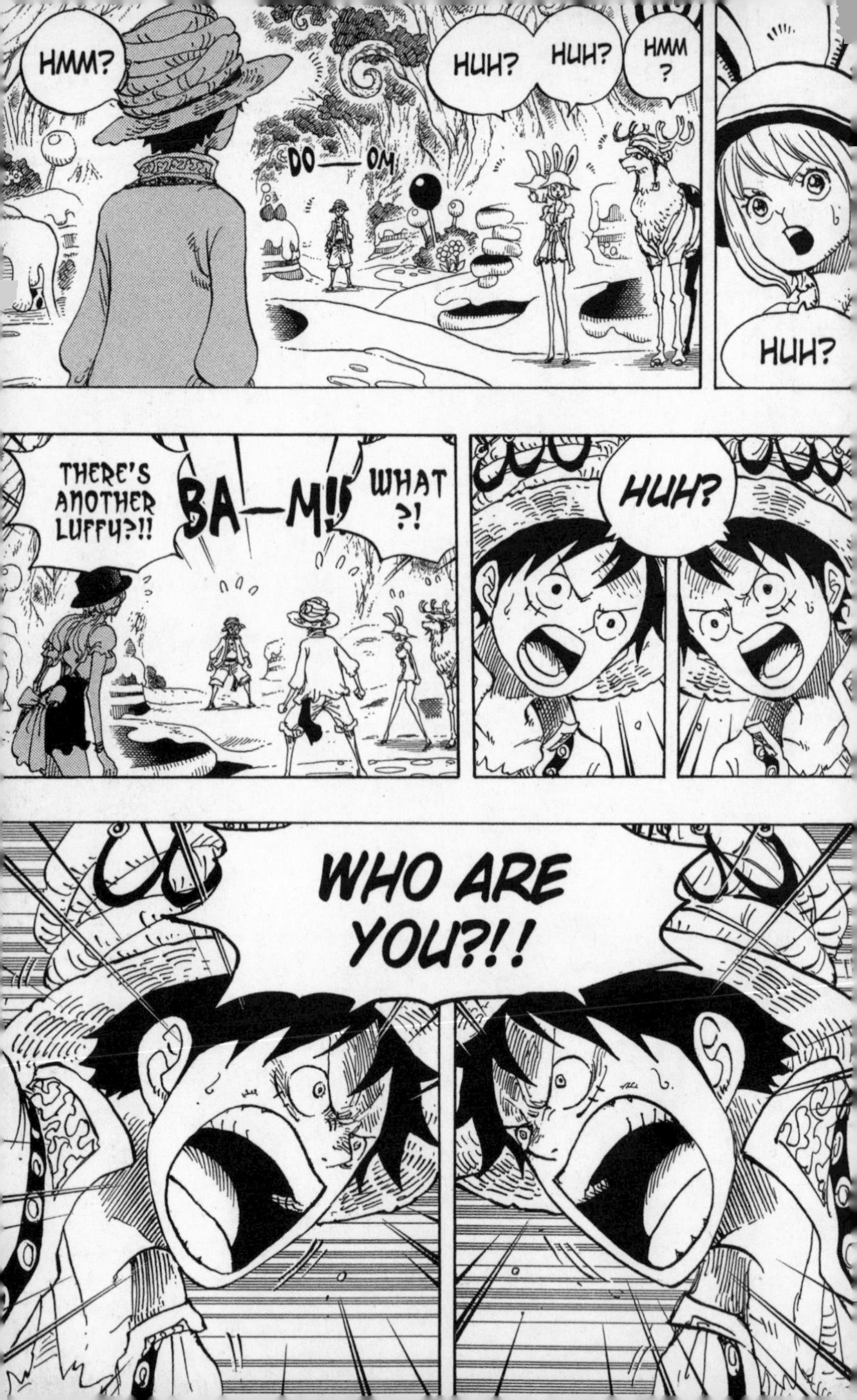
HUH?
HMM ?
HUH?
HUH?
DO—OM
HMM?
HUH?
WHAT ?!
BA—M!!
THERE'S ANOTHER LUFFY?!!
WHO ARE YOU?!!

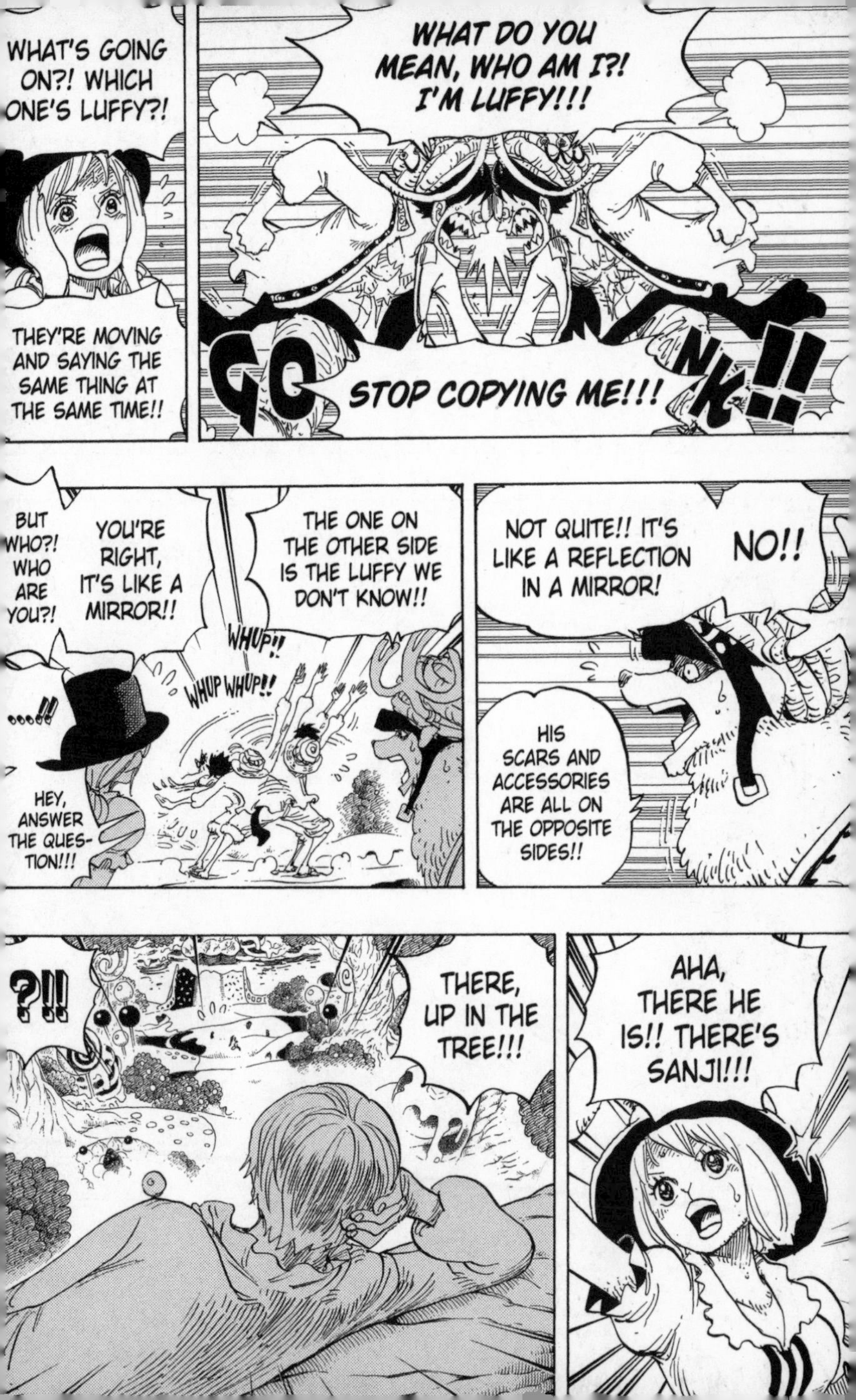
WHAT DO YOU MEAN, WHO AM I?! I'M LUFFY!!!
GONK!!
STOP COPYING ME!!!
WHAT'S GOING ON?! WHICH ONE'S LUFFY?!
THEY'RE MOVING AND SAYING THE SAME THING AT THE SAME TIME!!
NO!!
NOT QUITE!! IT'S LIKE A REFLECTION IN A MIRROR!
HIS SCARS AND ACCESSORIES ARE ALL ON THE OPPOSITE SIDES!!
THE ONE ON THE OTHER SIDE IS THE LUFFY WE DON'T KNOW!!
YOU'RE RIGHT, IT'S LIKE A MIRROR!!
BUT WHO?! WHO ARE YOU?!
WHUP!!
WHUP WHUP!!
...!!
HEY, ANSWER THE QUES-TION!!!
AHA, THERE HE IS!! THERE'S SANJI!!!
THERE, UP IN THE TREE!!!
?!!

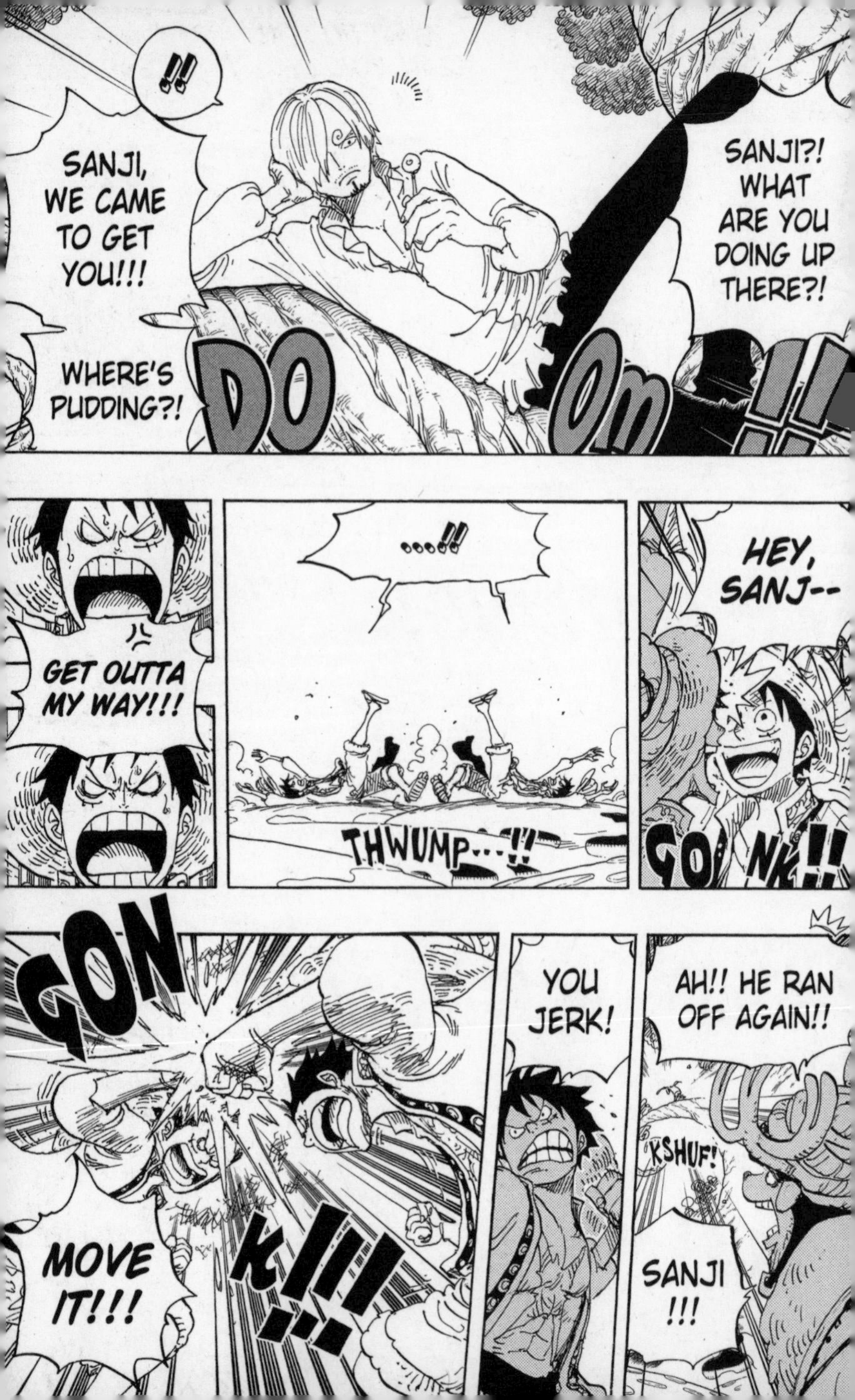
SANJI?! WHAT ARE YOU DOING UP THERE?!
!!
SANJI, WE CAME TO GET YOU!!!
WHERE'S PUDDING?!
DOOM!!
HEY, SANJ--
GONK!!
...!!
THWUMP...!!
GET OUTTA MY WAY!!!
AH!! HE RAN OFF AGAIN!!
KSHUF!
SANJI !!!
YOU JERK!
GON
K!!!
MOVE IT!!!

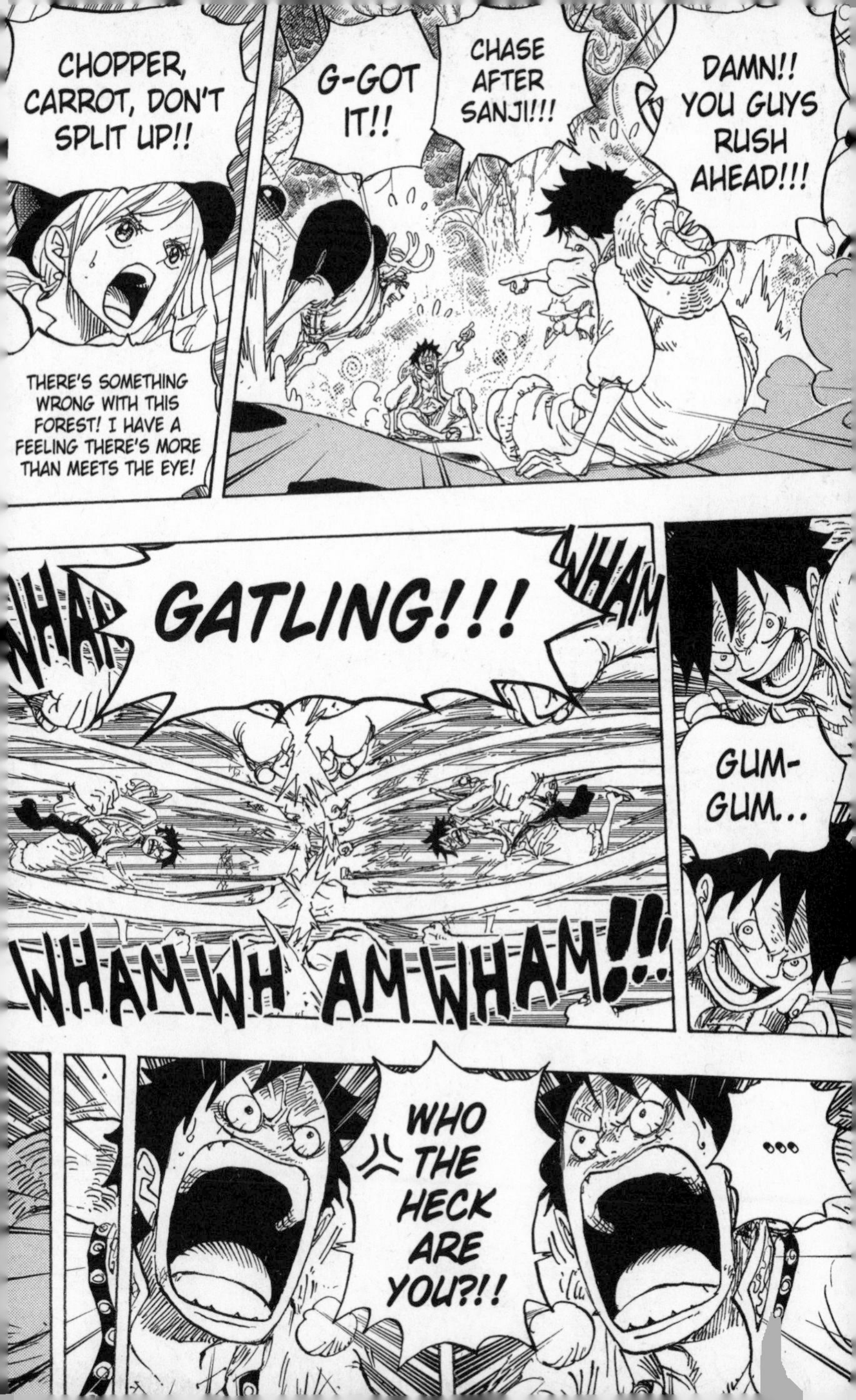
DAMN!! YOU GUYS RUSH AHEAD!!!
CHASE AFTER SANJI!!!
G-GOT IT!!
CHOPPER, CARROT, DON'T SPLIT UP!!
THERE'S SOMETHING WRONG WITH THIS FOREST! I HAVE A FEELING THERE'S MORE THAN MEETS THE EYE!
GUM-GUM...
WHAM
GATLING!!!
WHA
WHAM WH AM WHAM!!!
...
WHO THE HECK ARE YOU?!!

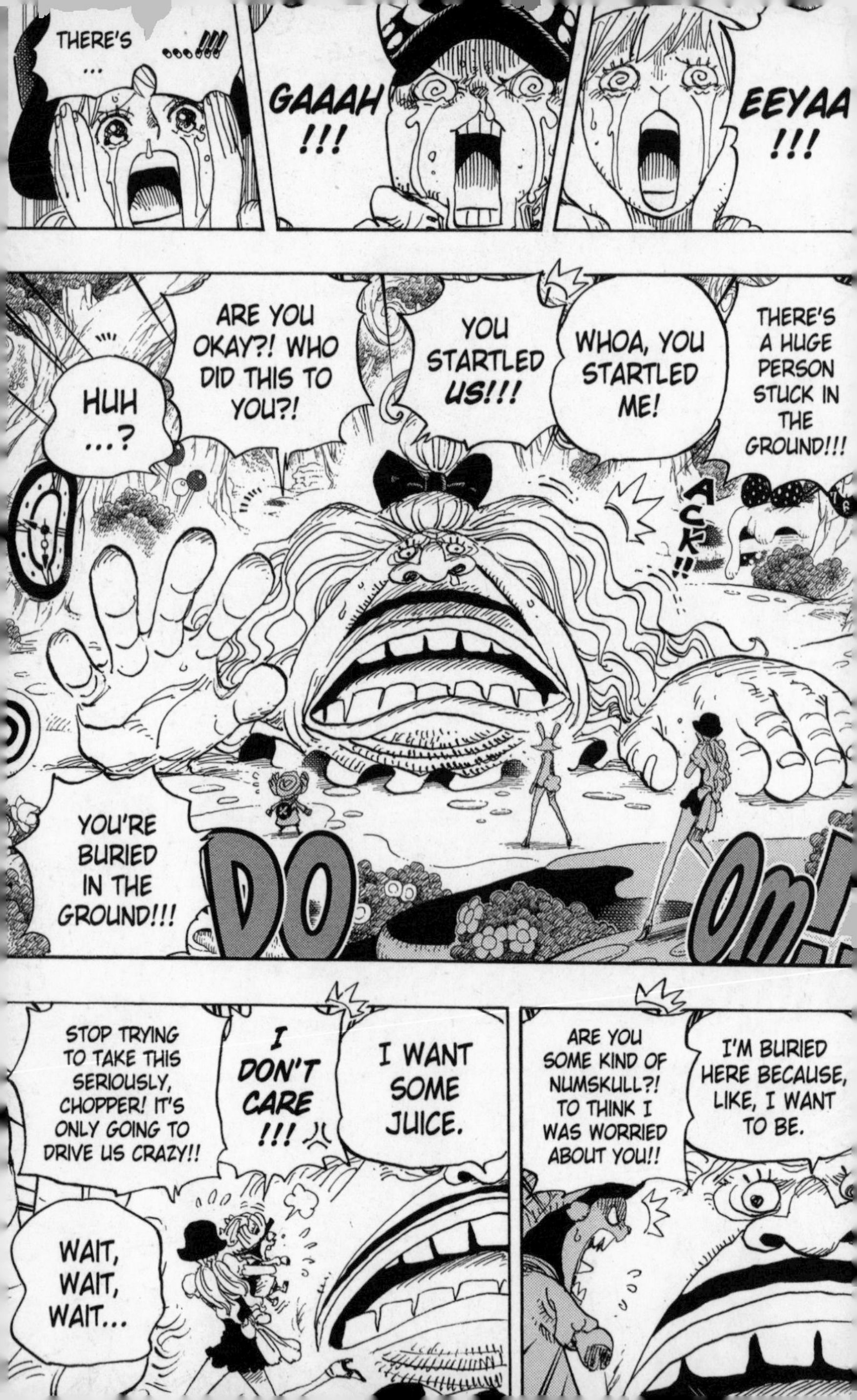
EEYAA !!!
GAAAH !!!
...!!!
THERE'S ...
THERE'S A HUGE PERSON STUCK IN THE GROUND!!!
WHOA, YOU STARTLED ME!
ACK!!
YOU STARTLED US!!!
ARE YOU OKAY?! WHO DID THIS TO YOU?!
HUH ...?
YOU'RE BURIED IN THE GROUND!!!
DO
Om!
I'M BURIED HERE BECAUSE, LIKE, I WANT TO BE.
ARE YOU SOME KIND OF NUMSKULL?! TO THINK I WAS WORRIED ABOUT YOU!!
I WANT SOME JUICE.
I DON'T CARE!!!
STOP TRYING TO TAKE THIS SERIOUSLY, CHOPPER! IT'S ONLY GOING TO DRIVE US CRAZY!!
WAIT, WAIT, WAIT...

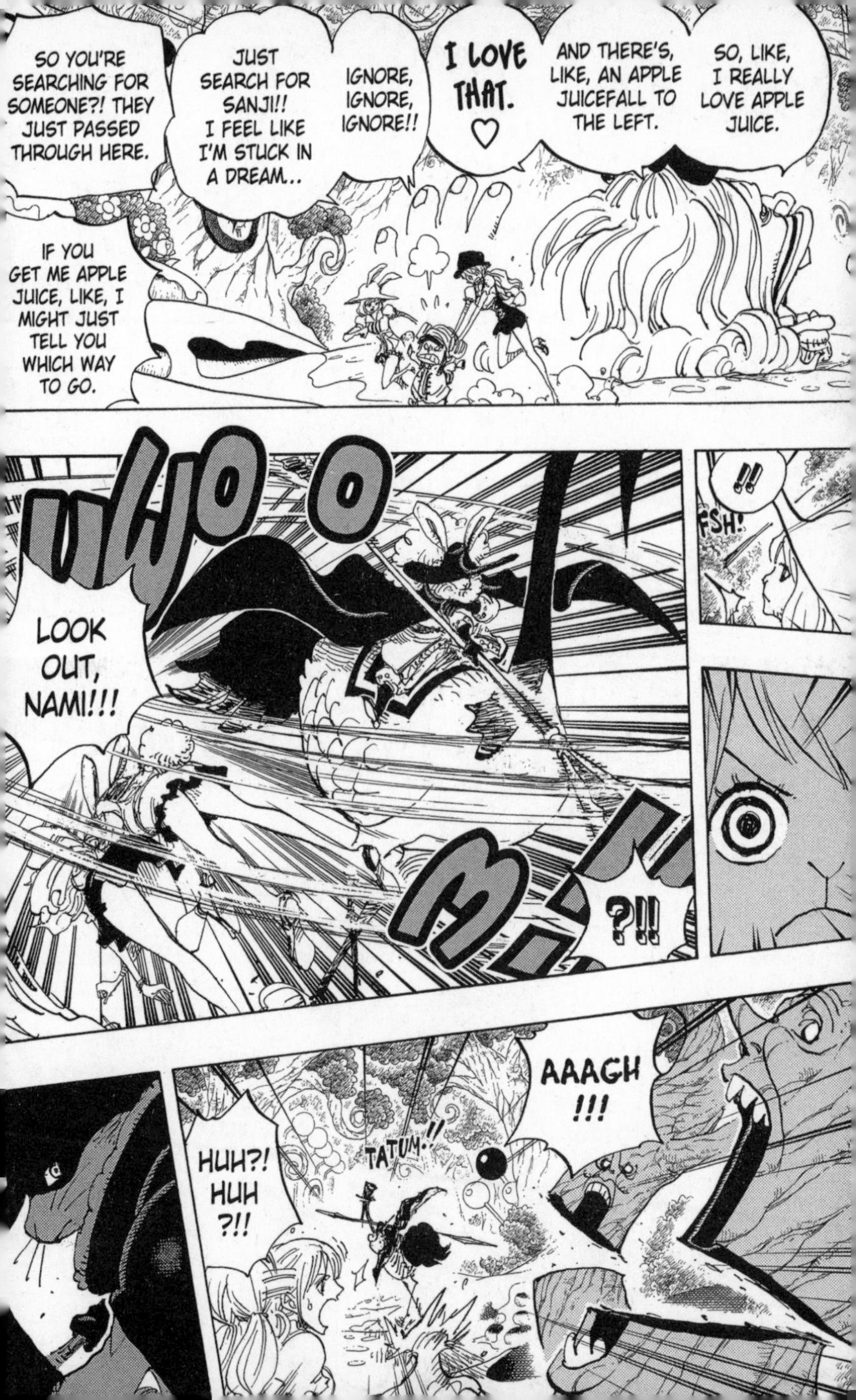
SO, LIKE, I REALLY LOVE APPLE JUICE.
AND THERE'S, LIKE, AN APPLE JUICEFALL TO THE LEFT.
I LOVE THAT. ♡
IGNORE, IGNORE, IGNORE!!
JUST SEARCH FOR SANJI!! I FEEL LIKE I'M STUCK IN A DREAM...
SO YOU'RE SEARCHING FOR SOMEONE?! THEY JUST PASSED THROUGH HERE.
IF YOU GET ME APPLE JUICE, LIKE, I MIGHT JUST TELL YOU WHICH WAY TO GO.
!!
FSH!
LOOK OUT, NAMI!!!
?!!
AAAGH !!!
TATUM!!
HUH?! HUH ?!!

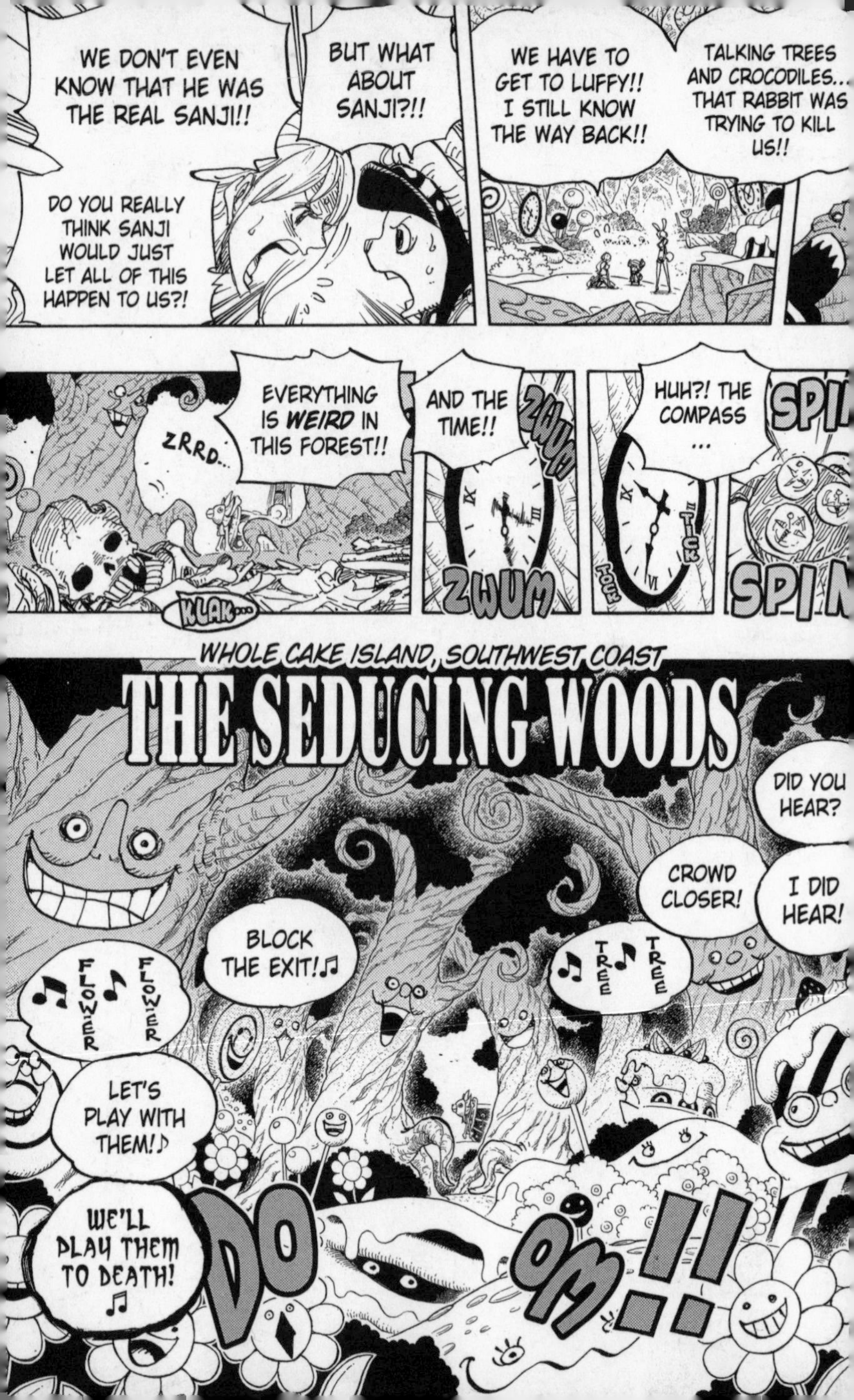
TALKING TREES AND CROCODILES... THAT RABBIT WAS TRYING TO KILL US!!
WE HAVE TO GET TO LUFFY!! I STILL KNOW THE WAY BACK!!
BUT WHAT ABOUT SANJI?!!
WE DON'T EVEN KNOW THAT HE WAS THE REAL SANJI!!
DO YOU REALLY THINK SANJI WOULD JUST LET ALL OF THIS HAPPEN TO US?!
SPI
SPIN
HUH?! THE COMPASS ...
TICK
TOCK
AND THE TIME!!
ZWUM
ZWUM
EVERYTHING IS *WEIRD* IN THIS FOREST!!
ZRRD..
KLAK...
WHOLE CAKE ISLAND, SOUTHWEST COAST
THE SEDUCING WOODS
DID YOU HEAR?
I DID HEAR!
CROWD CLOSER!
♪ TREE ♪ TREE
BLOCK THE EXIT!♫
♪ FLOWER ♪ FLOWER
LET'S PLAY WITH THEM!♪
WE'LL PLAY THEM TO DEATH! ♫
DOOM!!

KINGDOM OF GERMA

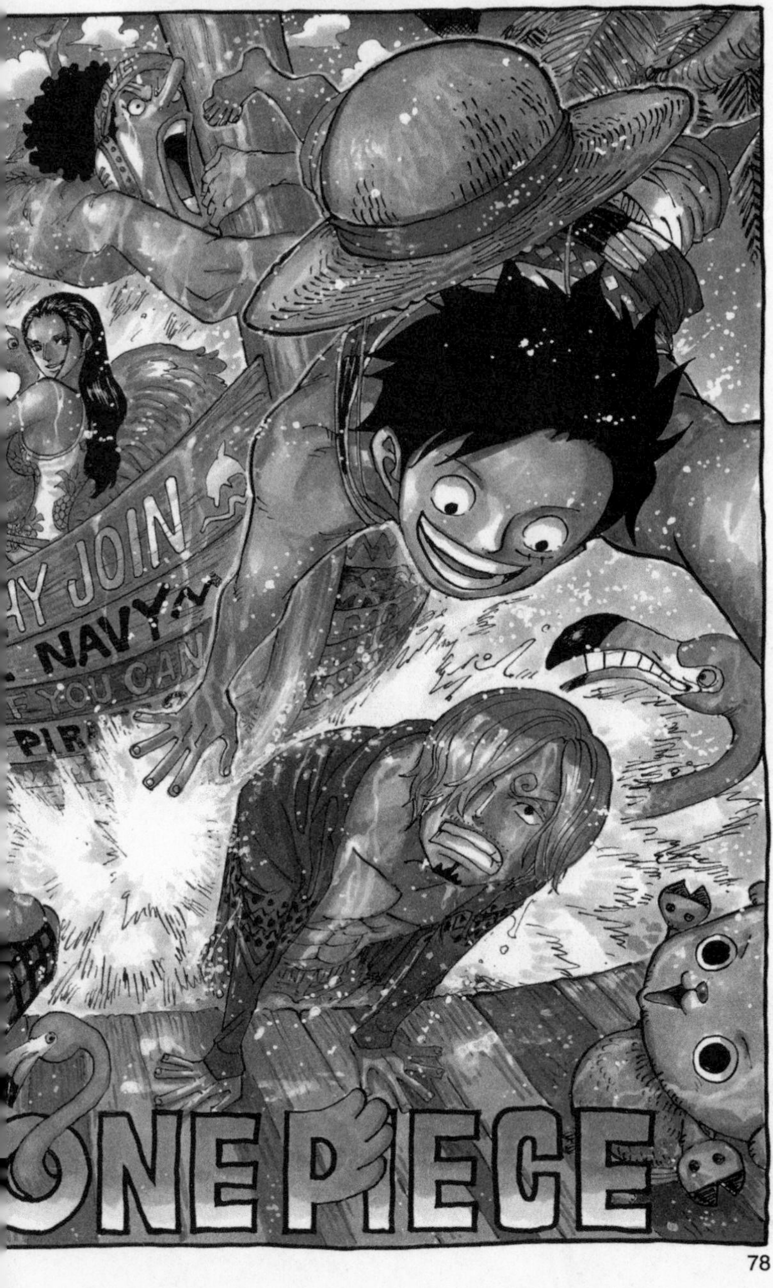

HY JOIN
NAVY!
F YOU CAN
PIR
ONE PIECE

Chapter 832:

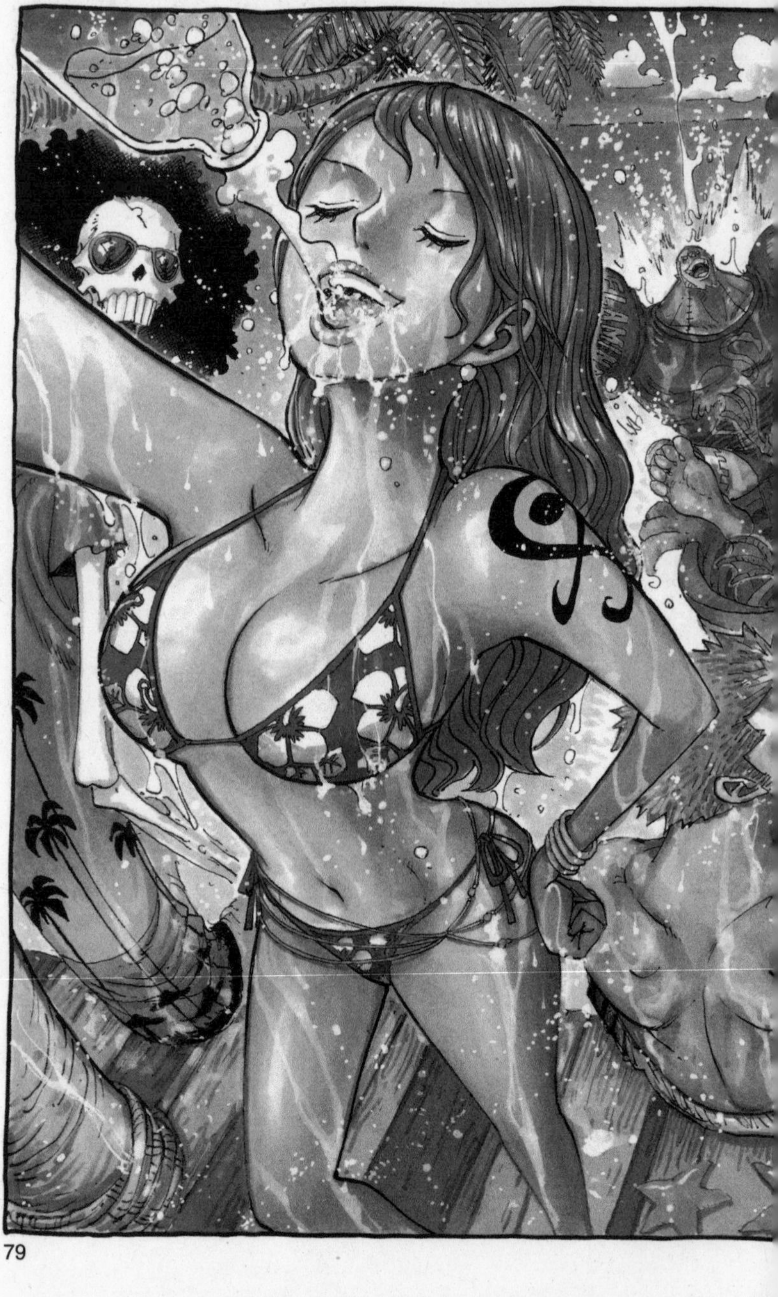

vol.83

ONE PIECE

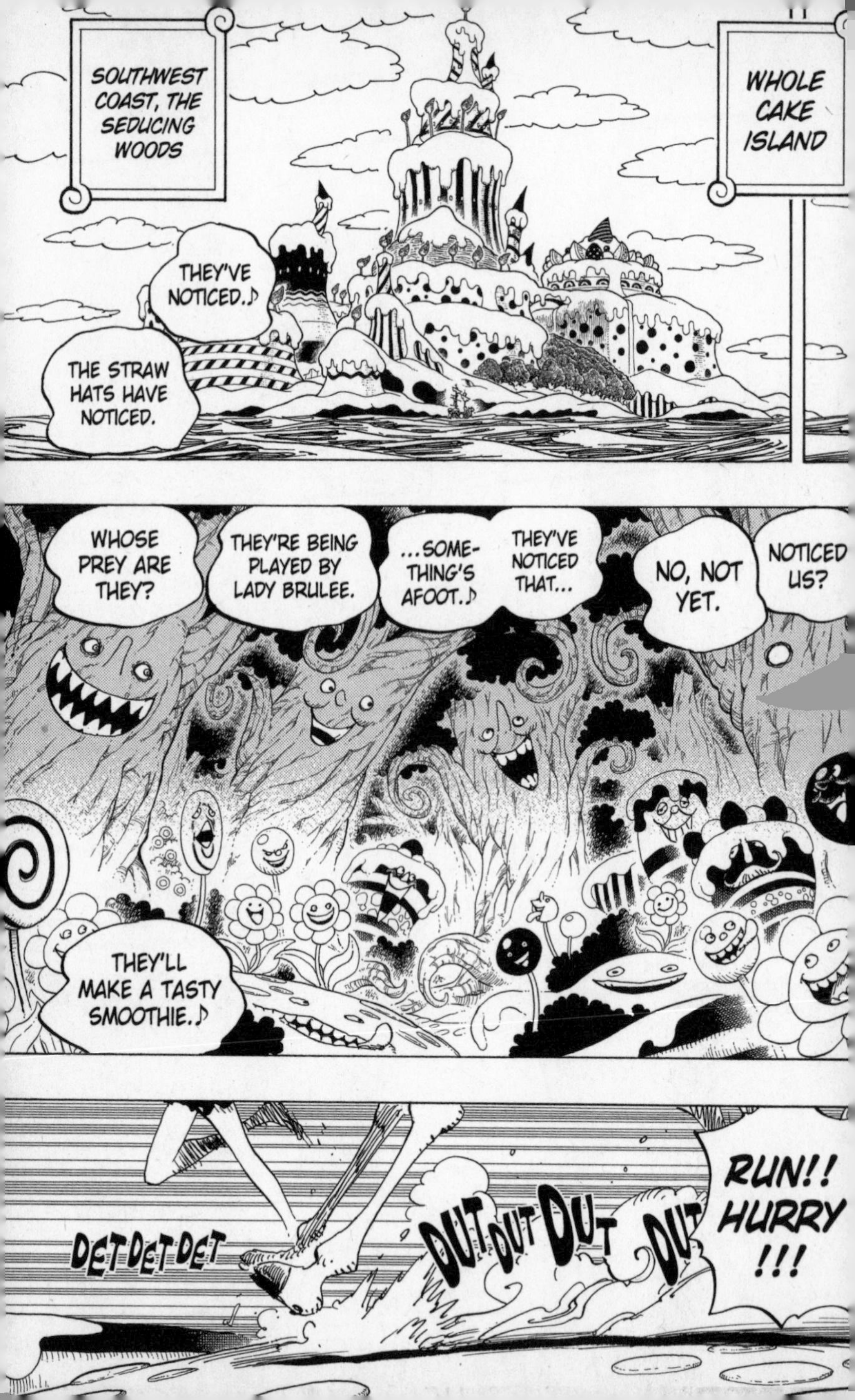
WHOLE CAKE ISLAND
SOUTHWEST COAST, THE SEDUCING WOODS
THEY'VE NOTICED.♪
THE STRAW HATS HAVE NOTICED.
NOTICED US?
NO, NOT YET.
THEY'VE NOTICED THAT...
...SOME-THING'S AFOOT.♪
THEY'RE BEING PLAYED BY LADY BRULEE.
WHOSE PREY ARE THEY?
THEY'LL MAKE A TASTY SMOOTHIE.♪
RUN!! HURRY!!!
DUT DUT DUT DUT
DET DET DET

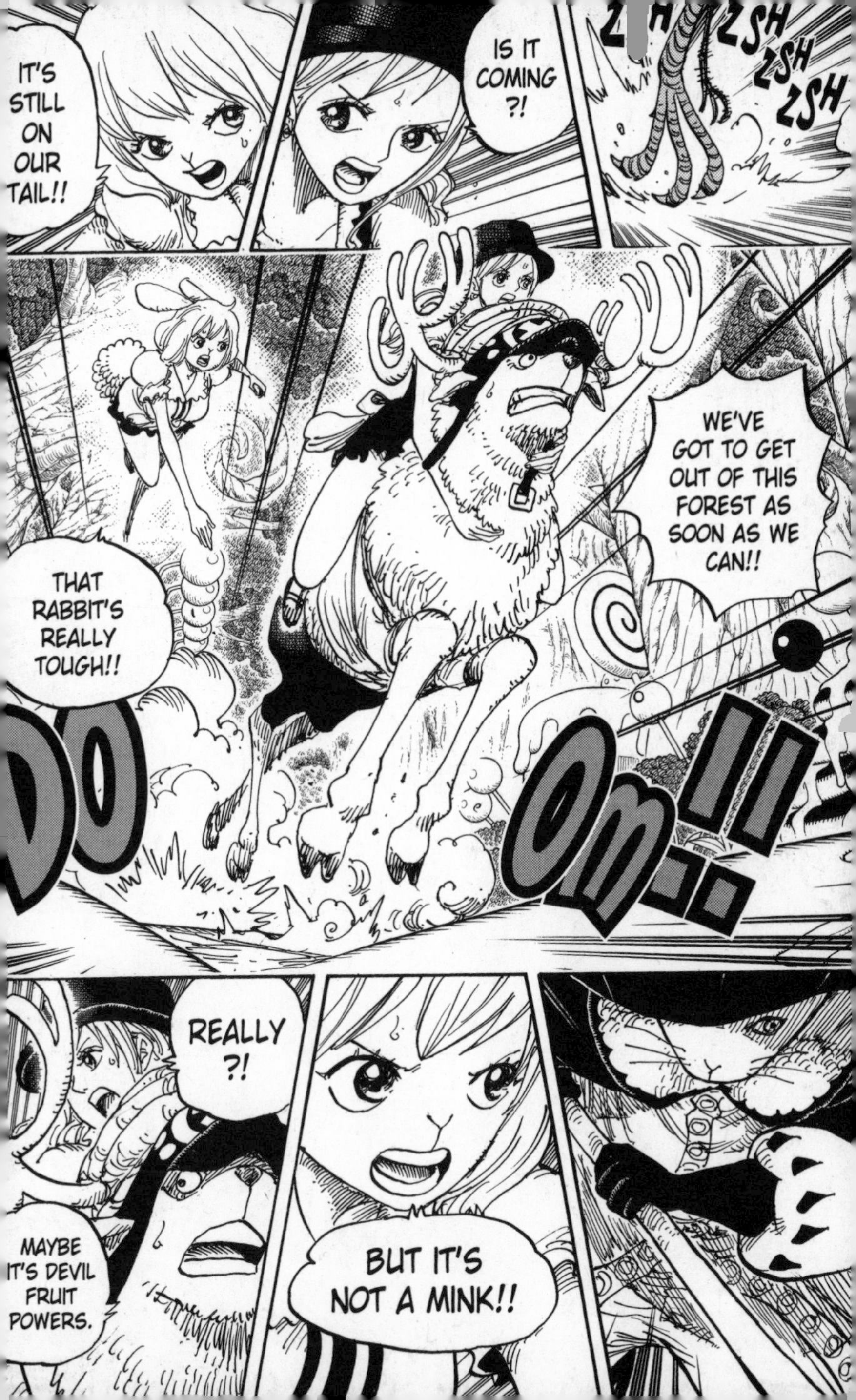
ZSH
ZSH
ZSH
IS IT COMING ?!
IT'S STILL ON OUR TAIL!!
WE'VE GOT TO GET OUT OF THIS FOREST AS SOON AS WE CAN!!
DOOM..!!
THAT RABBIT'S REALLY TOUGH!!
BUT IT'S NOT A MINK!!
REALLY ?!
MAYBE IT'S DEVIL FRUIT POWERS.

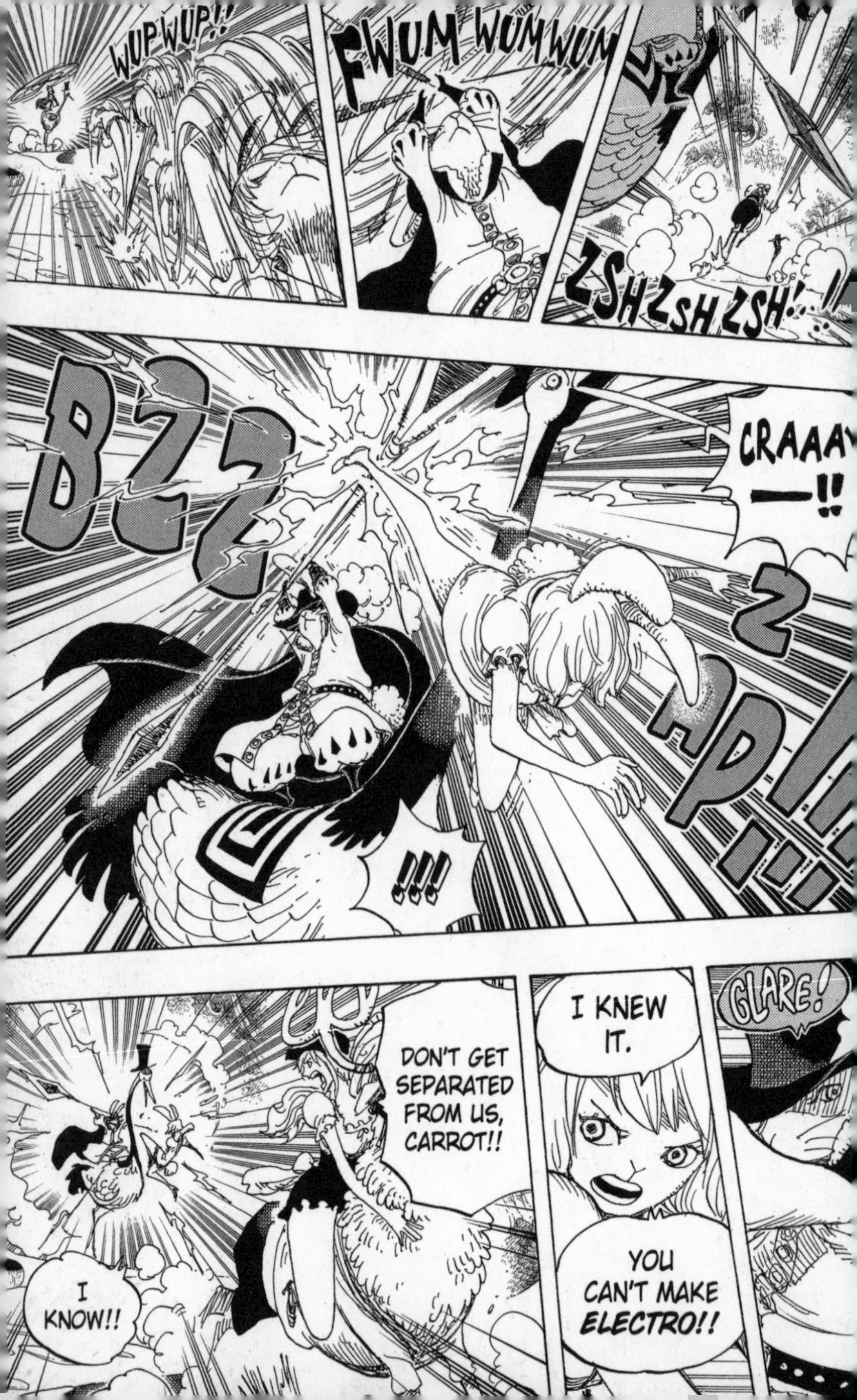
ZSH ZSH ZSH!!
FWUM WUM WUM
WUP WUP!!
CRAAAY —!!
ZZAP!!
BZZ
!!!
GLARE!
I KNEW IT.
YOU CAN'T MAKE *ELECTRO*!!
DON'T GET SEPARATED FROM US, CARROT!!
I KNOW!!

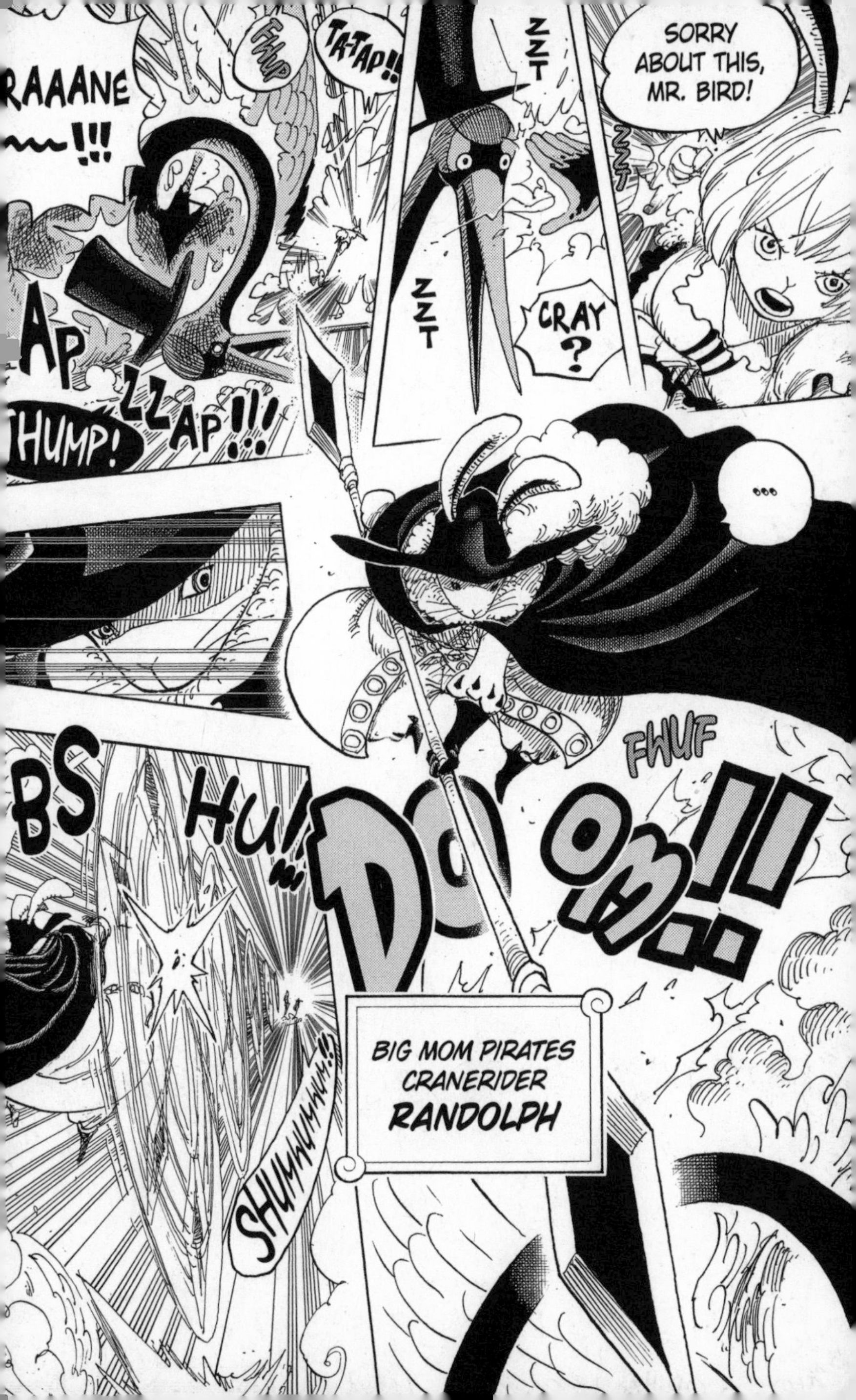

SORRY ABOUT THIS, MR. BIRD!
ZZT
CRAY ?
ZZT
ZZT
TA-TAP!!
FWP
RAAANE ~~!!!
AP
ZZAP!!!
THUMP!
...
FWUF
DOOM!!
BIG MOM PIRATES
CRANERIDER
RANDOLPH
HU!!
BS
SHUMMMMM!!

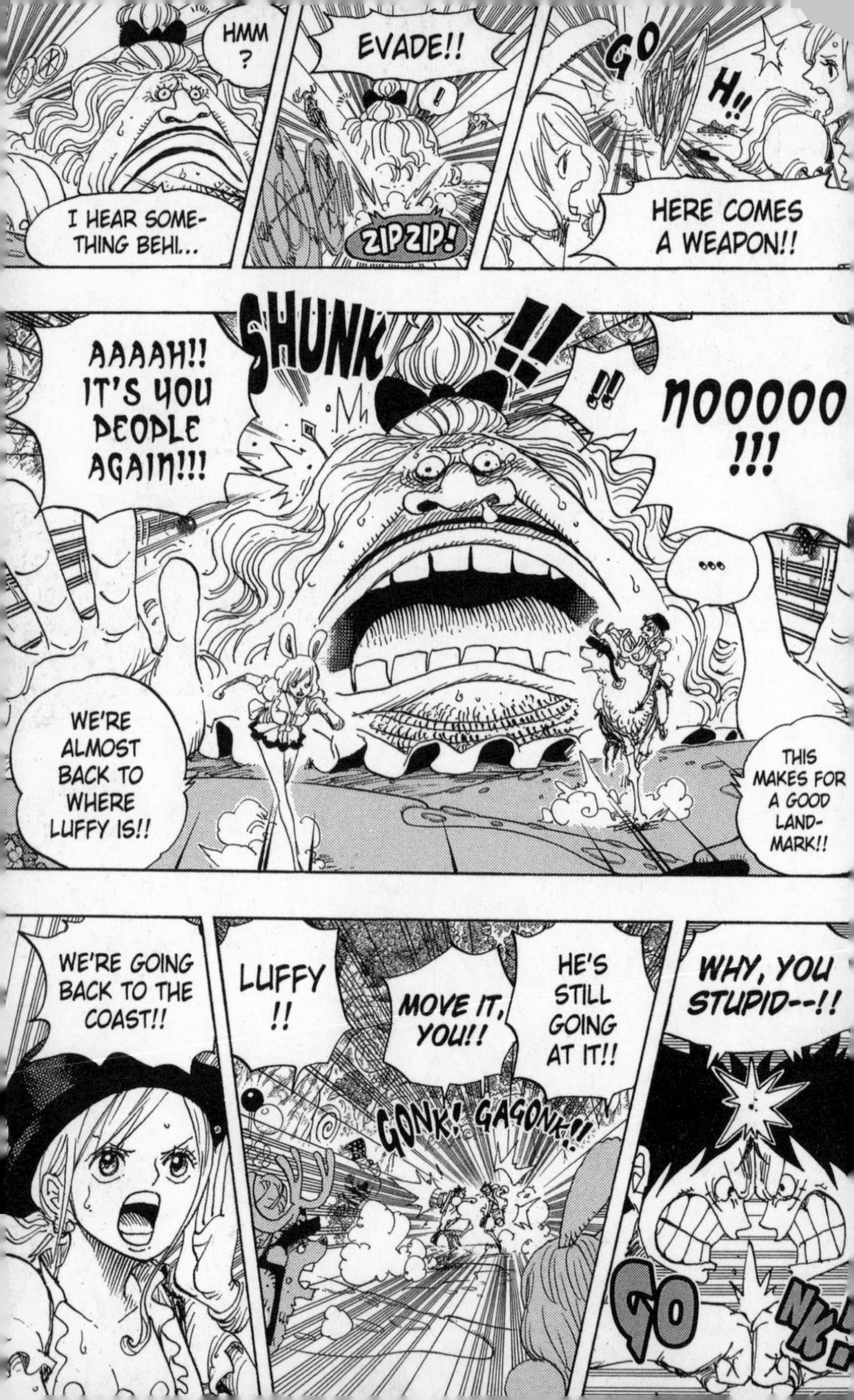
GO
H!!
HERE COMES A WEAPON!!
EVADE!!
!
ZIP ZIP!
HMM ?
I HEAR SOME-THING BEHI...
NOOOOO !!!
SHUNK
!!
!!
AAAAH!! IT'S YOU PEOPLE AGAIN!!!
...
THIS MAKES FOR A GOOD LAND-MARK!!
WE'RE ALMOST BACK TO WHERE LUFFY IS!!
WHY, YOU STUPID--!!
GO
NK!
HE'S STILL GOING AT IT!!
MOVE IT, YOU!!
LUFFY !!
GONK! GAGONK!!
WE'RE GOING BACK TO THE COAST!!

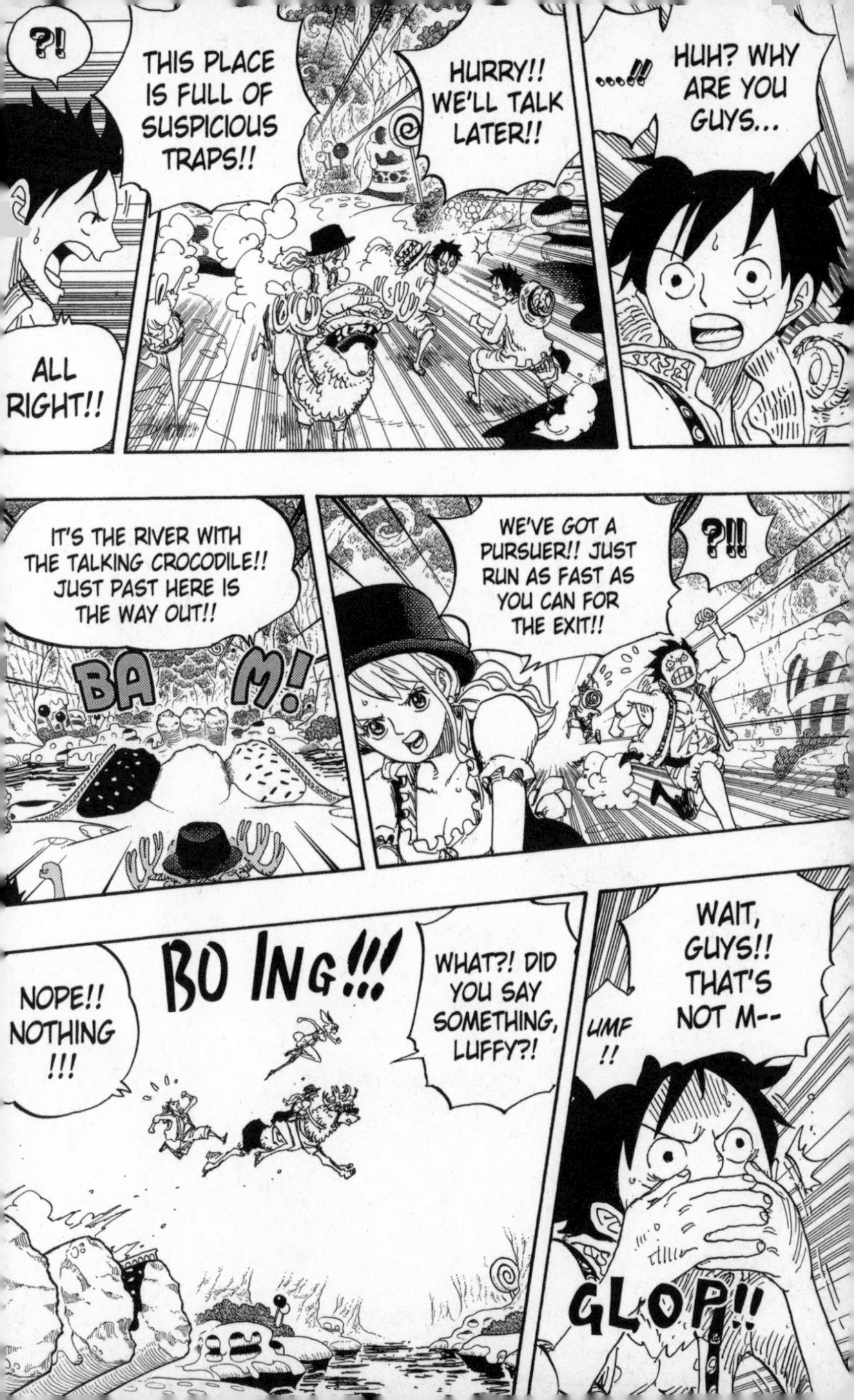
....!!
HUH? WHY ARE YOU GUYS...
HURRY!! WE'LL TALK LATER!!
THIS PLACE IS FULL OF SUSPICIOUS TRAPS!!
?!
ALL RIGHT!!
?!!
WE'VE GOT A PURSUER!! JUST RUN AS FAST AS YOU CAN FOR THE EXIT!!
IT'S THE RIVER WITH THE TALKING CROCODILE!! JUST PAST HERE IS THE WAY OUT!!
BAM!
WAIT, GUYS!! THAT'S NOT M--
UMF!!
GLOP!!
WHAT?! DID YOU SAY SOMETHING, LUFFY?!
BOING!!!
NOPE!! NOTHING!!!

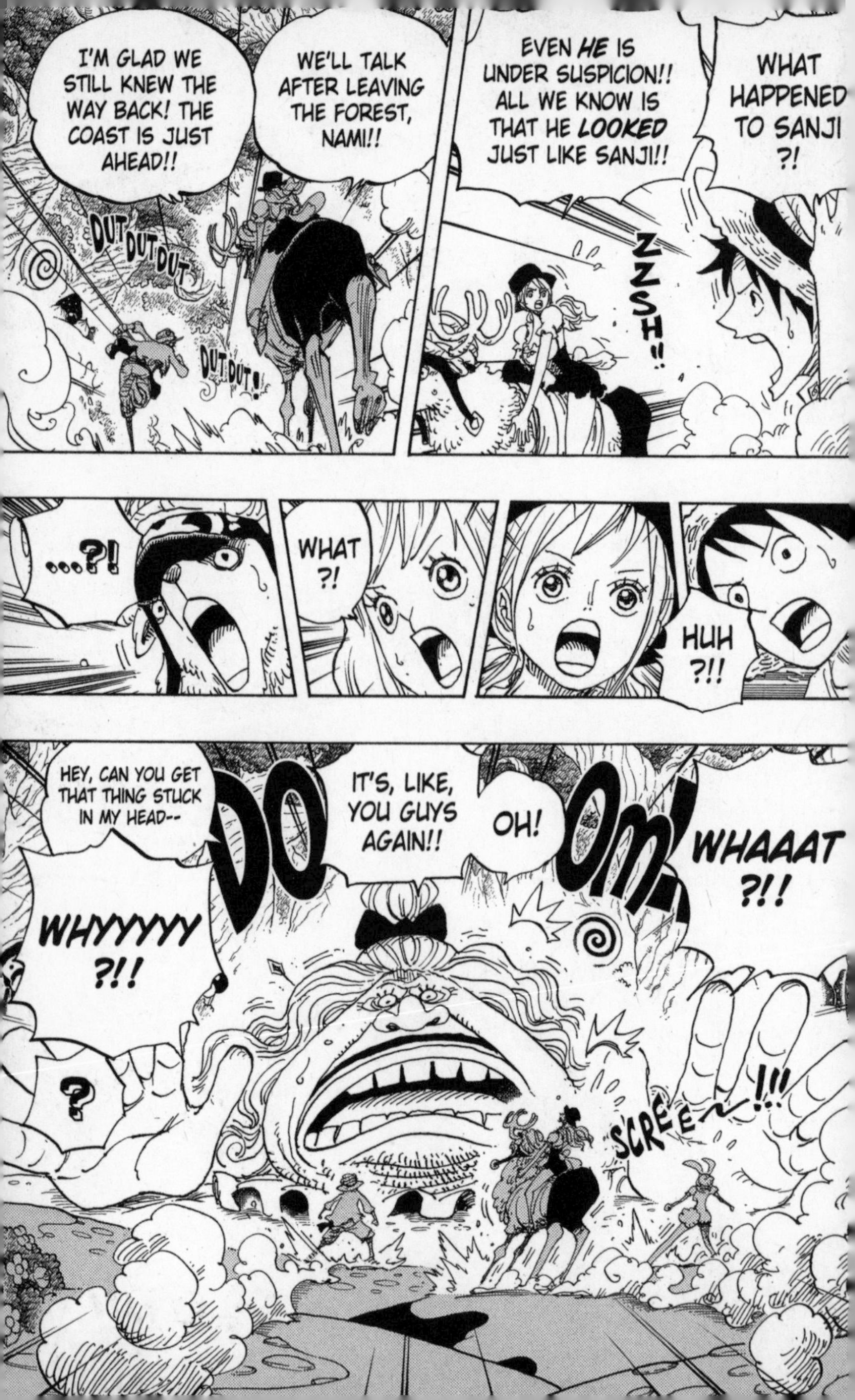
WHAT HAPPENED TO SANJI ?!
EVEN HE IS UNDER SUSPICION!! ALL WE KNOW IS THAT HE LOOKED JUST LIKE SANJI!!
ZZSH!!
WE'LL TALK AFTER LEAVING THE FOREST, NAMI!!
I'M GLAD WE STILL KNEW THE WAY BACK! THE COAST IS JUST AHEAD!!
DUT DUT DUT
DUT DUT!
HUH ?!!
WHAT ?!
...?!
WHAAAT ?!!
DOOM!
OH!
IT'S, LIKE, YOU GUYS AGAIN!!
HEY, CAN YOU GET THAT THING STUCK IN MY HEAD--
WHYYYYY ?!!
SCREE~!!!
?

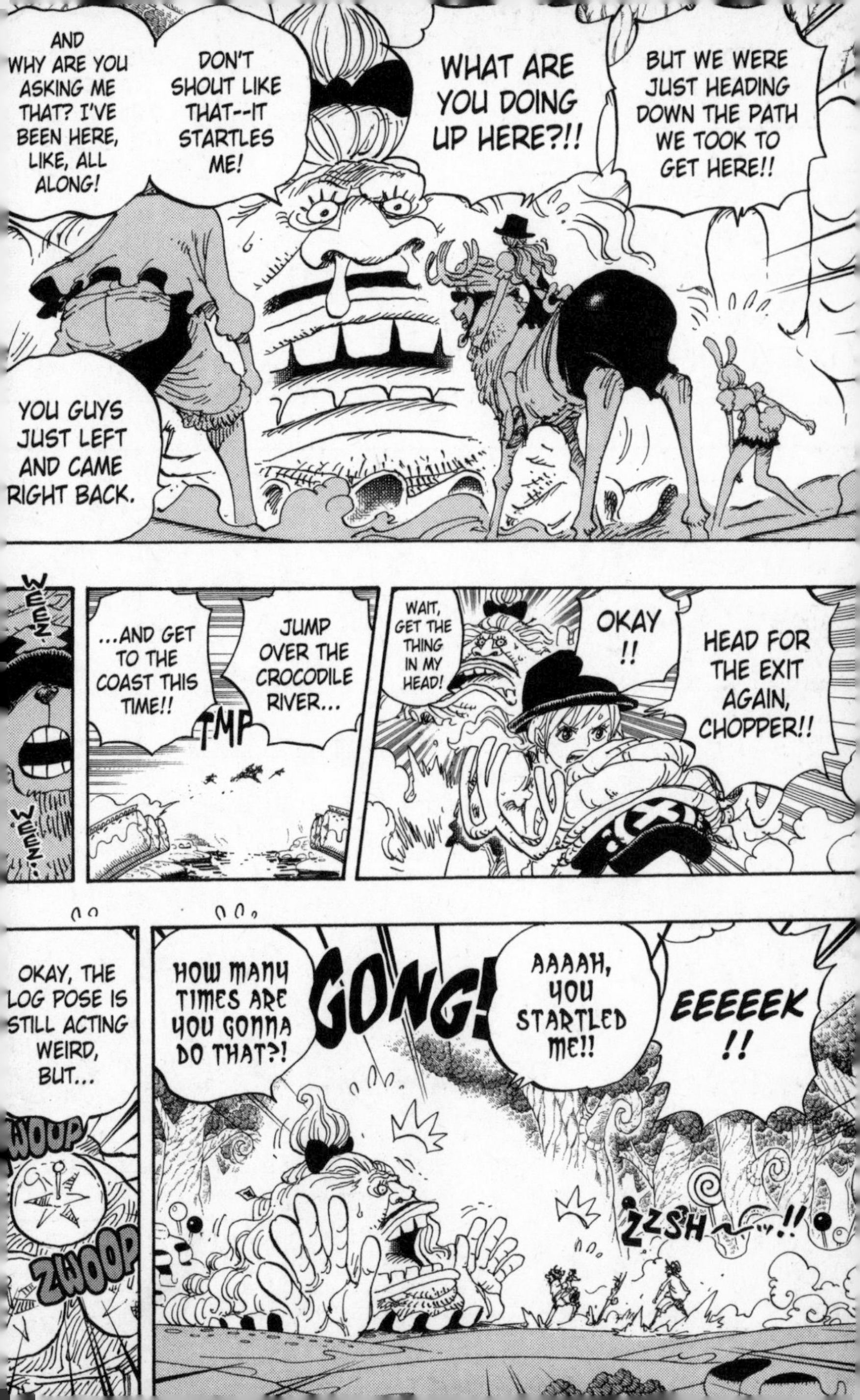
BUT WE WERE JUST HEADING DOWN THE PATH WE TOOK TO GET HERE!!
WHAT ARE YOU DOING UP HERE?!!
DON'T SHOUT LIKE THAT--IT STARTLES ME!
AND WHY ARE YOU ASKING ME THAT? I'VE BEEN HERE, LIKE, ALL ALONG!
YOU GUYS JUST LEFT AND CAME RIGHT BACK.
HEAD FOR THE EXIT AGAIN, CHOPPER!!
OKAY !!
WAIT, GET THE THING IN MY HEAD!
JUMP OVER THE CROCODILE RIVER...
...AND GET TO THE COAST THIS TIME!!
TMP
WEEZ
WEEZ..
EEEEEK !!
AAAAH, YOU STARTLED ME!!
GONG!
HOW MANY TIMES ARE YOU GONNA DO THAT?!
ZZSH~~...!!
OKAY, THE LOG POSE IS STILL ACTING WEIRD, BUT...
WOOP
ZWOOP

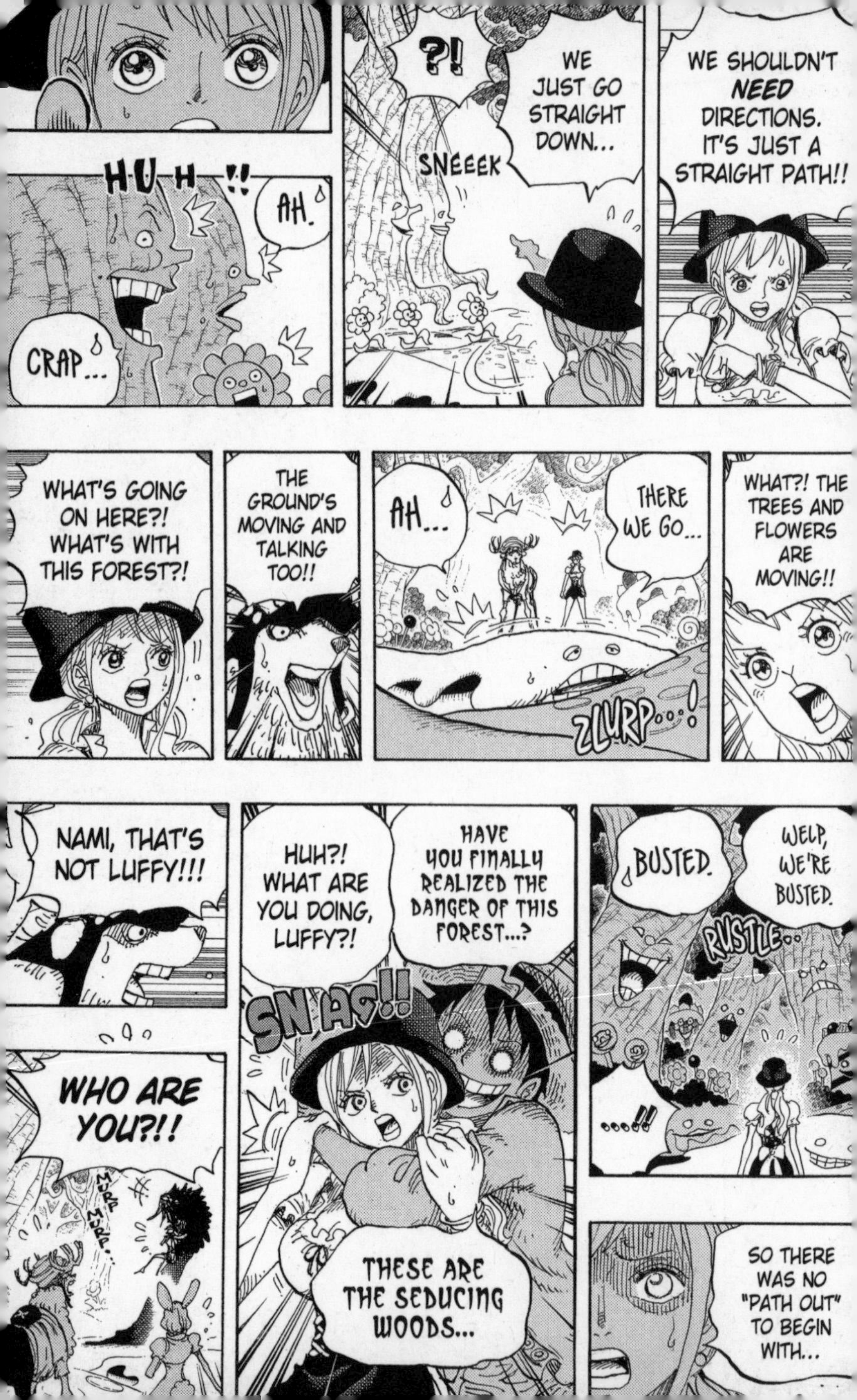
WE SHOULDN'T NEED DIRECTIONS. IT'S JUST A STRAIGHT PATH!!
WE JUST GO STRAIGHT DOWN...
?!
SNEEEK
AH.
HU H !!
CRAP...
WHAT?! THE TREES AND FLOWERS ARE MOVING!!
THERE WE GO...
AH...
ZLURP...!
THE GROUND'S MOVING AND TALKING TOO!!
WHAT'S GOING ON HERE?! WHAT'S WITH THIS FOREST?!
WELP, WE'RE BUSTED.
BUSTED.
RUSTLE
...!!
SO THERE WAS NO "PATH OUT" TO BEGIN WITH...
HAVE YOU FINALLY REALIZED THE DANGER OF THIS FOREST...?
HUH?! WHAT ARE YOU DOING, LUFFY?!
SNAG!!
THESE ARE THE SEDUCING WOODS...
NAMI, THAT'S NOT LUFFY!!!
WHO ARE YOU?!!
MURP MURP...

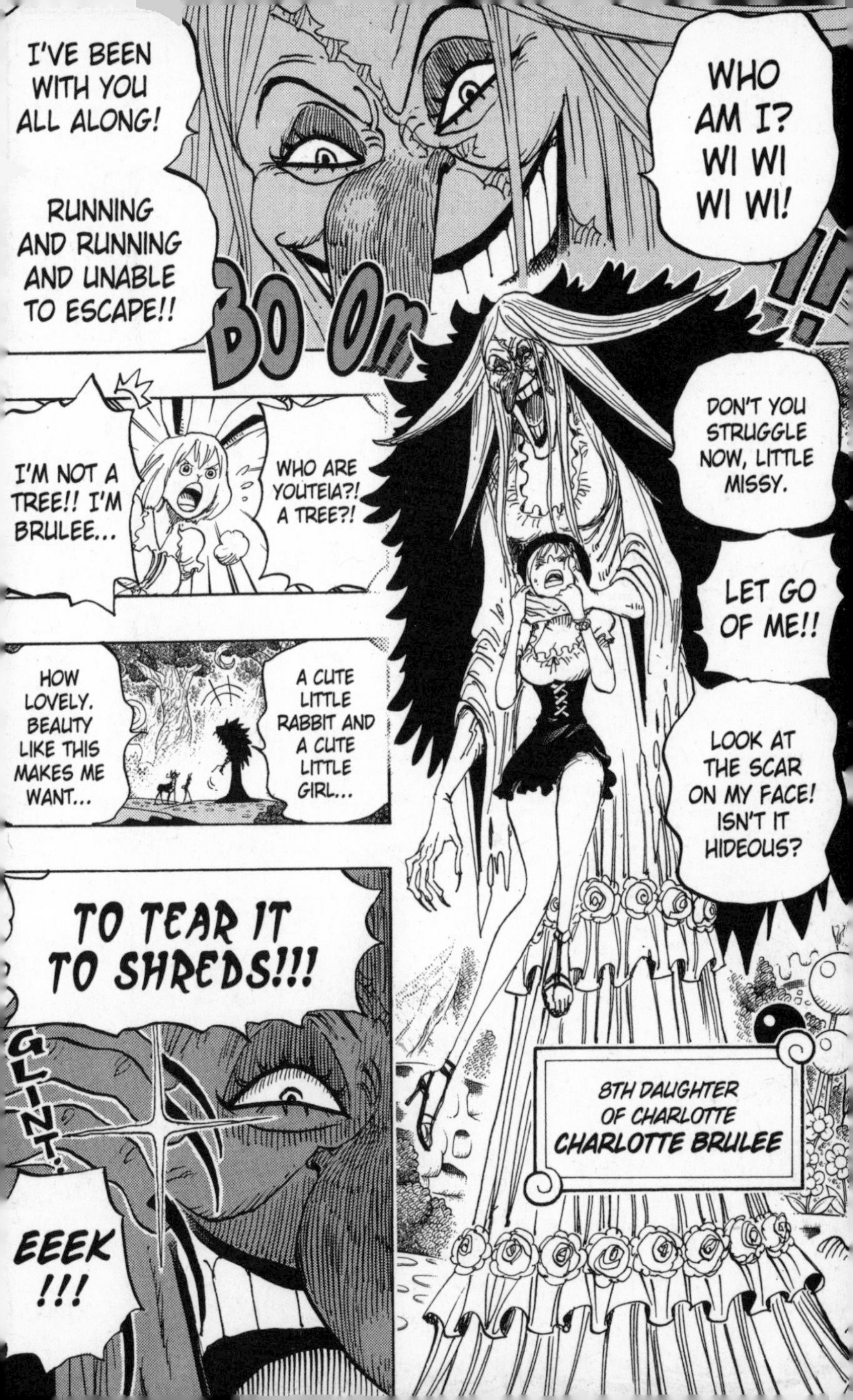
WHO AM I? WI WI WI WI!
I'VE BEEN WITH YOU ALL ALONG!
RUNNING AND RUNNING AND UNABLE TO ESCAPE!!
BOOM
!!
DON'T YOU STRUGGLE NOW, LITTLE MISSY.
LET GO OF ME!!
LOOK AT THE SCAR ON MY FACE! ISN'T IT HIDEOUS?
8TH DAUGHTER OF CHARLOTTE
CHARLOTTE BRULEE
WHO ARE YOUTEIA?! A TREE?!
I'M NOT A TREE!! I'M BRULEE...
A CUTE LITTLE RABBIT AND A CUTE LITTLE GIRL...
HOW LOVELY. BEAUTY LIKE THIS MAKES ME WANT...
TO TEAR IT TO SHREDS!!!
GLINT
EEEK !!!

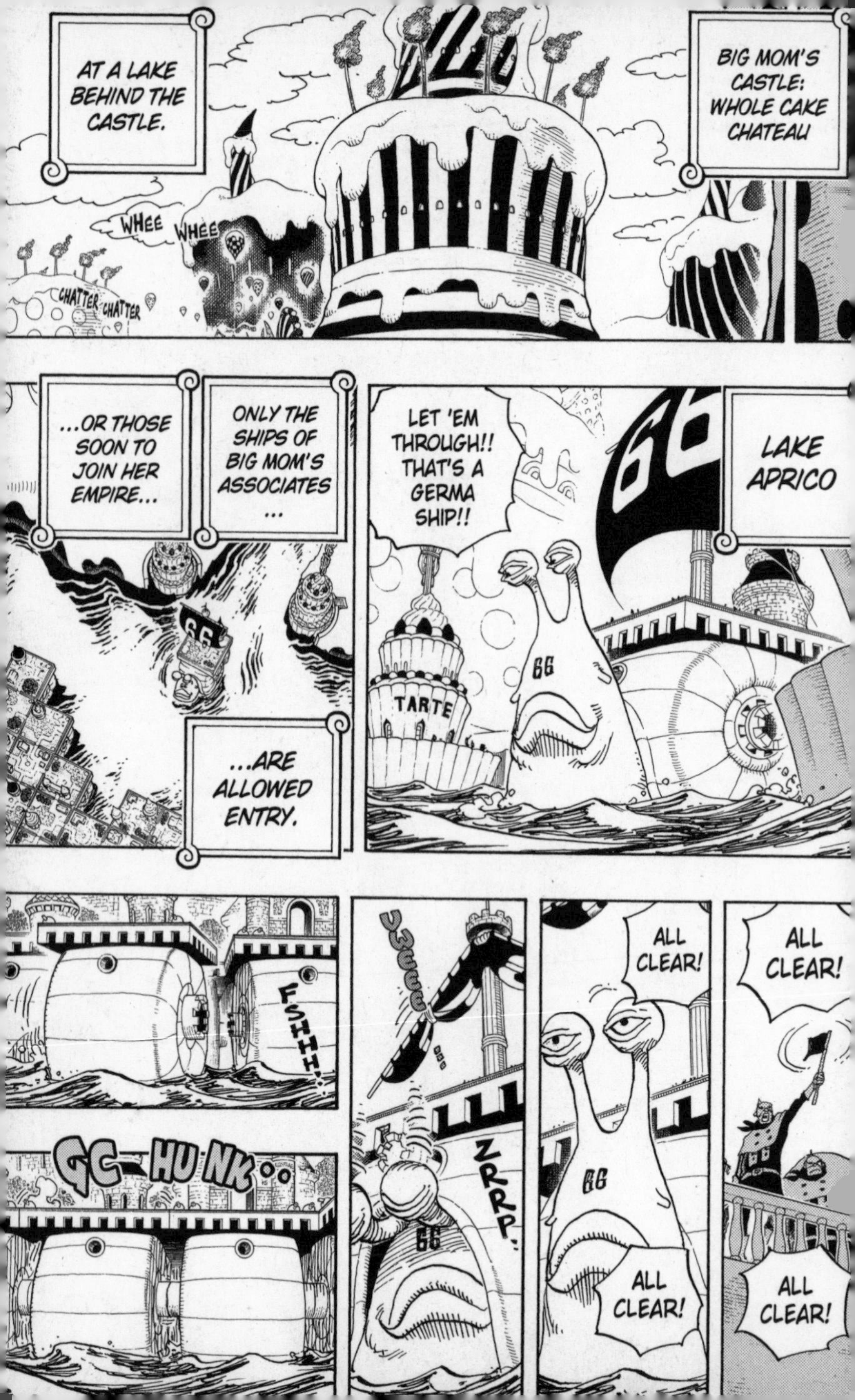
BIG MOM'S CASTLE: WHOLE CAKE CHATEAU
AT A LAKE BEHIND THE CASTLE.
WHEE
WHEE
CHATTER CHATTER
LAKE APRICO
LET 'EM THROUGH!! THAT'S A GERMA SHIP!!
TARTE
ONLY THE SHIPS OF BIG MOM'S ASSOCIATES ...
...OR THOSE SOON TO JOIN HER EMPIRE...
...ARE ALLOWED ENTRY.
ALL CLEAR!
ALL CLEAR!
ALL CLEAR!
ALL CLEAR!
ZRRP
FSHHH
GC-HUNK

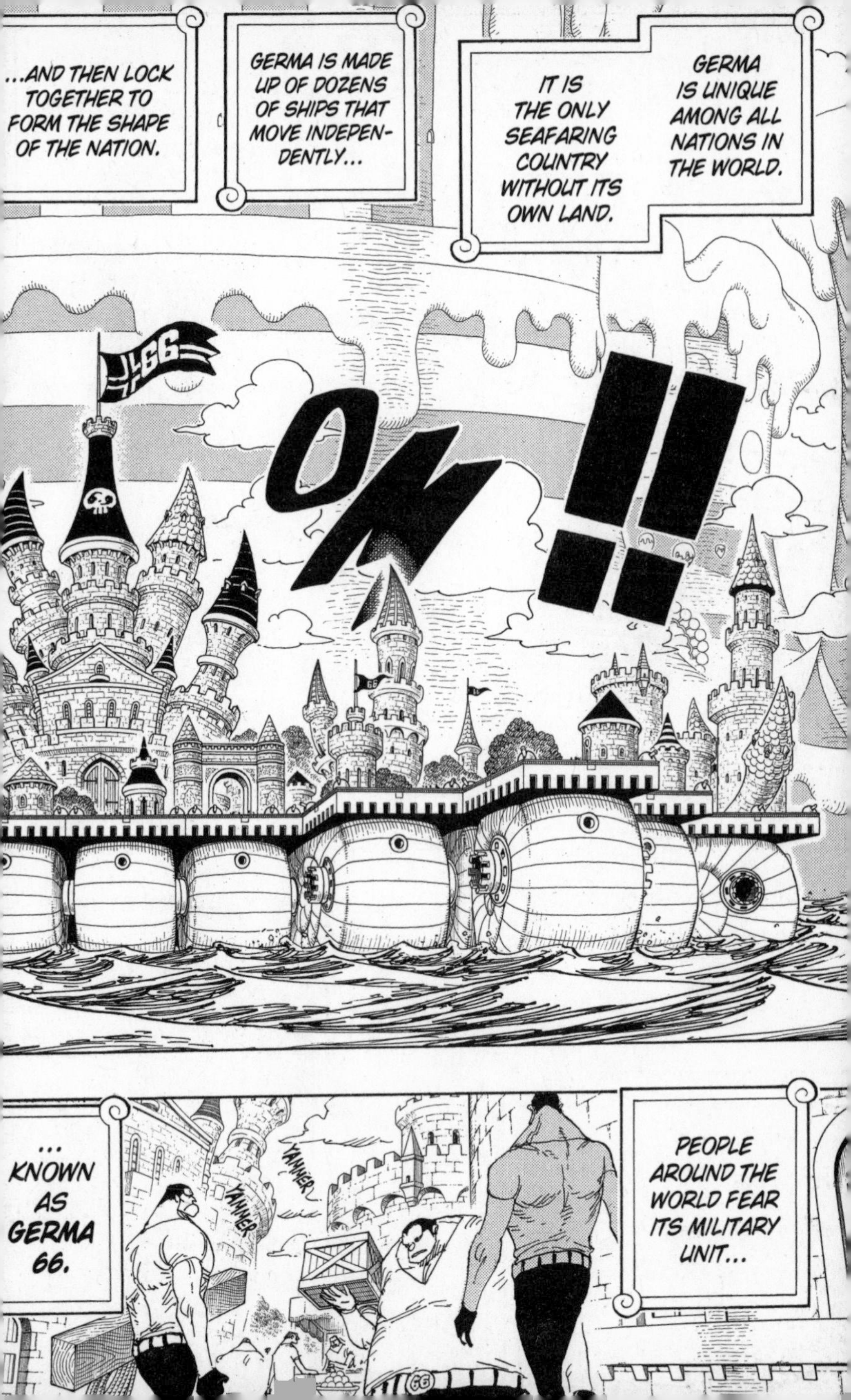
GERMA IS UNIQUE AMONG ALL NATIONS IN THE WORLD.
IT IS THE ONLY SEAFARING COUNTRY WITHOUT ITS OWN LAND.
GERMA IS MADE UP OF DOZENS OF SHIPS THAT MOVE INDEPEN-DENTLY...
...AND THEN LOCK TOGETHER TO FORM THE SHAPE OF THE NATION.
ON!!
PEOPLE AROUND THE WORLD FEAR ITS MILITARY UNIT...
YAMMER
YAMMER
... KNOWN AS GERMA 66.

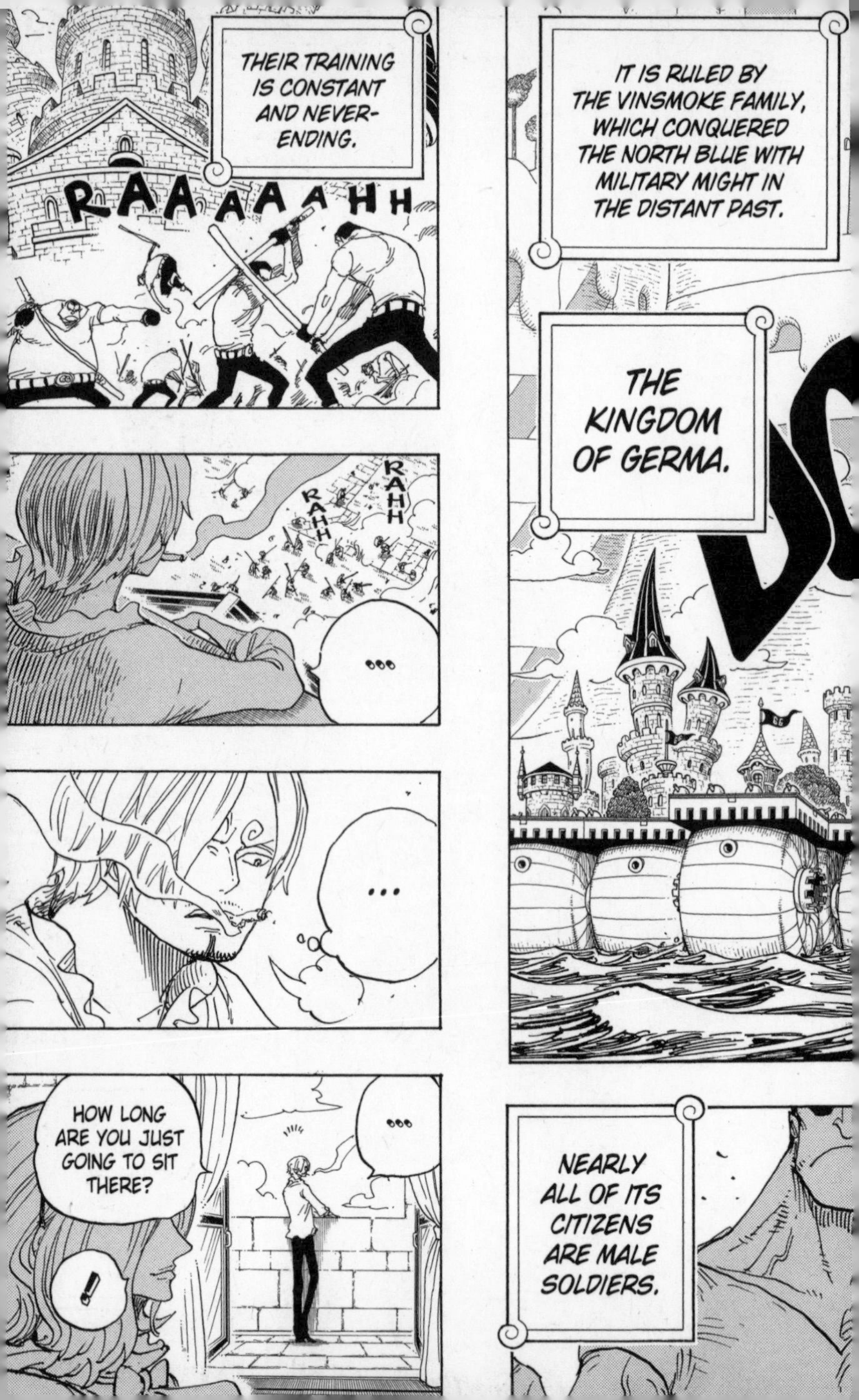
IT IS RULED BY THE VINSMOKE FAMILY, WHICH CONQUERED THE NORTH BLUE WITH MILITARY MIGHT IN THE DISTANT PAST.
THE KINGDOM OF GERMA.
NEARLY ALL OF ITS CITIZENS ARE MALE SOLDIERS.
THEIR TRAINING IS CONSTANT AND NEVER-ENDING.
RAAAAAHH
RAHH
RAHH
...
...
...
HOW LONG ARE YOU JUST GOING TO SIT THERE?
!

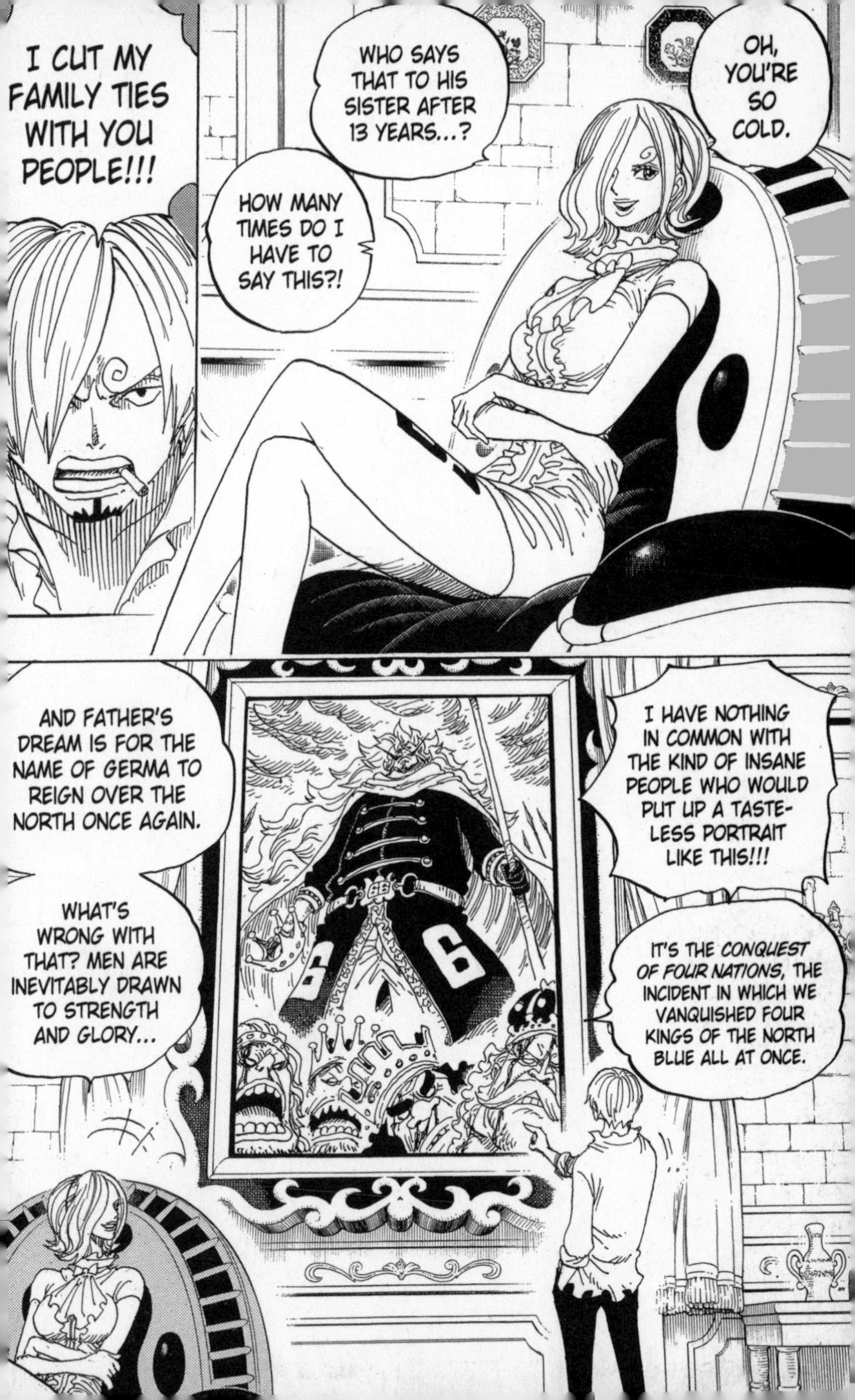
OH, YOU'RE SO COLD.
WHO SAYS THAT TO HIS SISTER AFTER 13 YEARS...?
HOW MANY TIMES DO I HAVE TO SAY THIS?!
I CUT MY FAMILY TIES WITH YOU PEOPLE!!!
I HAVE NOTHING IN COMMON WITH THE KIND OF INSANE PEOPLE WHO WOULD PUT UP A TASTE-LESS PORTRAIT LIKE THIS!!!
AND FATHER'S DREAM IS FOR THE NAME OF GERMA TO REIGN OVER THE NORTH ONCE AGAIN.
IT'S THE *CONQUEST OF FOUR NATIONS*, THE INCIDENT IN WHICH WE VANQUISHED FOUR KINGS OF THE NORTH BLUE ALL AT ONCE.
WHAT'S WRONG WITH THAT? MEN ARE INEVITABLY DRAWN TO STRENGTH AND GLORY...

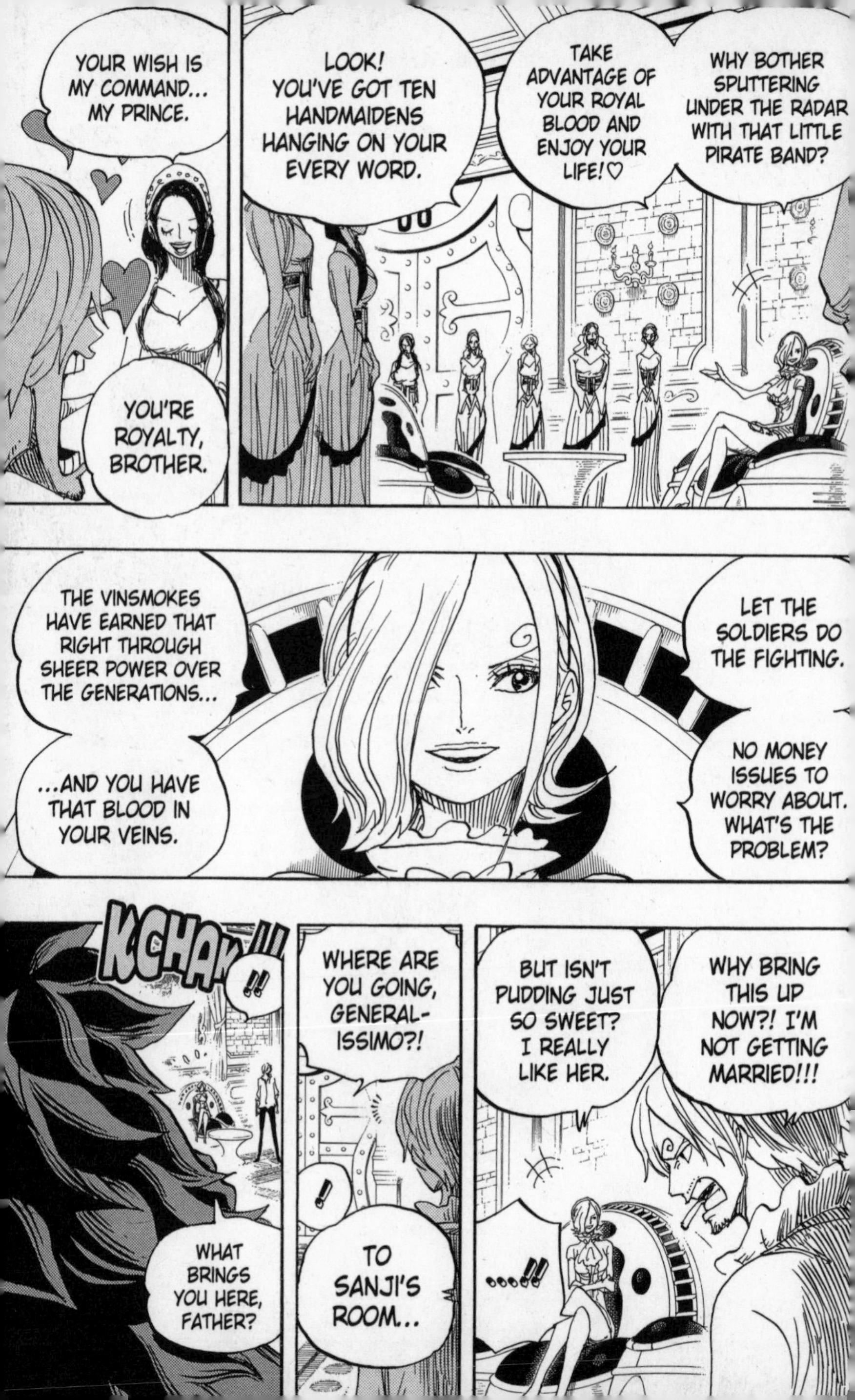

WHY BOTHER SPUTTERING UNDER THE RADAR WITH THAT LITTLE PIRATE BAND?
TAKE ADVANTAGE OF YOUR ROYAL BLOOD AND ENJOY YOUR LIFE!♡
LOOK! YOU'VE GOT TEN HANDMAIDENS HANGING ON YOUR EVERY WORD.
YOUR WISH IS MY COMMAND... MY PRINCE.
YOU'RE ROYALTY, BROTHER.
LET THE SOLDIERS DO THE FIGHTING.
NO MONEY ISSUES TO WORRY ABOUT. WHAT'S THE PROBLEM?
THE VINSMOKES HAVE EARNED THAT RIGHT THROUGH SHEER POWER OVER THE GENERATIONS...
...AND YOU HAVE THAT BLOOD IN YOUR VEINS.
WHY BRING THIS UP NOW?! I'M NOT GETTING MARRIED!!!
BUT ISN'T PUDDING JUST SO SWEET? I REALLY LIKE HER.
...!!
WHERE ARE YOU GOING, GENERAL-ISSIMO?!
!
TO SANJI'S ROOM...
KCHAK!!
!!
WHAT BRINGS YOU HERE, FATHER?

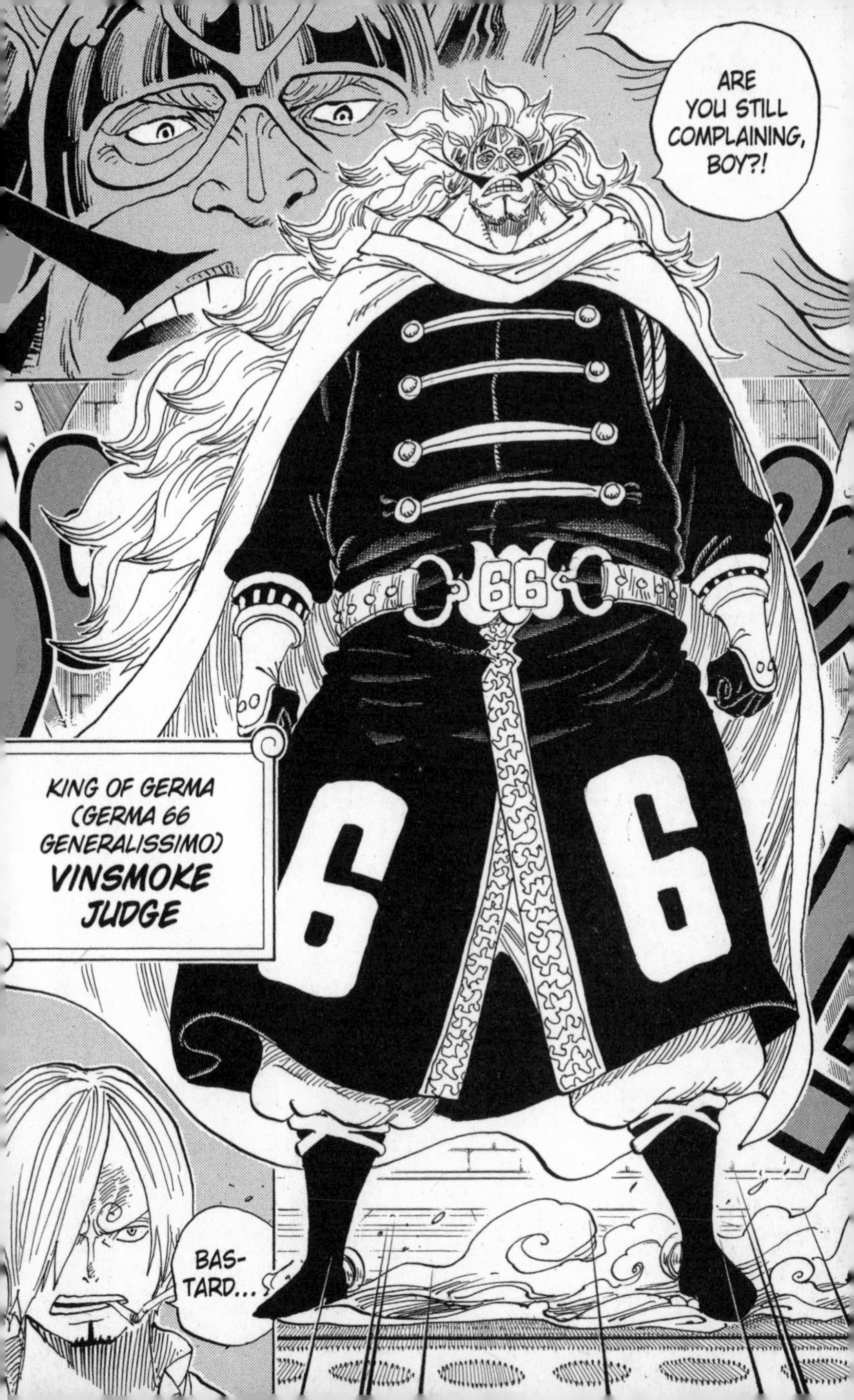
ARE YOU STILL COMPLAINING, BOY?!
KING OF GERMA (GERMA 66 GENERALISSIMO) VINSMOKE JUDGE
66
BAS-TARD...

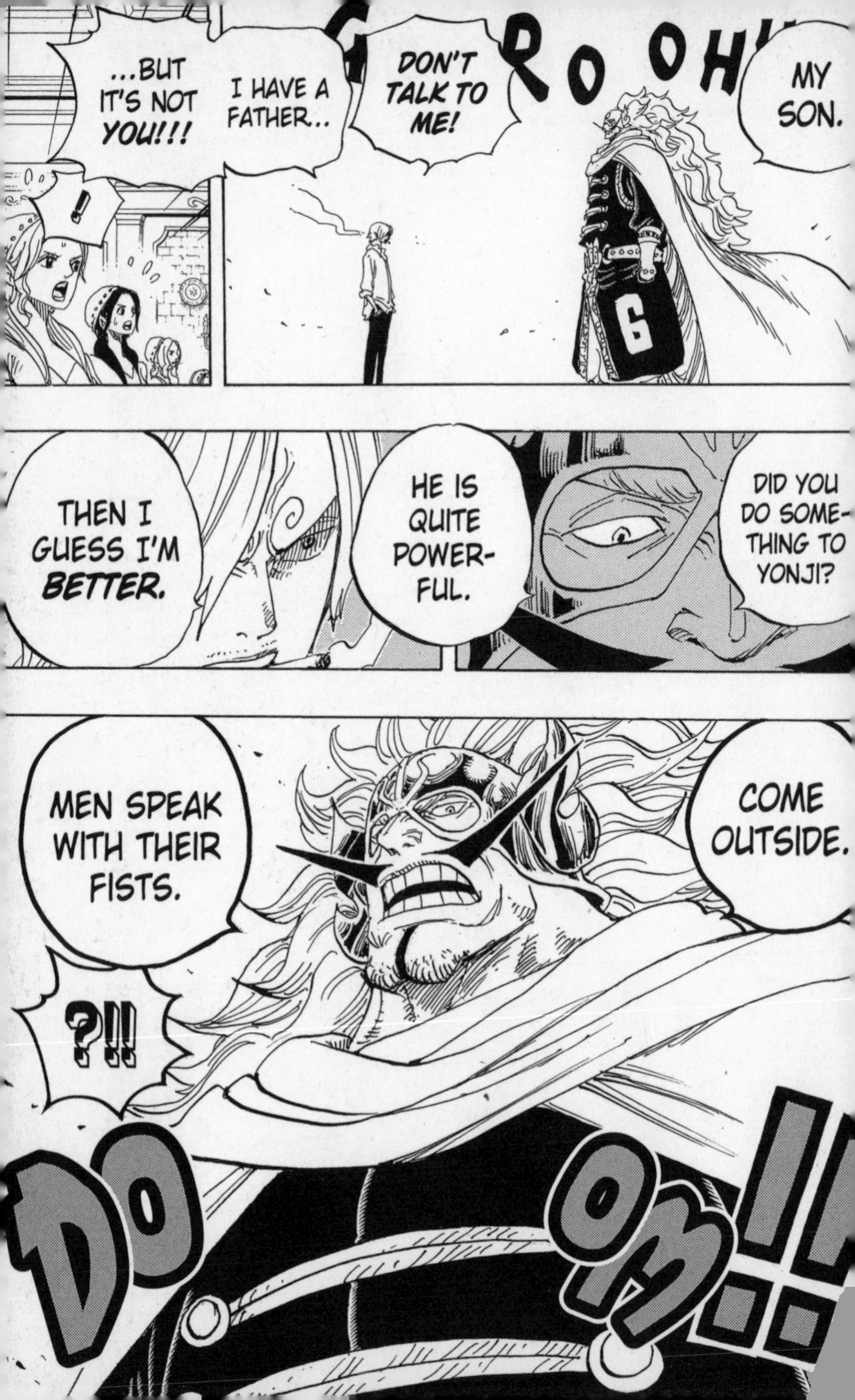
MY SON.
GROOH
DON'T TALK TO ME!
I HAVE A FATHER...
...BUT IT'S NOT YOU!!!
!
DID YOU DO SOME-THING TO YONJI?
HE IS QUITE POWER-FUL.
THEN I GUESS I'M BETTER.
COME OUTSIDE.
MEN SPEAK WITH THEIR FISTS.
?!!
DOOM!!

VINSMOKE JUDGE

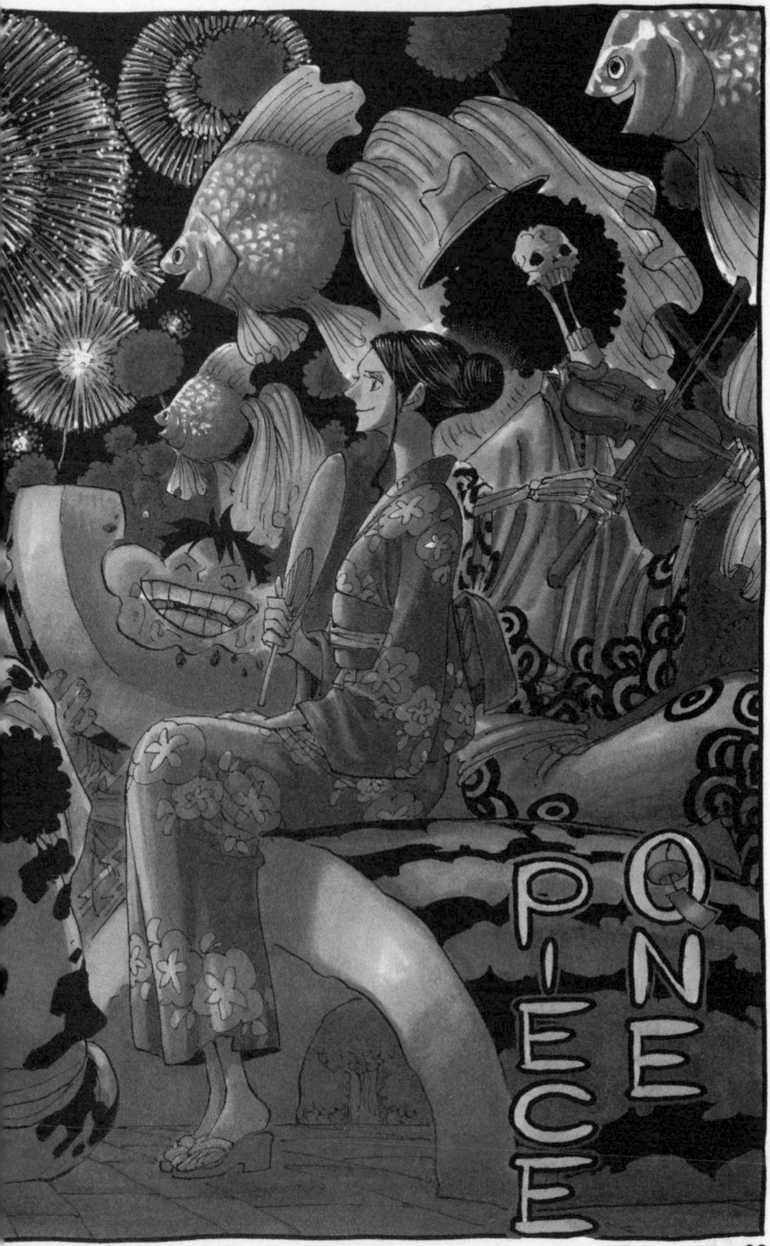
ONE PIECE

Chapter 833:

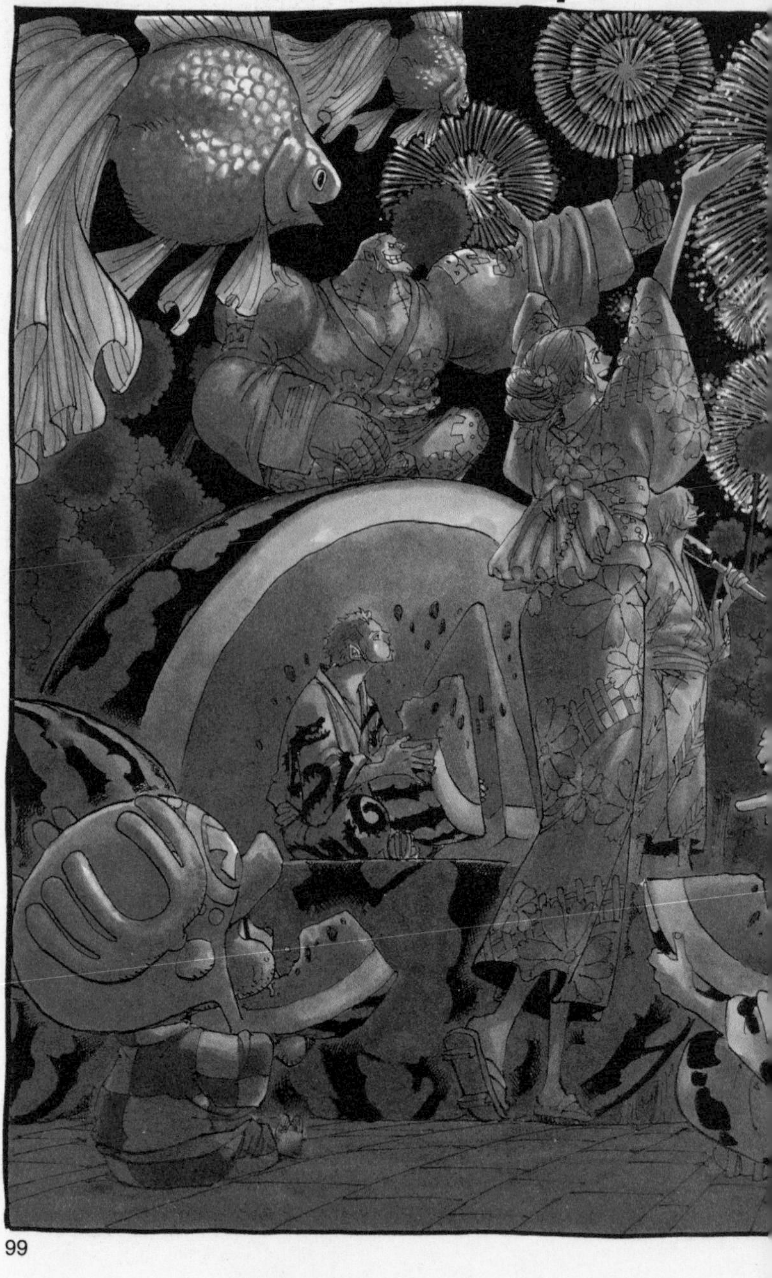

vol.83
ONE PIECE

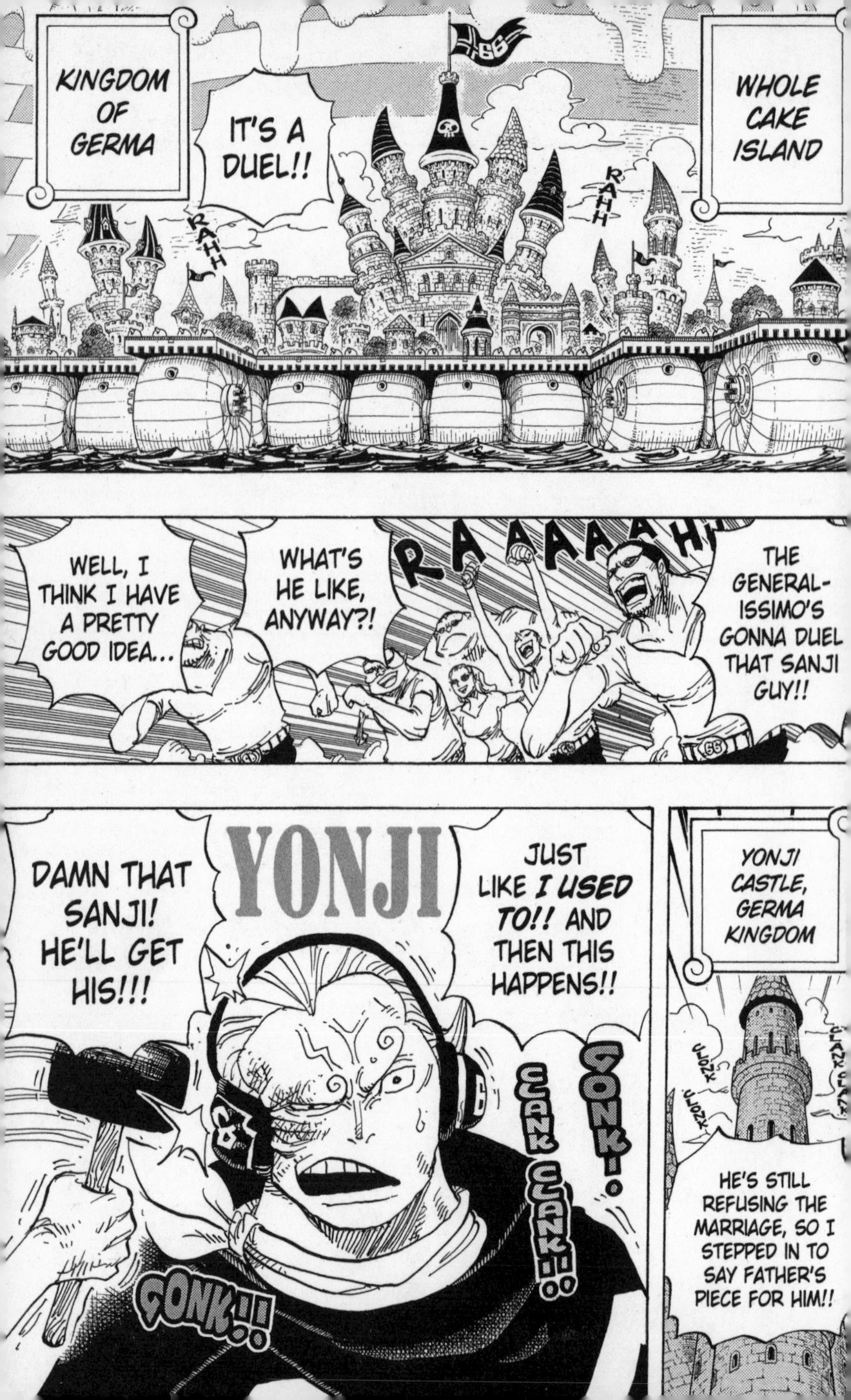
WHOLE CAKE ISLAND
RAHH
IT'S A DUEL!!
KINGDOM OF GERMA
RAHH
THE GENERAL-ISSIMO'S GONNA DUEL THAT SANJI GUY!!
RAAAAAH
WHAT'S HE LIKE, ANYWAY?!
WELL, I THINK I HAVE A PRETTY GOOD IDEA...
YONJI CASTLE, GERMA KINGDOM
CLANK CLANK
CLONK
CLONK
HE'S STILL REFUSING THE MARRIAGE, SO I STEPPED IN TO SAY FATHER'S PIECE FOR HIM!!
JUST LIKE *I USED TO!!* AND THEN THIS HAPPENS!!
YONJI
DAMN THAT SANJI! HE'LL GET HIS!!!
GONK!
CLANK CLANK CLANK!!
GONK!!

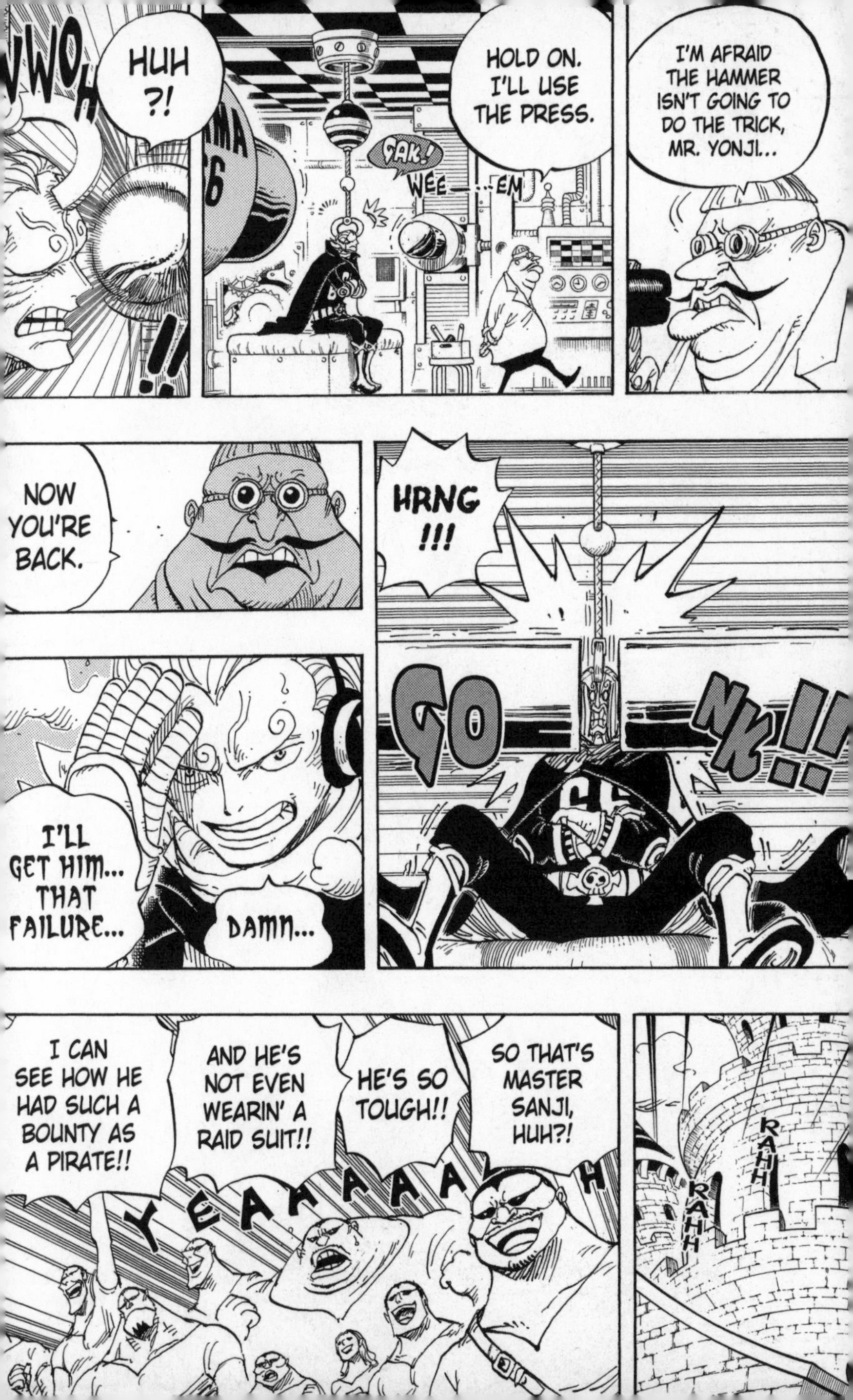
I'M AFRAID THE HAMMER ISN'T GOING TO DO THE TRICK, MR. YONJI...
HOLD ON. I'LL USE THE PRESS.
GAK!
WEE......EM
HUH ?!
VWOH
!!
HRNG !!!
GO
NK!!
NOW YOU'RE BACK.
I'LL GET HIM... THAT FAILURE...
DAMN...
RAHH
RAHH
SO THAT'S MASTER SANJI, HUH?!
HE'S SO TOUGH!!
AND HE'S NOT EVEN WEARIN' A RAID SUIT!!
I CAN SEE HOW HE HAD SUCH A BOUNTY AS A PIRATE!!
YEAAAAAAH

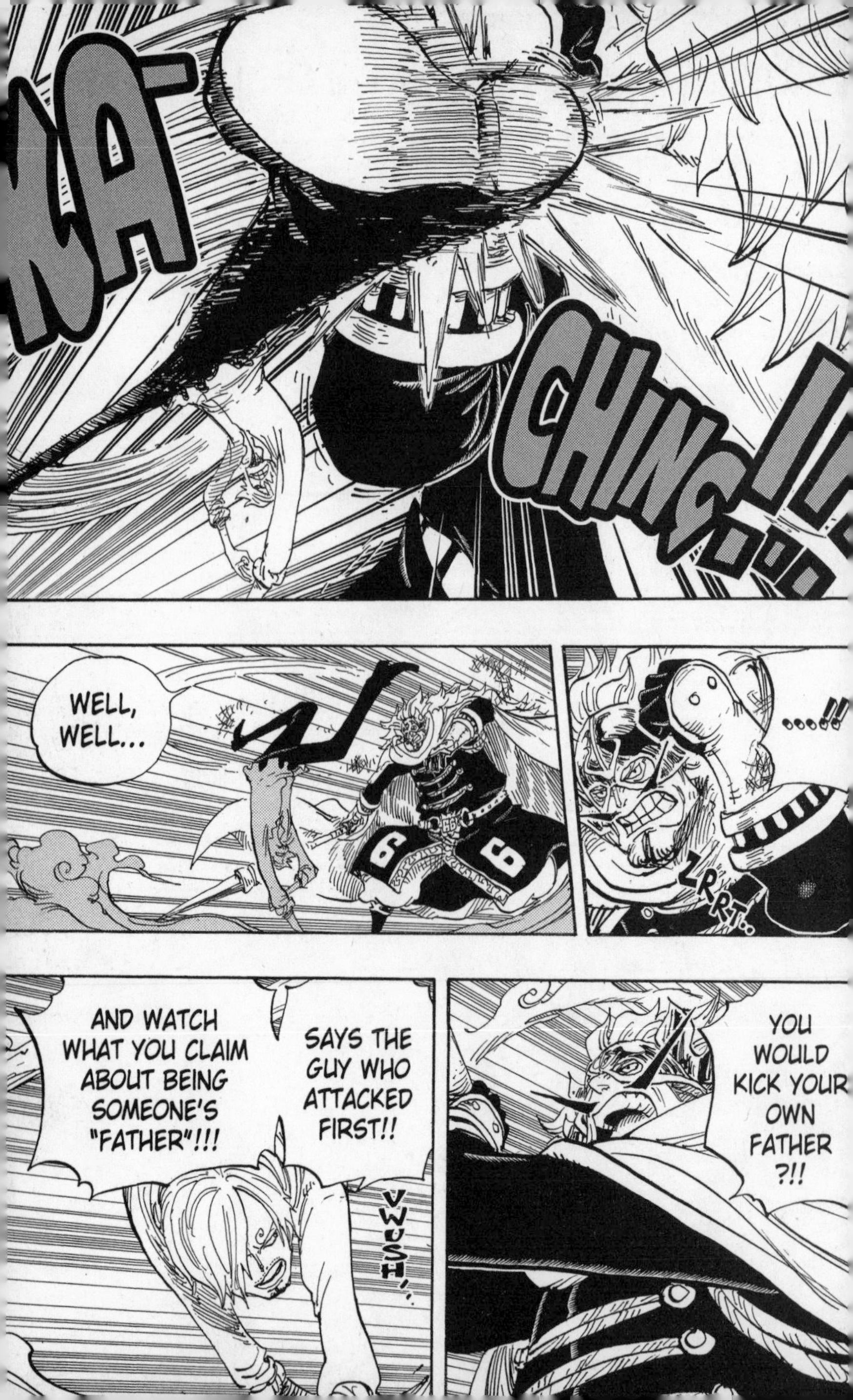
KA-
CHING..!!
...!!
ZRRT..
WELL, WELL...
YOU WOULD KICK YOUR OWN FATHER?!!
SAYS THE GUY WHO ATTACKED FIRST!!
AND WATCH WHAT YOU CLAIM ABOUT BEING SOMEONE'S "FATHER"!!!
VWUSH..

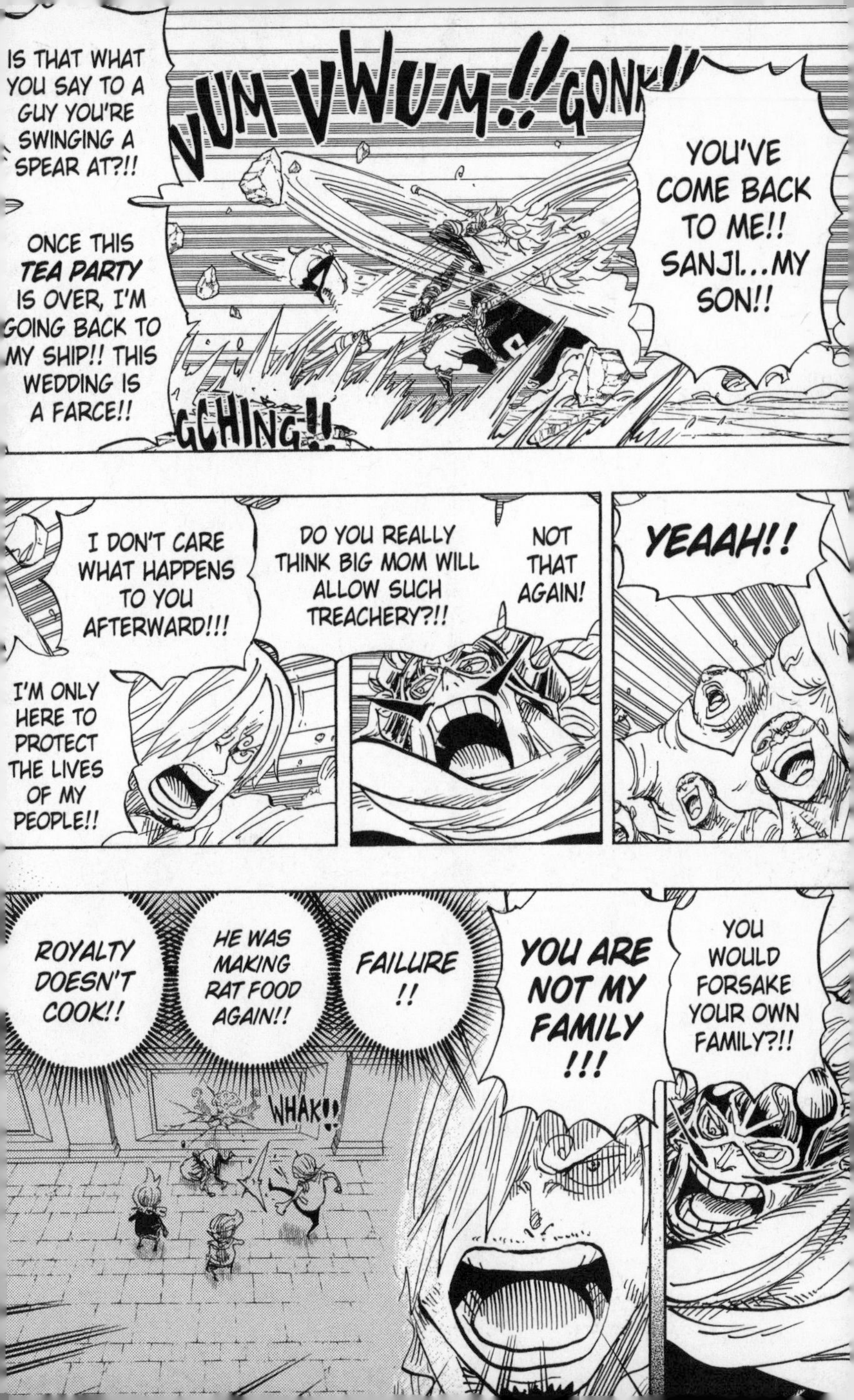

YOU'VE COME BACK TO ME!! SANJI...MY SON!!
VUM VWUM!! GONK!!
IS THAT WHAT YOU SAY TO A GUY YOU'RE SWINGING A SPEAR AT?!!
ONCE THIS *TEA PARTY* IS OVER, I'M GOING BACK TO MY SHIP!! THIS WEDDING IS A FARCE!!
GCHING!!
YEAAH!!
NOT THAT AGAIN!
DO YOU REALLY THINK BIG MOM WILL ALLOW SUCH TREACHERY?!!
I DON'T CARE WHAT HAPPENS TO YOU AFTERWARD!!!
I'M ONLY HERE TO PROTECT THE LIVES OF MY PEOPLE!!
YOU WOULD FORSAKE YOUR OWN FAMILY?!!
YOU ARE NOT MY FAMILY!!!
FAILURE!!
HE WAS MAKING RAT FOOD AGAIN!!
ROYALTY DOESN'T COOK!!
WHAK!!

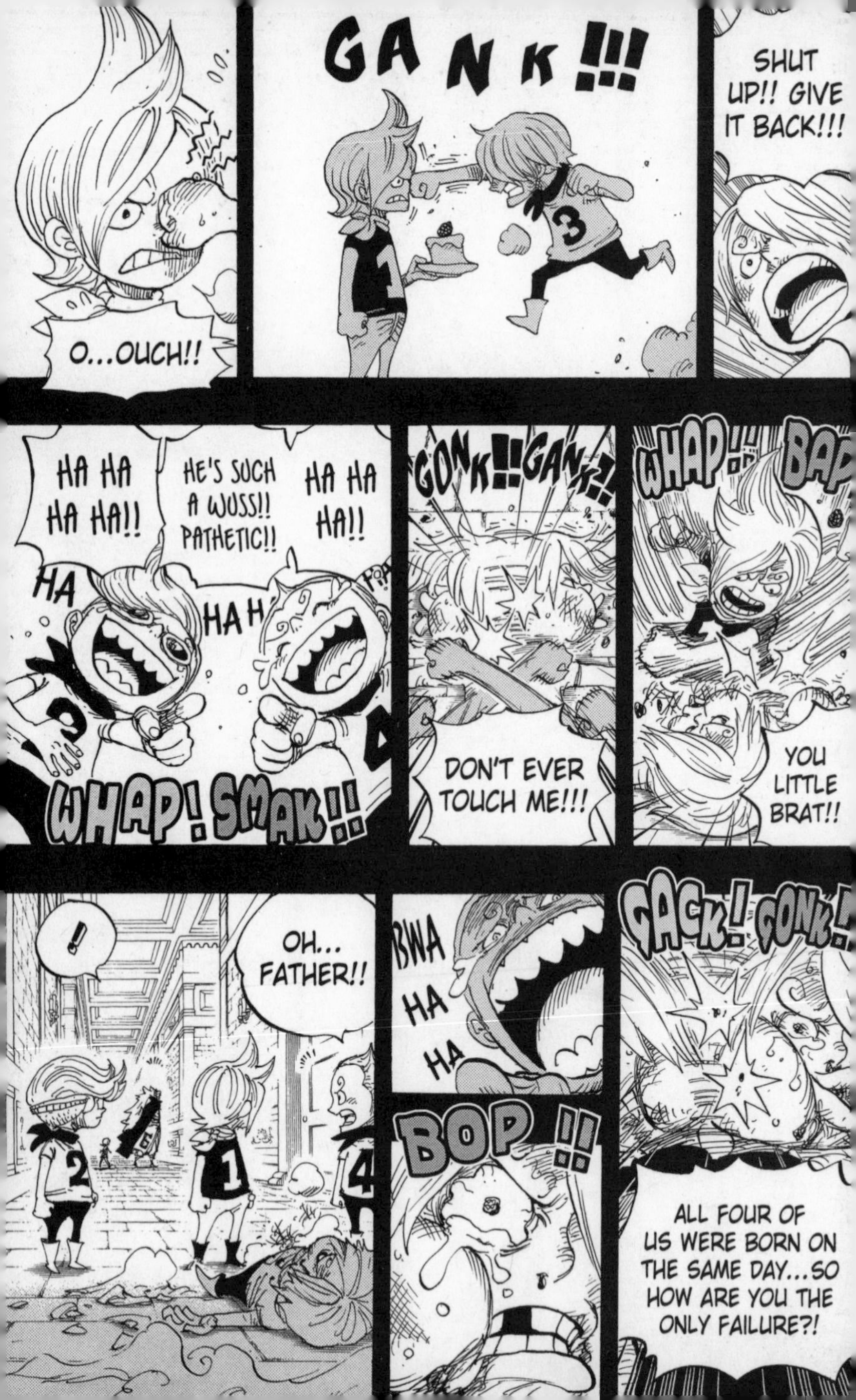
SHUT UP!! GIVE IT BACK!!!
GANK!!!
O...OUCH!!
WHAP!!
BAP
YOU LITTLE BRAT!!
GONK!! GANK!!
DON'T EVER TOUCH ME!!!
HA HA HA!!
HE'S SUCH A WUSS!! PATHETIC!!
HA HA HA HA!!
HA
HA H
WHAP! SMAK!!
GACK! GONK!
ALL FOUR OF US WERE BORN ON THE SAME DAY...SO HOW ARE YOU THE ONLY FAILURE?!
BWA HA HA
BOP!!
OH... FATHER!!
!

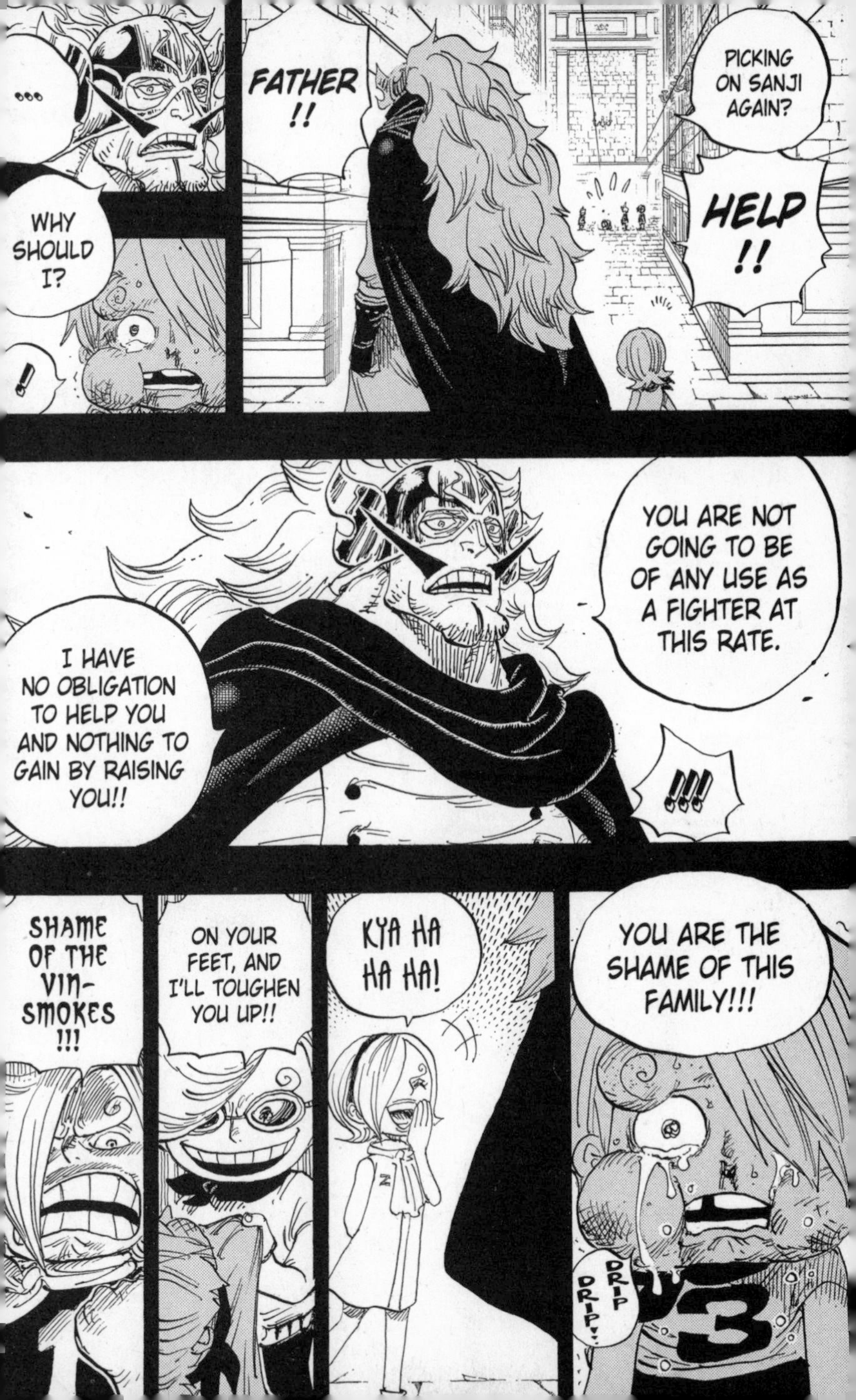
PICKING ON SANJI AGAIN?
HELP!!
FATHER!!
...
WHY SHOULD I?
!
YOU ARE NOT GOING TO BE OF ANY USE AS A FIGHTER AT THIS RATE.
I HAVE NO OBLIGATION TO HELP YOU AND NOTHING TO GAIN BY RAISING YOU!!
!!!
YOU ARE THE SHAME OF THIS FAMILY!!!
DRIP DRIP
KYA HA HA HA!
ON YOUR FEET, AND I'LL TOUGHEN YOU UP!!
SHAME OF THE VIN-SMOKES!!!

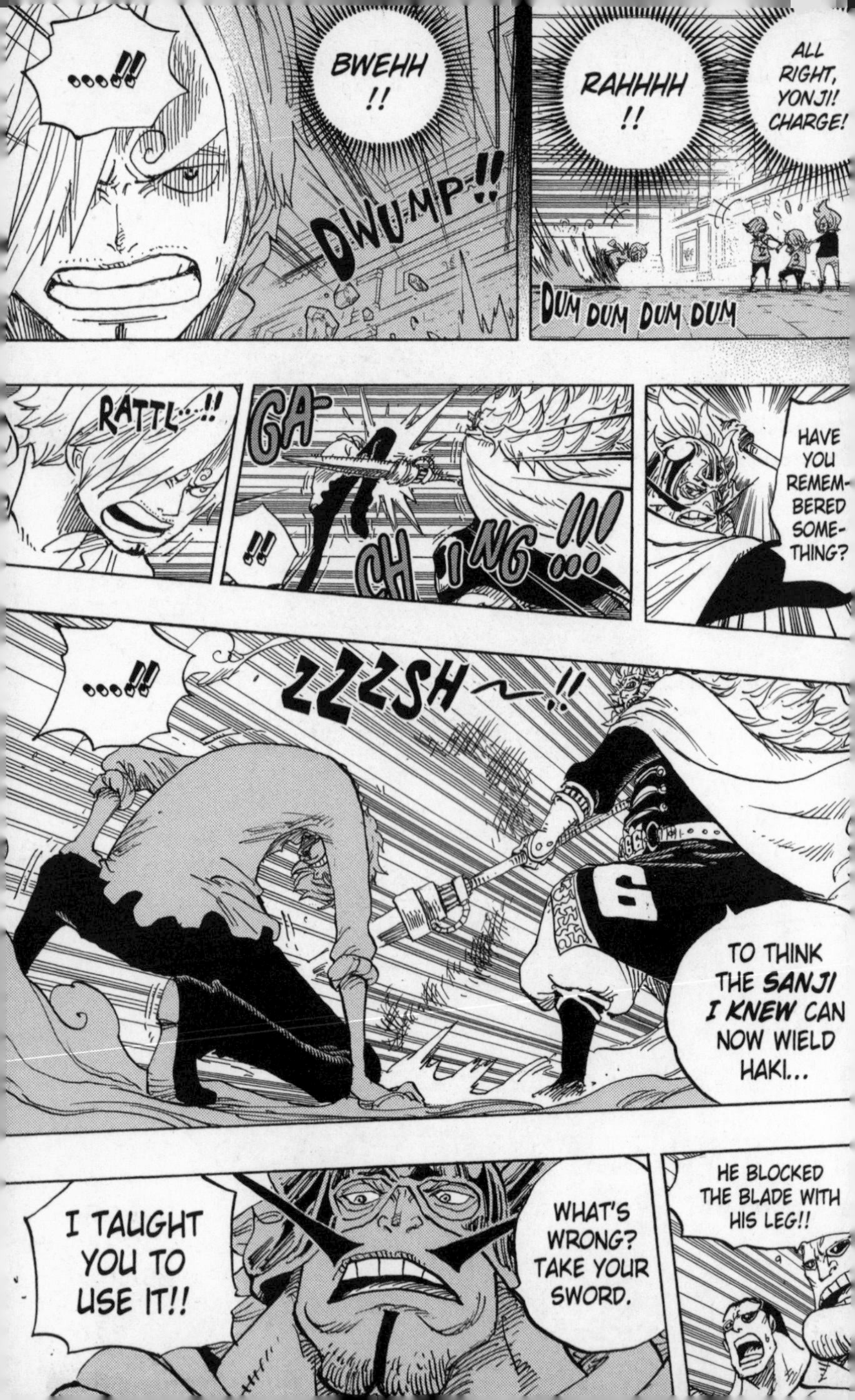
ALL RIGHT, YONJI! CHARGE!
RAHHHH!!
DUM DUM DUM DUM
BWEHH!!
DWUMP!!
....!!
HAVE YOU REMEMBERED SOMETHING?
GA-CHING...!!!
!!
RATTL...!!
ZZZSH~!!
TO THINK THE ***SANJI I KNEW*** CAN NOW WIELD HAKI...
....!!
HE BLOCKED THE BLADE WITH HIS LEG!!
WHAT'S WRONG? TAKE YOUR SWORD.
I TAUGHT YOU TO USE IT!!

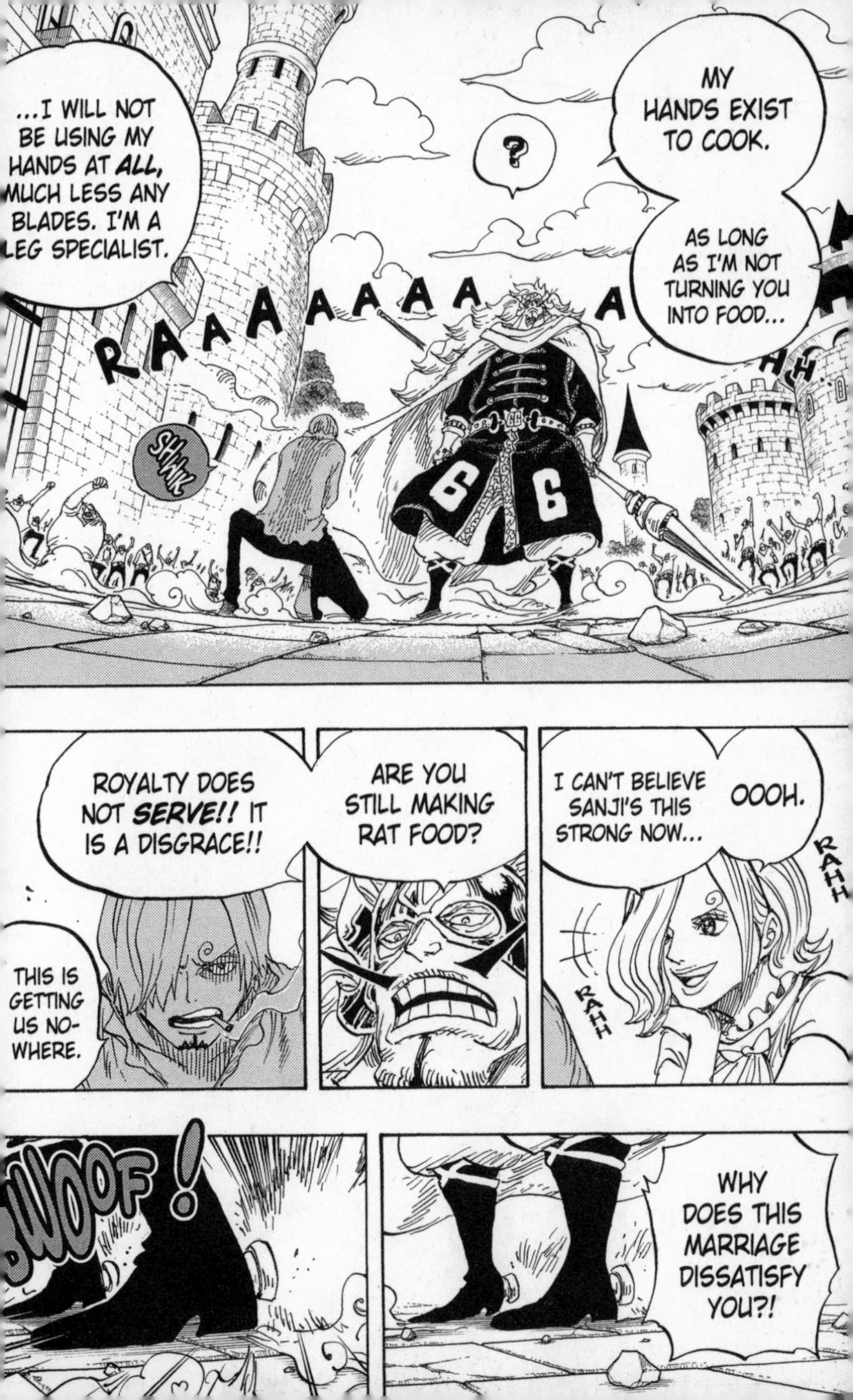
MY HANDS EXIST TO COOK.
AS LONG AS I'M NOT TURNING YOU INTO FOOD...
?
...I WILL NOT BE USING MY HANDS AT ***ALL,*** MUCH LESS ANY BLADES. I'M A LEG SPECIALIST.
RAAAAAAAA AHH
SHWK
OOOH.
I CAN'T BELIEVE SANJI'S THIS STRONG NOW...
RAHH
RAHH
ARE YOU STILL MAKING RAT FOOD?
ROYALTY DOES NOT ***SERVE!!*** IT IS A DISGRACE!!
THIS IS GETTING US NO-WHERE.
WHY DOES THIS MARRIAGE DISSATISFY YOU?!
WOOF!

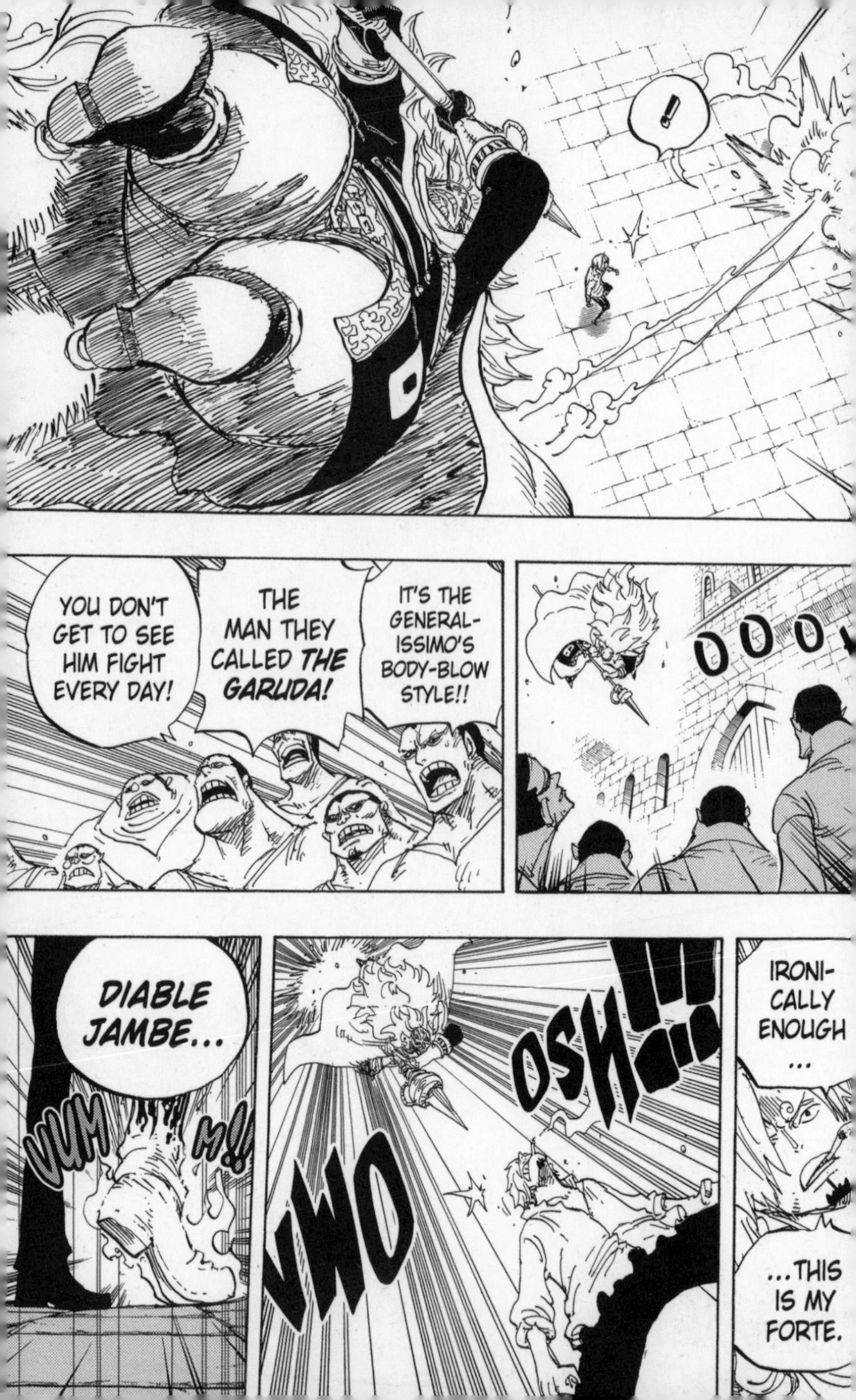
!
IT'S THE GENERAL-ISSIMO'S BODY-BLOW STYLE!!
THE MAN THEY CALLED ***THE GARUDA!***
YOU DON'T GET TO SEE HIM FIGHT EVERY DAY!
IRONI-CALLY ENOUGH ...
...THIS IS MY FORTE.
WHOOSH!!!
DIABLE JAMBE...

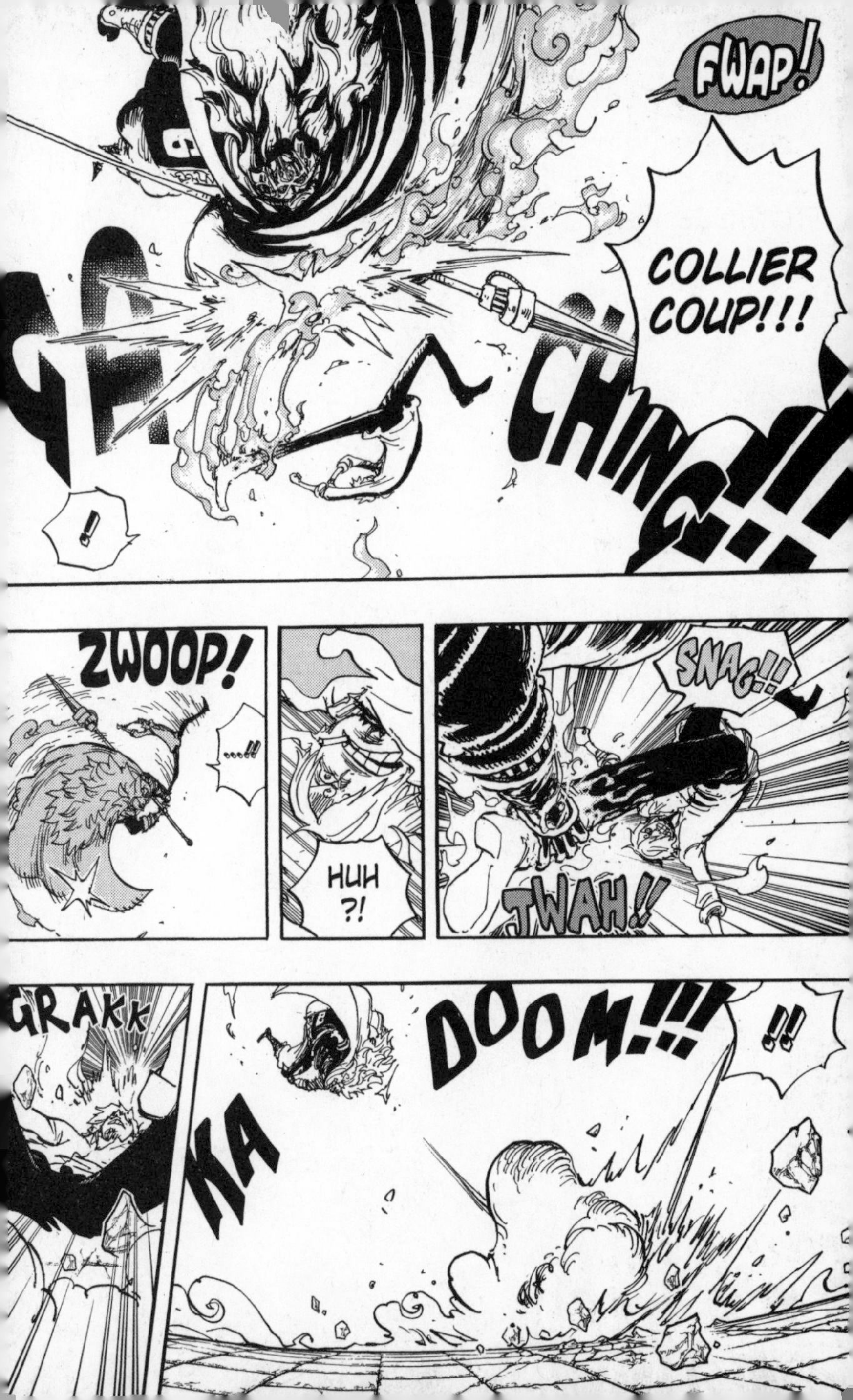
FWAP!
COLLIER COUP!!!
CHING!!!
!
SNAG!!
TWAH!!
HUH ?!
ZWOOP!
...!!
!!
DOOM!!!
KA
GRAKK

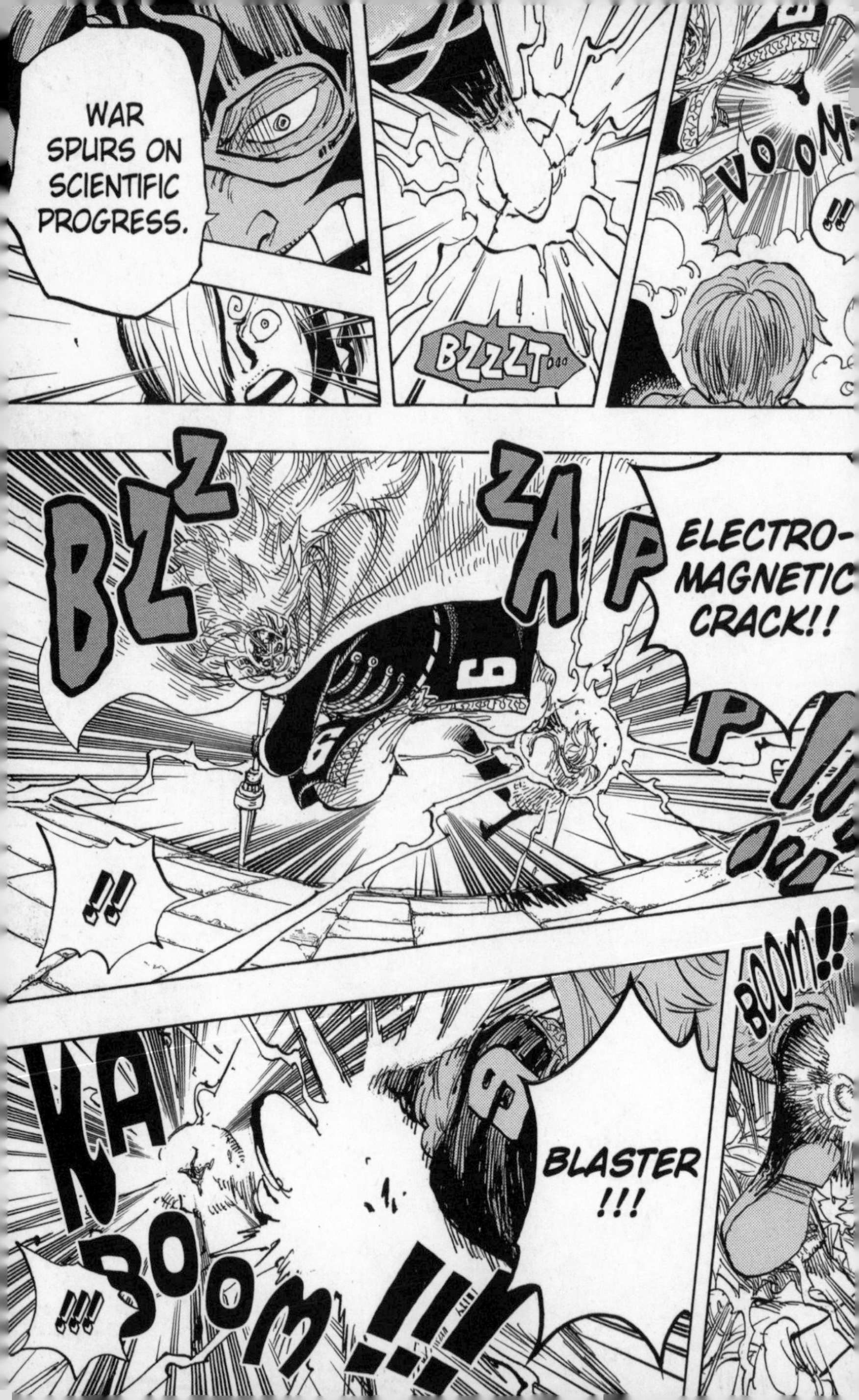
VOOM!!
BZZZT...
WAR SPURS ON SCIENTIFIC PROGRESS.
ELECTRO-MAGNETIC CRACK!!
ZAP
BZZ
BOOM!!
BLASTER !!!
KA BOOM!!!

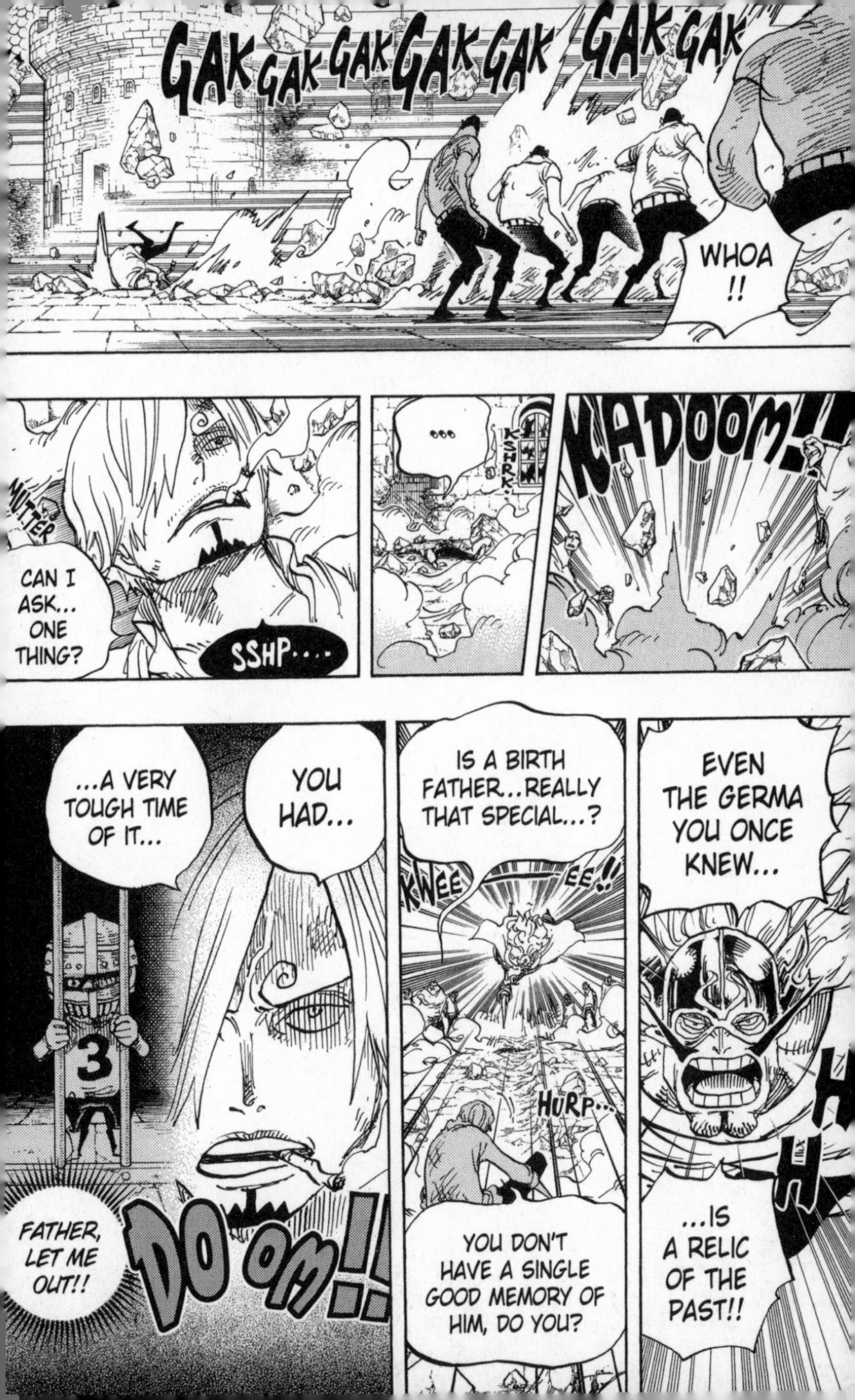
GAK GAK GAK GAK GAK GAK GAK
WHOA !!
KADOOM!!
...
KSHRK...
MUTTER
CAN I ASK... ONE THING?
SSHP....
EVEN THE GERMA YOU ONCE KNEW...
...IS A RELIC OF THE PAST!!
H H
IS A BIRTH FATHER...REALLY THAT SPECIAL...?
KWEEEE!!
HURP...
YOU DON'T HAVE A SINGLE GOOD MEMORY OF HIM, DO YOU?
YOU HAD...
...A VERY TOUGH TIME OF IT...
FATHER, LET ME OUT!!
DOOM!!

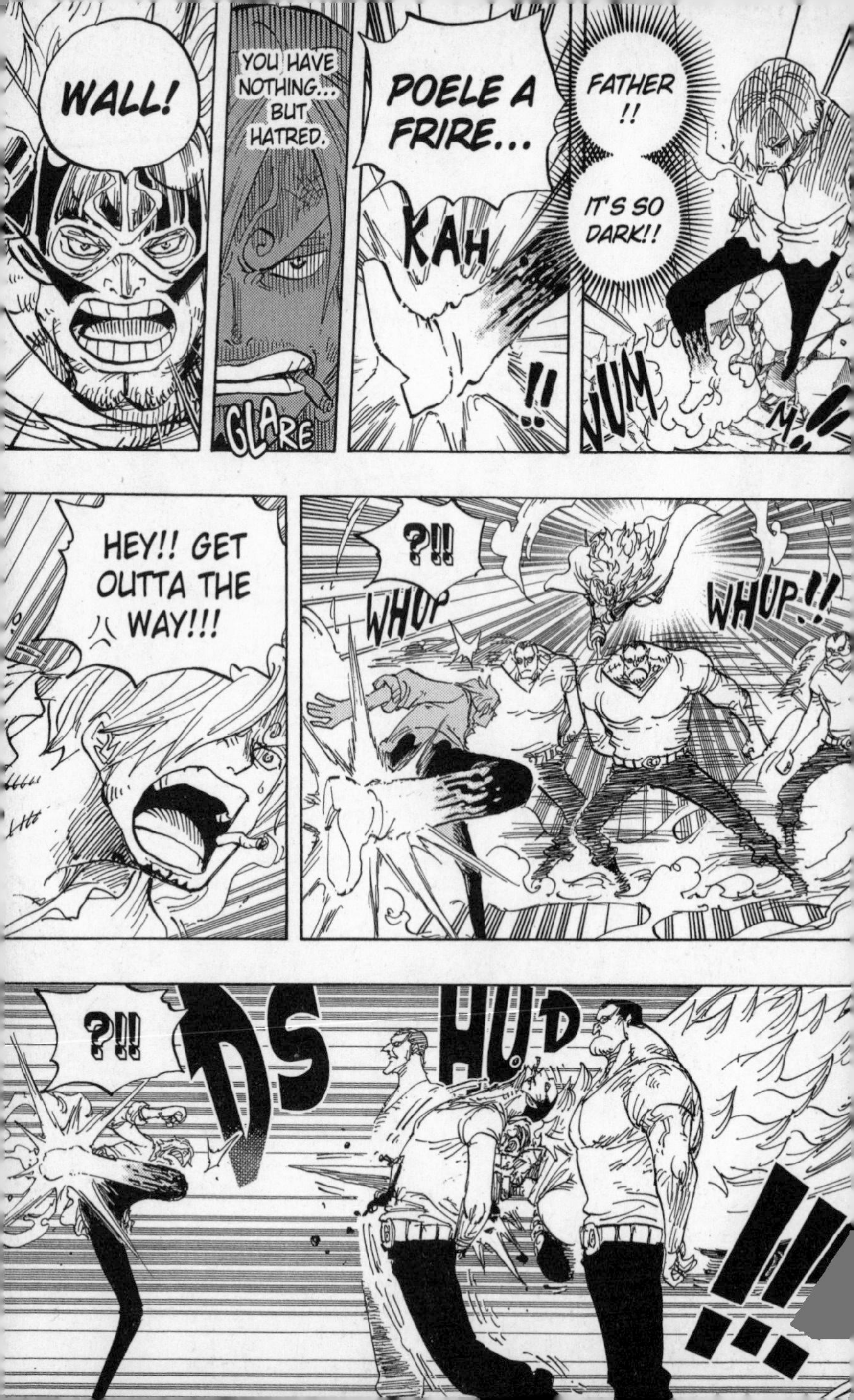
FATHER !!
IT'S SO DARK!!
M!!
VUM
POELE A FRIRE...
KAH
!!
YOU HAVE NOTHING... BUT HATRED.
GLARE
WALL!
?!!
WHUP!!
WHUP
HEY!! GET OUTTA THE WAY!!!
?!!
DS HUD
!!!

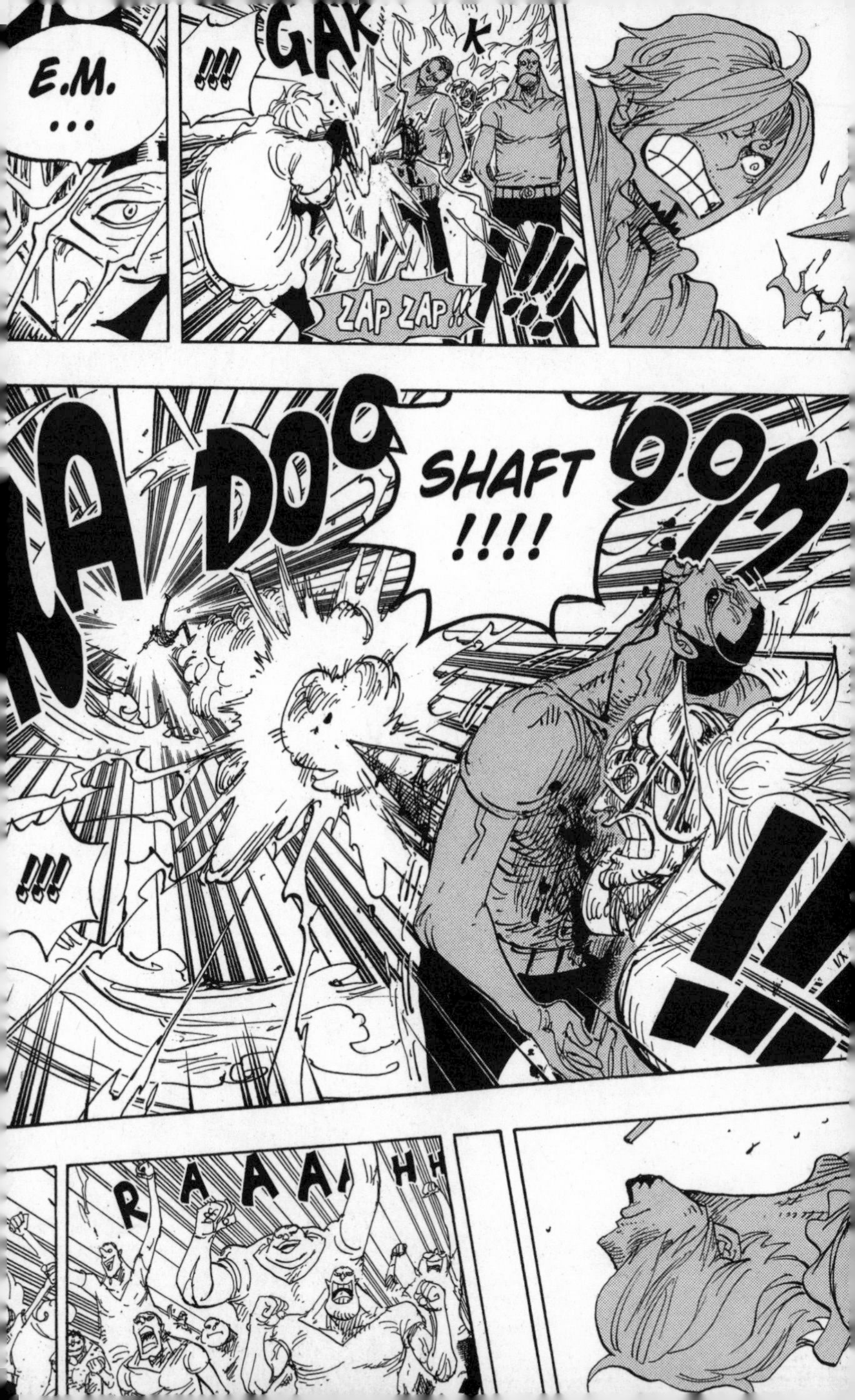
K
GAK
!!!
!!!
ZAP ZAP!!
E.M. ...
A DOO
SHAFT !!!!
OOM
!!!
!!!
RAAAHH

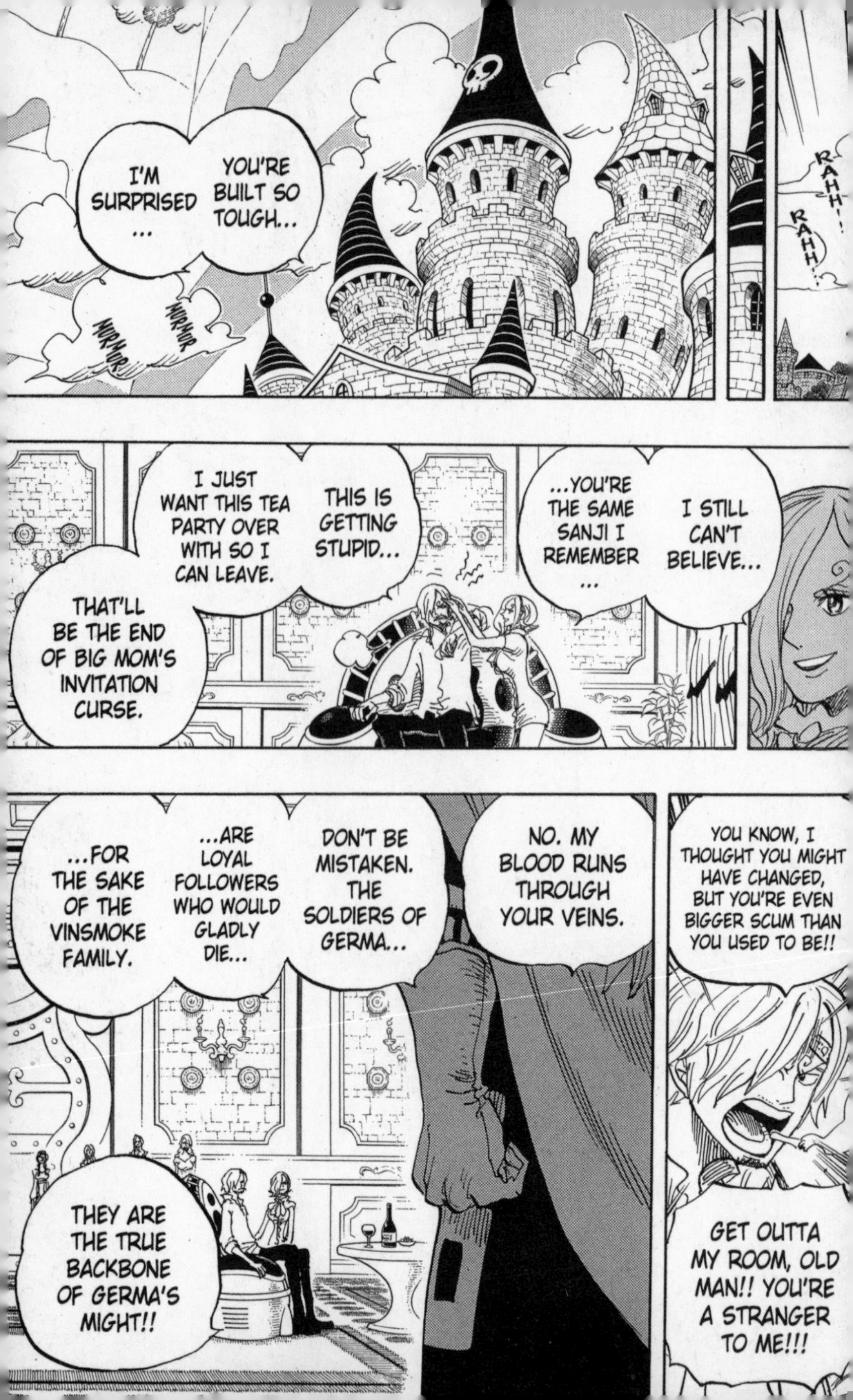
RAHH!!
RAHH!!
MURMUR
MURMUR
YOU'RE BUILT SO TOUGH...
I'M SURPRISED...
I STILL CAN'T BELIEVE...
...YOU'RE THE SAME SANJI I REMEMBER...
THIS IS GETTING STUPID...
I JUST WANT THIS TEA PARTY OVER WITH SO I CAN LEAVE.
THAT'LL BE THE END OF BIG MOM'S INVITATION CURSE.
YOU KNOW, I THOUGHT YOU MIGHT HAVE CHANGED, BUT YOU'RE EVEN BIGGER SCUM THAN YOU USED TO BE!!
GET OUTTA MY ROOM, OLD MAN!! YOU'RE A STRANGER TO ME!!!
NO. MY BLOOD RUNS THROUGH YOUR VEINS.
DON'T BE MISTAKEN. THE SOLDIERS OF GERMA...
...ARE LOYAL FOLLOWERS WHO WOULD GLADLY DIE...
...FOR THE SAKE OF THE VINSMOKE FAMILY.
THEY ARE THE TRUE BACKBONE OF GERMA'S MIGHT!!

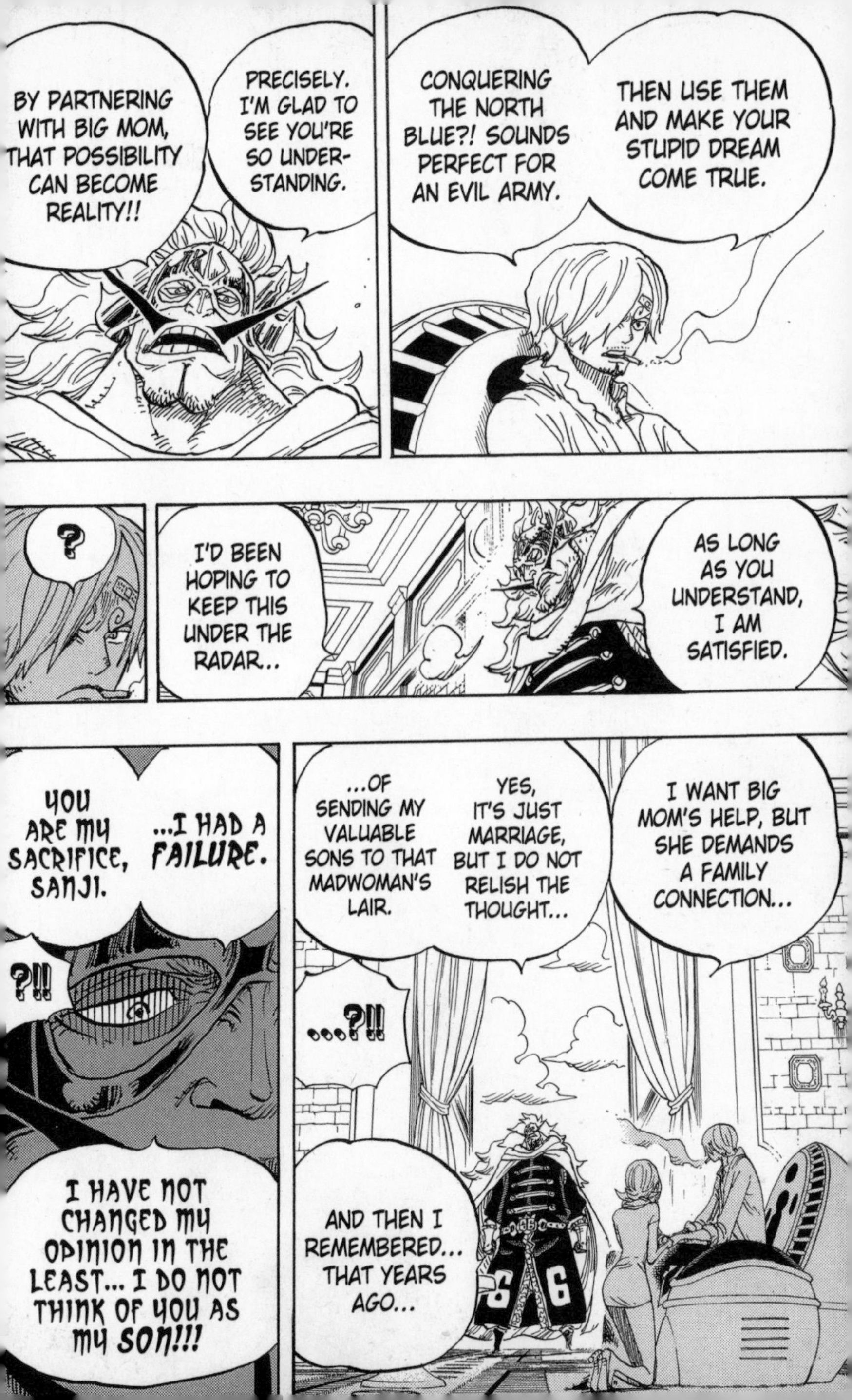
THEN USE THEM AND MAKE YOUR STUPID DREAM COME TRUE.
CONQUERING THE NORTH BLUE?! SOUNDS PERFECT FOR AN EVIL ARMY.
PRECISELY. I'M GLAD TO SEE YOU'RE SO UNDER-STANDING.
BY PARTNERING WITH BIG MOM, THAT POSSIBILITY CAN BECOME REALITY!!
AS LONG AS YOU UNDERSTAND, I AM SATISFIED.
I'D BEEN HOPING TO KEEP THIS UNDER THE RADAR...
?
I WANT BIG MOM'S HELP, BUT SHE DEMANDS A FAMILY CONNECTION...
YES, IT'S JUST MARRIAGE, BUT I DO NOT RELISH THE THOUGHT...
...OF SENDING MY VALUABLE SONS TO THAT MADWOMAN'S LAIR.
...?!!
AND THEN I REMEMBERED... THAT YEARS AGO...
...I HAD A FAILURE.
YOU ARE MY SACRIFICE, SANJI.
?!!
I HAVE NOT CHANGED MY OPINION IN THE LEAST... I DO NOT THINK OF YOU AS MY SON!!!

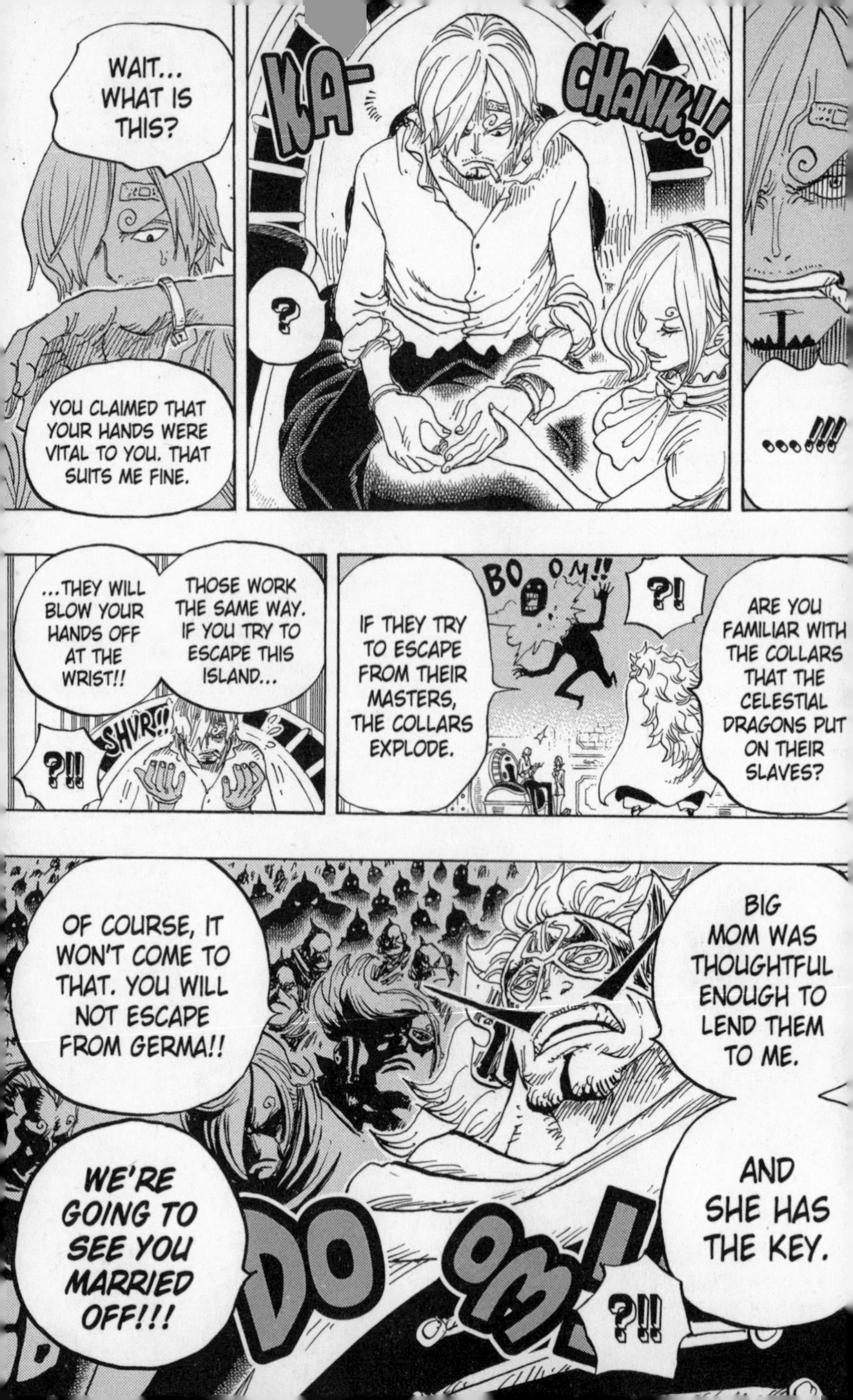
...!!!
KA-CHANK!!
?
WAIT... WHAT IS THIS?
YOU CLAIMED THAT YOUR HANDS WERE VITAL TO YOU. THAT SUITS ME FINE.
ARE YOU FAMILIAR WITH THE COLLARS THAT THE CELESTIAL DRAGONS PUT ON THEIR SLAVES?
?!
BOOM!!
IF THEY TRY TO ESCAPE FROM THEIR MASTERS, THE COLLARS EXPLODE.
THOSE WORK THE SAME WAY. IF YOU TRY TO ESCAPE THIS ISLAND...
...THEY WILL BLOW YOUR HANDS OFF AT THE WRIST!!
SHVR!!
?!!
BIG MOM WAS THOUGHTFUL ENOUGH TO LEND THEM TO ME.
OF COURSE, IT WON'T COME TO THAT. YOU WILL NOT ESCAPE FROM GERMA!!
AND SHE HAS THE KEY.
WE'RE GOING TO SEE YOU MARRIED OFF!!!
DOOM!
?!!

SBS

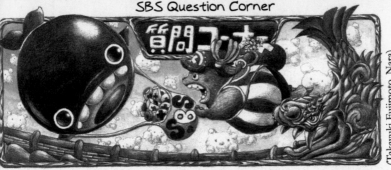

(Takayuki Fujimoto, Nara)

Me
45°
Mom
Oof!
H...how...?
SLUMP

Q: Odacchi!! In the SBS of Volume 82, you demonstrated the way to escape harm from Akainu, bears and ghosts. But when I tried that on my mom when she was angry, she hit me! Is my mom stronger than Akainu?

--Star Fairy

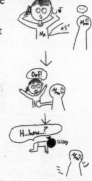

A: Whoa, hey! What did you expect?! Why would you do such a crazy thing?! That's the world's strongest creature!! She's stronger than Kaido!! Never try that again!
But your mom also loves you more than anyone else.

Q: I love the Dressrosa arc so much, I've read it multiple times, but I'm sending this question to the SBS because there's something I just can't put together. In Chapter 788, why did Viola and Doflamingo call each other "Dofy" and "Violet"? What was going on between them?

--Fuki

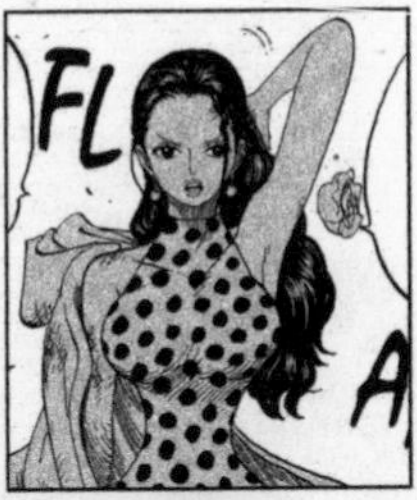

A: Hmm. A very insightful question. Well, there's some very deep backstory here, but I cannot tell you about it. I've told my editor, but it's a very grown-up story, and therefore I'm not showing it in One Piece, my manga for boys. You grown-ups reading this can use your imagination. Dressrosa is the land of passion!!

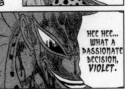

HEE HEE... WHAT A PASSIONATE DECISION, VIOLET.

Q: Hello, Odacchi! Heraclesun ends all of his statements with an "n" sound. Does that mean his real name is actually…Heracles?

--Uchi

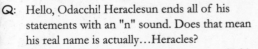

A: I couldn't say... It's an eternal enigman.

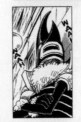

Chapter 834:
MY DREAM

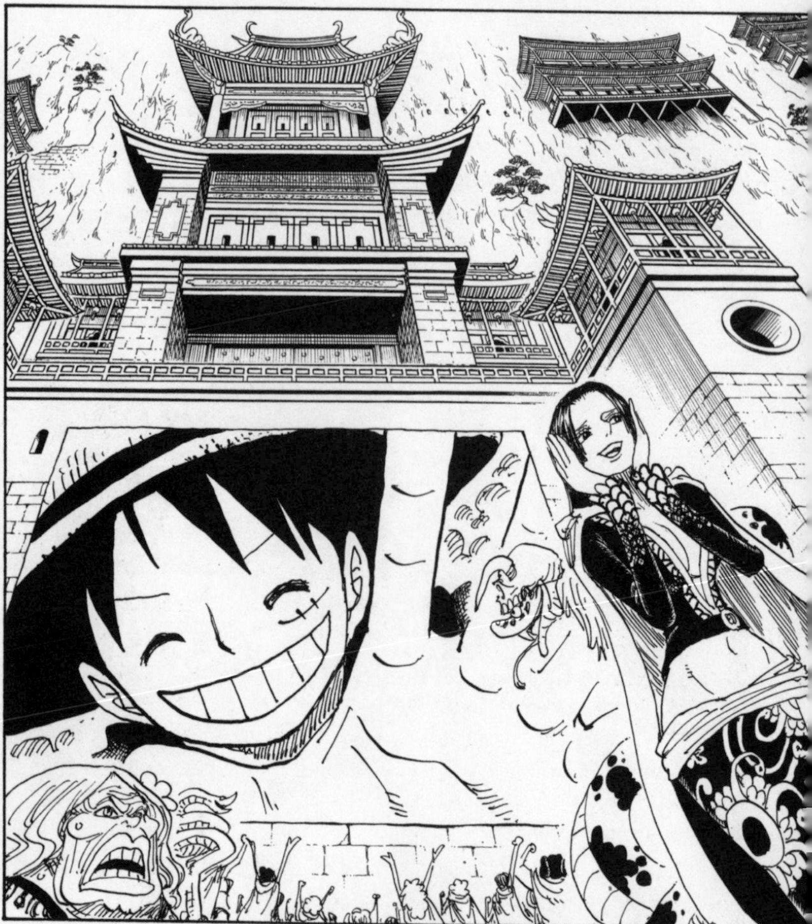

DECKS OF THE WORLD, 500-MILLION-MAN ARC,
VOL. 22: "THE ISLAND OF WOMEN"

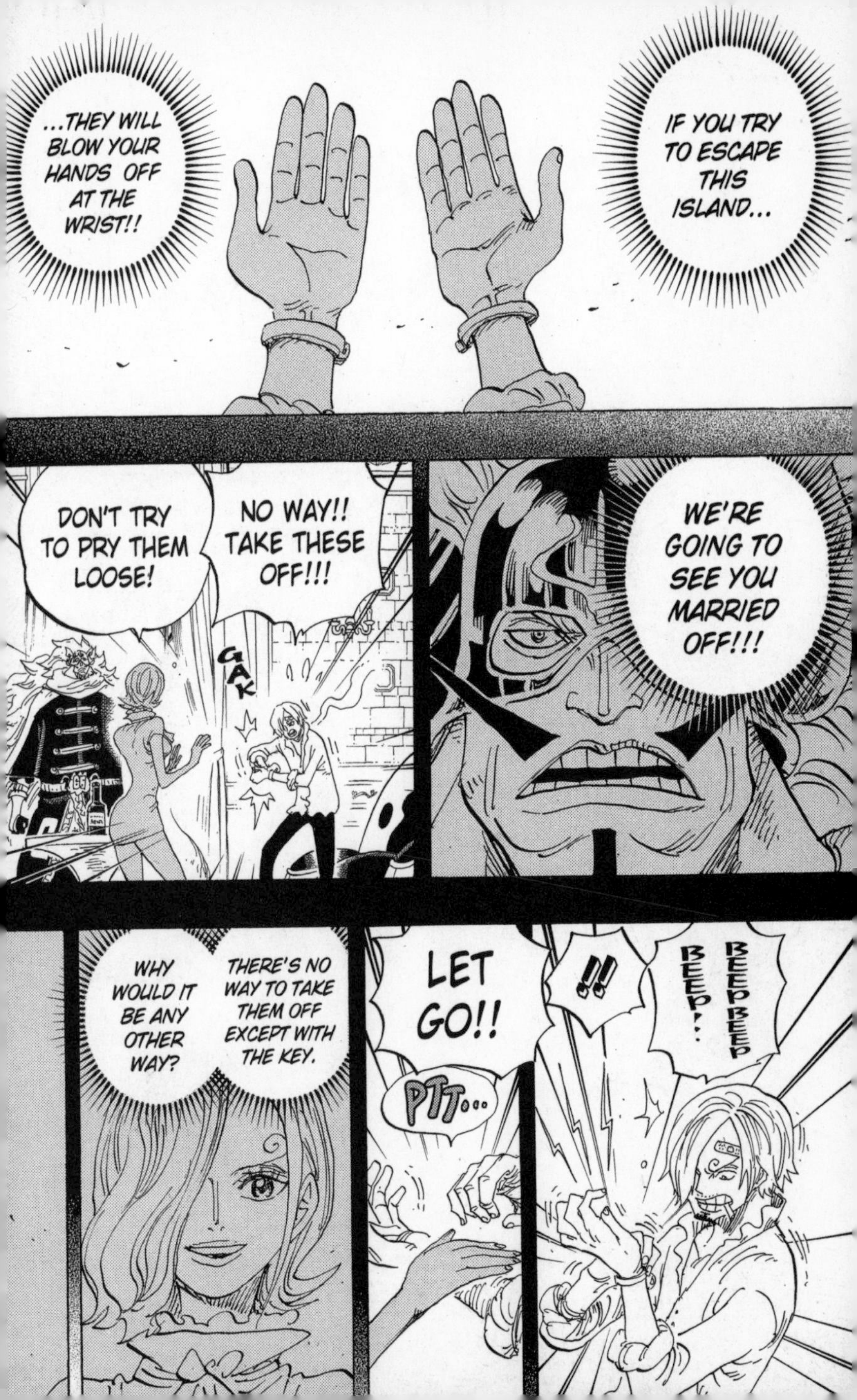
IF YOU TRY TO ESCAPE THIS ISLAND...
...THEY WILL BLOW YOUR HANDS OFF AT THE WRIST!!
WE'RE GOING TO SEE YOU MARRIED OFF!!!
NO WAY!! TAKE THESE OFF!!!
GAK
DON'T TRY TO PRY THEM LOOSE!
BEEPBEEP BEEP!!
!!
LET GO!!
PTT...
THERE'S NO WAY TO TAKE THEM OFF EXCEPT WITH THE KEY.
WHY WOULD IT BE ANY OTHER WAY?

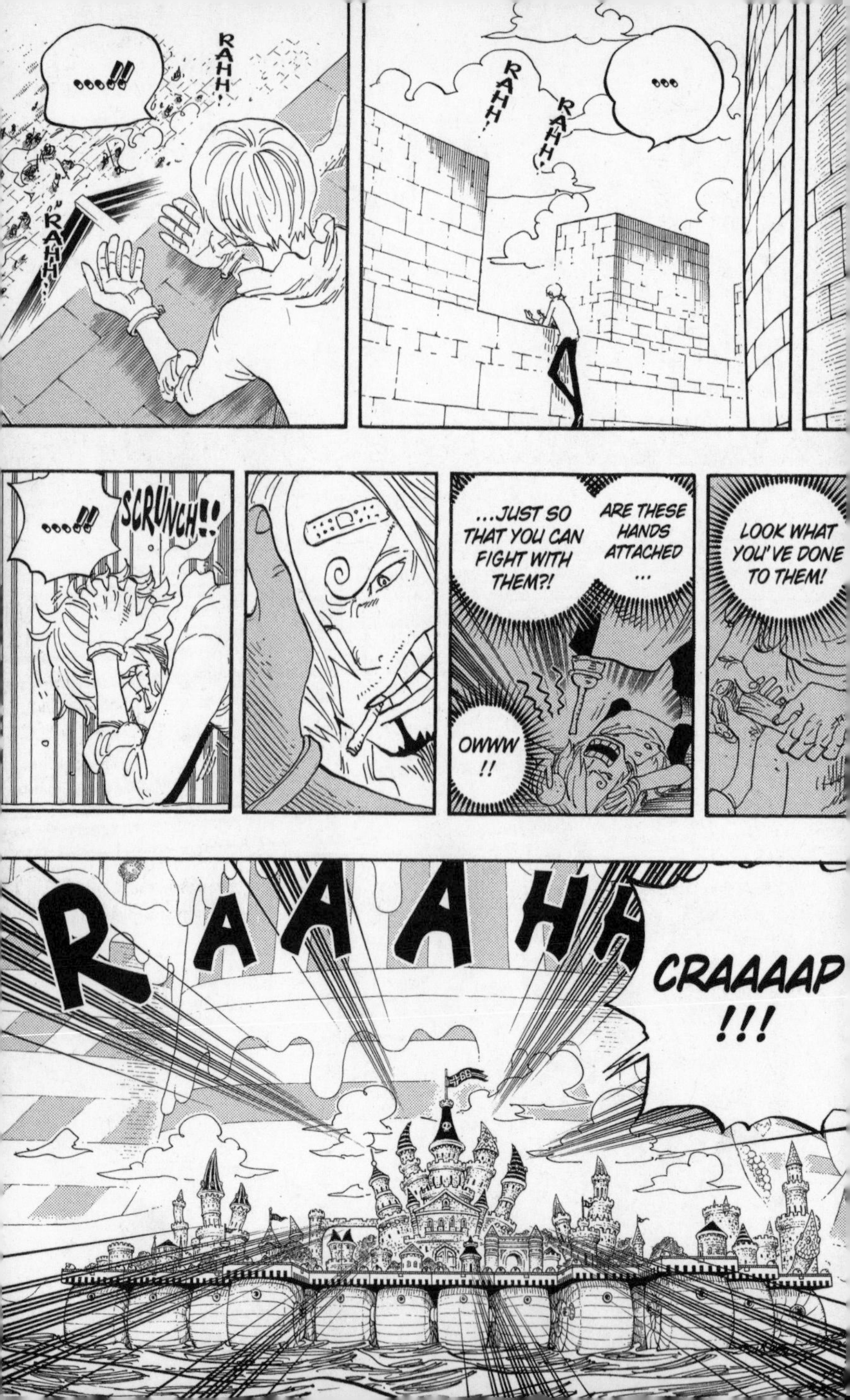
...
RAHH!
RAHH!
....!!
RAHH!
RAHH!
LOOK WHAT YOU'VE DONE TO THEM!
ARE THESE HANDS ATTACHED ...
...JUST SO THAT YOU CAN FIGHT WITH THEM?!
OWWW !!
....!!
SCRUNCH!!
RAAAH
CRAAAAP !!!

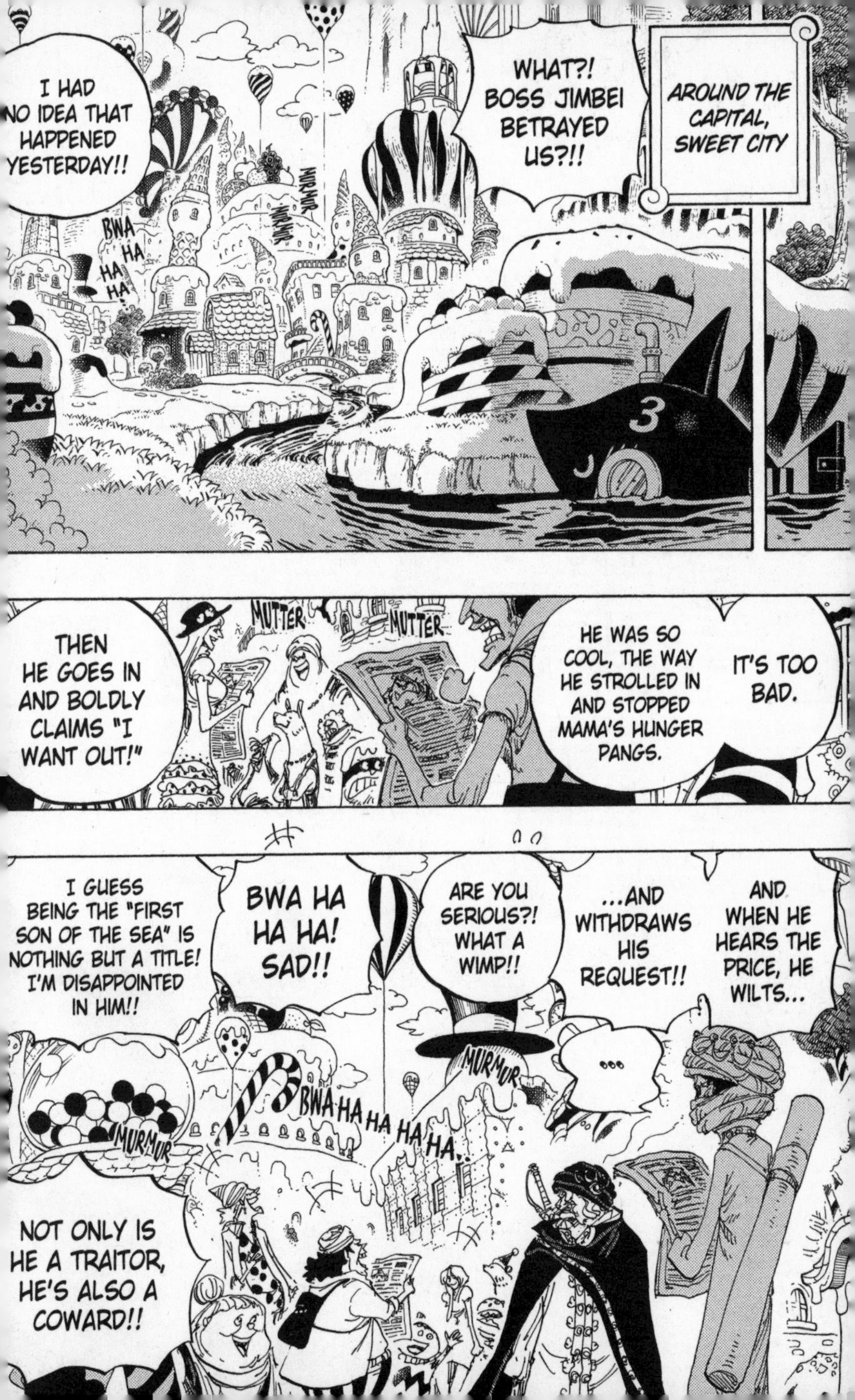
AROUND THE CAPITAL, SWEET CITY
WHAT?! BOSS JIMBEI BETRAYED US?!!
MURMUR MURMUR
BWA HA HA HA
I HAD NO IDEA THAT HAPPENED YESTERDAY!!
IT'S TOO BAD.
HE WAS SO COOL, THE WAY HE STROLLED IN AND STOPPED MAMA'S HUNGER PANGS.
MUTTER MUTTER
THEN HE GOES IN AND BOLDLY CLAIMS "I WANT OUT!"
AND WHEN HE HEARS THE PRICE, HE WILTS...
...AND WITHDRAWS HIS REQUEST!!
ARE YOU SERIOUS?! WHAT A WIMP!!
BWA HA HA HA! SAD!!
I GUESS BEING THE "FIRST SON OF THE SEA" IS NOTHING BUT A TITLE! I'M DISAPPOINTED IN HIM!!
...
MURMUR
BWA HA HA HA HA HA
MURMUR
NOT ONLY IS HE A TRAITOR, HE'S ALSO A COWARD!!

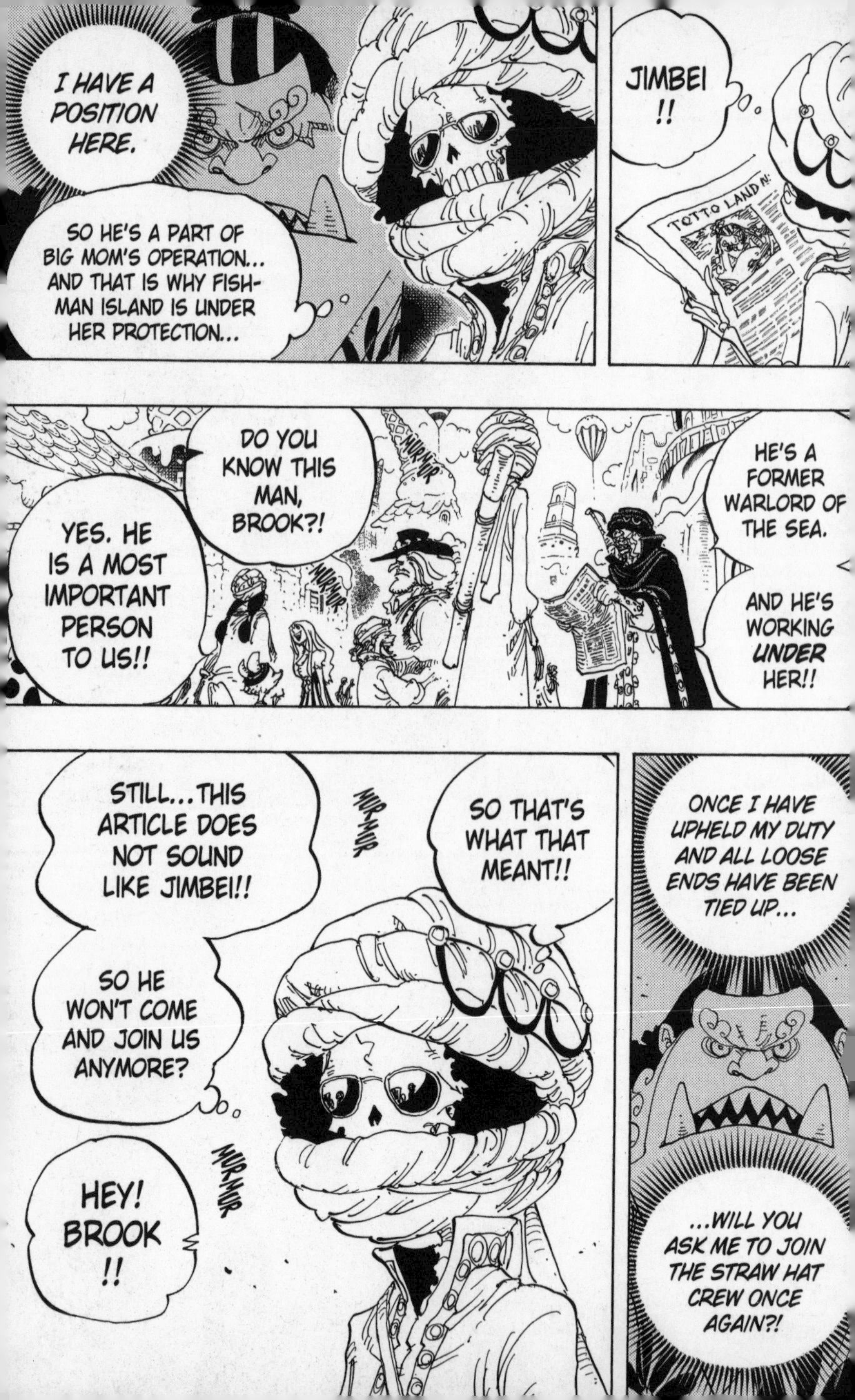
JIMBEI !!
I HAVE A POSITION HERE.
SO HE'S A PART OF BIG MOM'S OPERATION... AND THAT IS WHY FISH-MAN ISLAND IS UNDER HER PROTECTION...
HE'S A FORMER WARLORD OF THE SEA.
AND HE'S WORKING UNDER HER!!
MURMUR
DO YOU KNOW THIS MAN, BROOK?!
MURMUR
YES. HE IS A MOST IMPORTANT PERSON TO US!!
ONCE I HAVE UPHELD MY DUTY AND ALL LOOSE ENDS HAVE BEEN TIED UP...
...WILL YOU ASK ME TO JOIN THE STRAW HAT CREW ONCE AGAIN?!
SO THAT'S WHAT THAT MEANT!!
MUR MUR
STILL...THIS ARTICLE DOES NOT SOUND LIKE JIMBEI!!
SO HE WON'T COME AND JOIN US ANYMORE?
MURMUR
HEY! BROOK !!

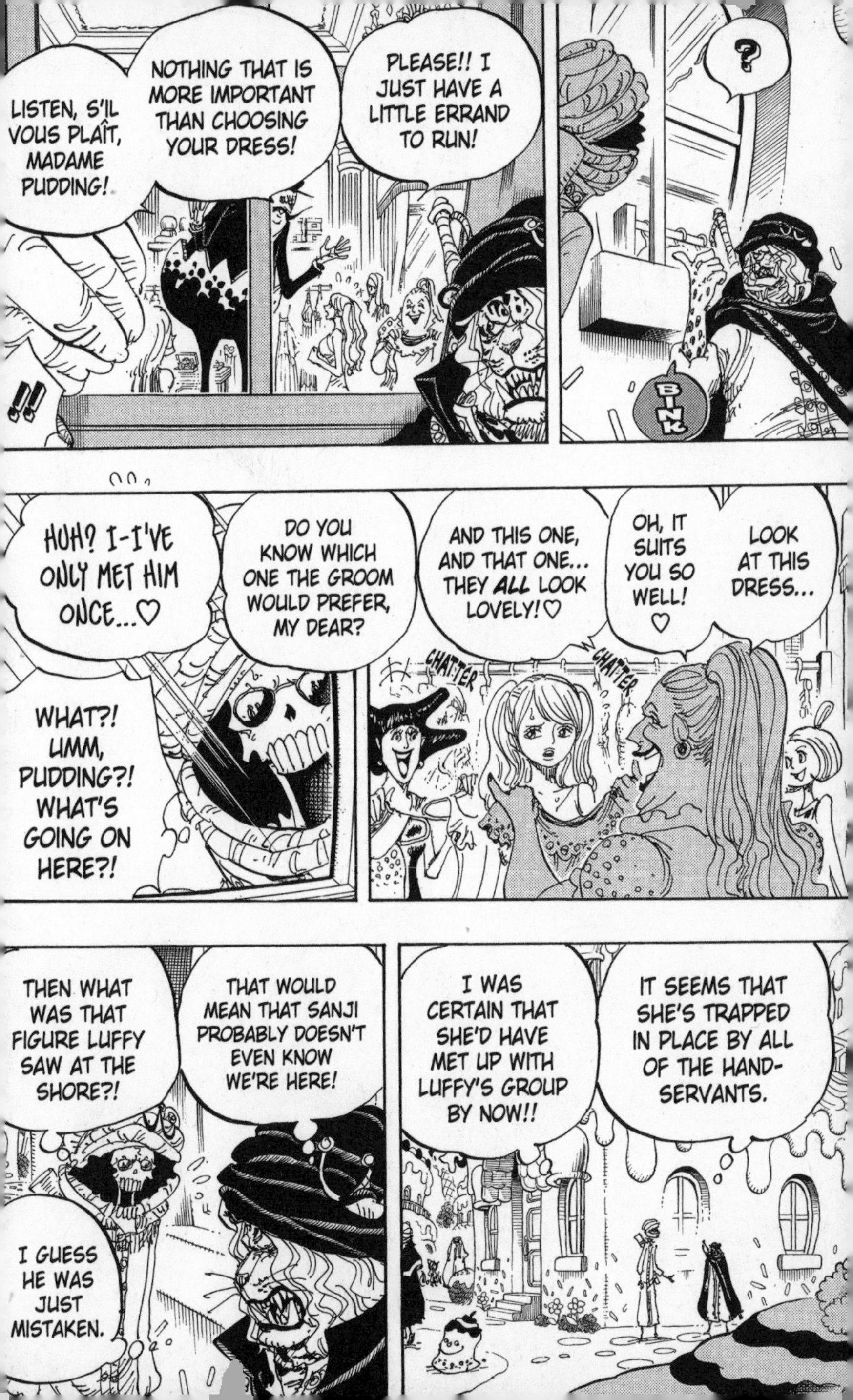
?
BINK
PLEASE!! I JUST HAVE A LITTLE ERRAND TO RUN!
NOTHING THAT IS MORE IMPORTANT THAN CHOOSING YOUR DRESS!
LISTEN, S'IL VOUS PLAÎT, MADAME PUDDING!
!!
LOOK AT THIS DRESS...
OH, IT SUITS YOU SO WELL! ♡
AND THIS ONE, AND THAT ONE... THEY *ALL* LOOK LOVELY! ♡
DO YOU KNOW WHICH ONE THE GROOM WOULD PREFER, MY DEAR?
HUH? I-I'VE ONLY MET HIM ONCE... ♡
CHATTER
CHATTER
WHAT?! UMM, PUDDING?! WHAT'S GOING ON HERE?!
IT SEEMS THAT SHE'S TRAPPED IN PLACE BY ALL OF THE HAND-SERVANTS.
I WAS CERTAIN THAT SHE'D HAVE MET UP WITH LUFFY'S GROUP BY NOW!!
THAT WOULD MEAN THAT SANJI PROBABLY DOESN'T EVEN KNOW WE'RE HERE!
THEN WHAT WAS THAT FIGURE LUFFY SAW AT THE SHORE?!
I GUESS HE WAS JUST MISTAKEN.

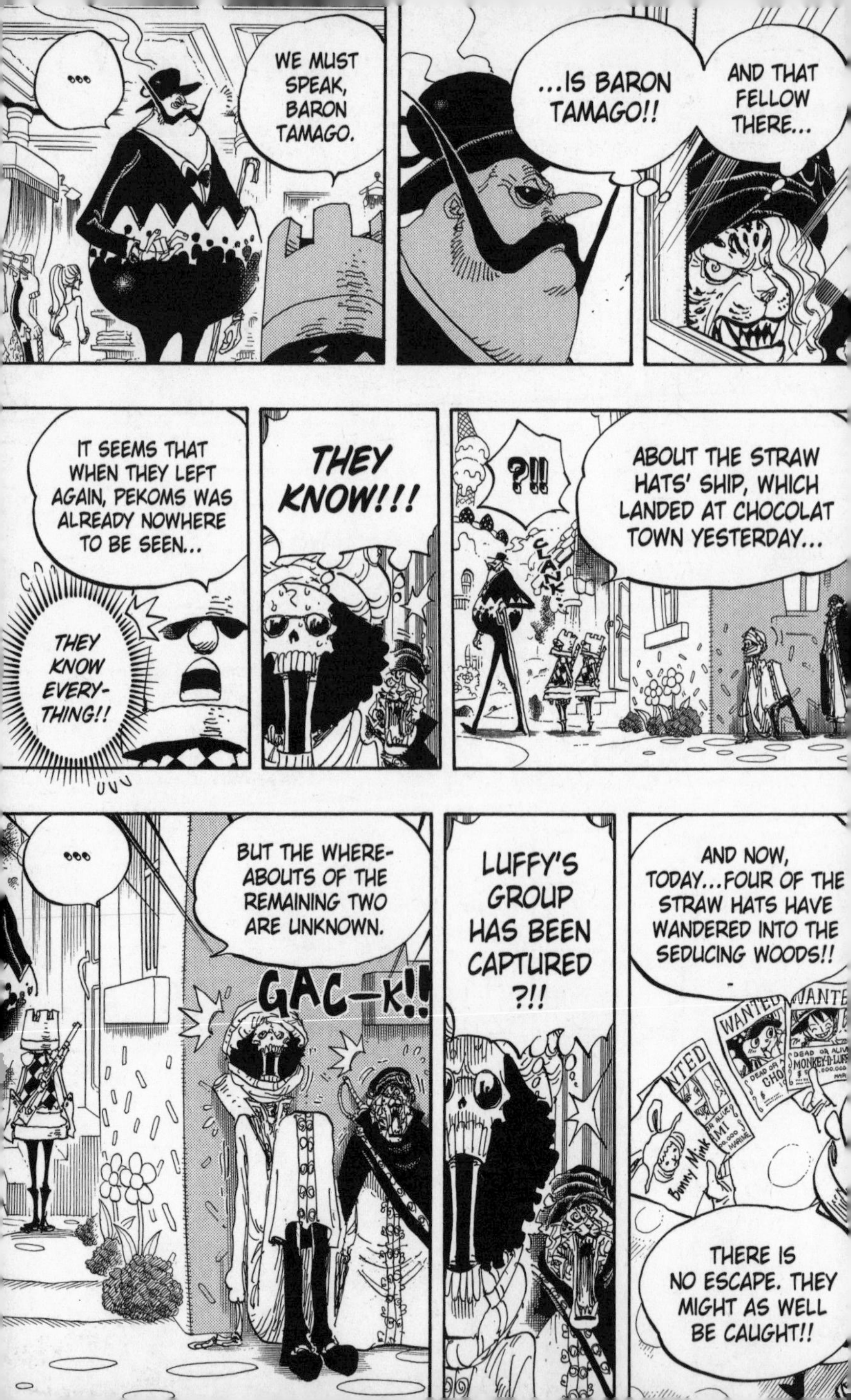
AND THAT FELLOW THERE...
...IS BARON TAMAGO!!
WE MUST SPEAK, BARON TAMAGO.
...
ABOUT THE STRAW HATS' SHIP, WHICH LANDED AT CHOCOLAT TOWN YESTERDAY...
?!!
CLANK
THEY KNOW!!!
IT SEEMS THAT WHEN THEY LEFT AGAIN, PEKOMS WAS ALREADY NOWHERE TO BE SEEN...
THEY KNOW EVERYTHING!!
AND NOW, TODAY...FOUR OF THE STRAW HATS HAVE WANDERED INTO THE SEDUCING WOODS!!
WANTED
WANTED
Bunny Mink
THERE IS NO ESCAPE. THEY MIGHT AS WELL BE CAUGHT!!
LUFFY'S GROUP HAS BEEN CAPTURED?!!
BUT THE WHEREABOUTS OF THE REMAINING TWO ARE UNKNOWN.
GAC—K!!
...

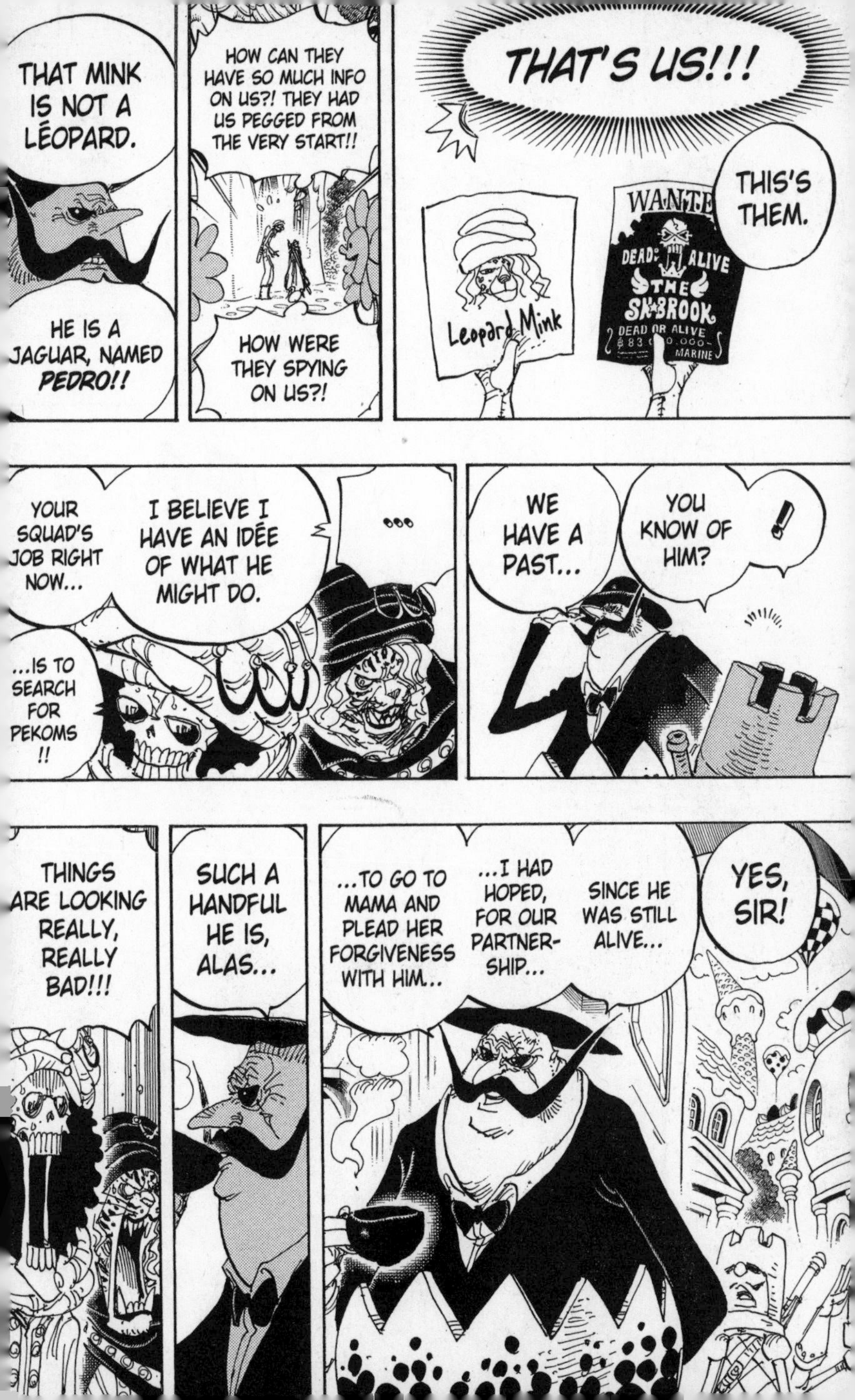
THAT'S US!!!
THIS'S THEM.
Leopard Mink
DEAD OR ALIVE
MARINE
HOW CAN THEY HAVE SO MUCH INFO ON US?! THEY HAD US PEGGED FROM THE VERY START!!
HOW WERE THEY SPYING ON US?!
THAT MINK IS NOT A LÉOPARD.
HE IS A JAGUAR, NAMED PEDRO!!
!
YOU KNOW OF HIM?
WE HAVE A PAST...
...
I BELIEVE I HAVE AN IDÉE OF WHAT HE MIGHT DO.
YOUR SQUAD'S JOB RIGHT NOW...
...IS TO SEARCH FOR PEKOMS!!
YES, SIR!
SINCE HE WAS STILL ALIVE...
...I HAD HOPED, FOR OUR PARTNERSHIP...
...TO GO TO MAMA AND PLEAD HER FORGIVENESS WITH HIM...
SUCH A HANDFUL HE IS, ALAS...
THINGS ARE LOOKING REALLY, REALLY BAD!!!

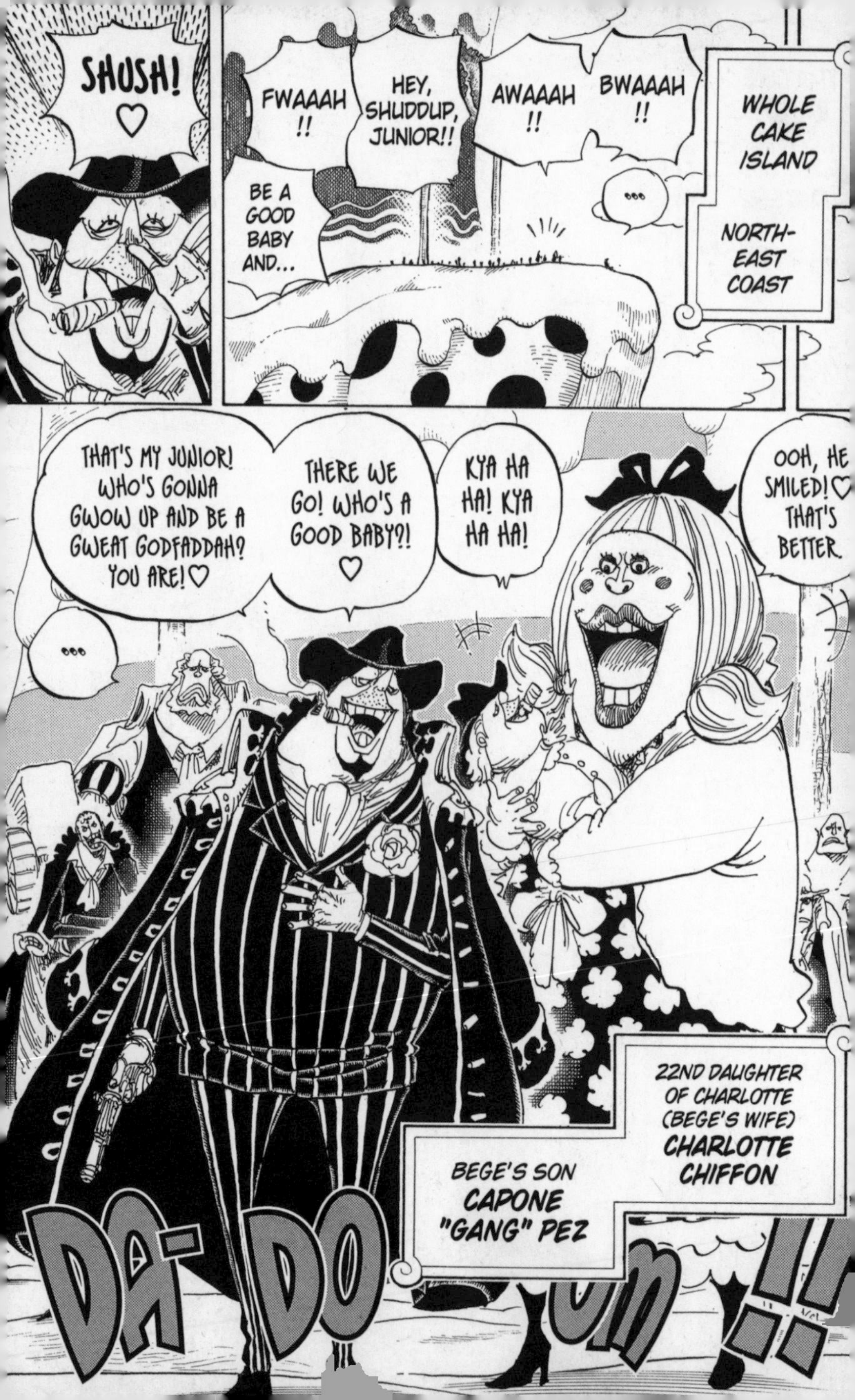
WHOLE CAKE ISLAND
NORTH-EAST COAST
BWAAAH !!
AWAAAH !!
HEY, SHUDDUP, JUNIOR!!
FWAAAH !!
...
BE A GOOD BABY AND...
SHUSH! ♡
OOH, HE SMILED! ♡ THAT'S BETTER.
KYA HA HA! KYA HA HA!
THERE WE GO! WHO'S A GOOD BABY?! ♡
THAT'S MY JUNIOR! WHO'S GONNA GWOW UP AND BE A GWEAT GODFADDAH? YOU ARE! ♡
...
22ND DAUGHTER OF CHARLOTTE (BEGE'S WIFE) CHARLOTTE CHIFFON
BEGE'S SON CAPONE "GANG" PEZ
DA-DOOM!!

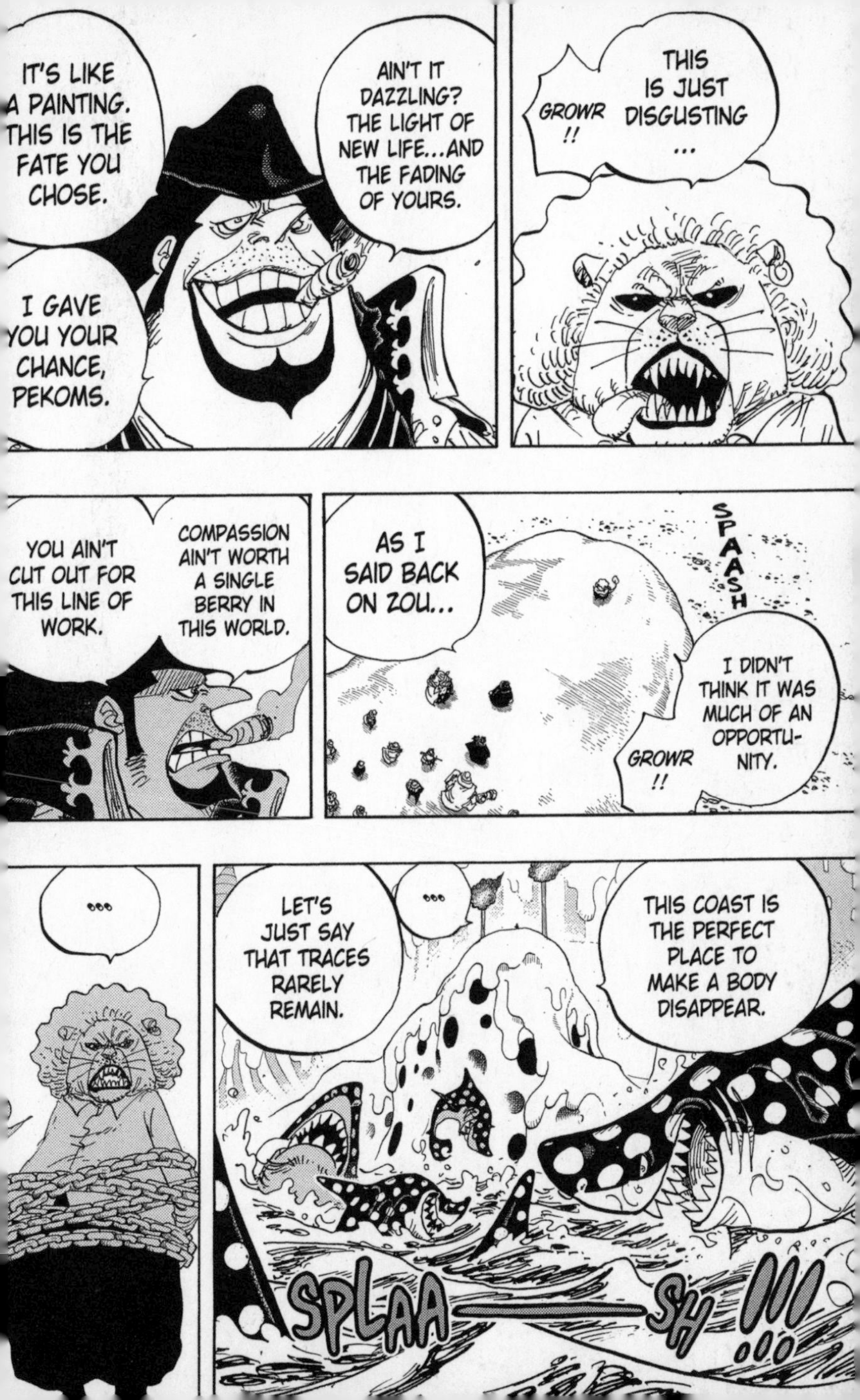

GROWR!!
THIS IS JUST DISGUSTING...
AIN'T IT DAZZLING? THE LIGHT OF NEW LIFE...AND THE FADING OF YOURS.
IT'S LIKE A PAINTING. THIS IS THE FATE YOU CHOSE.
I GAVE YOU YOUR CHANCE, PEKOMS.
SPAASH
AS I SAID BACK ON ZOU...
I DIDN'T THINK IT WAS MUCH OF AN OPPORTU-NITY.
GROWR!!
COMPASSION AIN'T WORTH A SINGLE BERRY IN THIS WORLD.
YOU AIN'T CUT OUT FOR THIS LINE OF WORK.
THIS COAST IS THE PERFECT PLACE TO MAKE A BODY DISAPPEAR.
...
LET'S JUST SAY THAT TRACES RARELY REMAIN.
SPLAA——SH!!!
...

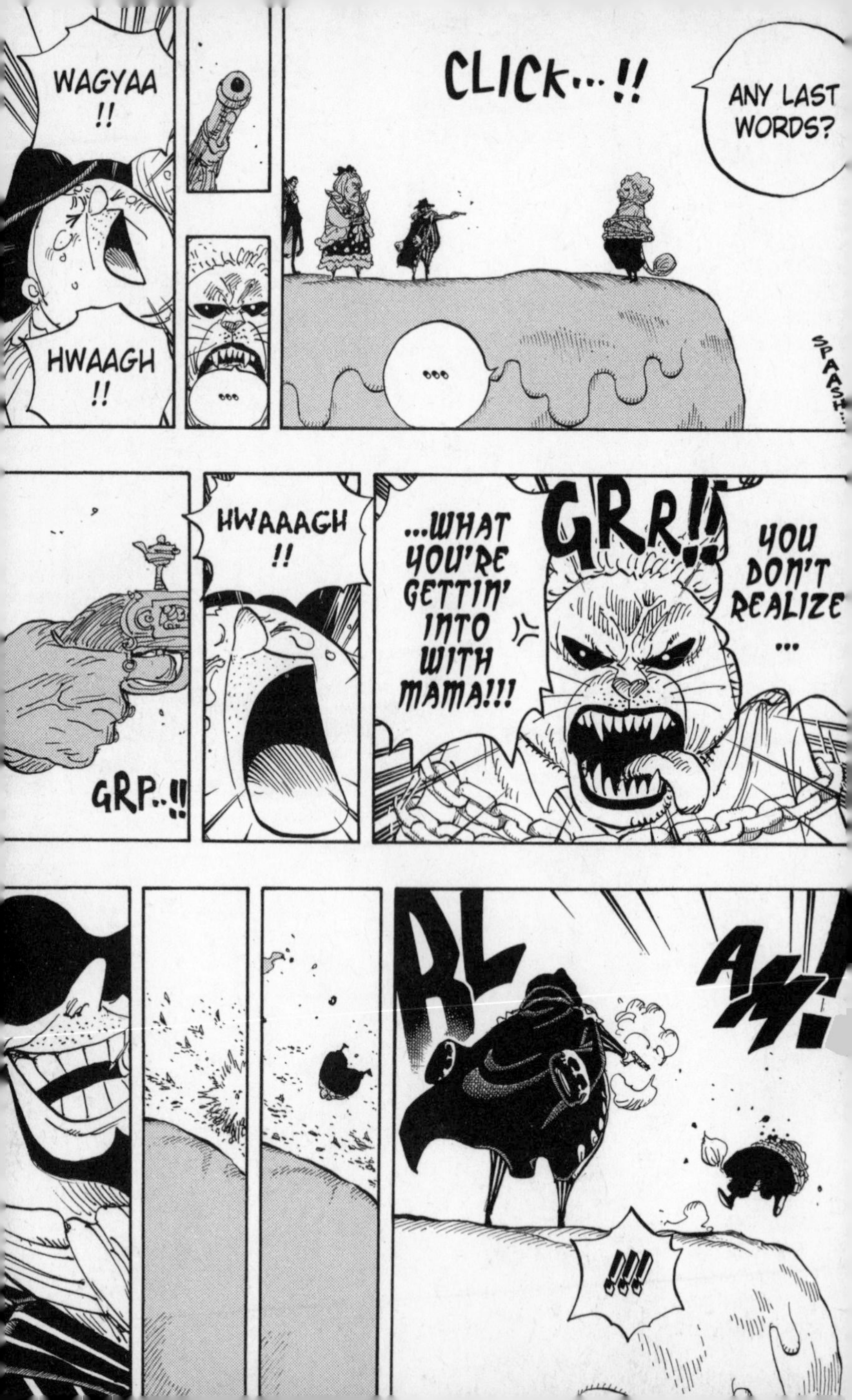

ANY LAST WORDS?
CLICK...!!
SPAASH...
...
...
WAGYAA!!
HWAAGH!!
YOU DON'T REALIZE...
GRR!!
...WHAT YOU'RE GETTIN' INTO WITH MAMA!!!
HWAAAGH!!
GRP..!!
BL
AM!
!!!

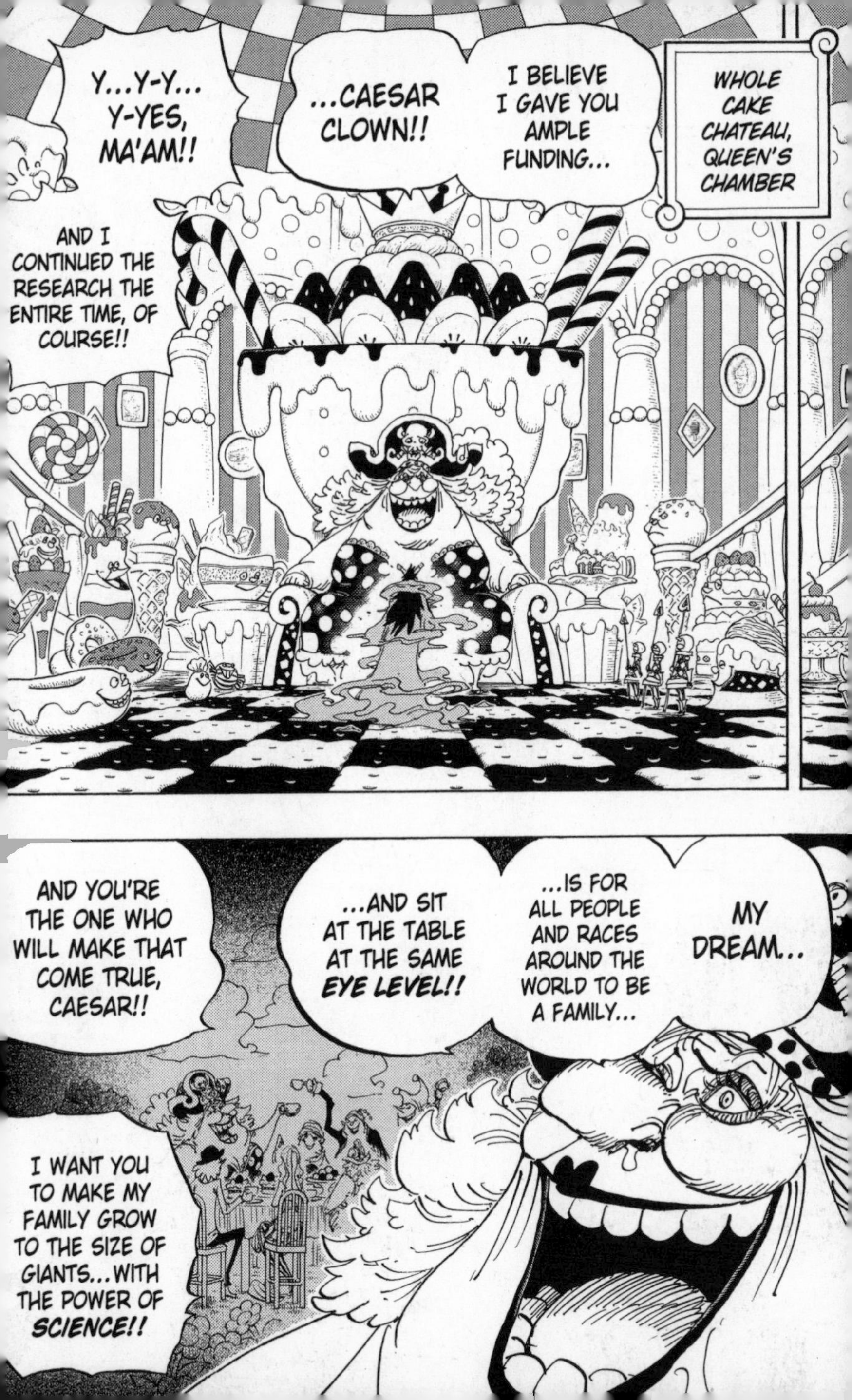
WHOLE CAKE CHATEAU, QUEEN'S CHAMBER
I BELIEVE I GAVE YOU AMPLE FUNDING...
...CAESAR CLOWN!!
Y...Y-Y... Y-YES, MA'AM!!
AND I CONTINUED THE RESEARCH THE ENTIRE TIME, OF COURSE!!
MY DREAM...
...IS FOR ALL PEOPLE AND RACES AROUND THE WORLD TO BE A FAMILY...
...AND SIT AT THE TABLE AT THE SAME EYE LEVEL!!
AND YOU'RE THE ONE WHO WILL MAKE THAT COME TRUE, CAESAR!!
I WANT YOU TO MAKE MY FAMILY GROW TO THE SIZE OF GIANTS...WITH THE POWER OF SCIENCE!!

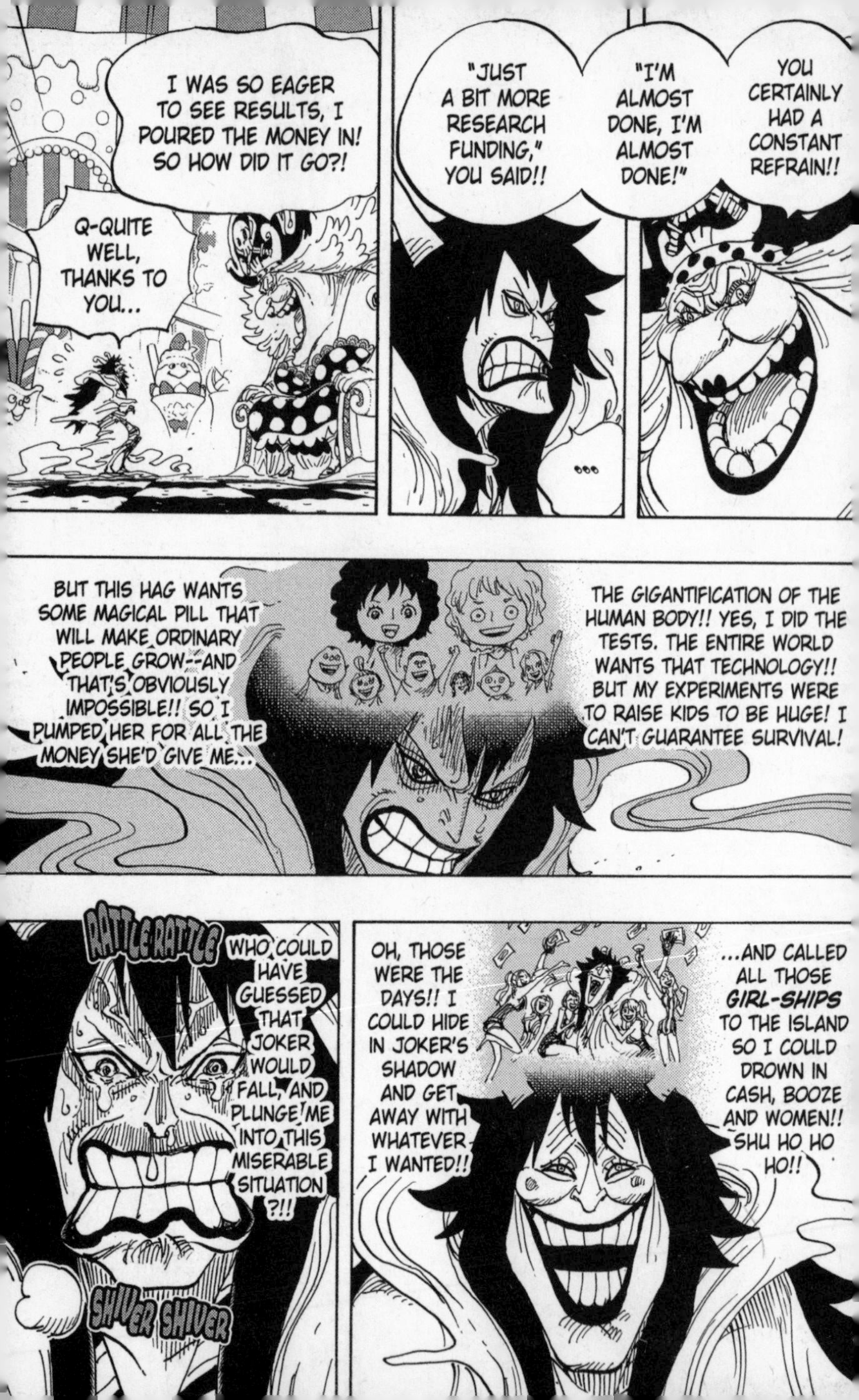
YOU CERTAINLY HAD A CONSTANT REFRAIN!!
"I'M ALMOST DONE, I'M ALMOST DONE!"
"JUST A BIT MORE RESEARCH FUNDING," YOU SAID!!
...
I WAS SO EAGER TO SEE RESULTS, I POURED THE MONEY IN! SO HOW DID IT GO?!
Q-QUITE WELL, THANKS TO YOU...
THE GIGANTIFICATION OF THE HUMAN BODY!! YES, I DID THE TESTS. THE ENTIRE WORLD WANTS THAT TECHNOLOGY!! BUT MY EXPERIMENTS WERE TO RAISE KIDS TO BE HUGE! I CAN'T GUARANTEE SURVIVAL!
BUT THIS HAG WANTS SOME MAGICAL PILL THAT WILL MAKE ORDINARY PEOPLE GROW--AND THAT'S OBVIOUSLY IMPOSSIBLE!! SO I PUMPED HER FOR ALL THE MONEY SHE'D GIVE ME...
OH, THOSE WERE THE DAYS!! I COULD HIDE IN JOKER'S SHADOW AND GET AWAY WITH WHATEVER I WANTED!!
...AND CALLED ALL THOSE *GIRL-SHIPS* TO THE ISLAND SO I COULD DROWN IN CASH, BOOZE AND WOMEN!! SHU HO HO HO!!
RATTLE RATTLE
WHO COULD HAVE GUESSED THAT JOKER WOULD FALL, AND PLUNGE ME INTO THIS MISERABLE SITUATION?!!
SHIVER SHIVER

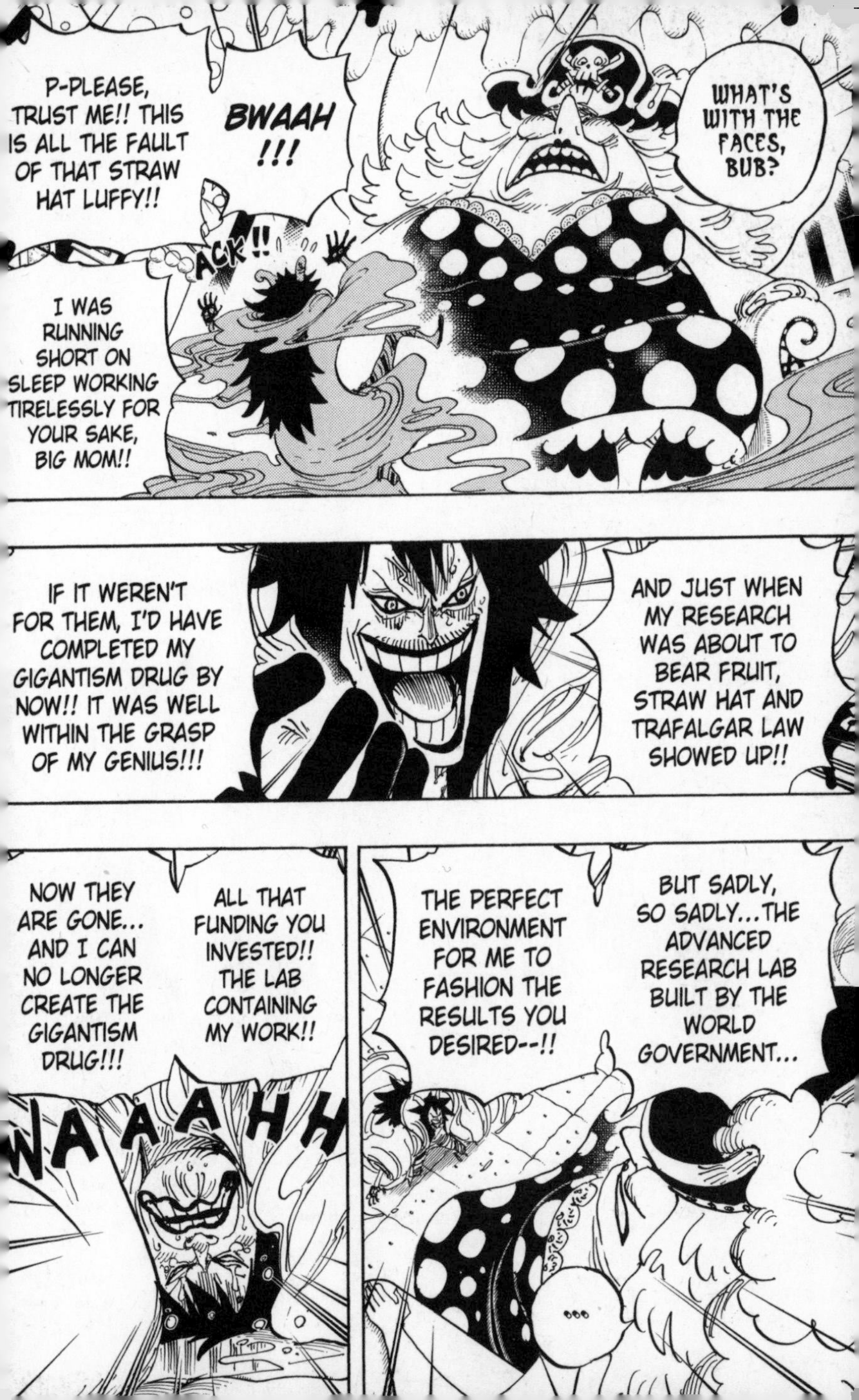
WHAT'S WITH THE FACES, BUB?
BWAAH!!!
P-PLEASE, TRUST ME!! THIS IS ALL THE FAULT OF THAT STRAW HAT LUFFY!!
ACK!!
I WAS RUNNING SHORT ON SLEEP WORKING TIRELESSLY FOR YOUR SAKE, BIG MOM!!
AND JUST WHEN MY RESEARCH WAS ABOUT TO BEAR FRUIT, STRAW HAT AND TRAFALGAR LAW SHOWED UP!!
IF IT WEREN'T FOR THEM, I'D HAVE COMPLETED MY GIGANTISM DRUG BY NOW!! IT WAS WELL WITHIN THE GRASP OF MY GENIUS!!!
BUT SADLY, SO SADLY...THE ADVANCED RESEARCH LAB BUILT BY THE WORLD GOVERNMENT...
THE PERFECT ENVIRONMENT FOR ME TO FASHION THE RESULTS YOU DESIRED--!!
...
ALL THAT FUNDING YOU INVESTED!! THE LAB CONTAINING MY WORK!!
NOW THEY ARE GONE... AND I CAN NO LONGER CREATE THE GIGANTISM DRUG!!!
WAAAHH

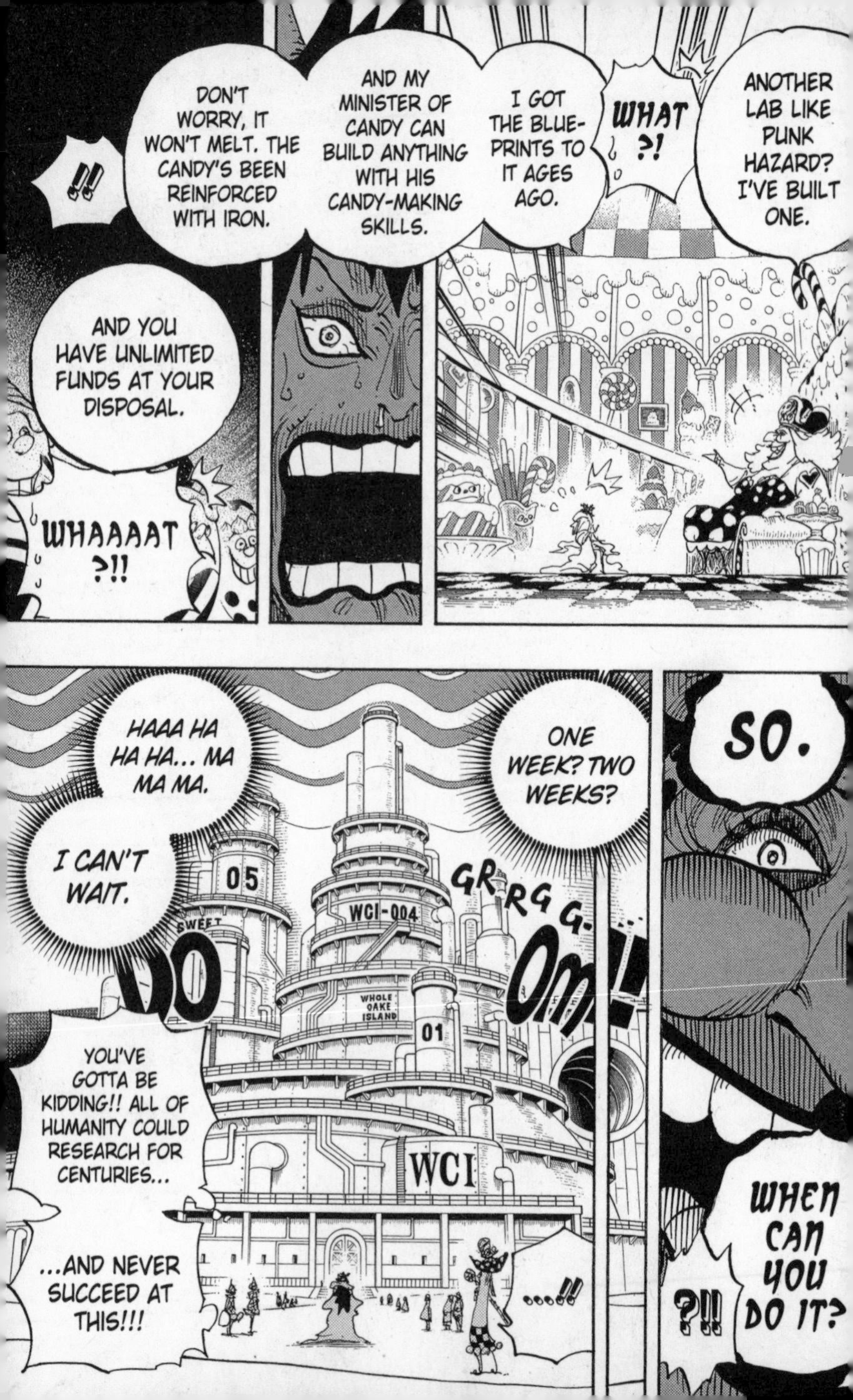
ANOTHER LAB LIKE PUNK HAZARD? I'VE BUILT ONE.
WHAT ?!
I GOT THE BLUE-PRINTS TO IT AGES AGO.
AND MY MINISTER OF CANDY CAN BUILD ANYTHING WITH HIS CANDY-MAKING SKILLS.
DON'T WORRY, IT WON'T MELT. THE CANDY'S BEEN REINFORCED WITH IRON.
!!
AND YOU HAVE UNLIMITED FUNDS AT YOUR DISPOSAL.
WHAAAAT ?!!
SO.
WHEN CAN YOU DO IT?
?!!
ONE WEEK? TWO WEEKS?
HAAA HA HA HA... MA MA MA.
I CAN'T WAIT.
GRRG G-
05
SWEET
WCI-004
WHOLE CAKE ISLAND
01
WCI
DO
OM!!
...!!
YOU'VE GOTTA BE KIDDING!! ALL OF HUMANITY COULD RESEARCH FOR CENTURIES...
...AND NEVER SUCCEED AT THIS!!!

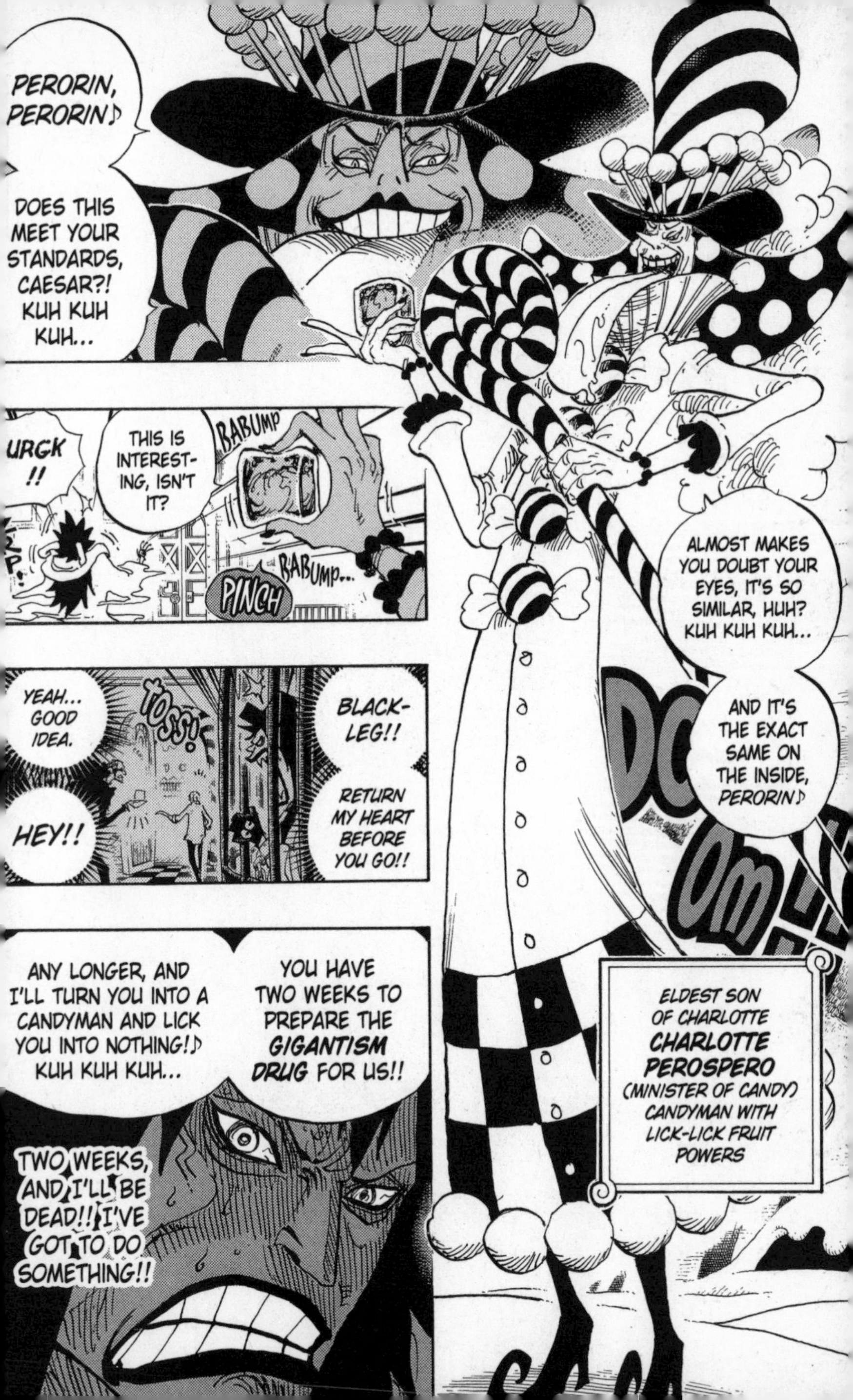
PERORIN, PERORIN♪
DOES THIS MEET YOUR STANDARDS, CAESAR?! KUH KUH KUH...
ALMOST MAKES YOU DOUBT YOUR EYES, IT'S SO SIMILAR, HUH? KUH KUH KUH...
AND IT'S THE EXACT SAME ON THE INSIDE, PERORIN♪
DOOM
ELDEST SON OF CHARLOTTE
CHARLOTTE PEROSPERO
(MINISTER OF CANDY)
CANDYMAN WITH LICK-LICK FRUIT POWERS
BABUMP
THIS IS INTERESTING, ISN'T IT?
URGK !!
PINCH
BABUMP...
BLACK-LEG!!
RETURN MY HEART BEFORE YOU GO!!
TOSS
YEAH... GOOD IDEA.
HEY!!
YOU HAVE TWO WEEKS TO PREPARE THE GIGANTISM DRUG FOR US!!
ANY LONGER, AND I'LL TURN YOU INTO A CANDYMAN AND LICK YOU INTO NOTHING!♪ KUH KUH KUH...
TWO WEEKS, AND I'LL BE DEAD!! I'VE GOT TO DO SOMETHING!!

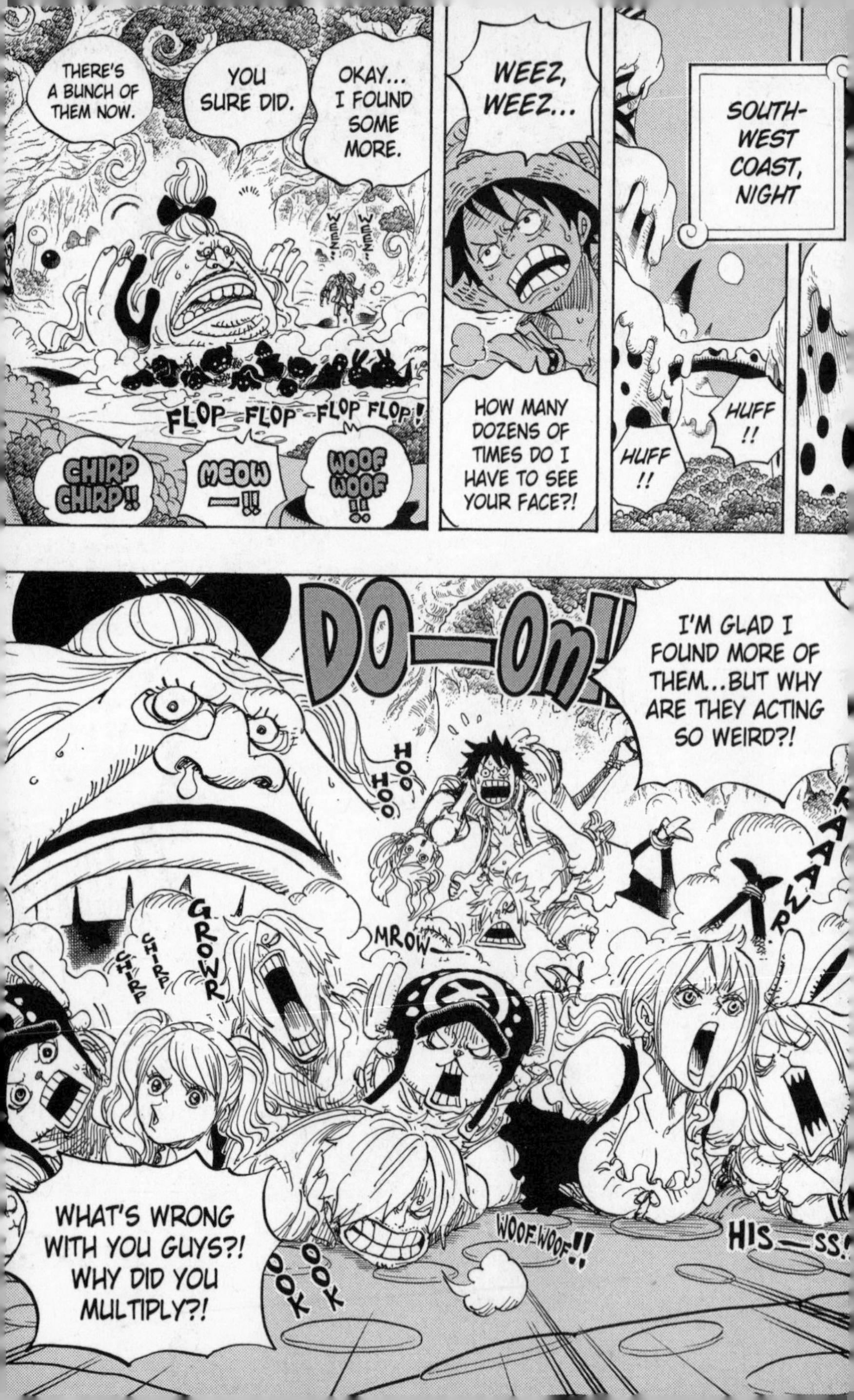
SOUTH-WEST COAST, NIGHT
HUFF!!
HUFF!!
WEEZ, WEEZ...
HOW MANY DOZENS OF TIMES DO I HAVE TO SEE YOUR FACE?!
OKAY... I FOUND SOME MORE.
YOU SURE DID.
THERE'S A BUNCH OF THEM NOW.
WEEZ... WEEZ...
FLOP FLOP FLOP FLOP!
WOOF WOOF!!
MEOW—!!
CHIRP CHIRP!!
I'M GLAD I FOUND MORE OF THEM...BUT WHY ARE THEY ACTING SO WEIRD?!
DO—OM!!
HOO HOO HOO
RAAAAWR
MROW—
GROWR
CHIRP CHIRP
HIS—SS
WOOF WOOF!!
OOOK OOOK
WHAT'S WRONG WITH YOU GUYS?! WHY DID YOU MULTIPLY?!

KINGDOM OF SOUL

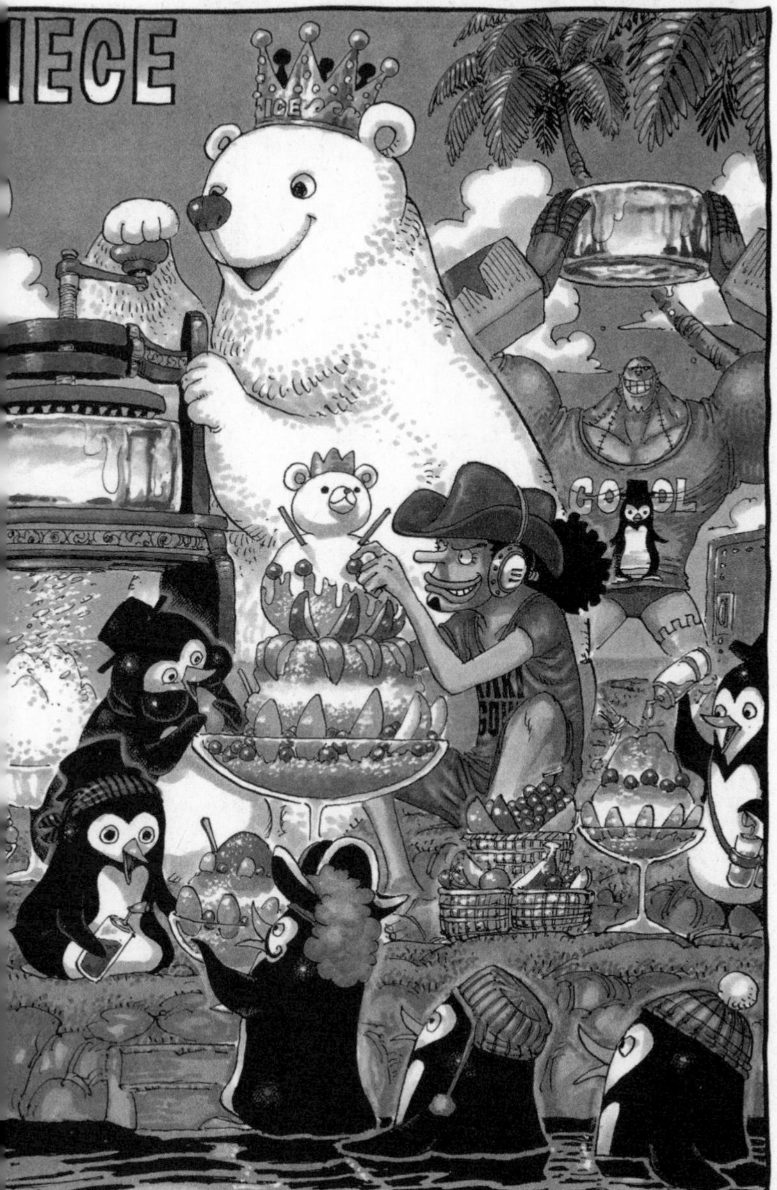
IECE
ICE
COOL

Chapter 835:

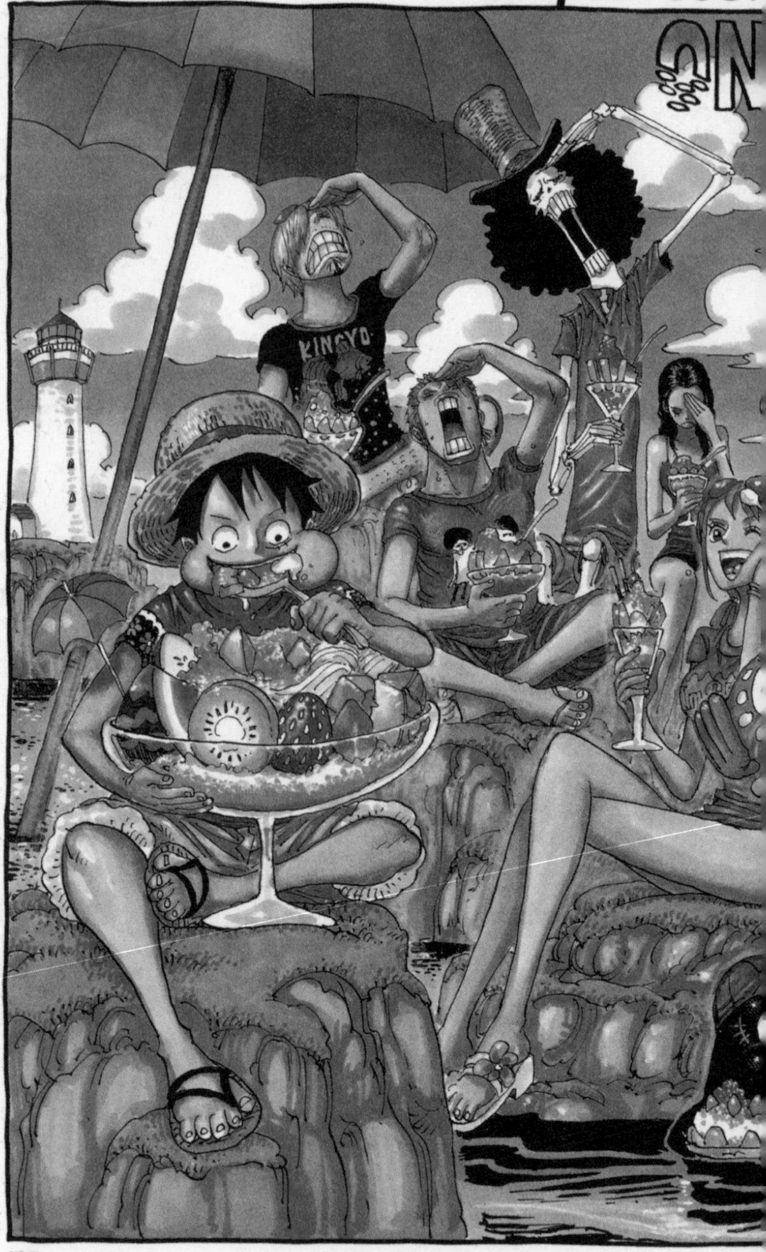
KINGYO

vol.**83**

ONE PIECE

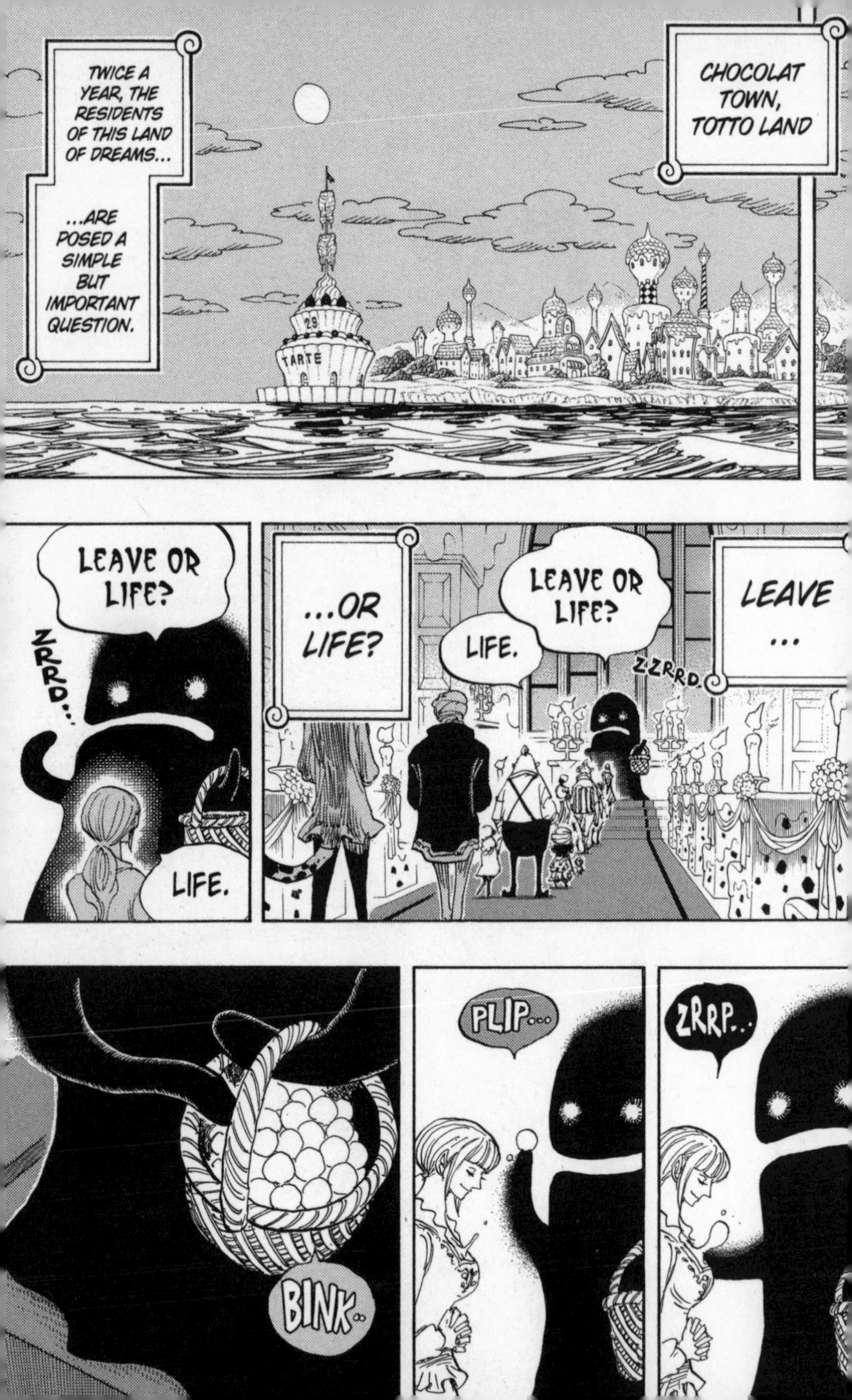
CHOCOLAT TOWN, TOTTO LAND
TWICE A YEAR, THE RESIDENTS OF THIS LAND OF DREAMS...
...ARE POSED A SIMPLE BUT IMPORTANT QUESTION.
29
TARTE
LEAVE ...
ZZRRD
LEAVE OR LIFE?
LIFE.
...OR LIFE?
LEAVE OR LIFE?
ZRRD...
LIFE.
ZRRP..
PLIP...
BINK

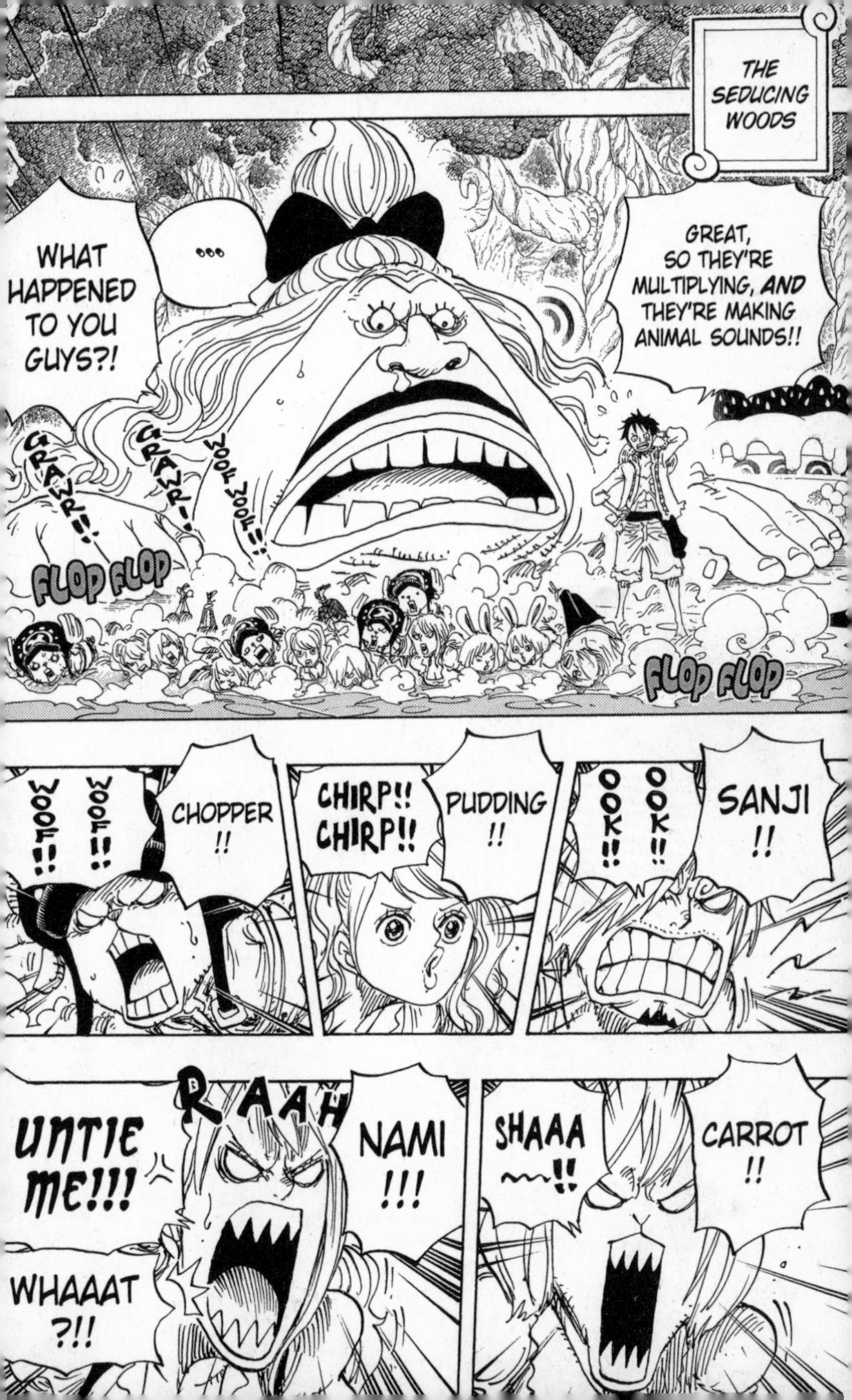
THE SEDUCING WOODS
GREAT, SO THEY'RE MULTIPLYING, AND THEY'RE MAKING ANIMAL SOUNDS!!
...
WHAT HAPPENED TO YOU GUYS?!
GRAWR!!
GRAWR!!
WOOF WOOF!!
FLOP FLOP
FLOP FLOP
SANJI !!
OOK!! OOK!!
PUDDING !!
CHIRP!! CHIRP!!
CHOPPER !!
WOOF!! WOOF!!
CARROT !!
SHAAA~!!
NAMI !!!
RAAH
UNTIE ME!!!
WHAAAT ?!!

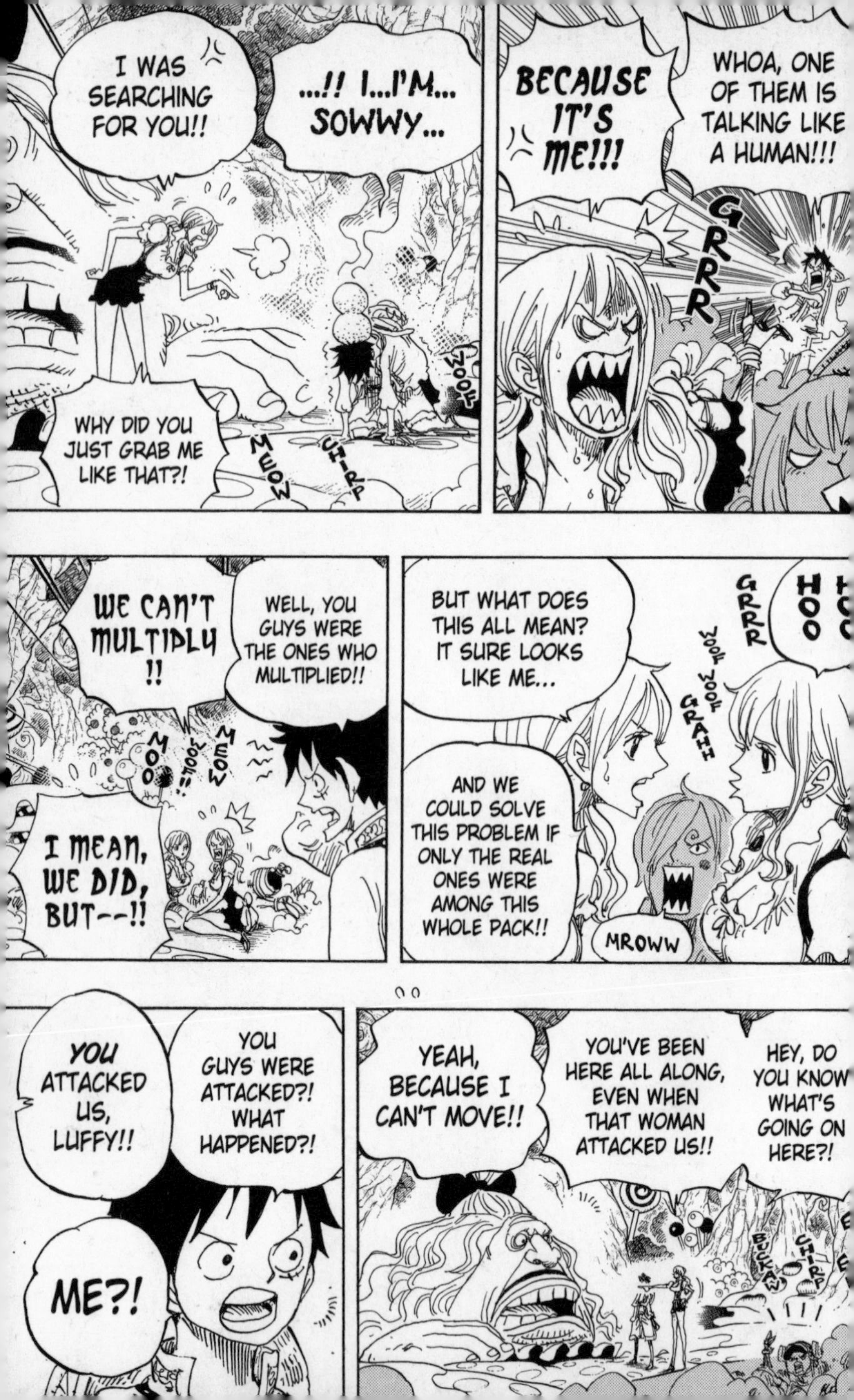
WHOA, ONE OF THEM IS TALKING LIKE A HUMAN!!!
BECAUSE IT'S ME!!!
GRRR
...!! I...I'M... SOWWY...
I WAS SEARCHING FOR YOU!!
WOOF
CHIRP
MEOW
WHY DID YOU JUST GRAB ME LIKE THAT?!
HOO
GRRR
WOOF WOOF
GRAHH
BUT WHAT DOES THIS ALL MEAN? IT SURE LOOKS LIKE ME...
AND WE COULD SOLVE THIS PROBLEM IF ONLY THE REAL ONES WERE AMONG THIS WHOLE PACK!!
MROWW
WELL, YOU GUYS WERE THE ONES WHO MULTIPLIED!!
WE CAN'T MULTIPLY!!
MEOW
WOOF!!
MOO
I MEAN, WE DID, BUT--!!
HEY, DO YOU KNOW WHAT'S GOING ON HERE?!
YOU'VE BEEN HERE ALL ALONG, EVEN WHEN THAT WOMAN ATTACKED US!!
YEAH, BECAUSE I CAN'T MOVE!!
CHIRP
BUCKAW
YOU GUYS WERE ATTACKED?! WHAT HAPPENED?!
YOU ATTACKED US, LUFFY!!
ME?!

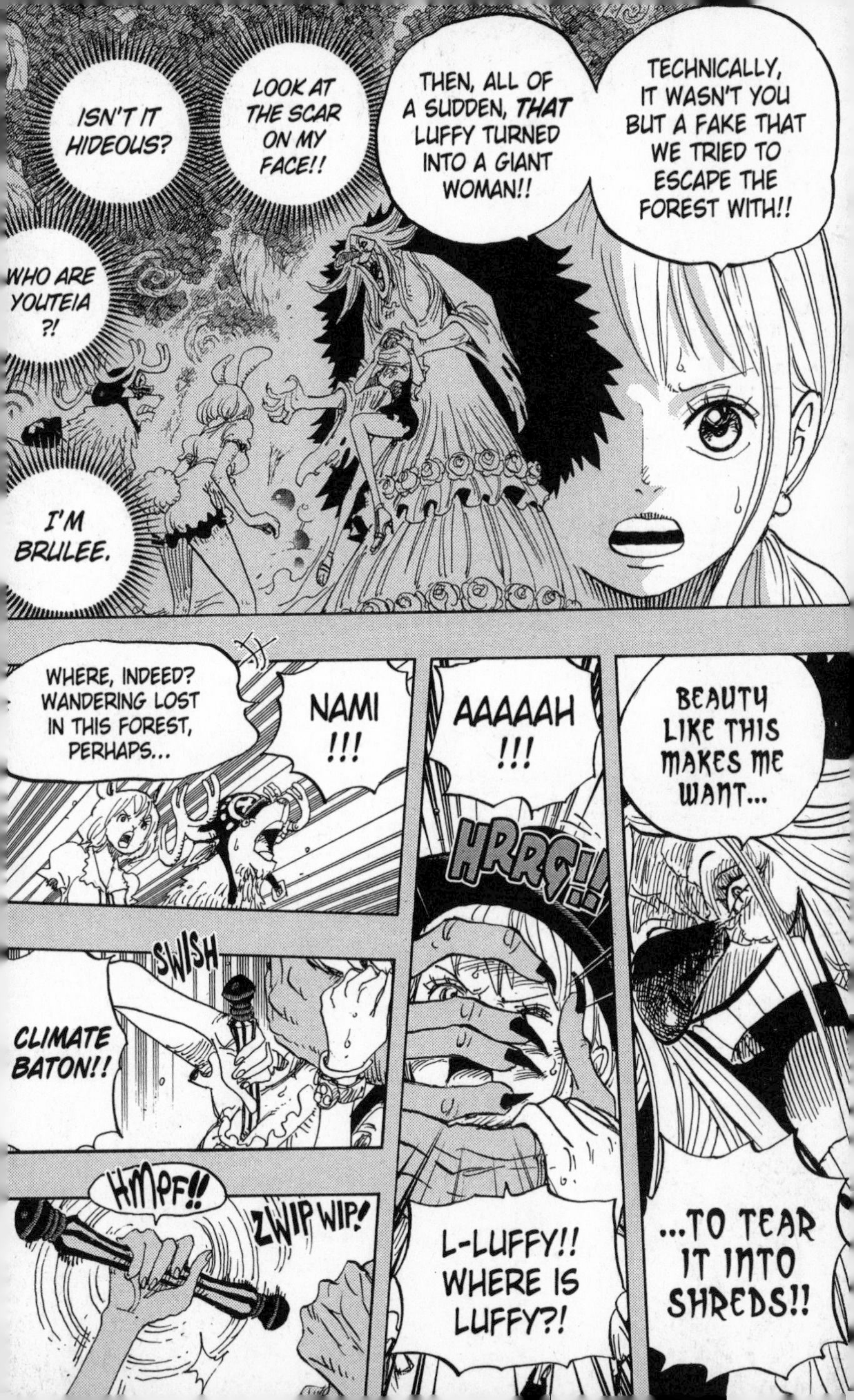
TECHNICALLY, IT WASN'T YOU BUT A FAKE THAT WE TRIED TO ESCAPE THE FOREST WITH!!
THEN, ALL OF A SUDDEN, *THAT* LUFFY TURNED INTO A GIANT WOMAN!!
LOOK AT THE SCAR ON MY FACE!!
ISN'T IT HIDEOUS?
WHO ARE YOUTEIA ?!
I'M BRULEE.
BEAUTY LIKE THIS MAKES ME WANT...
...TO TEAR IT INTO SHREDS!!
AAAAAH !!!
HRRG!!
L-LUFFY!! WHERE IS LUFFY?!
NAMI !!!
WHERE, INDEED? WANDERING LOST IN THIS FOREST, PERHAPS...
SWISH
CLIMATE BATON!!
ZWIP WIP!
HMPF!!

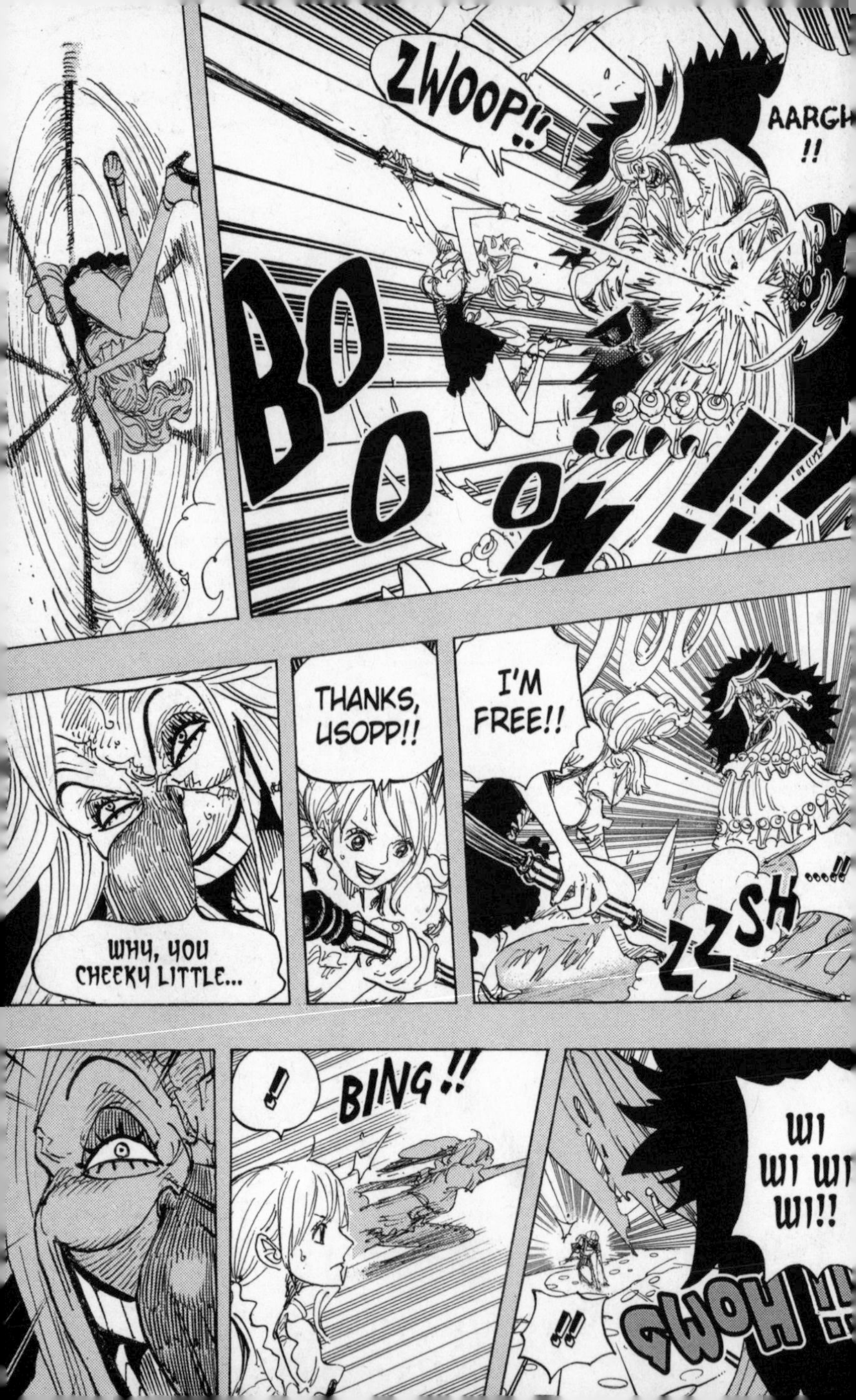
AARGH!!
ZWOOP!!
BOOOM!!!
I'M FREE!!
ZZSH...!!
THANKS, USOPP!!
WHY, YOU CHEEKY LITTLE...
WI WI WI WI!!
GWOH!!
!!
BING!!
!

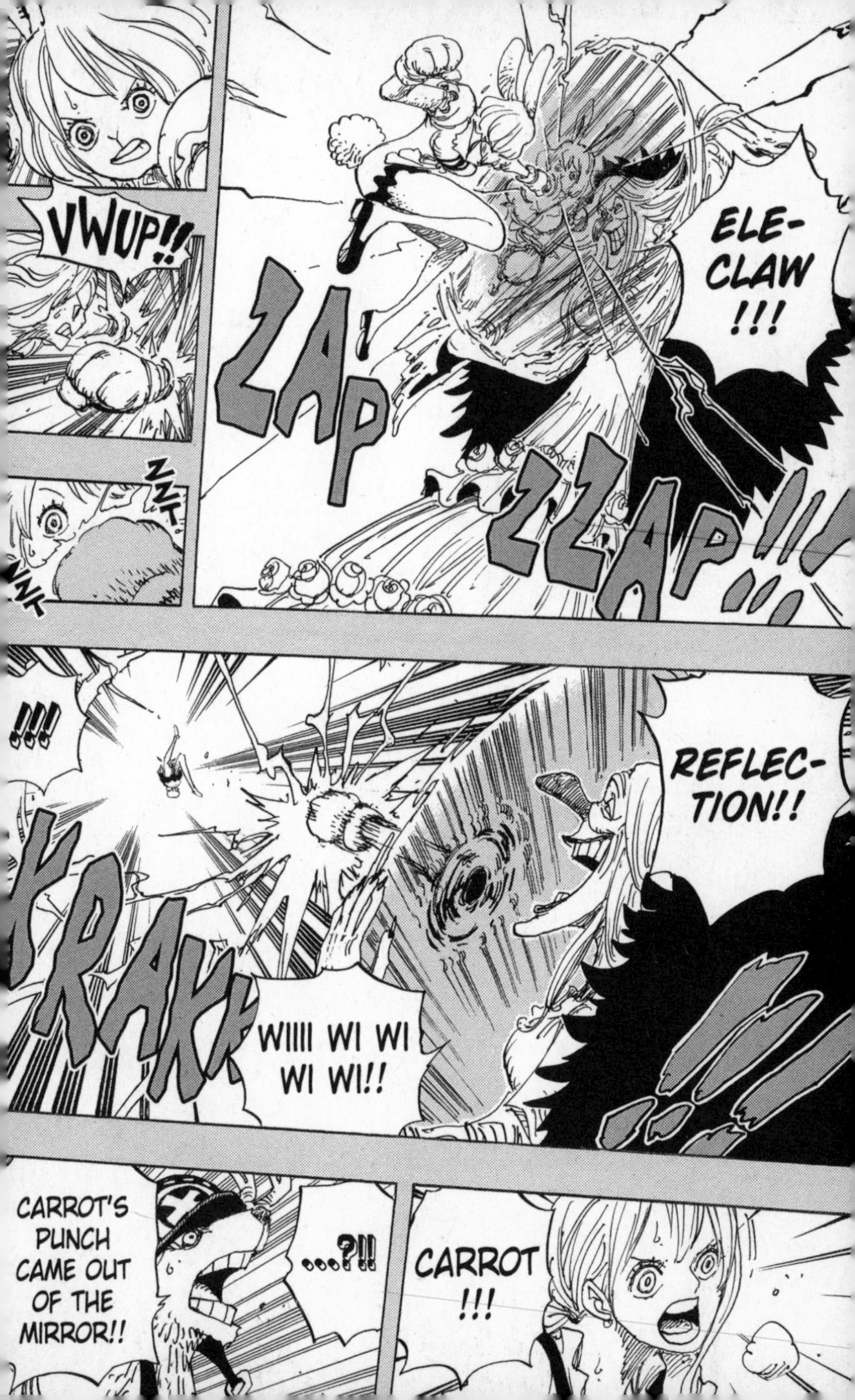
ELE-CLAW!!!
ZAP
ZZAP!!!
VWUP!!
ZNNT
NNK
REFLECTION!!
!!!
WIIII WI WI WI WI!!
KRAKK
!!!
CARROT!!!
...?!!
CARROT'S PUNCH CAME OUT OF THE MIRROR!!

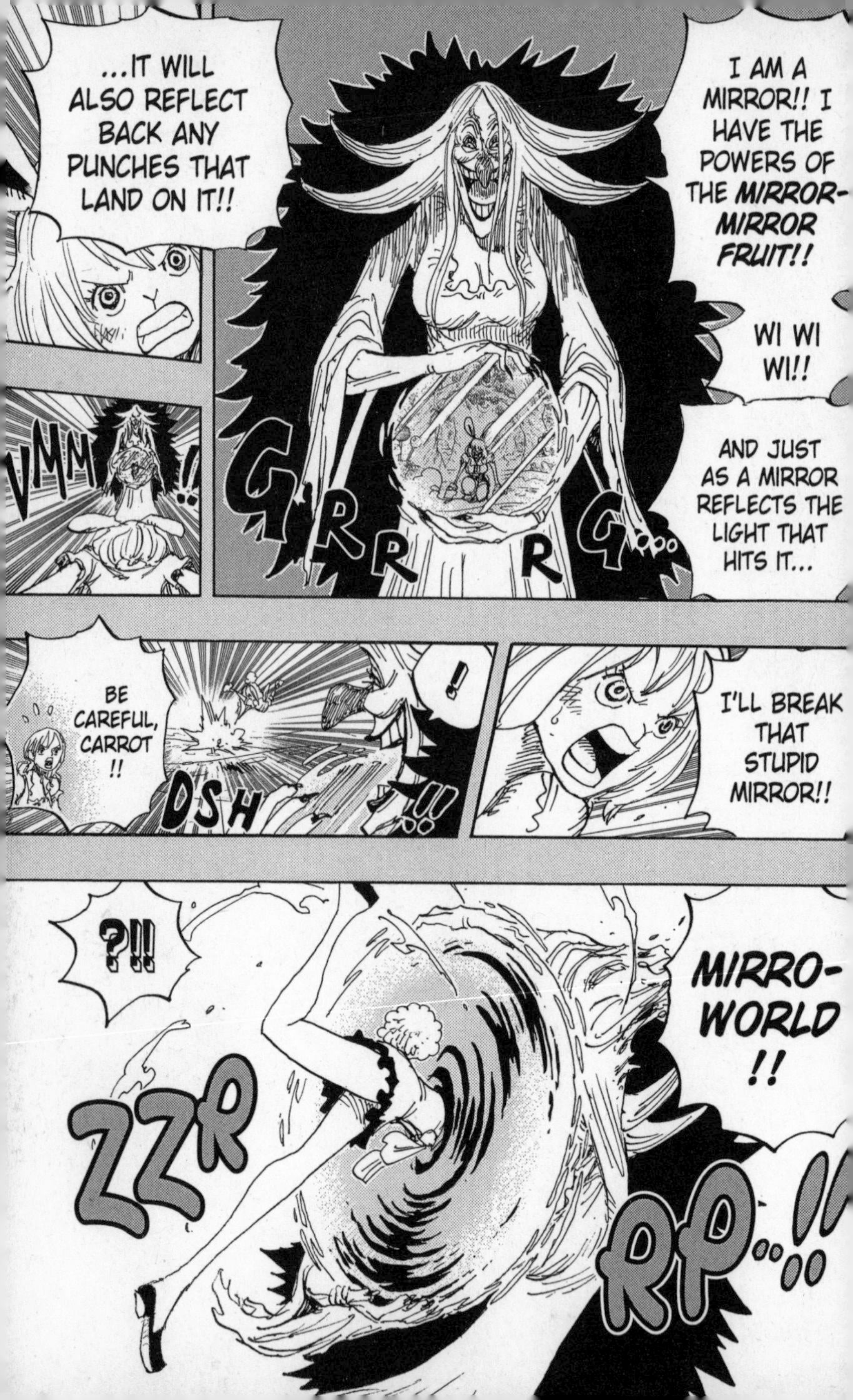
I AM A MIRROR!! I HAVE THE POWERS OF THE MIRROR-MIRROR FRUIT!!
WI WI WI!!
AND JUST AS A MIRROR REFLECTS THE LIGHT THAT HITS IT...
GRRRG...
...IT WILL ALSO REFLECT BACK ANY PUNCHES THAT LAND ON IT!!
VMM!!
I'LL BREAK THAT STUPID MIRROR!!
!
DSH!!
BE CAREFUL, CARROT!!
MIRRO-WORLD!!
?!!
ZZRRP...!!

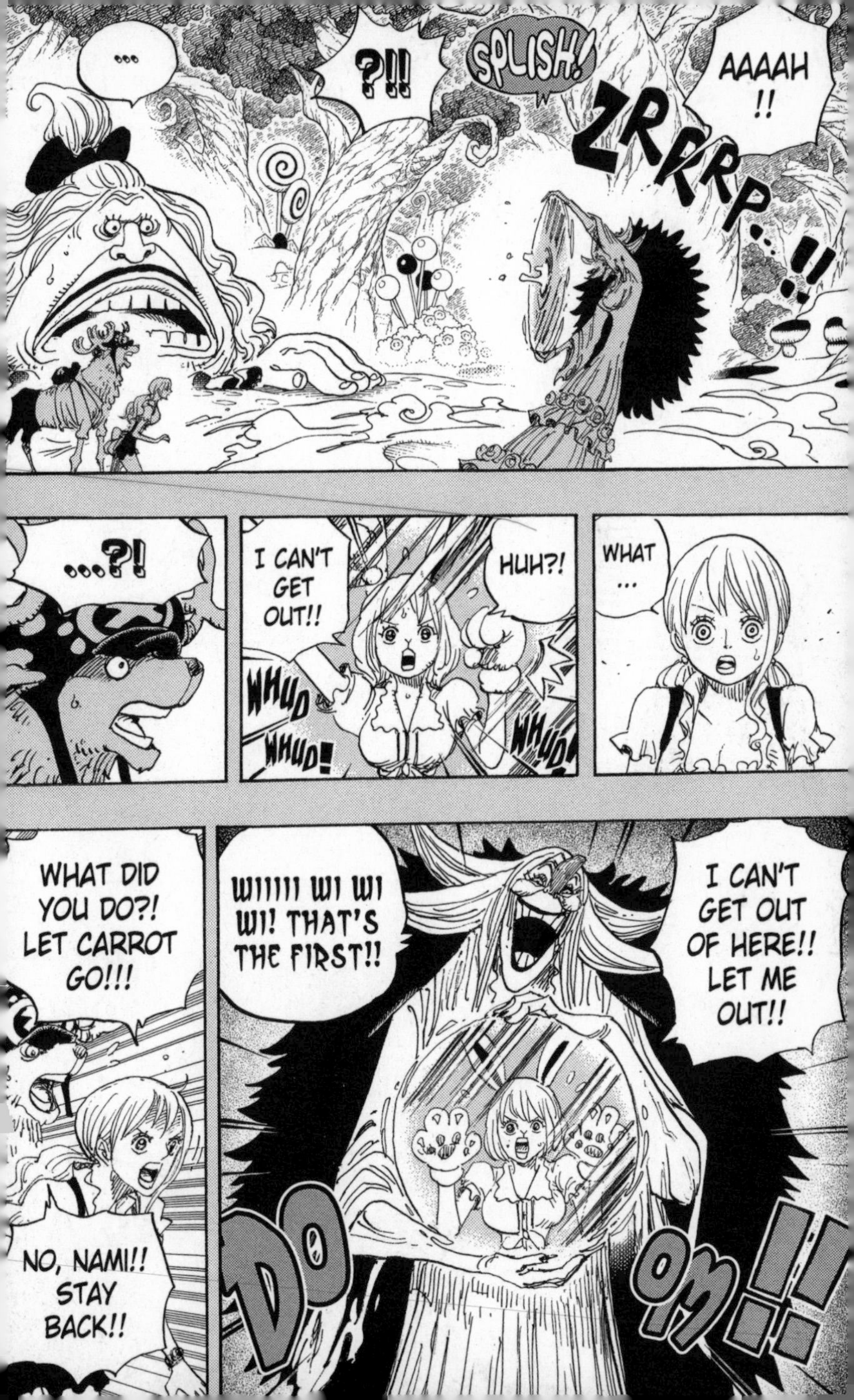
AAAAH !!
SPLISH!
ZRRRP...!!
?!!
...
WHAT ...
HUH?!
I CAN'T GET OUT!!
WHUD
WHUD WHUD!
...?!
I CAN'T GET OUT OF HERE!! LET ME OUT!!
WIIIII WI WI WI! THAT'S THE FIRST!!
DOOM!!
WHAT DID YOU DO?! LET CARROT GO!!!
NO, NAMI!! STAY BACK!!

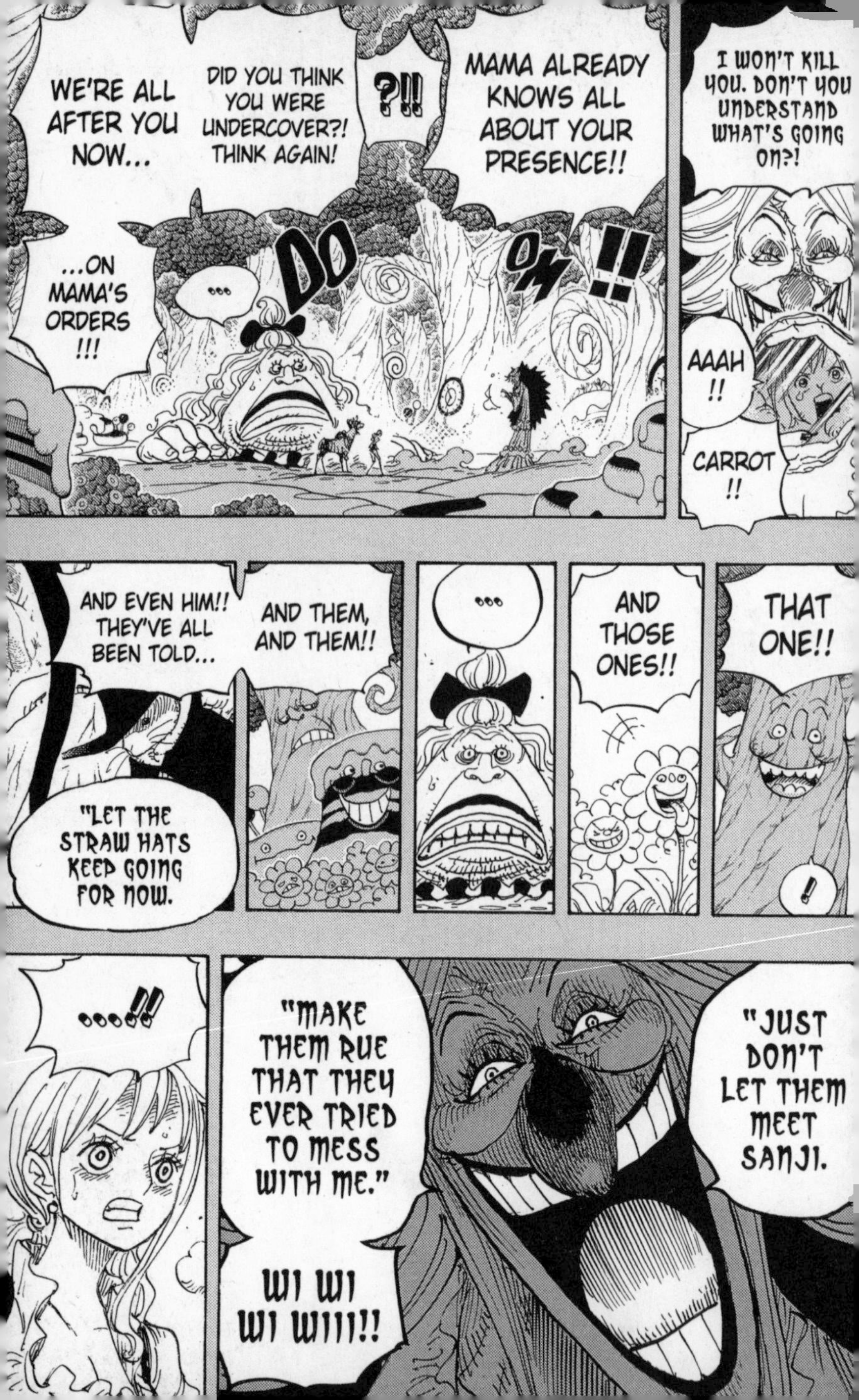
I WON'T KILL YOU. DON'T YOU UNDERSTAND WHAT'S GOING ON?!
AAAH !!
CARROT !!
MAMA ALREADY KNOWS ALL ABOUT YOUR PRESENCE!!
?!!
DID YOU THINK YOU WERE UNDERCOVER?! THINK AGAIN!
WE'RE ALL AFTER YOU NOW...
DOOM!!
...
...ON MAMA'S ORDERS !!!
THAT ONE!!
!
AND THOSE ONES!!
...
AND THEM, AND THEM!!
AND EVEN HIM!! THEY'VE ALL BEEN TOLD...
"LET THE STRAW HATS KEEP GOING FOR NOW.
"JUST DON'T LET THEM MEET SANJI.
"MAKE THEM RUE THAT THEY EVER TRIED TO MESS WITH ME."
WI WI WI WIII!!
...!!

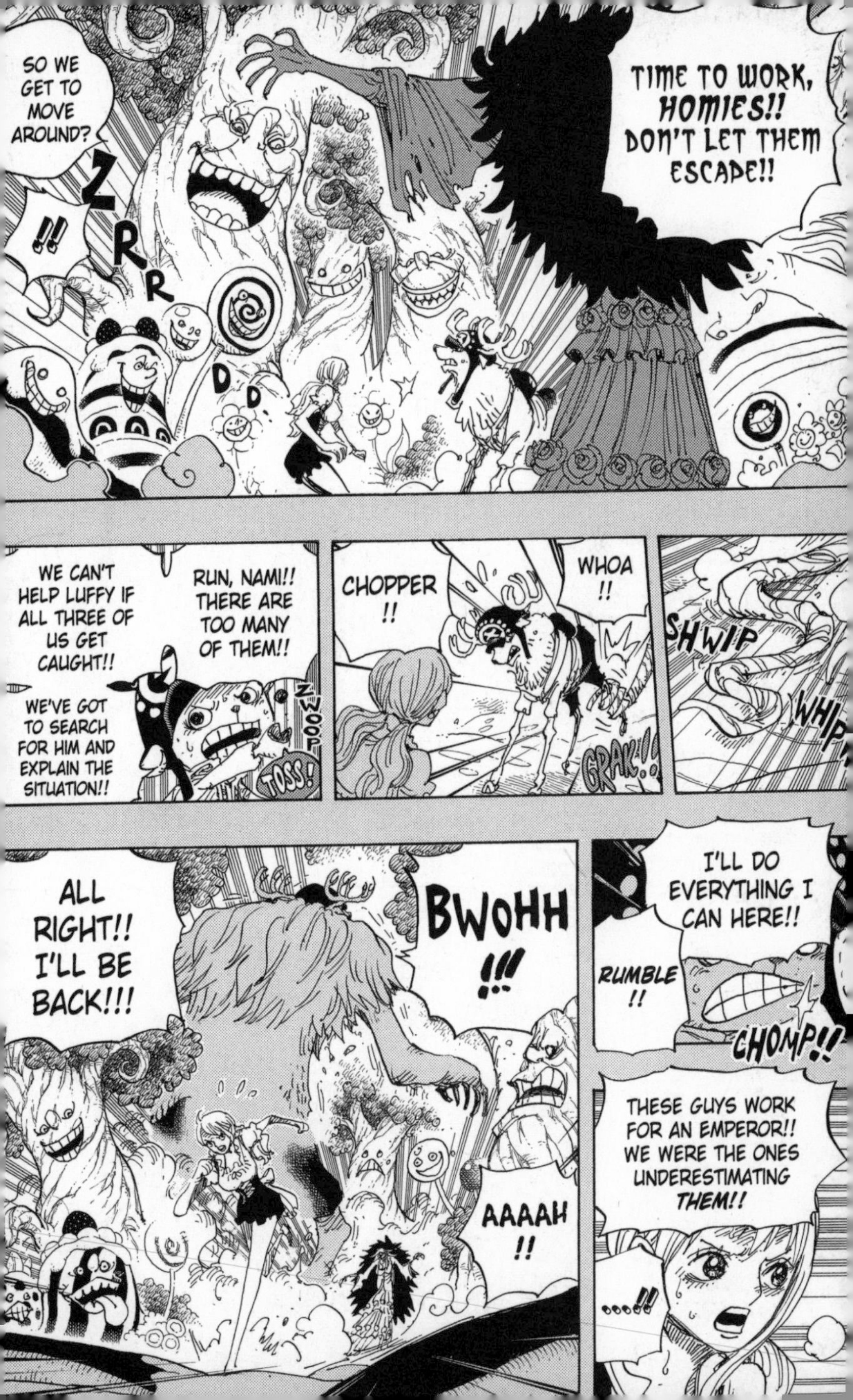
TIME TO WORK, HOMIES!! DON'T LET THEM ESCAPE!!
SO WE GET TO MOVE AROUND?
!!
ZRRR
DD
SHWIP
WHIP
WHOA!!
CHOPPER!!
CRAK!!
RUN, NAMI!! THERE ARE TOO MANY OF THEM!!
WE CAN'T HELP LUFFY IF ALL THREE OF US GET CAUGHT!!
WE'VE GOT TO SEARCH FOR HIM AND EXPLAIN THE SITUATION!!
ZWOOP
TOSS!
I'LL DO EVERYTHING I CAN HERE!!
RUMBLE!!
CHOMP!!
THESE GUYS WORK FOR AN EMPEROR!! WE WERE THE ONES UNDERESTIMATING THEM!!
...!!
BWOHH!!!
ALL RIGHT!! I'LL BE BACK!!!
AAAAH!!

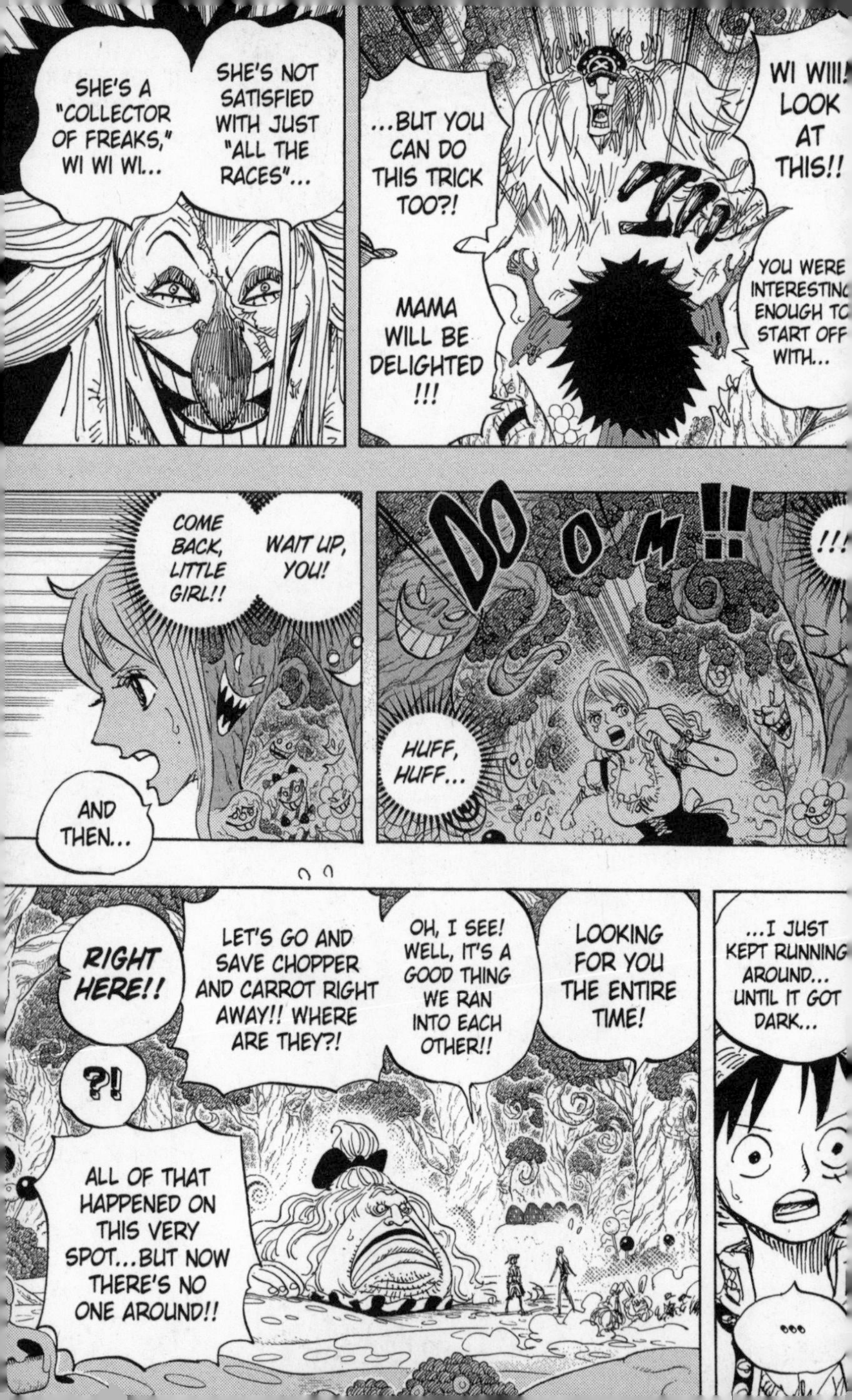
WI WIII! LOOK AT THIS!!
YOU WERE INTERESTING ENOUGH TO START OFF WITH...
...BUT YOU CAN DO THIS TRICK TOO?!
MAMA WILL BE DELIGHTED!!!
SHE'S NOT SATISFIED WITH JUST "ALL THE RACES"...
SHE'S A "COLLECTOR OF FREAKS," WI WI WI...
!!!
DOOM!!
HUFF, HUFF...
WAIT UP, YOU!
COME BACK, LITTLE GIRL!!
AND THEN...
...I JUST KEPT RUNNING AROUND... UNTIL IT GOT DARK...
...
LOOKING FOR YOU THE ENTIRE TIME!
OH, I SEE! WELL, IT'S A GOOD THING WE RAN INTO EACH OTHER!!
LET'S GO AND SAVE CHOPPER AND CARROT RIGHT AWAY!! WHERE ARE THEY?!
RIGHT HERE!!
?!
ALL OF THAT HAPPENED ON THIS VERY SPOT...BUT NOW THERE'S NO ONE AROUND!!

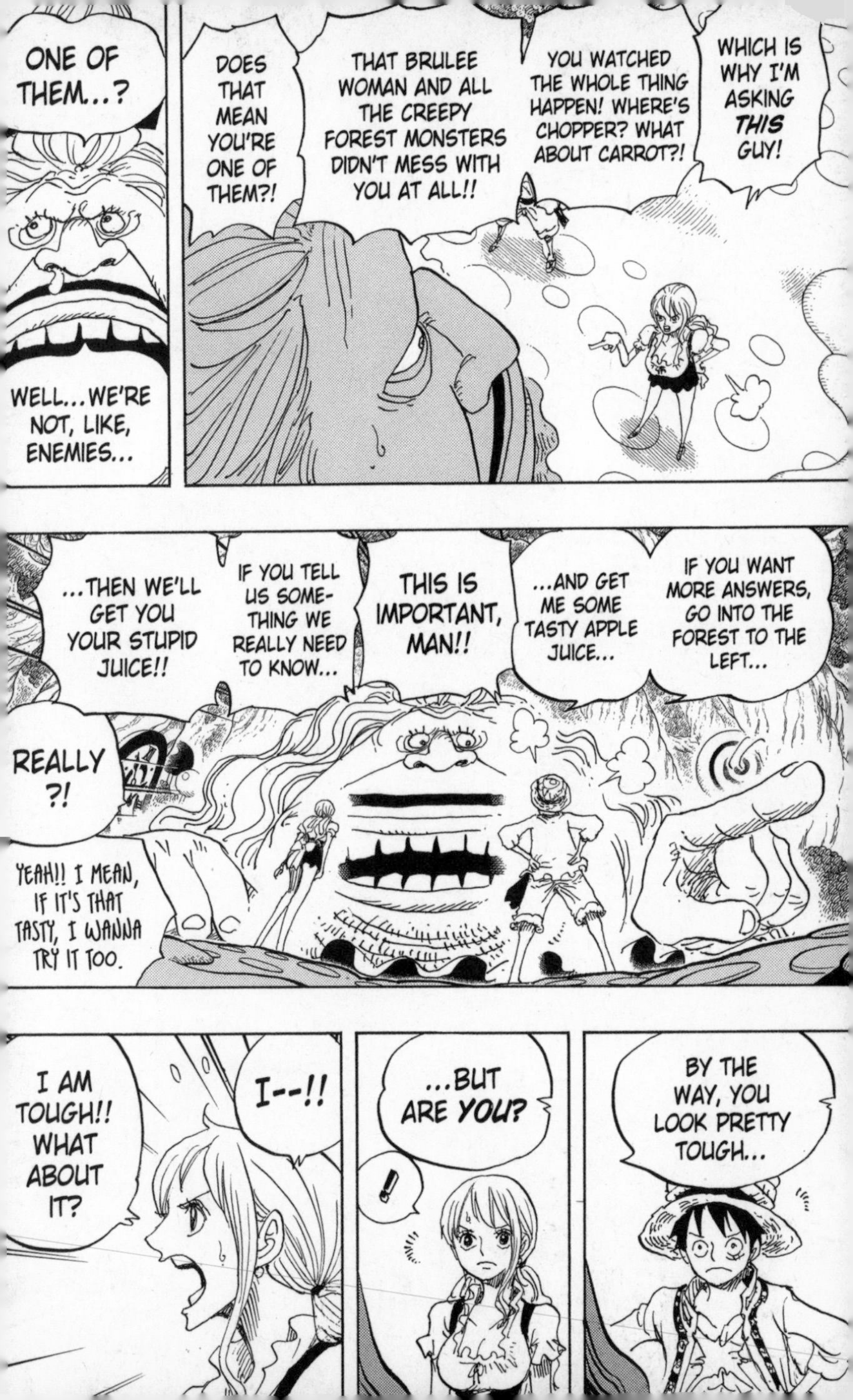
WHICH IS WHY I'M ASKING THIS GUY!
YOU WATCHED THE WHOLE THING HAPPEN! WHERE'S CHOPPER? WHAT ABOUT CARROT?!
THAT BRULEE WOMAN AND ALL THE CREEPY FOREST MONSTERS DIDN'T MESS WITH YOU AT ALL!!
DOES THAT MEAN YOU'RE ONE OF THEM?!
ONE OF THEM...?
WELL...WE'RE NOT, LIKE, ENEMIES...
IF YOU WANT MORE ANSWERS, GO INTO THE FOREST TO THE LEFT...
...AND GET ME SOME TASTY APPLE JUICE...
THIS IS IMPORTANT, MAN!!
IF YOU TELL US SOME-THING WE REALLY NEED TO KNOW...
...THEN WE'LL GET YOU YOUR STUPID JUICE!!
REALLY ?!
YEAH!! I MEAN, IF IT'S THAT TASTY, I WANNA TRY IT TOO.
BY THE WAY, YOU LOOK PRETTY TOUGH...
...BUT ARE YOU?
!
I--!!
I AM TOUGH!! WHAT ABOUT IT?

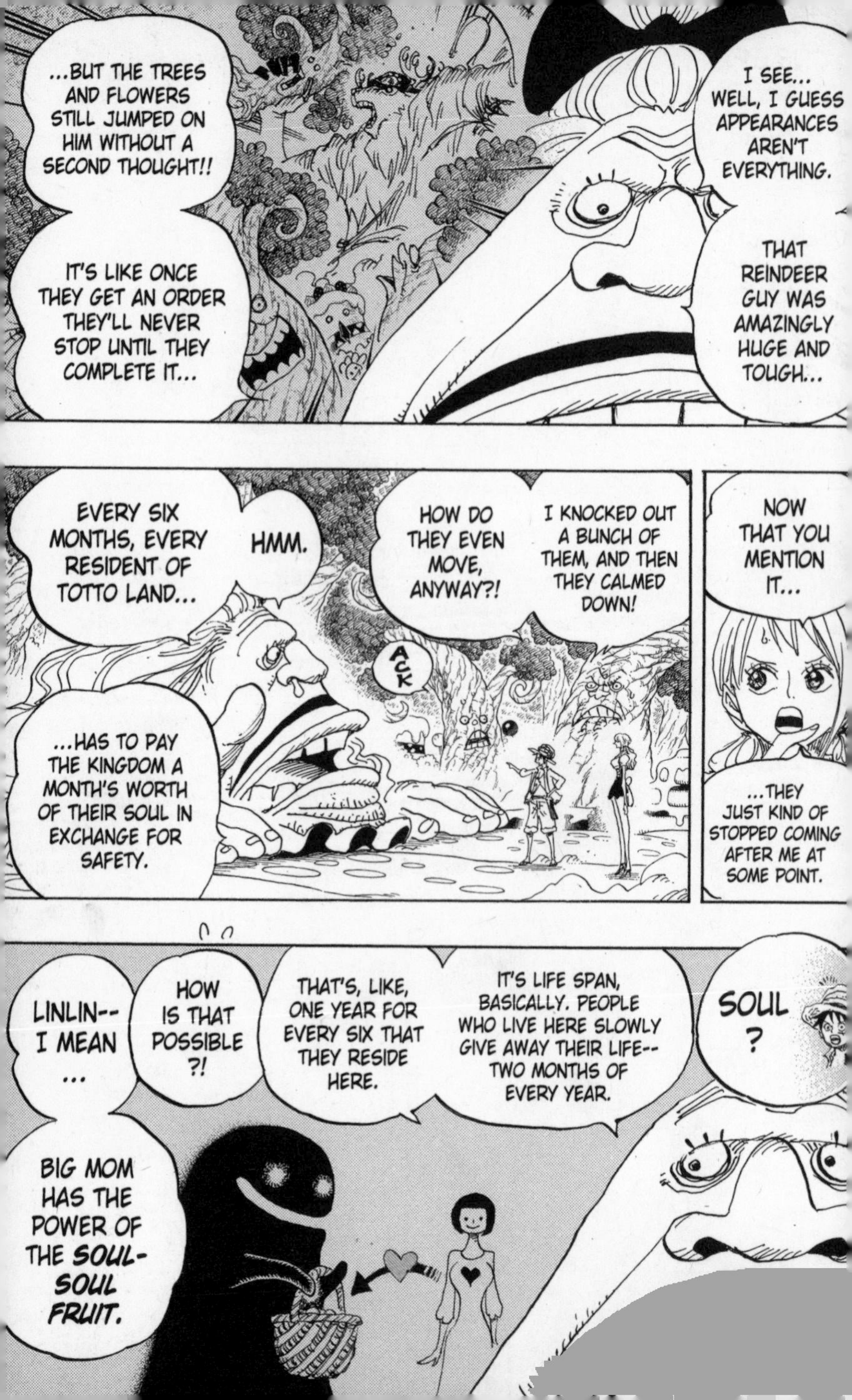
I SEE... WELL, I GUESS APPEARANCES AREN'T EVERYTHING.
THAT REINDEER GUY WAS AMAZINGLY HUGE AND TOUGH...
...BUT THE TREES AND FLOWERS STILL JUMPED ON HIM WITHOUT A SECOND THOUGHT!!
IT'S LIKE ONCE THEY GET AN ORDER THEY'LL NEVER STOP UNTIL THEY COMPLETE IT...
NOW THAT YOU MENTION IT...
...THEY JUST KIND OF STOPPED COMING AFTER ME AT SOME POINT.
I KNOCKED OUT A BUNCH OF THEM, AND THEN THEY CALMED DOWN!
HOW DO THEY EVEN MOVE, ANYWAY?!
HMM.
EVERY SIX MONTHS, EVERY RESIDENT OF TOTTO LAND...
ACK
...HAS TO PAY THE KINGDOM A MONTH'S WORTH OF THEIR SOUL IN EXCHANGE FOR SAFETY.
SOUL?
IT'S LIFE SPAN, BASICALLY. PEOPLE WHO LIVE HERE SLOWLY GIVE AWAY THEIR LIFE-- TWO MONTHS OF EVERY YEAR.
THAT'S, LIKE, ONE YEAR FOR EVERY SIX THAT THEY RESIDE HERE.
HOW IS THAT POSSIBLE?!
LINLIN-- I MEAN...
BIG MOM HAS THE POWER OF THE SOUL-SOUL FRUIT.

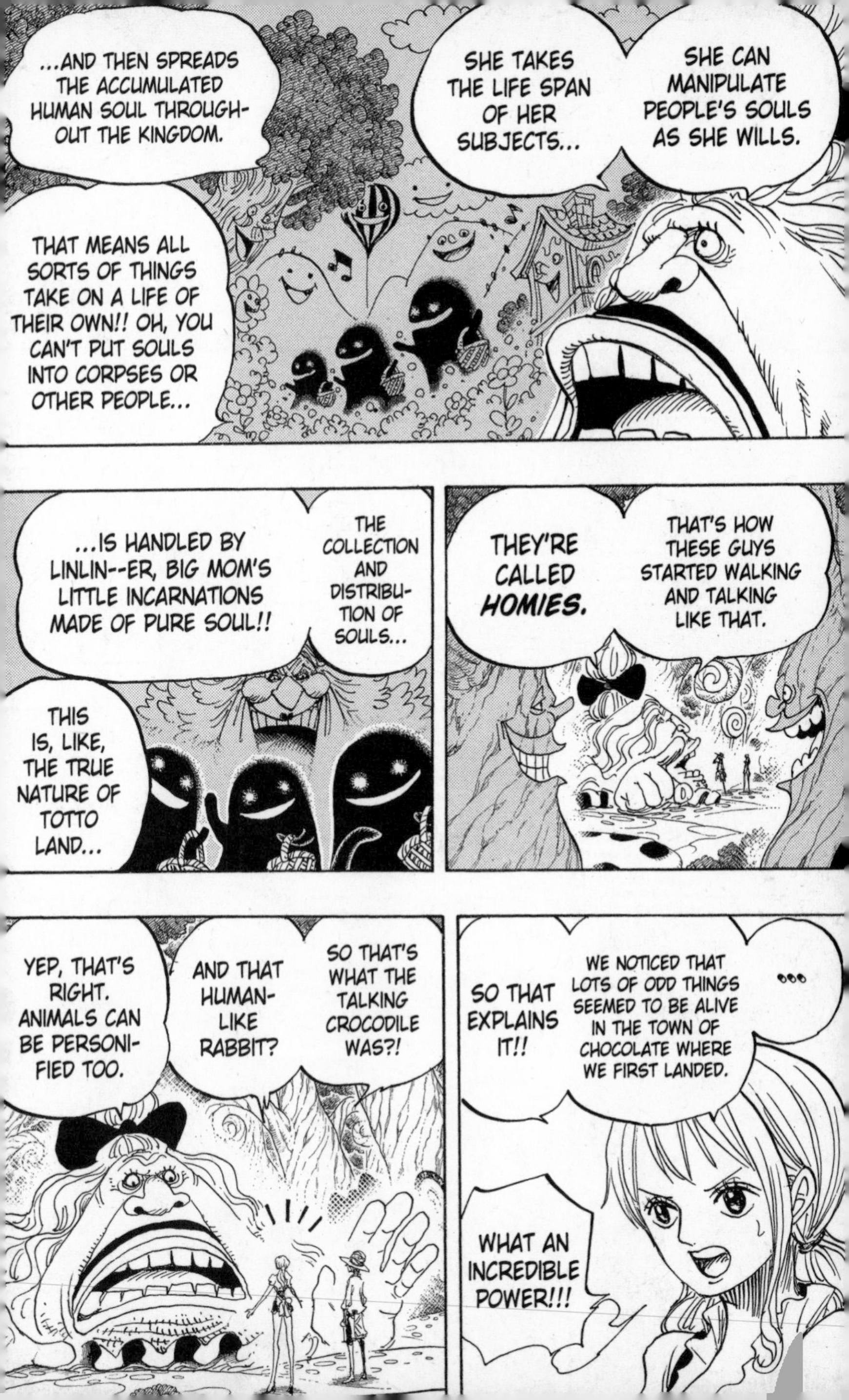
SHE CAN MANIPULATE PEOPLE'S SOULS AS SHE WILLS.
SHE TAKES THE LIFE SPAN OF HER SUBJECTS...
...AND THEN SPREADS THE ACCUMULATED HUMAN SOUL THROUGH-OUT THE KINGDOM.
THAT MEANS ALL SORTS OF THINGS TAKE ON A LIFE OF THEIR OWN!! OH, YOU CAN'T PUT SOULS INTO CORPSES OR OTHER PEOPLE...
THAT'S HOW THESE GUYS STARTED WALKING AND TALKING LIKE THAT.
THEY'RE CALLED ***HOMIES.***
THE COLLECTION AND DISTRIBU-TION OF SOULS...
...IS HANDLED BY LINLIN--ER, BIG MOM'S LITTLE INCARNATIONS MADE OF PURE SOUL!!
THIS IS, LIKE, THE TRUE NATURE OF TOTTO LAND...
...
WE NOTICED THAT LOTS OF ODD THINGS SEEMED TO BE ALIVE IN THE TOWN OF CHOCOLATE WHERE WE FIRST LANDED.
SO THAT EXPLAINS IT!!
WHAT AN INCREDIBLE POWER!!!
SO THAT'S WHAT THE TALKING CROCODILE WAS?!
AND THAT HUMAN-LIKE RABBIT?
YEP, THAT'S RIGHT. ANIMALS CAN BE PERSONI-FIED TOO.

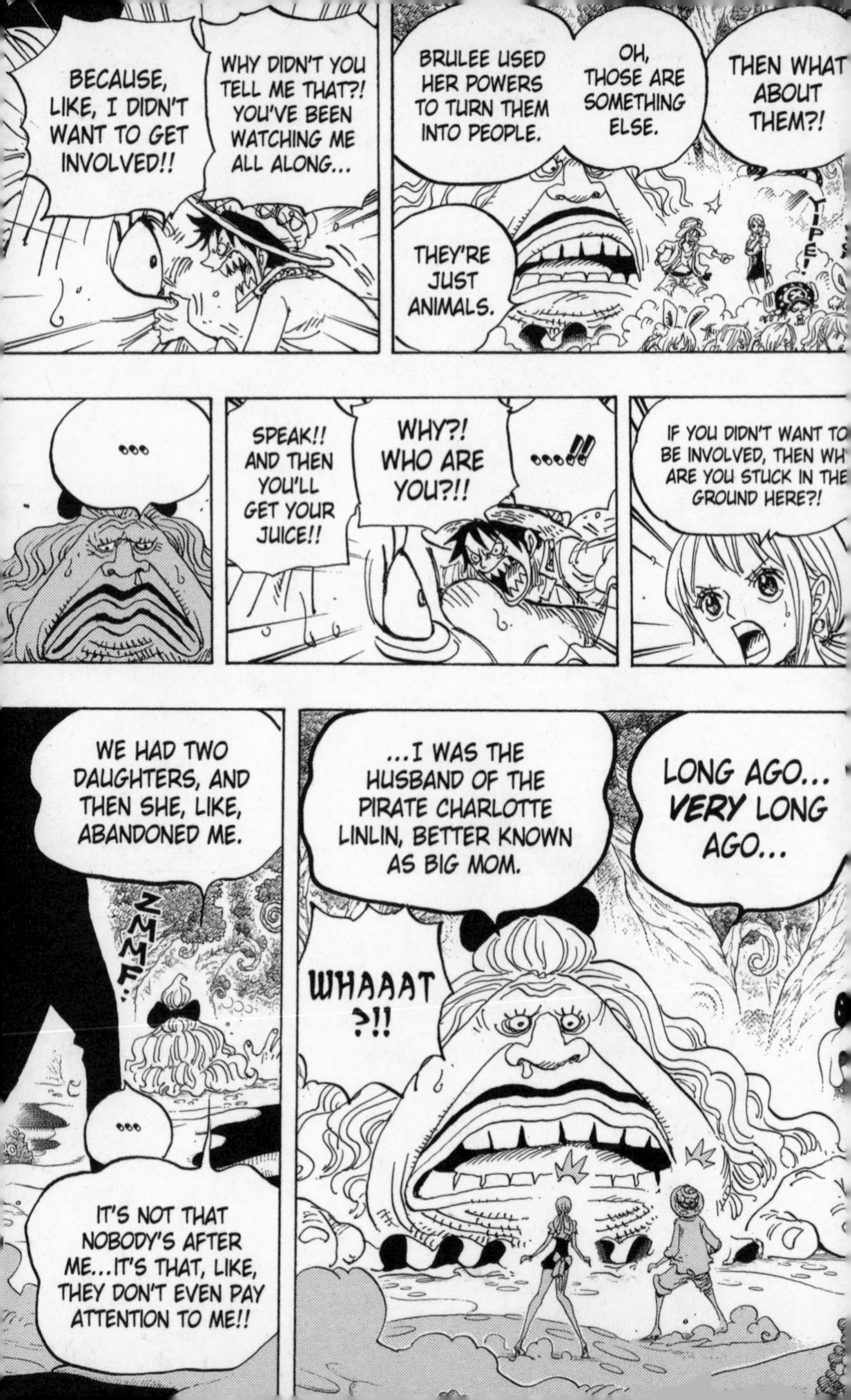
THEN WHAT ABOUT THEM?!
OH, THOSE ARE SOMETHING ELSE.
BRULEE USED HER POWERS TO TURN THEM INTO PEOPLE.
THEY'RE JUST ANIMALS.
YIPE!
WHY DIDN'T YOU TELL ME THAT?! YOU'VE BEEN WATCHING ME ALL ALONG...
BECAUSE, LIKE, I DIDN'T WANT TO GET INVOLVED!!
IF YOU DIDN'T WANT TO BE INVOLVED, THEN WH ARE YOU STUCK IN THE GROUND HERE?!
...!!
WHY?! WHO ARE YOU?!!
SPEAK!! AND THEN YOU'LL GET YOUR JUICE!!
...
LONG AGO... VERY LONG AGO...
...I WAS THE HUSBAND OF THE PIRATE CHARLOTTE LINLIN, BETTER KNOWN AS BIG MOM.
WHAAAT ?!!
WE HAD TWO DAUGHTERS, AND THEN SHE, LIKE, ABANDONED ME.
ZMMF
...
IT'S NOT THAT NOBODY'S AFTER ME...IT'S THAT, LIKE, THEY DON'T EVEN PAY ATTENTION TO ME!!

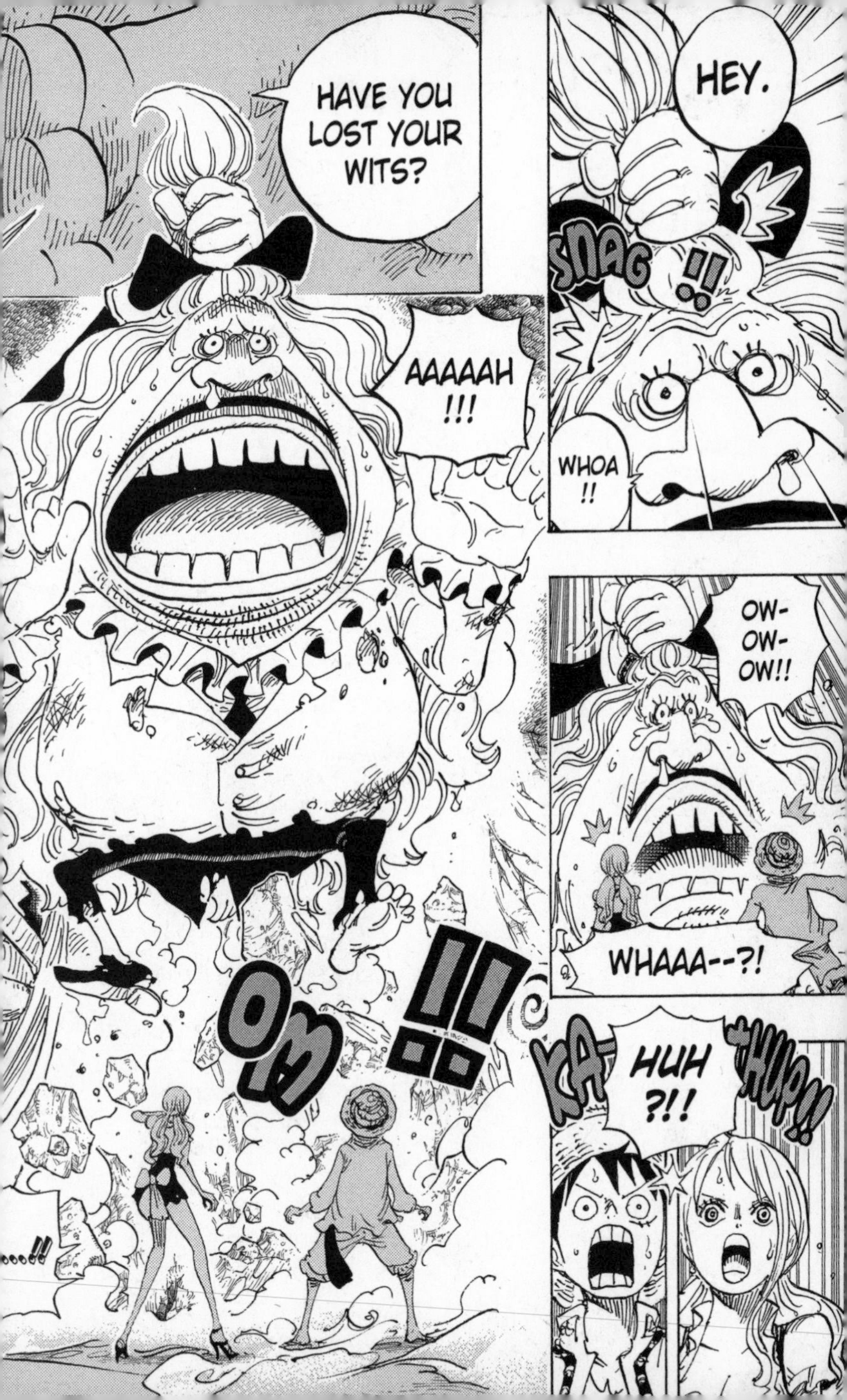
HEY.
SNAG!!
WHOA!!
HAVE YOU LOST YOUR WITS?
AAAAAH!!!
OM!!
....!!
OW-OW-OW!!
WHAAA--?!
KA-THUD!!
HUH?!!

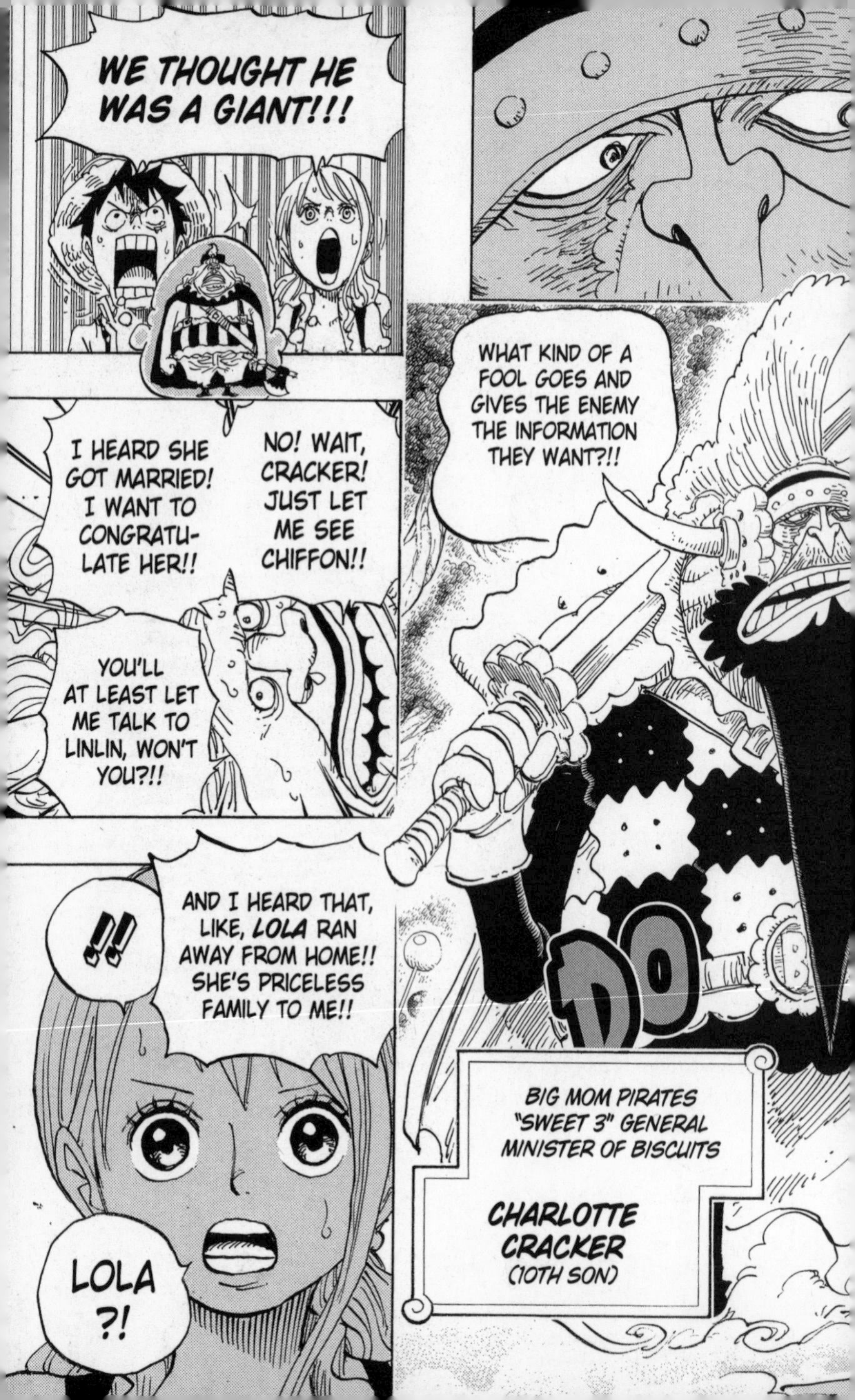
WE THOUGHT HE WAS A GIANT!!!
WHAT KIND OF A FOOL GOES AND GIVES THE ENEMY THE INFORMATION THEY WANT?!!
DO
BIG MOM PIRATES "SWEET 3" GENERAL MINISTER OF BISCUITS
CHARLOTTE CRACKER (10TH SON)
NO! WAIT, CRACKER! JUST LET ME SEE CHIFFON!!
I HEARD SHE GOT MARRIED! I WANT TO CONGRATU-LATE HER!!
YOU'LL AT LEAST LET ME TALK TO LINLIN, WON'T YOU?!!
AND I HEARD THAT, LIKE, *LOLA* RAN AWAY FROM HOME!! SHE'S PRICELESS FAMILY TO ME!!
!!
LOLA ?!

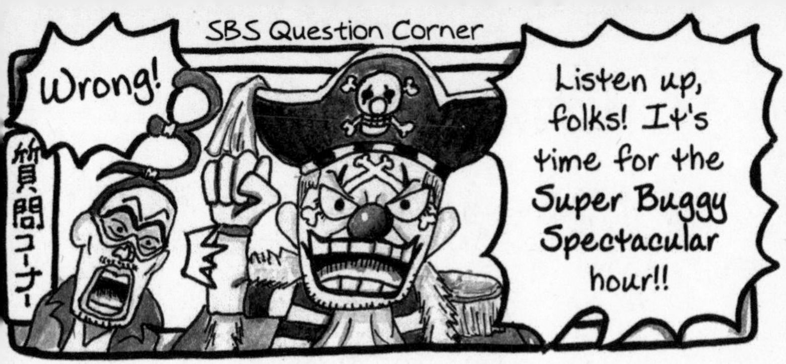
SBS Question Corner
Listen up, folks! It's time for the Super Buggy Spectacular hour!!
Wrong!
質問コーナー

(Hayato Asami, Kanagawa)

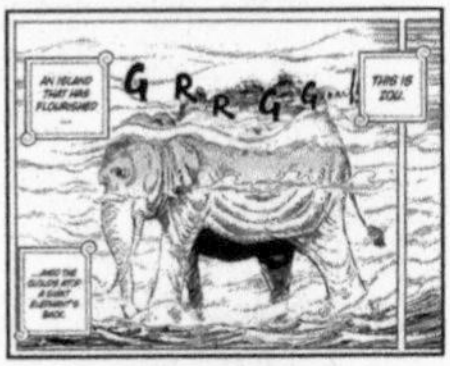
THIS IS ZOU.

Q: Odacchi, here's a question! What's up with Zou's legs? Are those ultra-long legs that would make the inhabitants of Long Ring Long Land jealous?!?!

--Shokotan

A: Ah. This is a very interesting question. Indeed, if you think of it being proportioned like a normal elephant, that would mean the sea is very shallow! As a matter of fact, this elephant belongs to the species *elephus dalí*, which is known for having one extra leg joint, and extremely long legs. Maybe you'll see it in the manga someday, or maybe not, but that's the explanation.

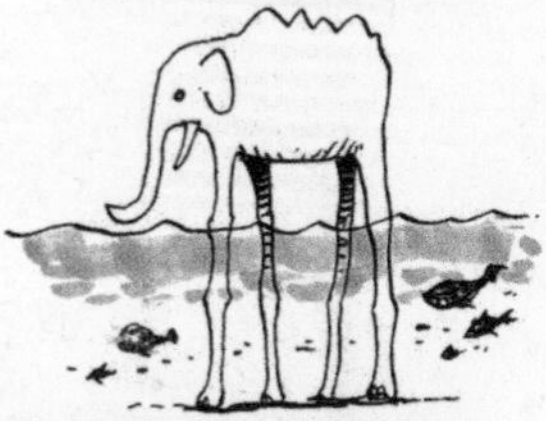

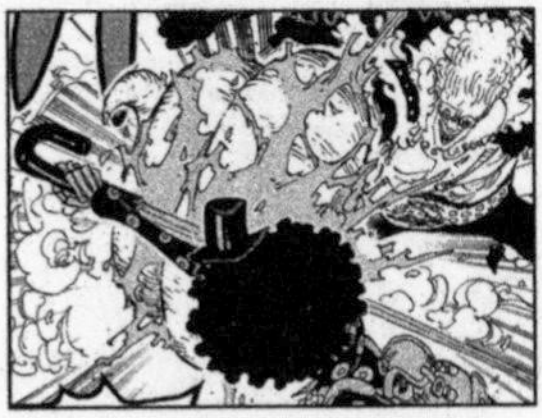

Q: Am I the only one who thinks the special attack move "Sheep's Head" in Chapter 195 looks like a **poop?** I'm so obsessed with this that I can't even eat tapioca pudding with my chopsticks anymore.

--My friend can drink coffee black

A: It looks like poop to me too.

Q: Hi, Oda Sensei. Did you know that the world's finest coffee is extracted from elephant dung? I'm sure a thousand-year-old elephant produces some truly well-aged dung, so get right in there and pull out those beans!

--Sanadacchi

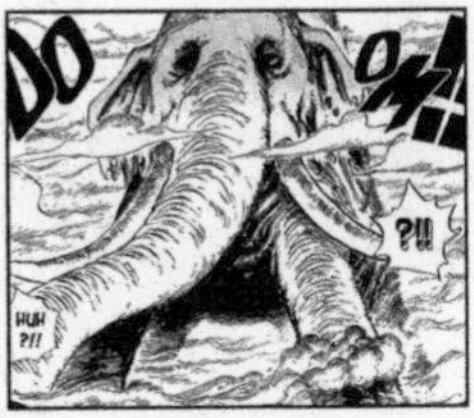
?!!
HUH ?!!

A: I never heard this before!! I looked it up!! It's true!!
I understand the reasoning, but I think I'll pass on this one!! No thanks.

Chapter 836:
LOLA'S VIVRE CARD

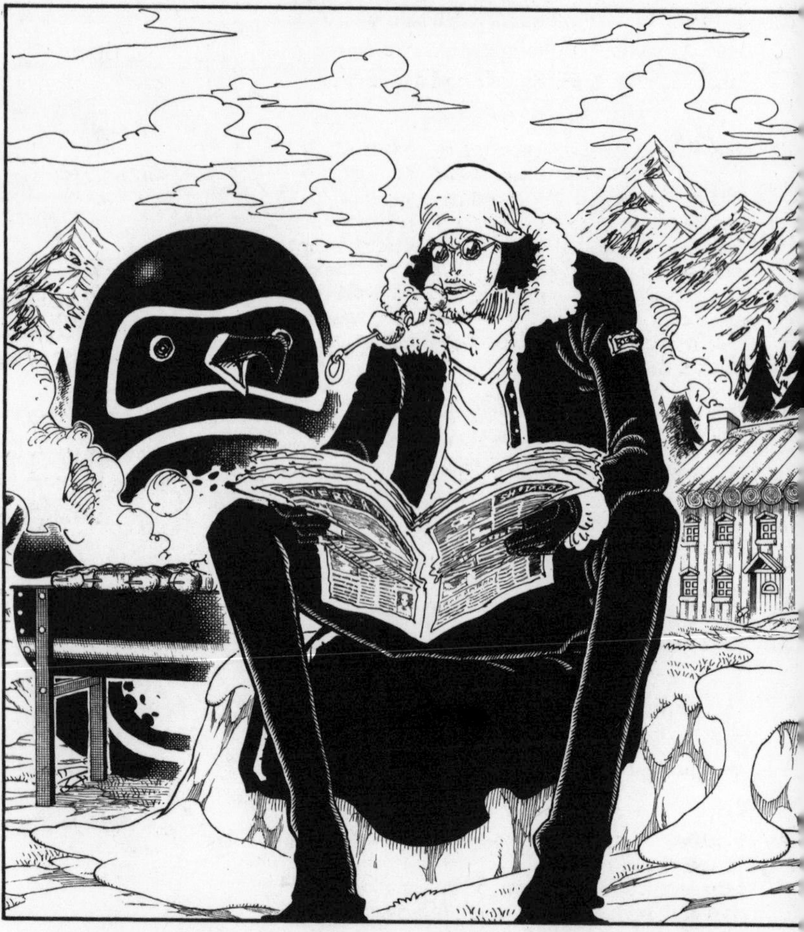

DECKS OF THE WORLD, 500-MILLION-MAN ARC,
VOL. 23: "AOKIJI ON A CERTAIN ISLAND"

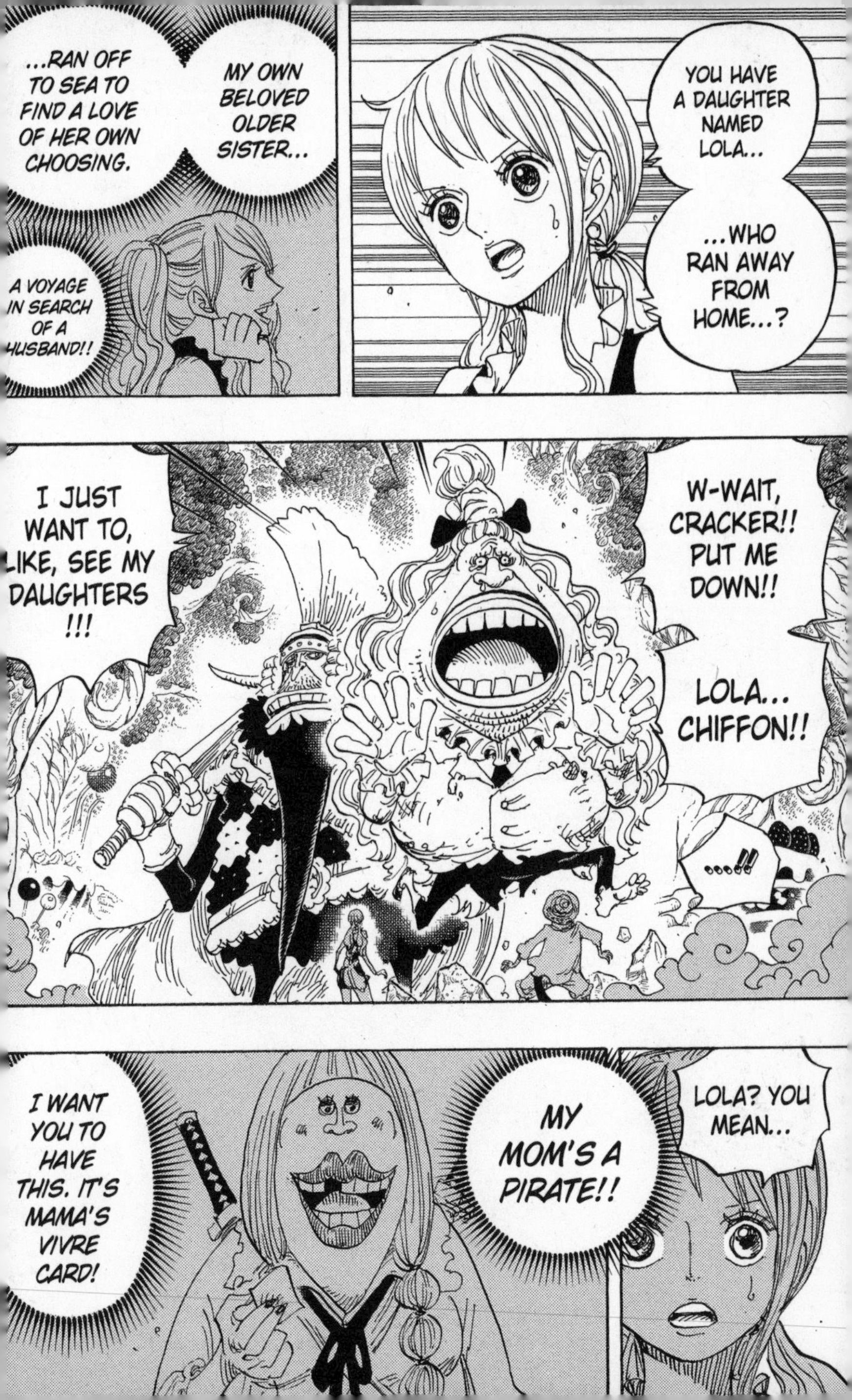
YOU HAVE A DAUGHTER NAMED LOLA...
...WHO RAN AWAY FROM HOME...?
MY OWN BELOVED OLDER SISTER...
...RAN OFF TO SEA TO FIND A LOVE OF HER OWN CHOOSING.
A VOYAGE IN SEARCH OF A HUSBAND!!
W-WAIT, CRACKER!! PUT ME DOWN!!
LOLA... CHIFFON!!
....!!
I JUST WANT TO, LIKE, SEE MY DAUGHTERS!!!
LOLA? YOU MEAN...
MY MOM'S A PIRATE!!
I WANT YOU TO HAVE THIS. IT'S MAMA'S VIVRE CARD!

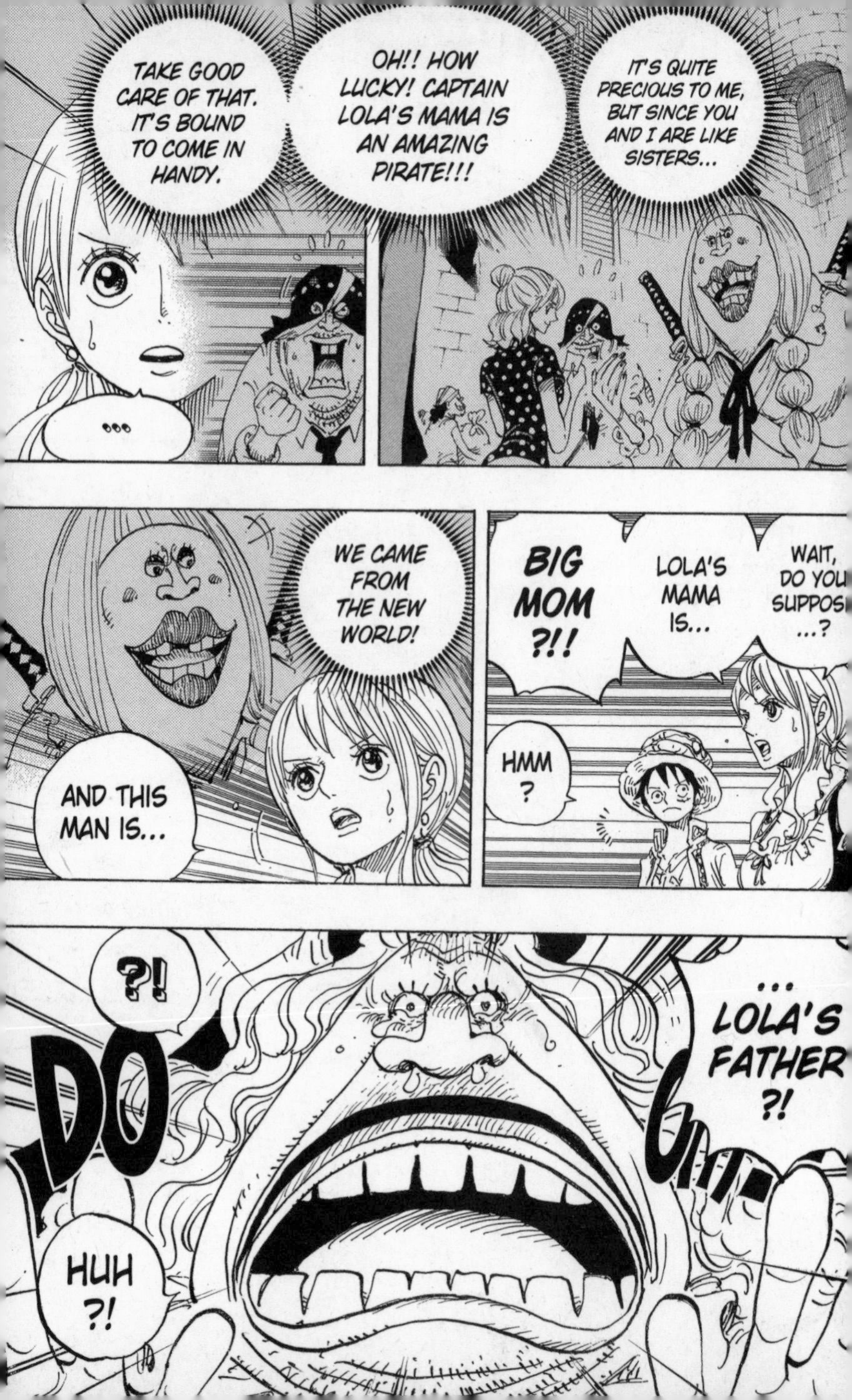
IT'S QUITE PRECIOUS TO ME, BUT SINCE YOU AND I ARE LIKE SISTERS...
OH!! HOW LUCKY! CAPTAIN LOLA'S MAMA IS AN AMAZING PIRATE!!!
TAKE GOOD CARE OF THAT. IT'S BOUND TO COME IN HANDY.
...
WAIT, DO YOU SUPPOS ...?
LOLA'S MAMA IS...
BIG MOM ?!!
HMM ?
WE CAME FROM THE NEW WORLD!
AND THIS MAN IS...
... LOLA'S FATHER ?!
?!
DO
HUH ?!

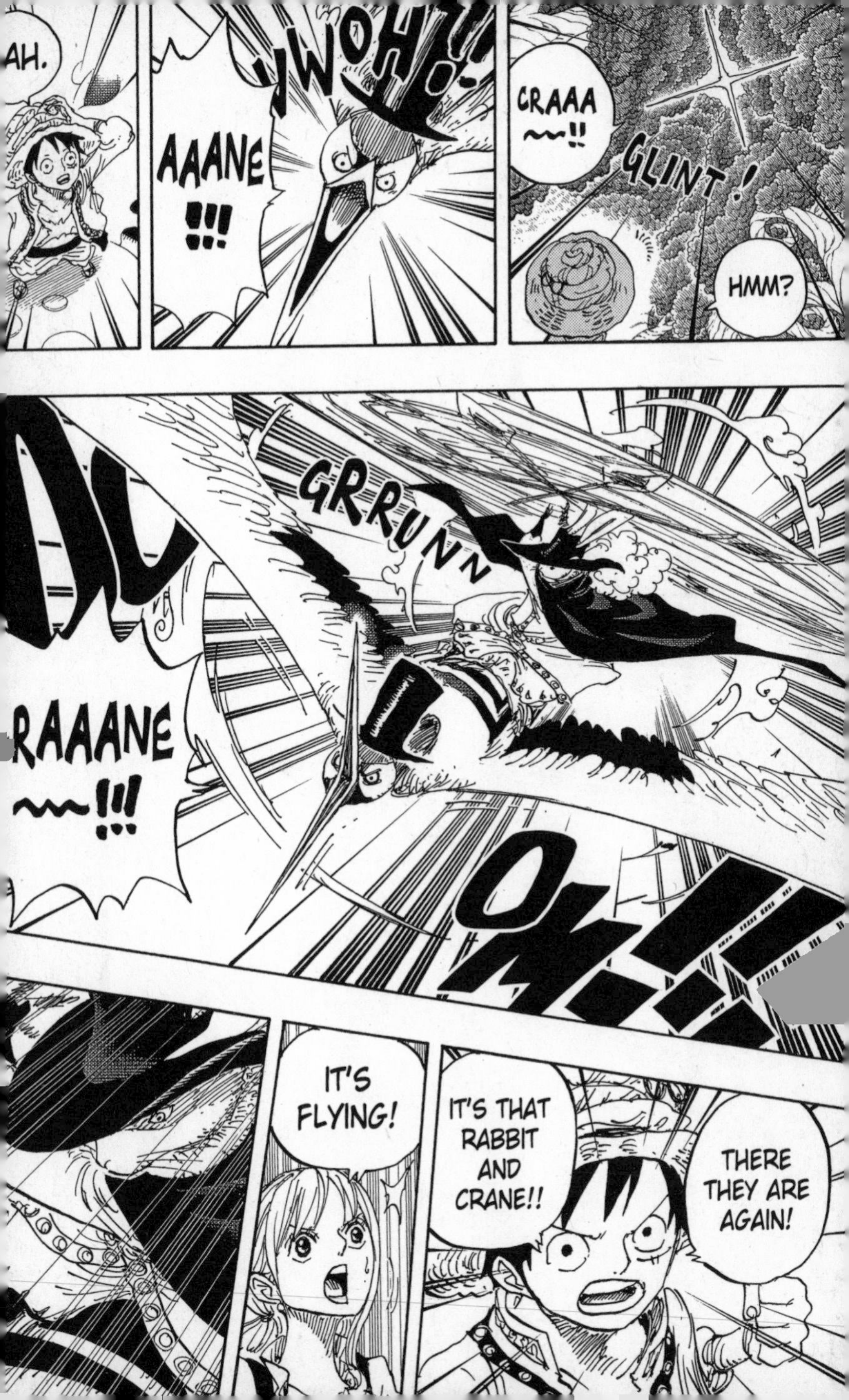
CRAAA ~~!!
GLINT!
HMM?
WOH!!
AAANE!!!
AH.
RAAANE ~~!!!
GRRUNN
OH!!
THERE THEY ARE AGAIN!
IT'S THAT RABBIT AND CRANE!!
IT'S FLYING!

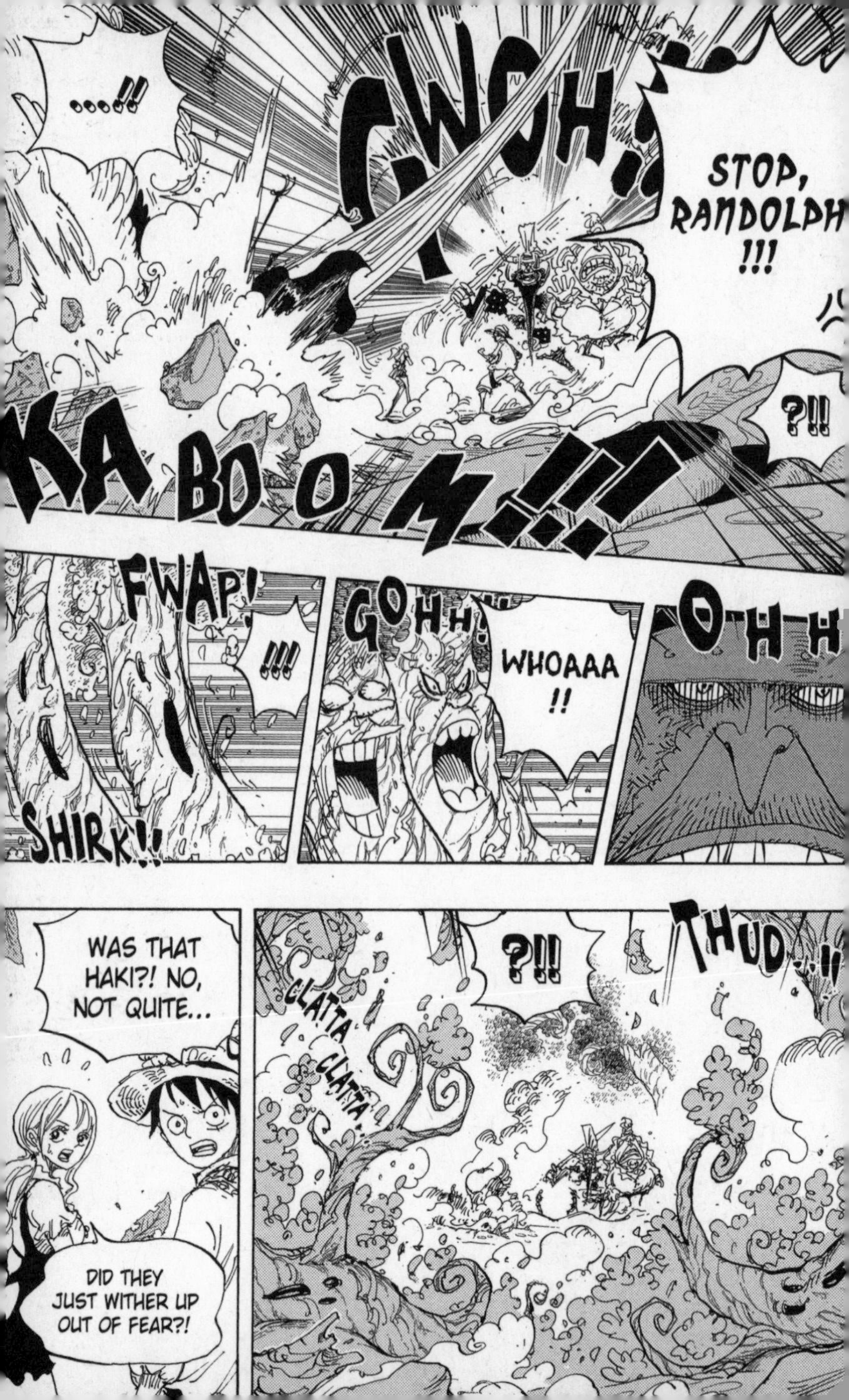
STOP, RANDOLPH!!!
GWOH..
...!!
?!!
KABOOM!!!
OHH
GOHH!!
WHOAAA!!
FWAP!
!!!
SHIRK!!
THUD..!!
?!!
CLATTA CLATTA
WAS THAT HAKI?! NO, NOT QUITE...
DID THEY JUST WITHER UP OUT OF FEAR?!

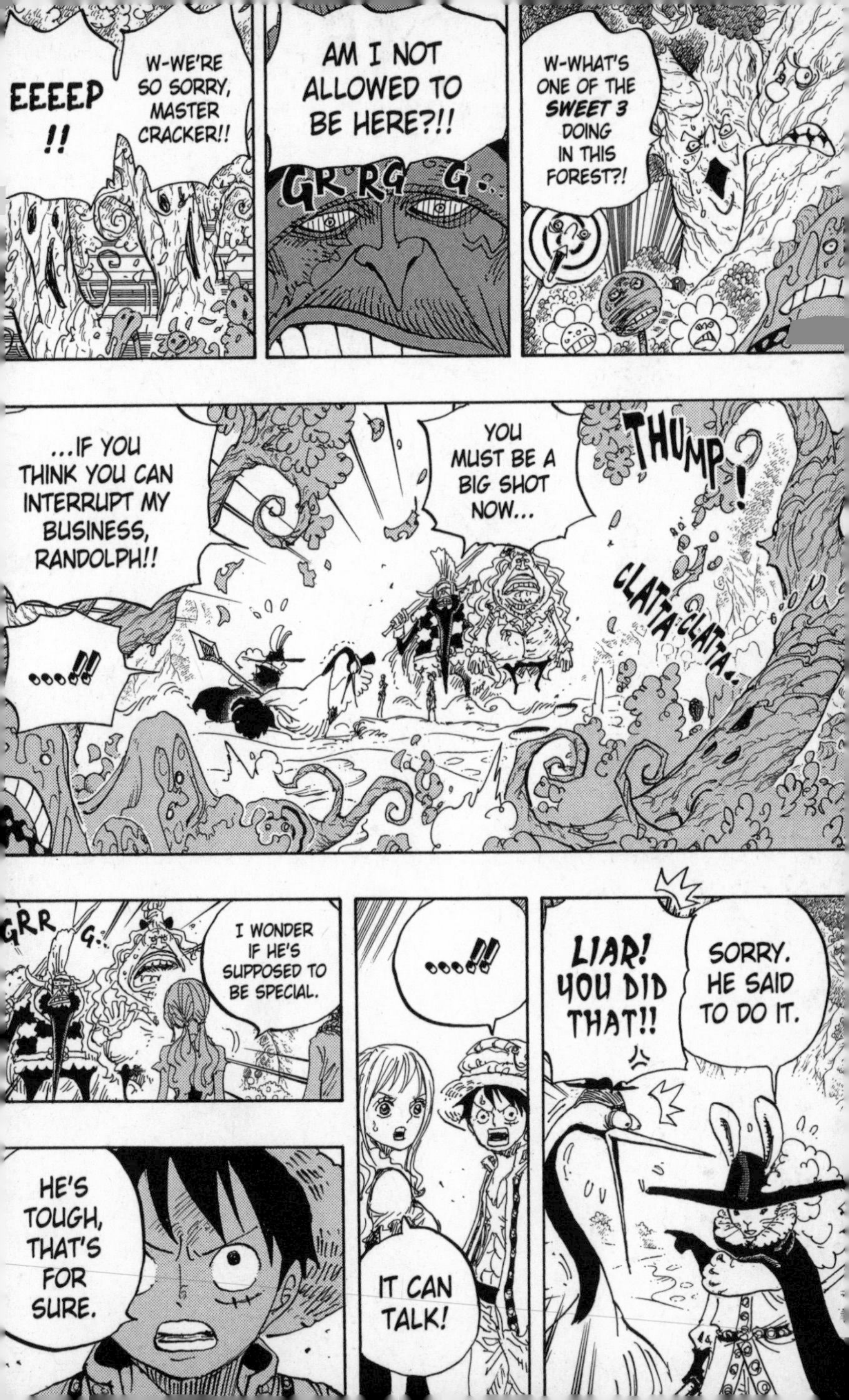
W-WHAT'S ONE OF THE SWEET 3 DOING IN THIS FOREST?!
GRRG G..
AM I NOT ALLOWED TO BE HERE?!!
W-WE'RE SO SORRY, MASTER CRACKER!!
EEEEP!!
THUMP!
YOU MUST BE A BIG SHOT NOW...
CLATTA CLATTA..
...IF YOU THINK YOU CAN INTERRUPT MY BUSINESS, RANDOLPH!!
...!!
SORRY. HE SAID TO DO IT.
LIAR! YOU DID THAT!!
...!!
IT CAN TALK!
I WONDER IF HE'S SUPPOSED TO BE SPECIAL.
GRR G..
HE'S TOUGH, THAT'S FOR SURE.

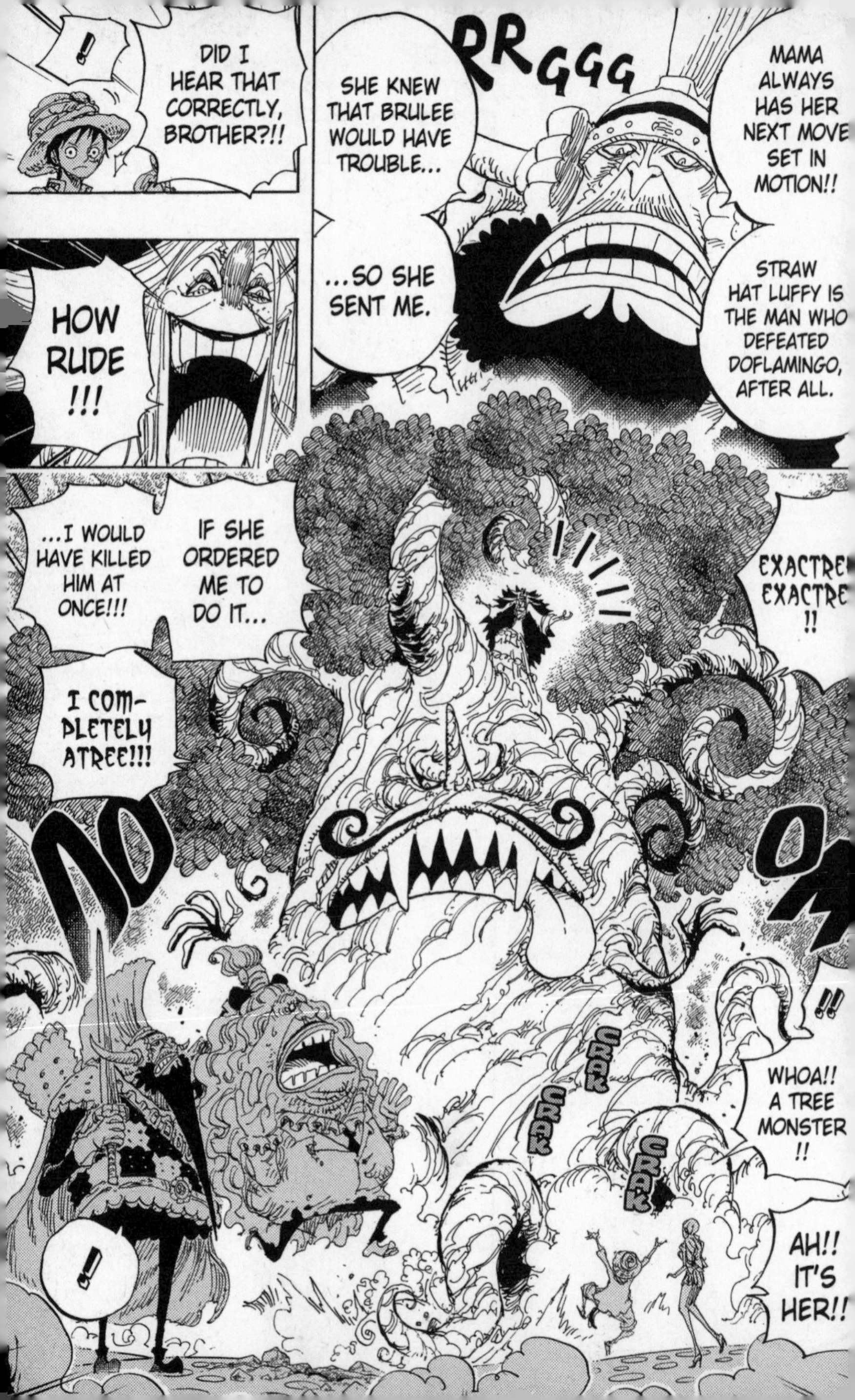
MAMA ALWAYS HAS HER NEXT MOVE SET IN MOTION!!
STRAW HAT LUFFY IS THE MAN WHO DEFEATED DOFLAMINGO, AFTER ALL.
RRGGG
SHE KNEW THAT BRULEE WOULD HAVE TROUBLE...
...SO SHE SENT ME.
DID I HEAR THAT CORRECTLY, BROTHER?!!
!
HOW RUDE!!!
EXACTRE EXACTRE!!
IF SHE ORDERED ME TO DO IT...
...I WOULD HAVE KILLED HIM AT ONCE!!!
I COMPLETELY ATREE!!!
OM
DO
!!
WHOA!! A TREE MONSTER!!
CRAK
CRAK
CRAK
AH!! IT'S HER!!
!

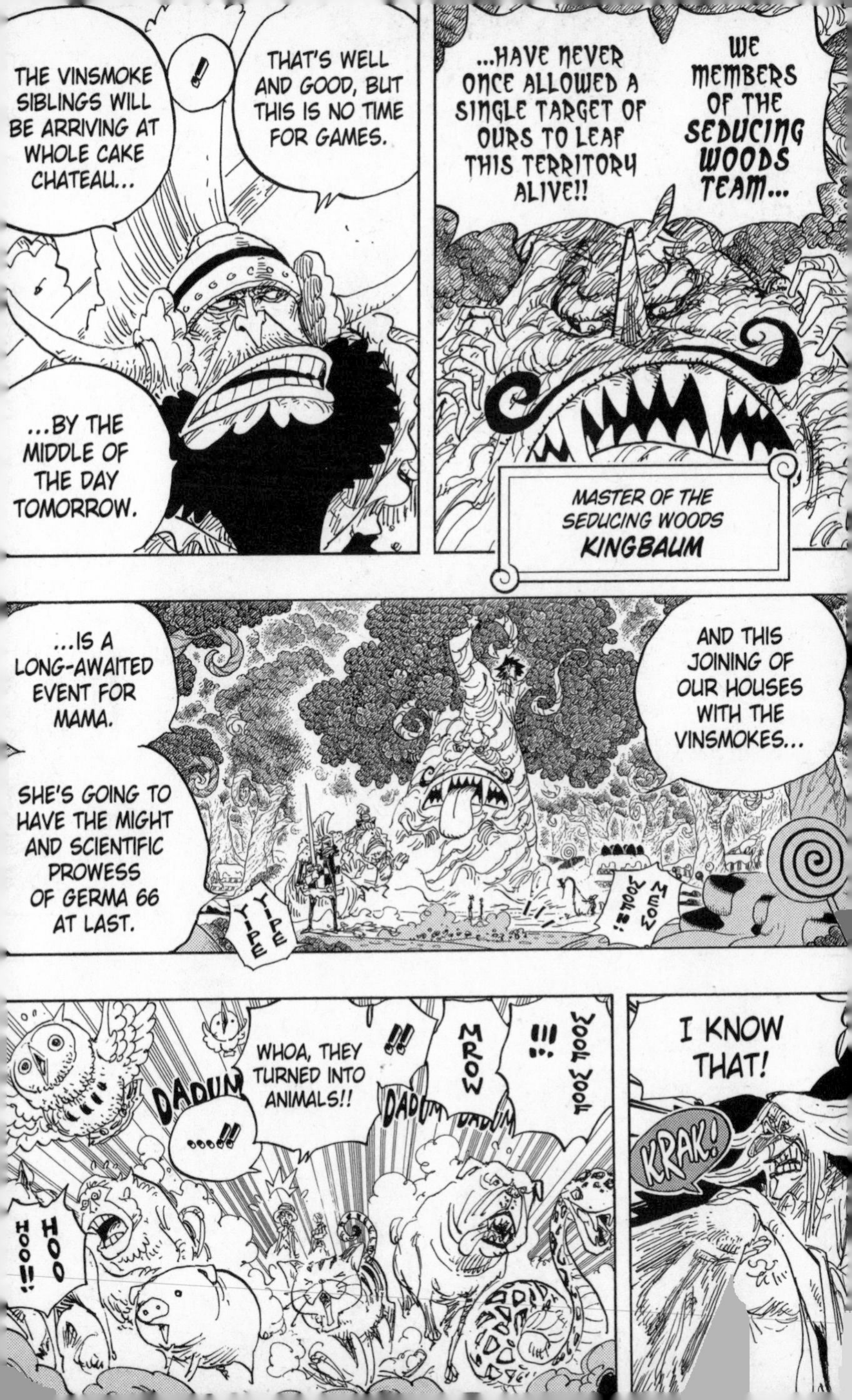
WE MEMBERS OF THE SEDUCING WOODS TEAM...
...HAVE NEVER ONCE ALLOWED A SINGLE TARGET OF OURS TO LEAF THIS TERRITORY ALIVE!!
MASTER OF THE SEDUCING WOODS KINGBAUM
THAT'S WELL AND GOOD, BUT THIS IS NO TIME FOR GAMES.
!
THE VINSMOKE SIBLINGS WILL BE ARRIVING AT WHOLE CAKE CHATEAU...
...BY THE MIDDLE OF THE DAY TOMORROW.
AND THIS JOINING OF OUR HOUSES WITH THE VINSMOKES...
MEOW
WOOF!!
YIPE YIPE
...IS A LONG-AWAITED EVENT FOR MAMA.
SHE'S GOING TO HAVE THE MIGHT AND SCIENTIFIC PROWESS OF GERMA 66 AT LAST.
I KNOW THAT!
KRAK!
WOOF WOOF
!!!
MROW
DADUM DADUM
!!
WHOA, THEY TURNED INTO ANIMALS!!
DADUM
...!!
HOO HOO!!

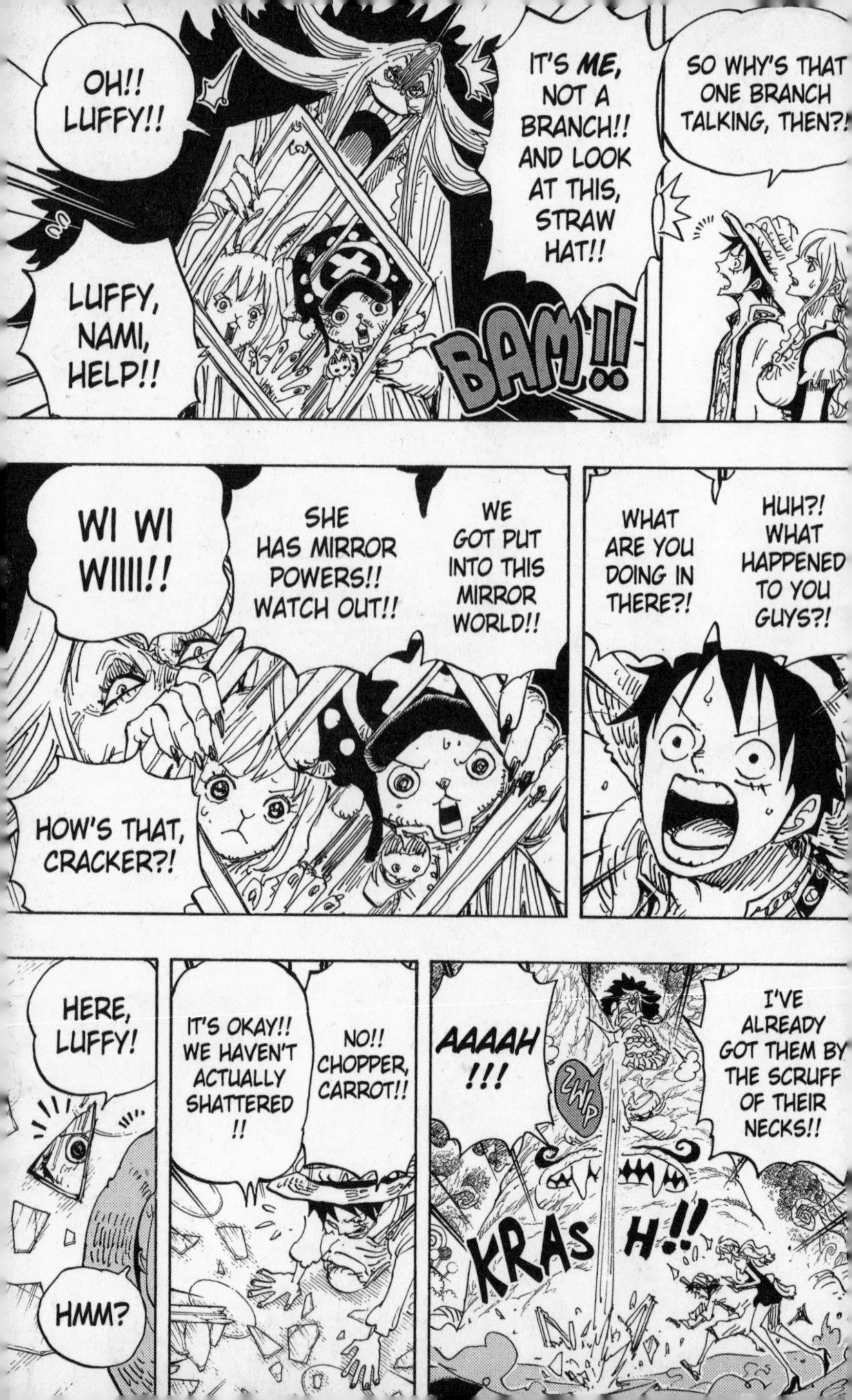
SO WHY'S THAT ONE BRANCH TALKING, THEN?!
IT'S ME, NOT A BRANCH!! AND LOOK AT THIS, STRAW HAT!!
OH!! LUFFY!!
BAM!!
LUFFY, NAMI, HELP!!
HUH?! WHAT HAPPENED TO YOU GUYS?!
WHAT ARE YOU DOING IN THERE?!
WE GOT PUT INTO THIS MIRROR WORLD!!
SHE HAS MIRROR POWERS!! WATCH OUT!!
WI WI WIIIII!!
HOW'S THAT, CRACKER?!
I'VE ALREADY GOT THEM BY THE SCRUFF OF THEIR NECKS!!
AAAAH!!!
ZWIP
KRASH!!
NO!! CHOPPER, CARROT!!
IT'S OKAY!! WE HAVEN'T ACTUALLY SHATTERED!!
HERE, LUFFY!
HMM?

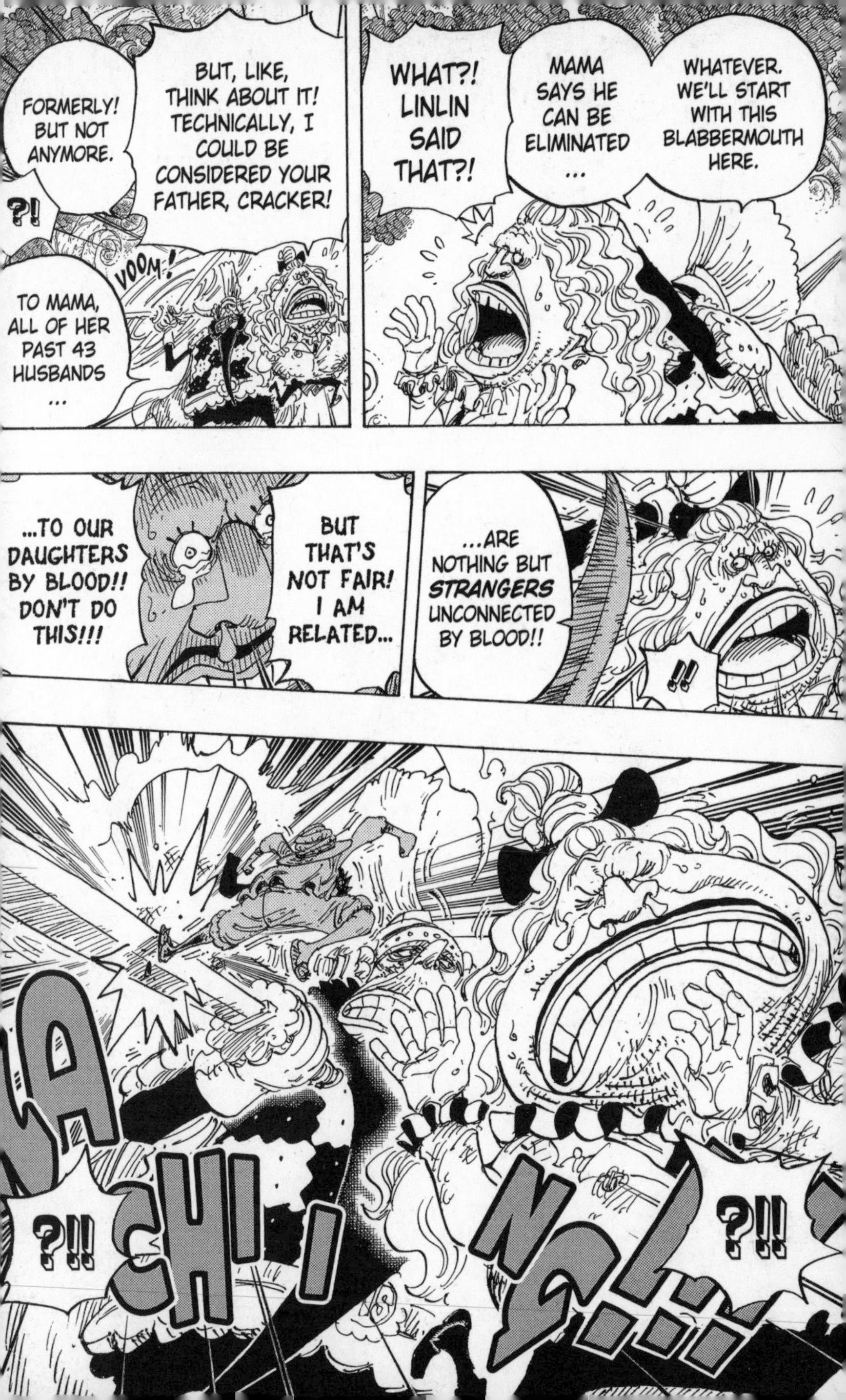
WHATEVER. WE'LL START WITH THIS BLABBERMOUTH HERE.
MAMA SAYS HE CAN BE ELIMINATED ...
WHAT?! LINLIN SAID THAT?!
BUT, LIKE, THINK ABOUT IT! TECHNICALLY, I COULD BE CONSIDERED YOUR FATHER, CRACKER!
FORMERLY! BUT NOT ANYMORE.
?!
VOOM!
TO MAMA, ALL OF HER PAST 43 HUSBANDS ...
...ARE NOTHING BUT *STRANGERS* UNCONNECTED BY BLOOD!!
!!
BUT THAT'S NOT FAIR! I AM RELATED...
...TO OUR DAUGHTERS BY BLOOD!! DON'T DO THIS!!!
?!!
A CHI N...
?!!

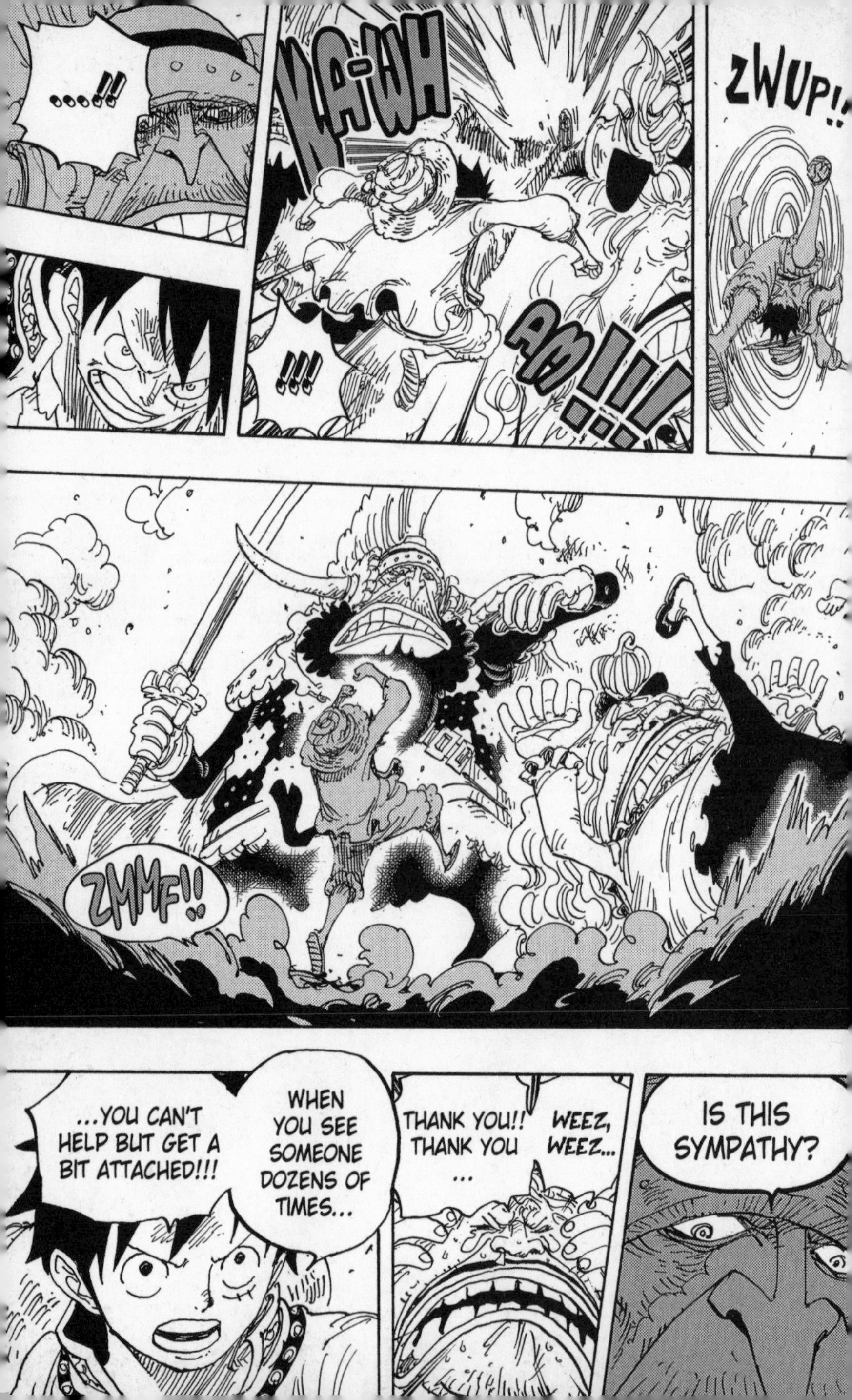
ZWUP!!
KA-WH
AM!!!!
!!!
....!!
ZMMF!!
IS THIS SYMPATHY?
WEEZ, WEEZ...
THANK YOU!! THANK YOU ...
WHEN YOU SEE SOMEONE DOZENS OF TIMES...
...YOU CAN'T HELP BUT GET A BIT ATTACHED!!!

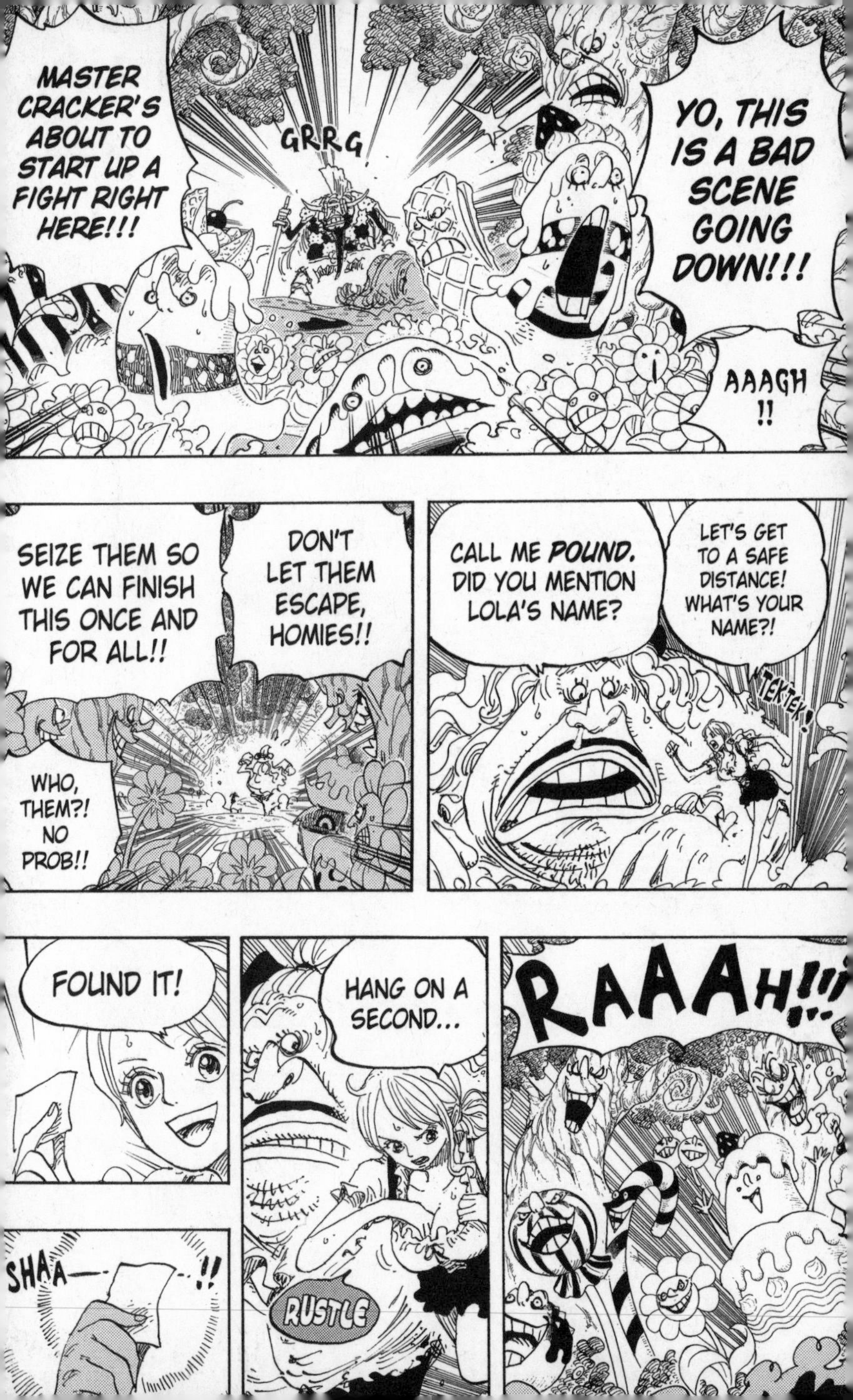
YO, THIS IS A BAD SCENE GOING DOWN!!!
GRRG
MASTER CRACKER'S ABOUT TO START UP A FIGHT RIGHT HERE!!!
AAAGH!!
LET'S GET TO A SAFE DISTANCE! WHAT'S YOUR NAME?!
CALL ME *POUND.* DID YOU MENTION LOLA'S NAME?
TEK TEK!
DON'T LET THEM ESCAPE, HOMIES!!
SEIZE THEM SO WE CAN FINISH THIS ONCE AND FOR ALL!!
WHO, THEM?! NO PROB!!
RAAAH!!!
HANG ON A SECOND...
RUSTLE
FOUND IT!
SHAA—!!

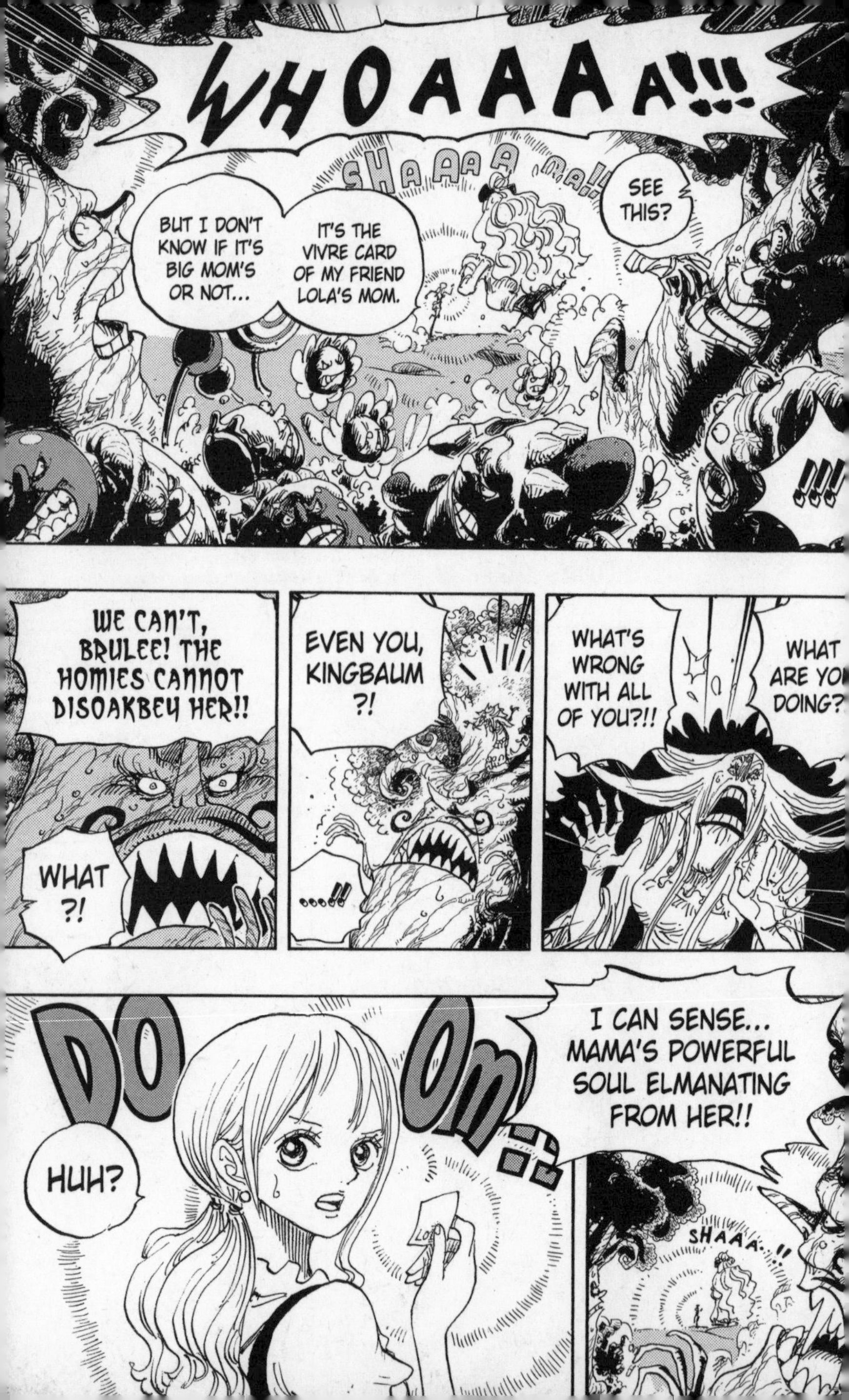
WHOAAAA!!!
SEE THIS?
SHAAAAMA!!
IT'S THE VIVRE CARD OF MY FRIEND LOLA'S MOM.
BUT I DON'T KNOW IF IT'S BIG MOM'S OR NOT...
!!!
WHAT ARE YO DOING?
WHAT'S WRONG WITH ALL OF YOU?!!
EVEN YOU, KINGBAUM ?!
...!!
WE CAN'T, BRULEE! THE HOMIES CANNOT DISOAKBEY HER!!
WHAT ?!
I CAN SENSE... MAMA'S POWERFUL SOUL ELMANATING FROM HER!!
SHAAA...!!
DOOM..!!
HUH?

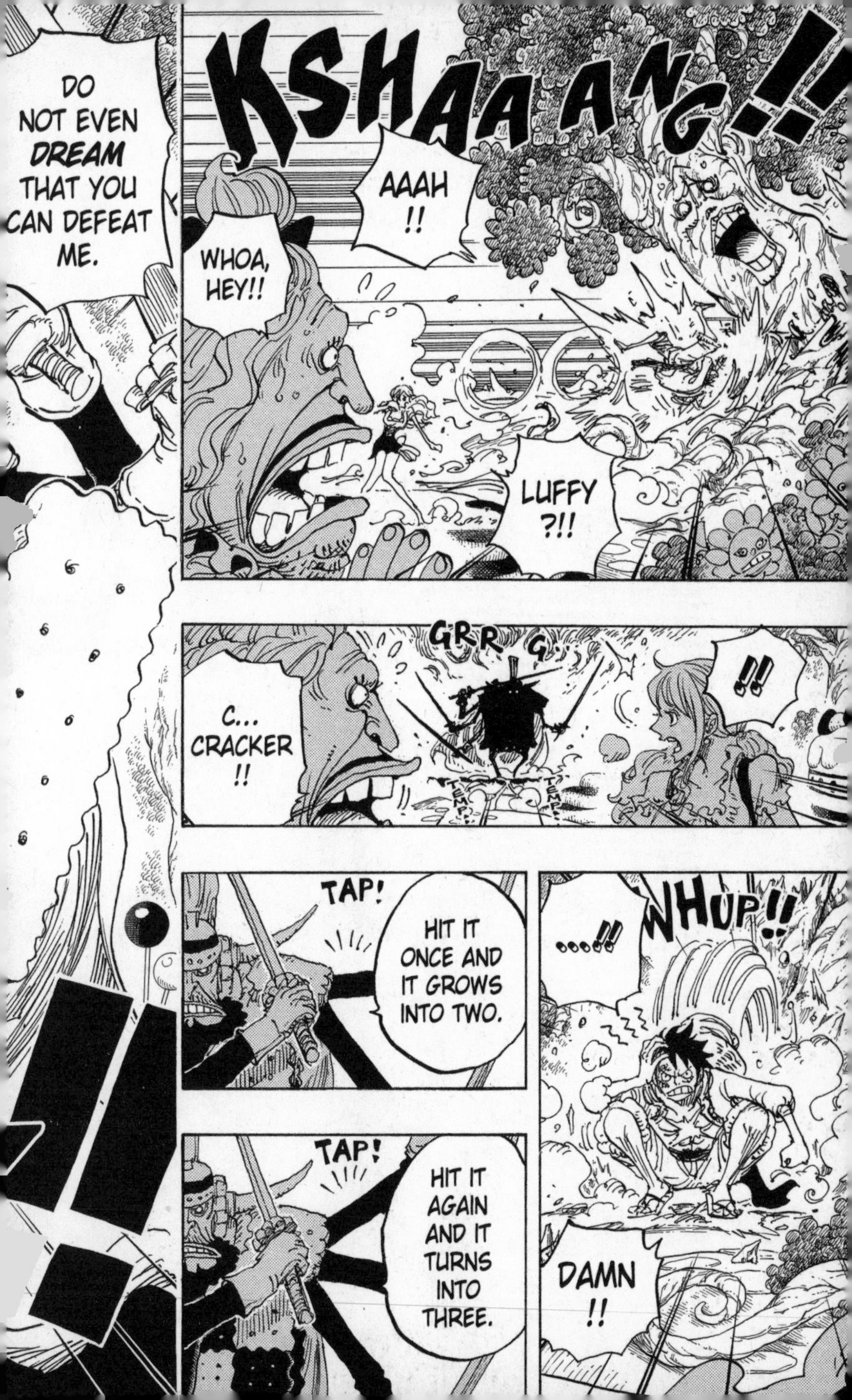
KSHAAANG!!
AAAH!!
WHOA, HEY!!
LUFFY?!!
GRRG
!!
C... CRACKER!!
TEMP...
TEMP...
WHUP!!
....!!
DAMN!!
TAP!
HIT IT ONCE AND IT GROWS INTO TWO.
TAP!
HIT IT AGAIN AND IT TURNS INTO THREE.
DO NOT EVEN *DREAM* THAT YOU CAN DEFEAT ME.

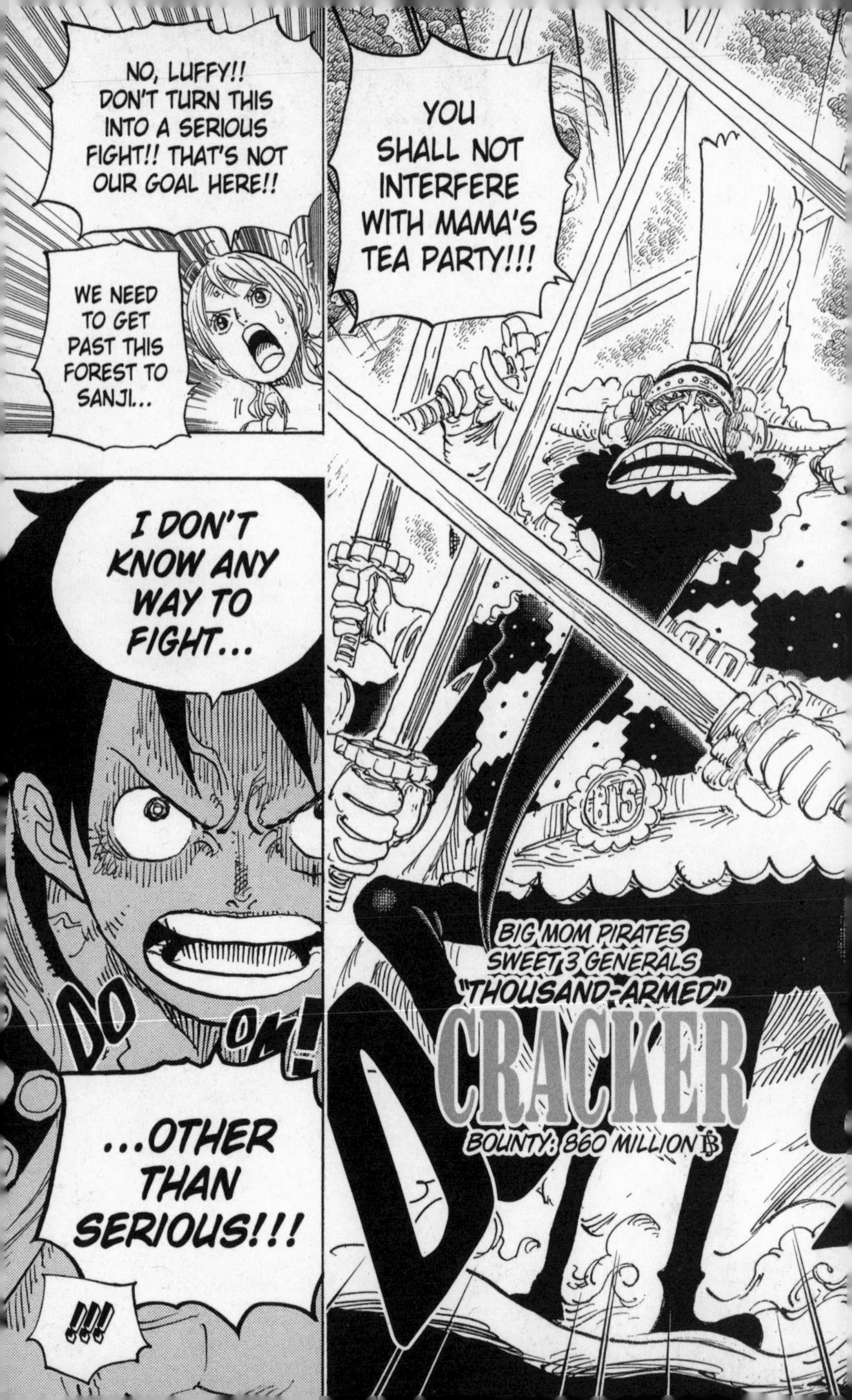

YOU SHALL NOT INTERFERE WITH MAMA'S TEA PARTY!!!
BIG MOM PIRATES
SWEET 3 GENERALS
"THOUSAND-ARMED"
CRACKER
BOUNTY: 860 MILLION ฿
NO, LUFFY!! DON'T TURN THIS INTO A SERIOUS FIGHT!! THAT'S NOT OUR GOAL HERE!!
WE NEED TO GET PAST THIS FOREST TO SANJI...
I DON'T KNOW ANY WAY TO FIGHT...
DOOM!
...OTHER THAN SERIOUS!!!
!!!

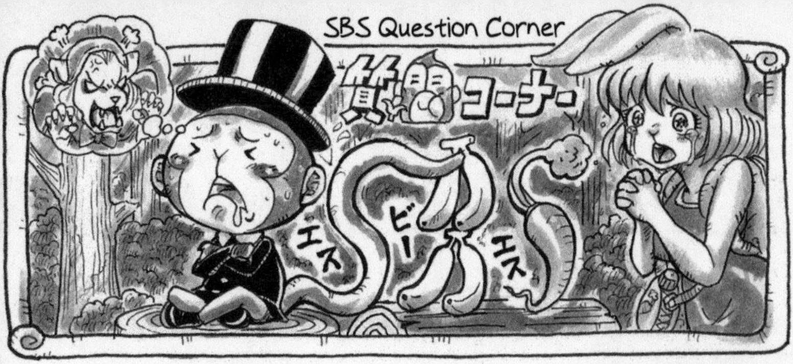
SBS Question Corner
質問コーナー
エス
ビー
エス

(Hippo Iron, Saitama)

Q: Heso, Mr. Oda!! Pumpkins are a special crop in Skypiea. And it was Noland the botanist who introduced the pumpkin to Jaya, the original island, correct? And I've noticed there are plenty of pumpkins in Dressrosa too! Is it possible that when Noland met the Tontattas on his travels, he learned how to grow pumpkins from them? Tell me!

--Kamiki

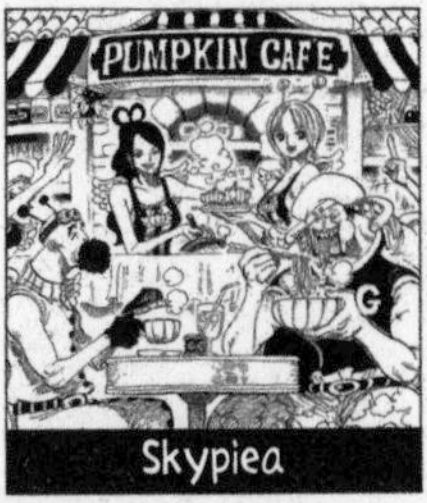
PUMPKIN CAFE
Skypiea

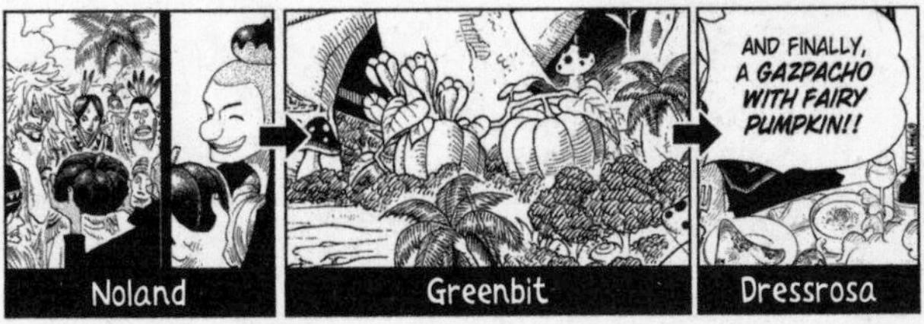
AND FINALLY, A GAZPACHO WITH FAIRY PUMPKIN!!
Noland
Greenbit
Dressrosa

A: That's correct--perfect answer. Pumpkins are very nutritious, so it looks like the crop took root wherever Noland brought it. Perhaps it's a sign of the trust he earned from those he met too.

Q: I have a question about Vito the Phantom Gun from the Firetank Pirates. He's got extraordinarily large hands, but his suit seems to be normal-sized. So how does he get his hands through the sleeves?

--Stark Yohn

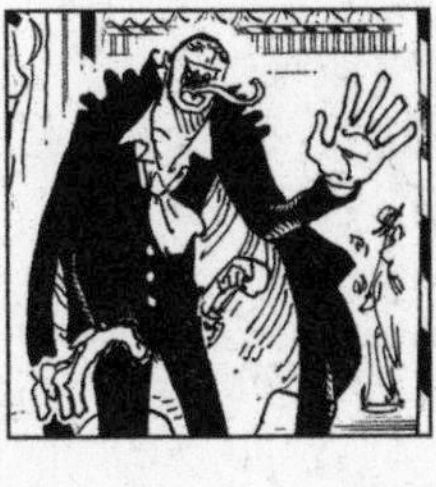

A: Like this!!

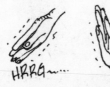

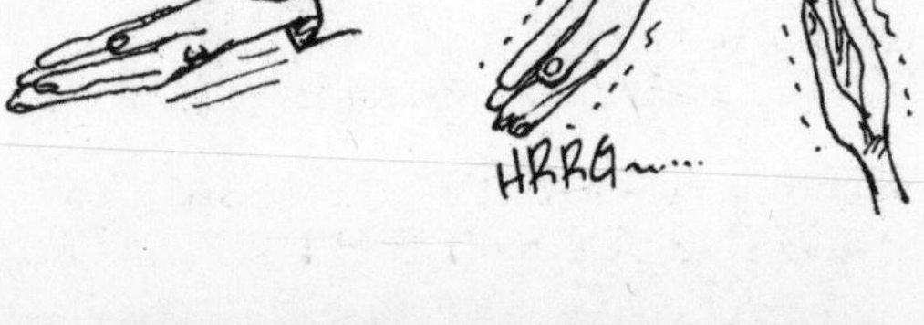
HRRG~....

Chapter 837: LUFFY VS. CRACKER THE GENERAL

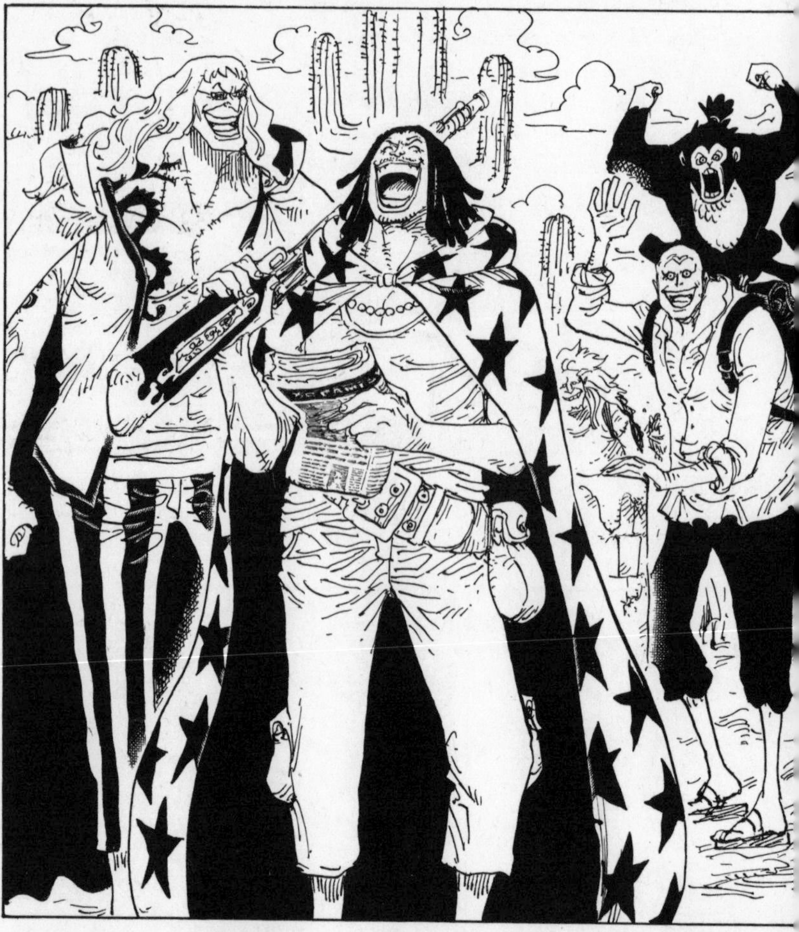

DECKS OF THE WORLD, 500-MILLION-MAN ARC, VOL. 24:
"A CERTAIN RUINED ISLAND--RED-HAIR PIRATES"

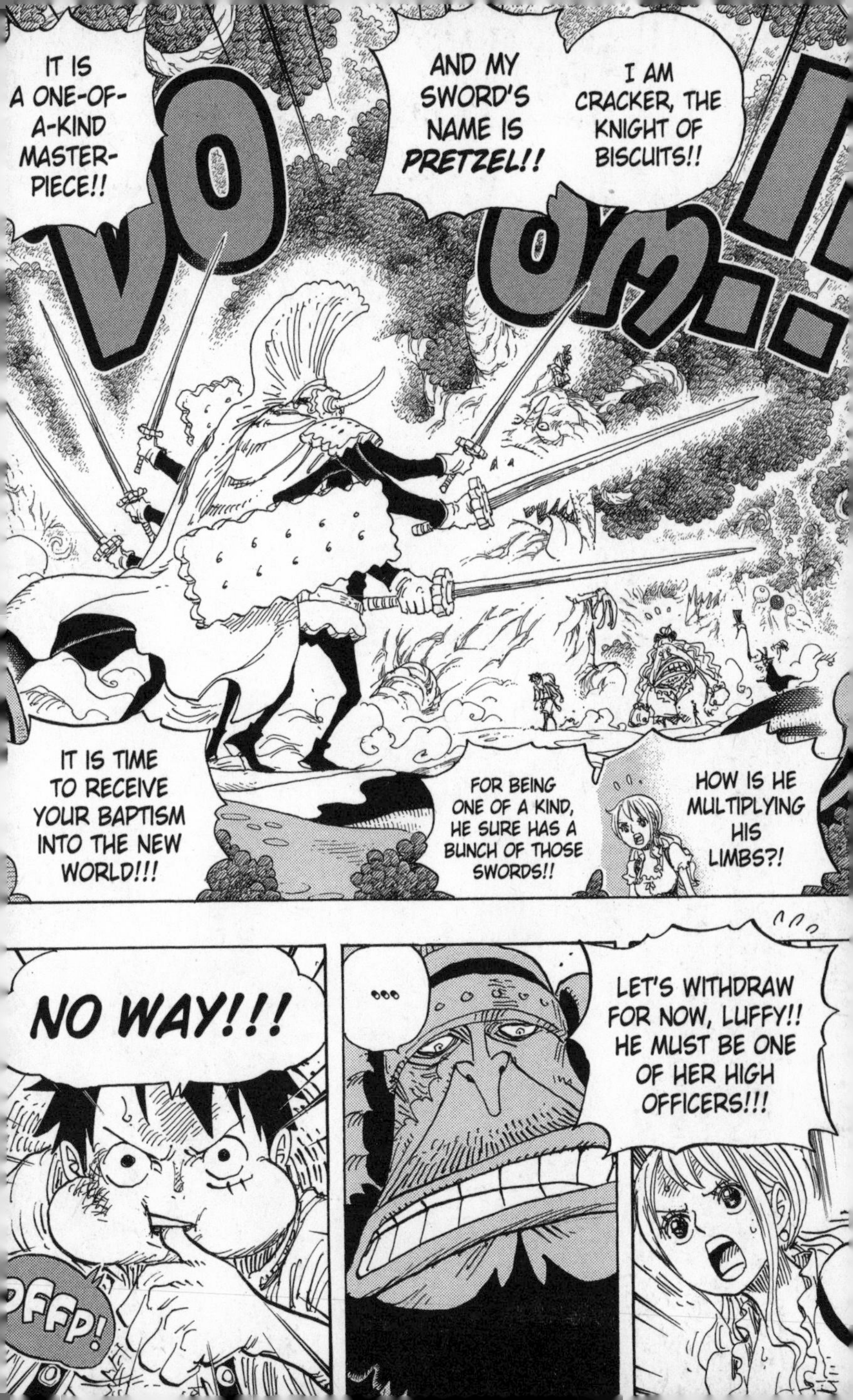
I AM CRACKER, THE KNIGHT OF BISCUITS!!
AND MY SWORD'S NAME IS PRETZEL!!
IT IS A ONE-OF-A-KIND MASTERPIECE!!
VOOM!!
HOW IS HE MULTIPLYING HIS LIMBS?!
FOR BEING ONE OF A KIND, HE SURE HAS A BUNCH OF THOSE SWORDS!!
IT IS TIME TO RECEIVE YOUR BAPTISM INTO THE NEW WORLD!!!
LET'S WITHDRAW FOR NOW, LUFFY!! HE MUST BE ONE OF HER HIGH OFFICERS!!!
...
NO WAY!!!
FFP!

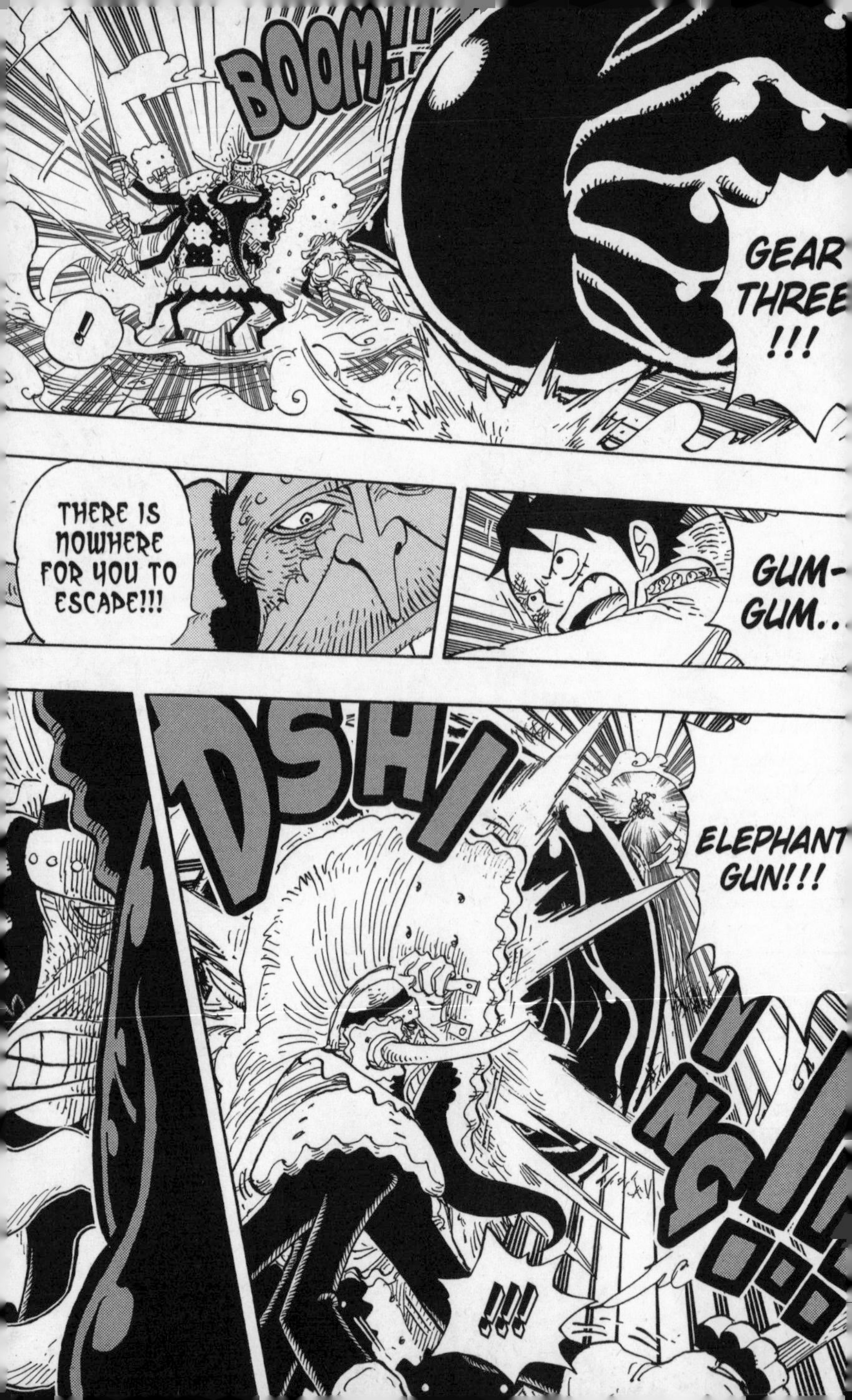
GEAR THREE!!!
BOOM!!
!
GUM-GUM...
THERE IS NOWHERE FOR YOU TO ESCAPE!!!
ELEPHANT GUN!!!
DSHING!!
!!!

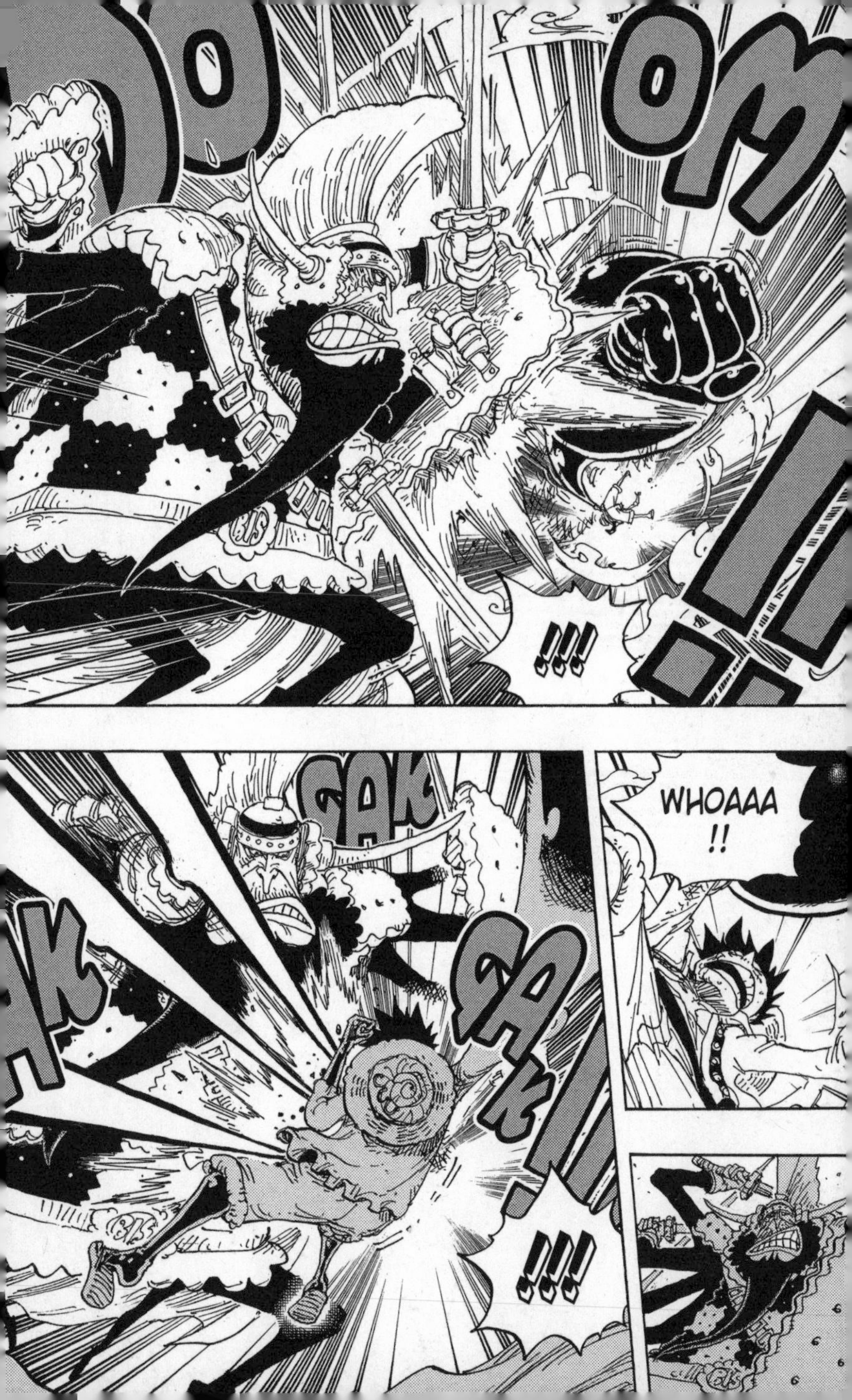
OOM
!!!
WHOAAA !!
GAK
GAK
!!!

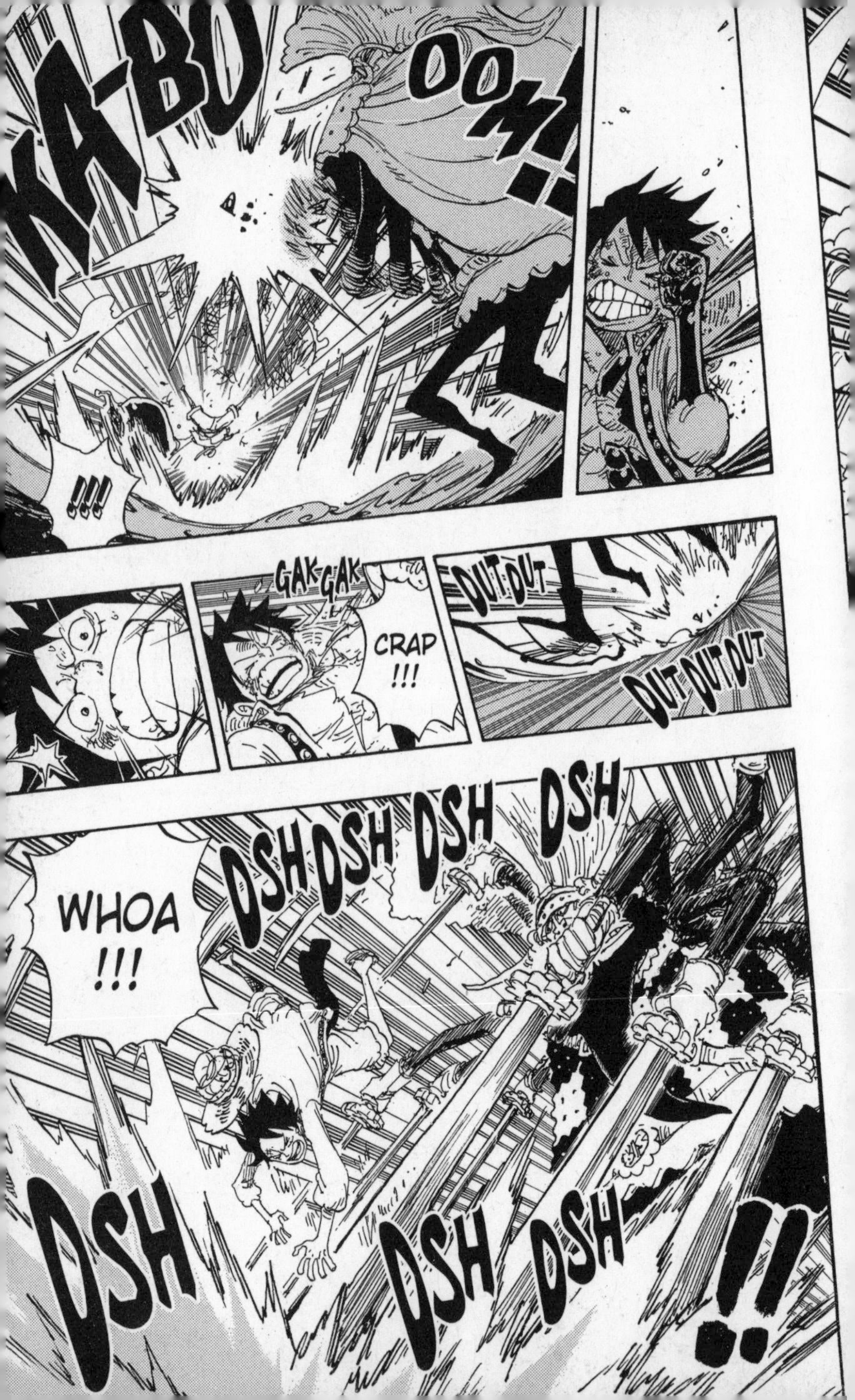

KA-BOOOOM!!
!!!
DUT DUT
DUT DUT DUT
GAK GAK
CRAP !!!
DSH DSH DSH DSH
WHOA !!!
DSH
DSH DSH!!

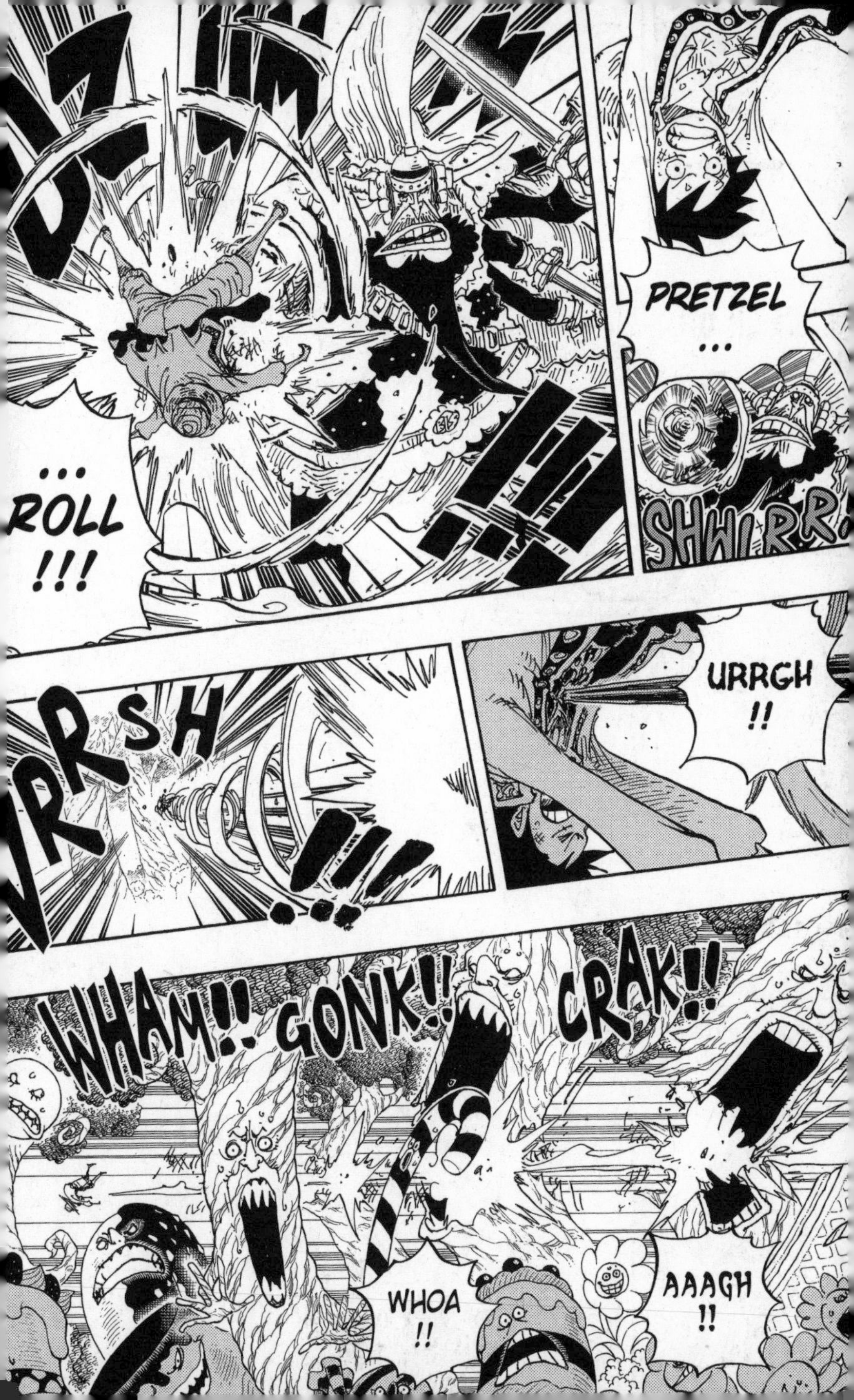
PRETZEL ...
SHWIRR
... ROLL !!!
URRGH !!
VRRSH
CRAK!!
GONK!!
WHAM!!
AAAGH !!
WHOA !!

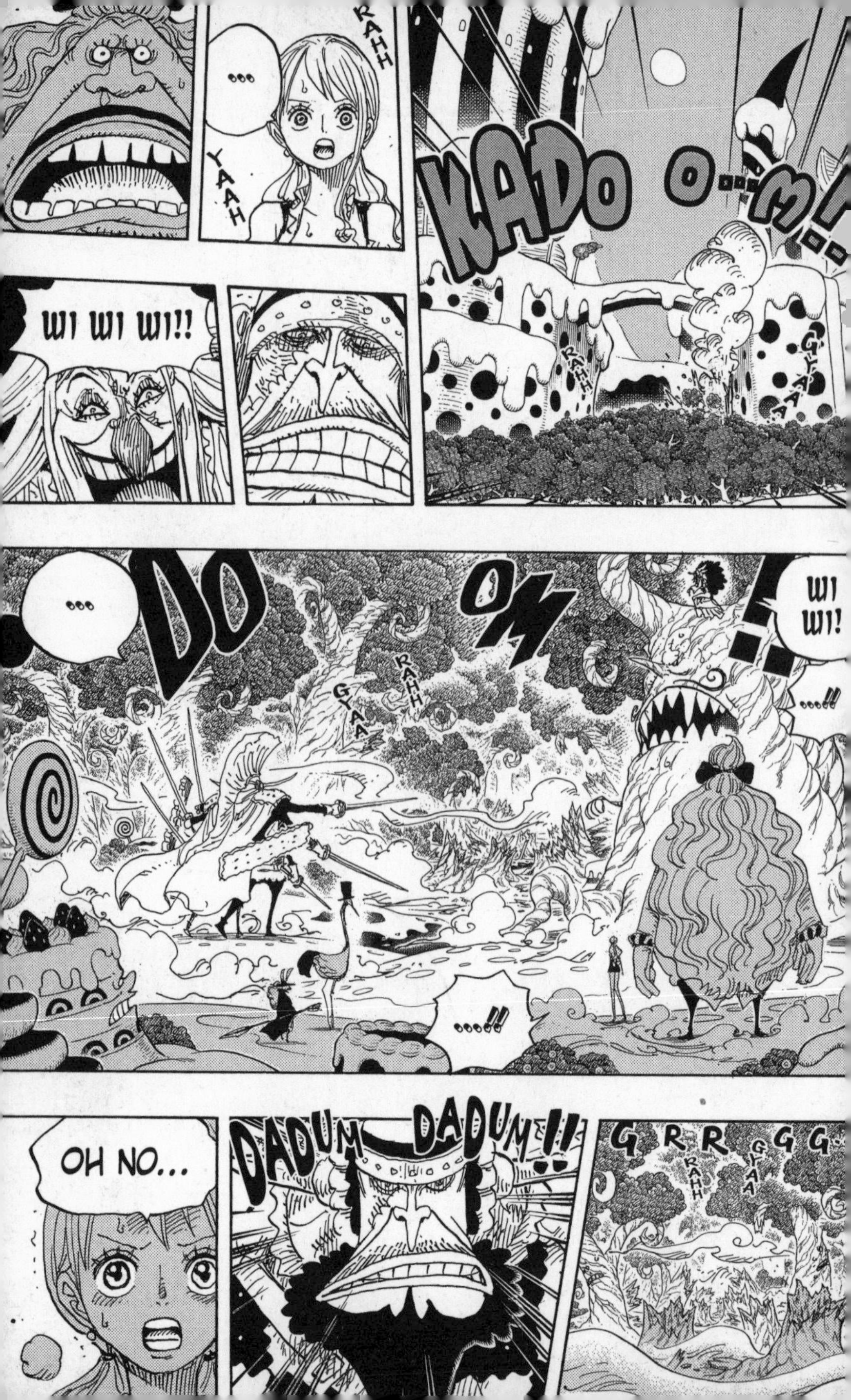
KADO O...M!!
RAHH
GYAAA
...
RAHH
YAAH
WI WI WI!!
WI WI!
...!!
DOON!!
RAHH
GYAA
...
...!!
GRRRGG
RAHH
GYAA
DADUM DADUM!!
OH NO...

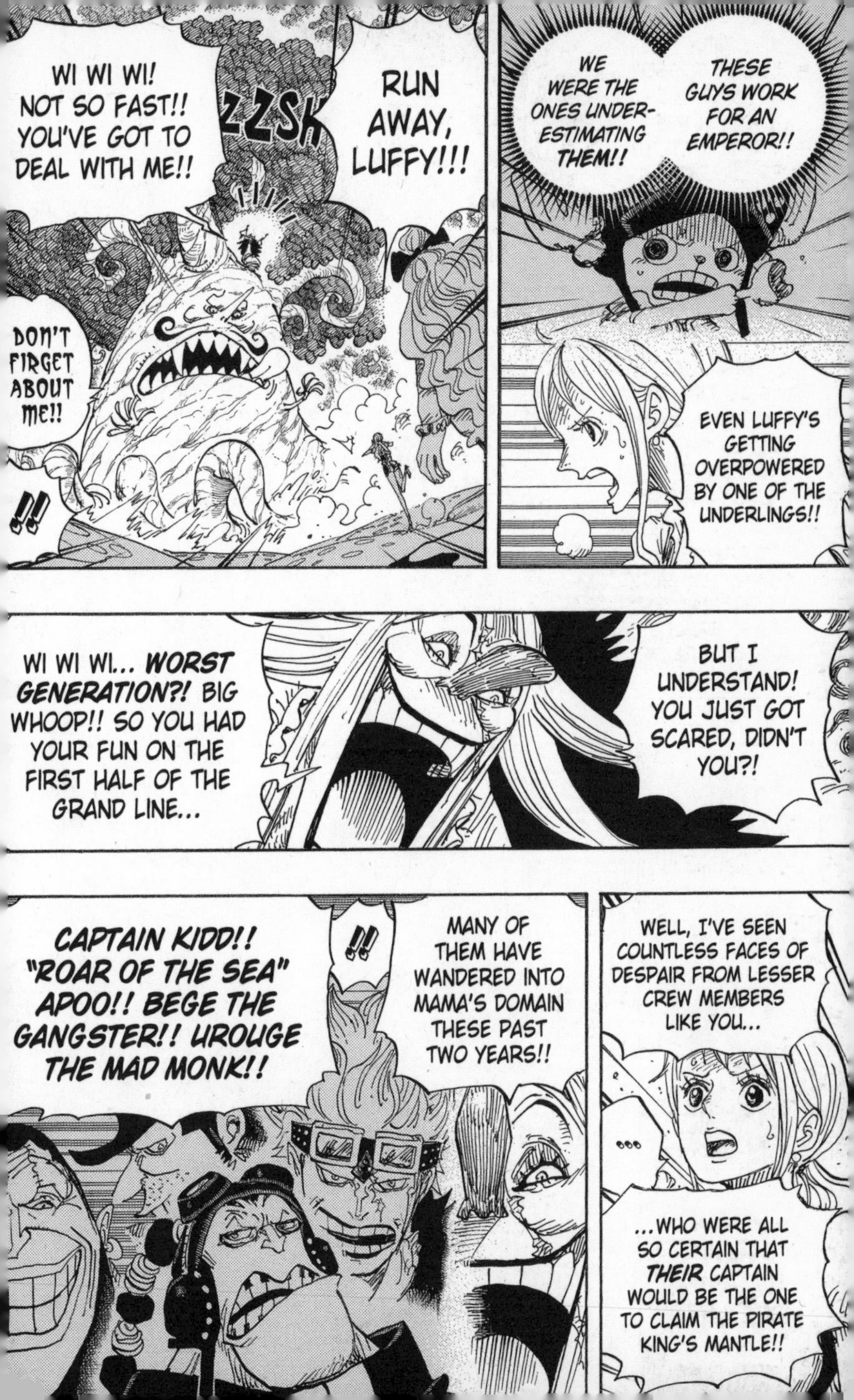
THESE GUYS WORK FOR AN EMPEROR!!
WE WERE THE ONES UNDER-ESTIMATING THEM!!
EVEN LUFFY'S GETTING OVERPOWERED BY ONE OF THE UNDERLINGS!!
RUN AWAY, LUFFY!!!
ZZSH
WI WI WI! NOT SO FAST!! YOU'VE GOT TO DEAL WITH ME!!
DON'T FIRGET ABOUT ME!!
!!
BUT I UNDERSTAND! YOU JUST GOT SCARED, DIDN'T YOU?!
WI WI WI... *WORST GENERATION?!* BIG WHOOP!! SO YOU HAD YOUR FUN ON THE FIRST HALF OF THE GRAND LINE...
WELL, I'VE SEEN COUNTLESS FACES OF DESPAIR FROM LESSER CREW MEMBERS LIKE YOU...
...
...WHO WERE ALL SO CERTAIN THAT *THEIR* CAPTAIN WOULD BE THE ONE TO CLAIM THE PIRATE KING'S MANTLE!!
MANY OF THEM HAVE WANDERED INTO MAMA'S DOMAIN THESE PAST TWO YEARS!!
!!
CAPTAIN KIDD!! "ROAR OF THE SEA" APOO!! BEGE THE GANGSTER!! UROUGE THE MAD MONK!!

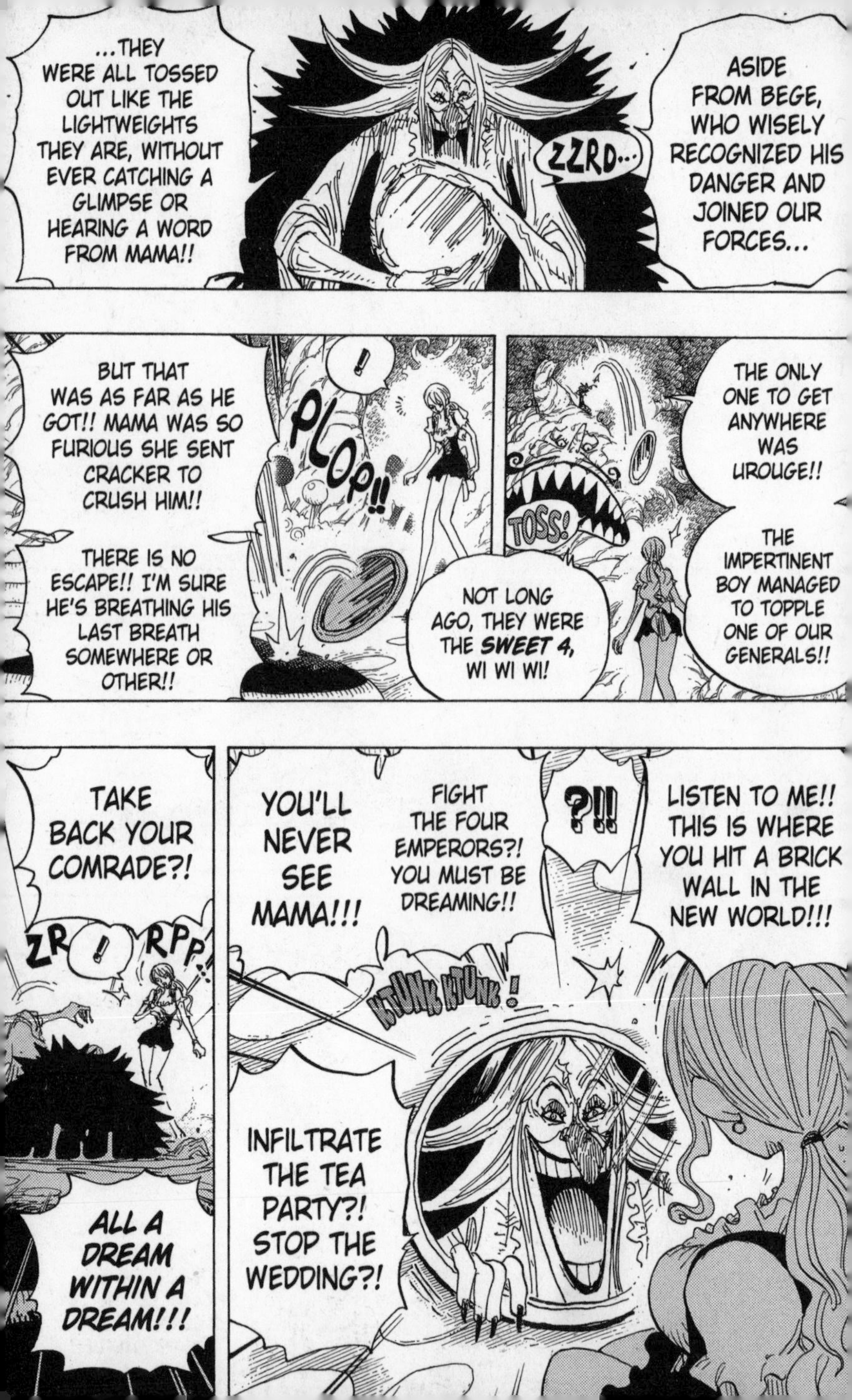
ASIDE FROM BEGE, WHO WISELY RECOGNIZED HIS DANGER AND JOINED OUR FORCES...
ZZRD...
...THEY WERE ALL TOSSED OUT LIKE THE LIGHTWEIGHTS THEY ARE, WITHOUT EVER CATCHING A GLIMPSE OR HEARING A WORD FROM MAMA!!
THE ONLY ONE TO GET ANYWHERE WAS UROUGE!!
THE IMPERTINENT BOY MANAGED TO TOPPLE ONE OF OUR GENERALS!!
TOSS!
NOT LONG AGO, THEY WERE THE ***SWEET 4***, WI WI WI!
!
PLOP!!
BUT THAT WAS AS FAR AS HE GOT!! MAMA WAS SO FURIOUS SHE SENT CRACKER TO CRUSH HIM!!
THERE IS NO ESCAPE!! I'M SURE HE'S BREATHING HIS LAST BREATH SOMEWHERE OR OTHER!!
LISTEN TO ME!! THIS IS WHERE YOU HIT A BRICK WALL IN THE NEW WORLD!!!
?!!
FIGHT THE FOUR EMPERORS?! YOU MUST BE DREAMING!!
YOU'LL NEVER SEE MAMA!!!
KTUNK KTUNK!
INFILTRATE THE TEA PARTY?! STOP THE WEDDING?!
TAKE BACK YOUR COMRADE?!
ZRRPP
!
ALL A DREAM WITHIN A DREAM!!!

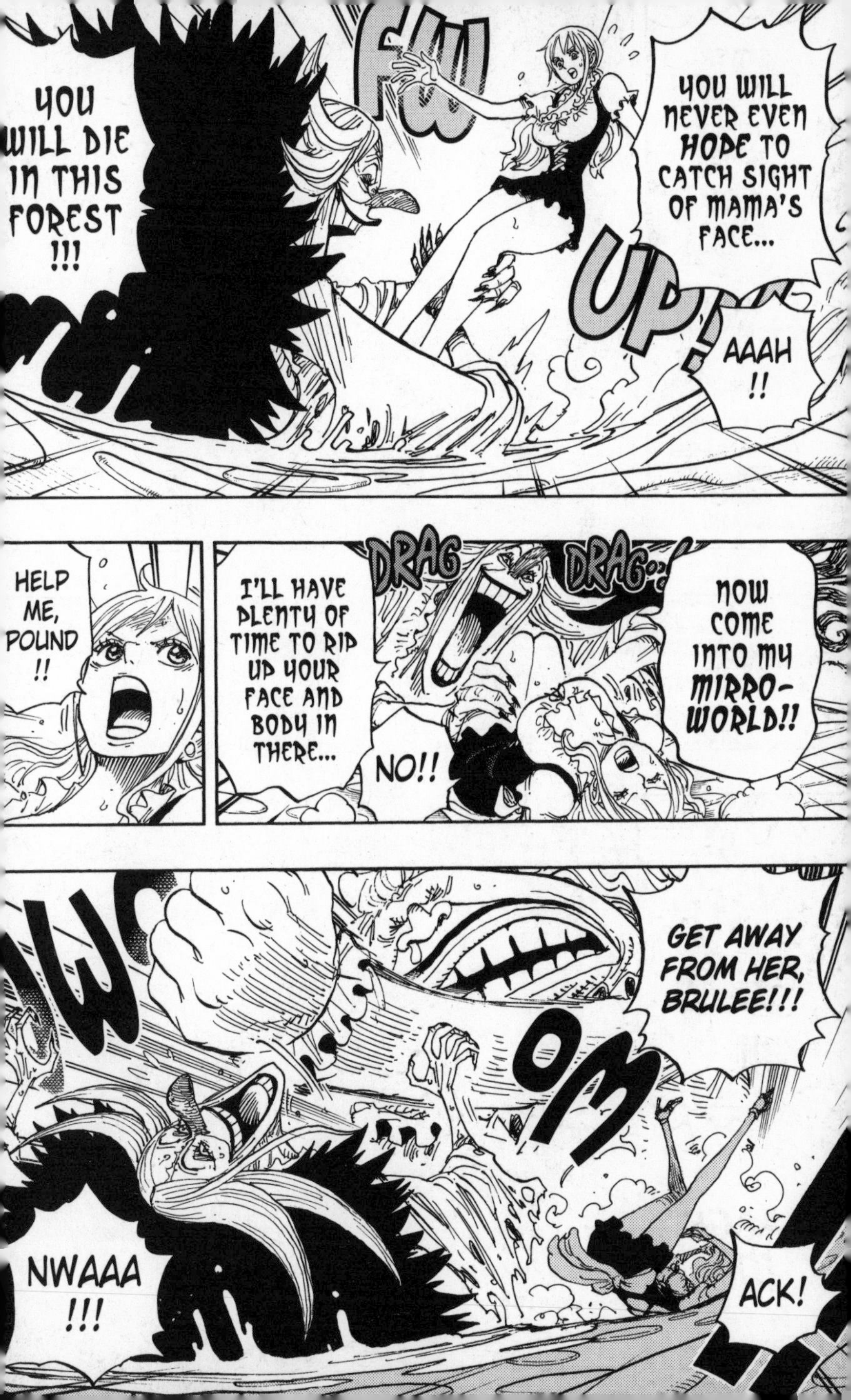
YOU WILL NEVER EVEN HOPE TO CATCH SIGHT OF MAMA'S FACE...
YOU WILL DIE IN THIS FOREST!!!
AAAH!!
NOW COME INTO MY MIRRO-WORLD!!
DRAG
DRAG
I'LL HAVE PLENTY OF TIME TO RIP UP YOUR FACE AND BODY IN THERE...
NO!!
HELP ME, POUND!!
GET AWAY FROM HER, BRULEE!!!
ACK!
NWAAA!!!

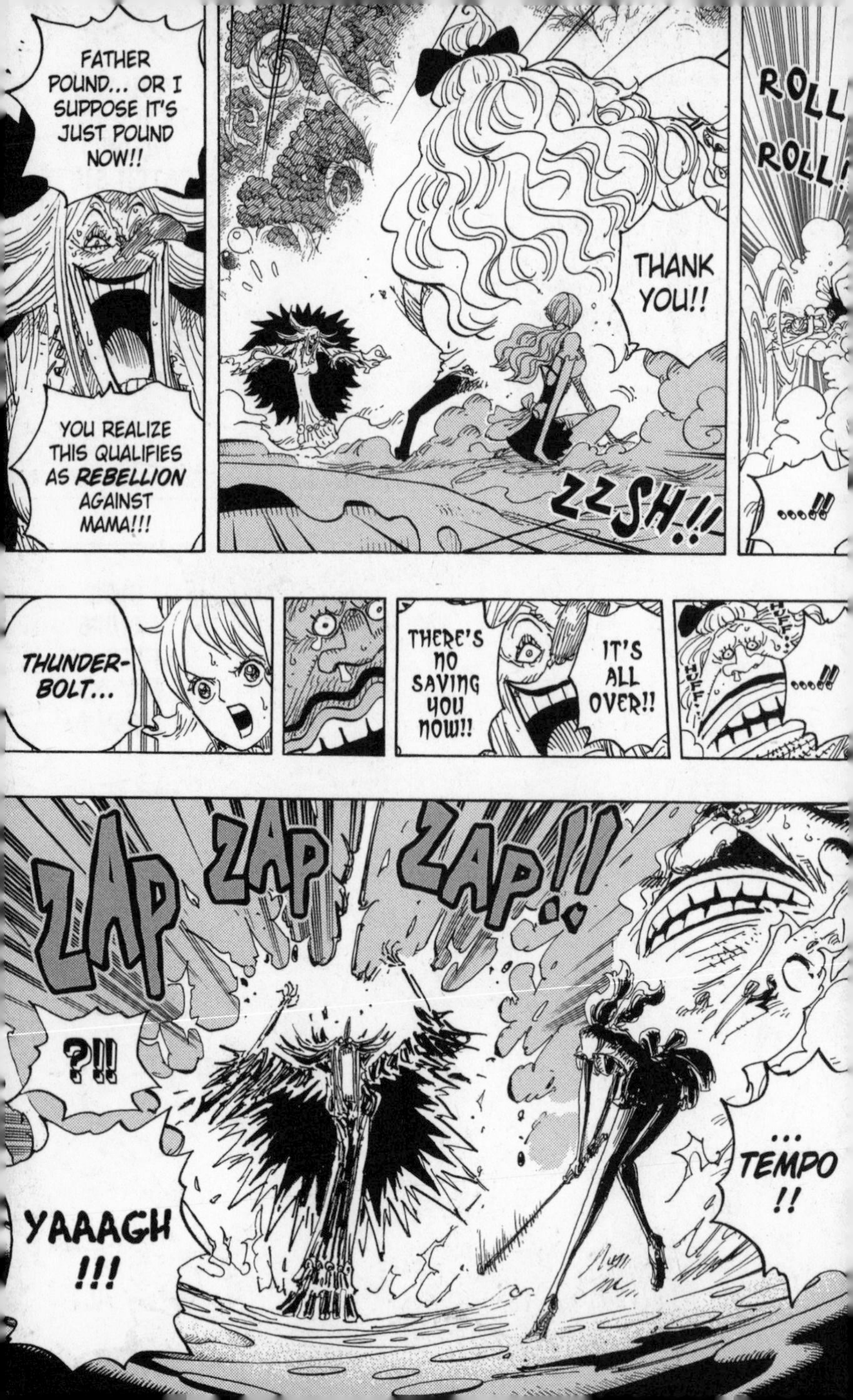
ROLL ROLL!!
...!!
THANK YOU!!
ZZSH!!
FATHER POUND... OR I SUPPOSE IT'S JUST POUND NOW!!
YOU REALIZE THIS QUALIFIES AS *REBELLION* AGAINST MAMA!!!
HUFF HUFF
...!!
IT'S ALL OVER!!
THERE'S NO SAVING YOU NOW!!
THUNDER-BOLT...
ZAP ZAP ZAP!!
...TEMPO!!
?!!
YAAAGH!!!

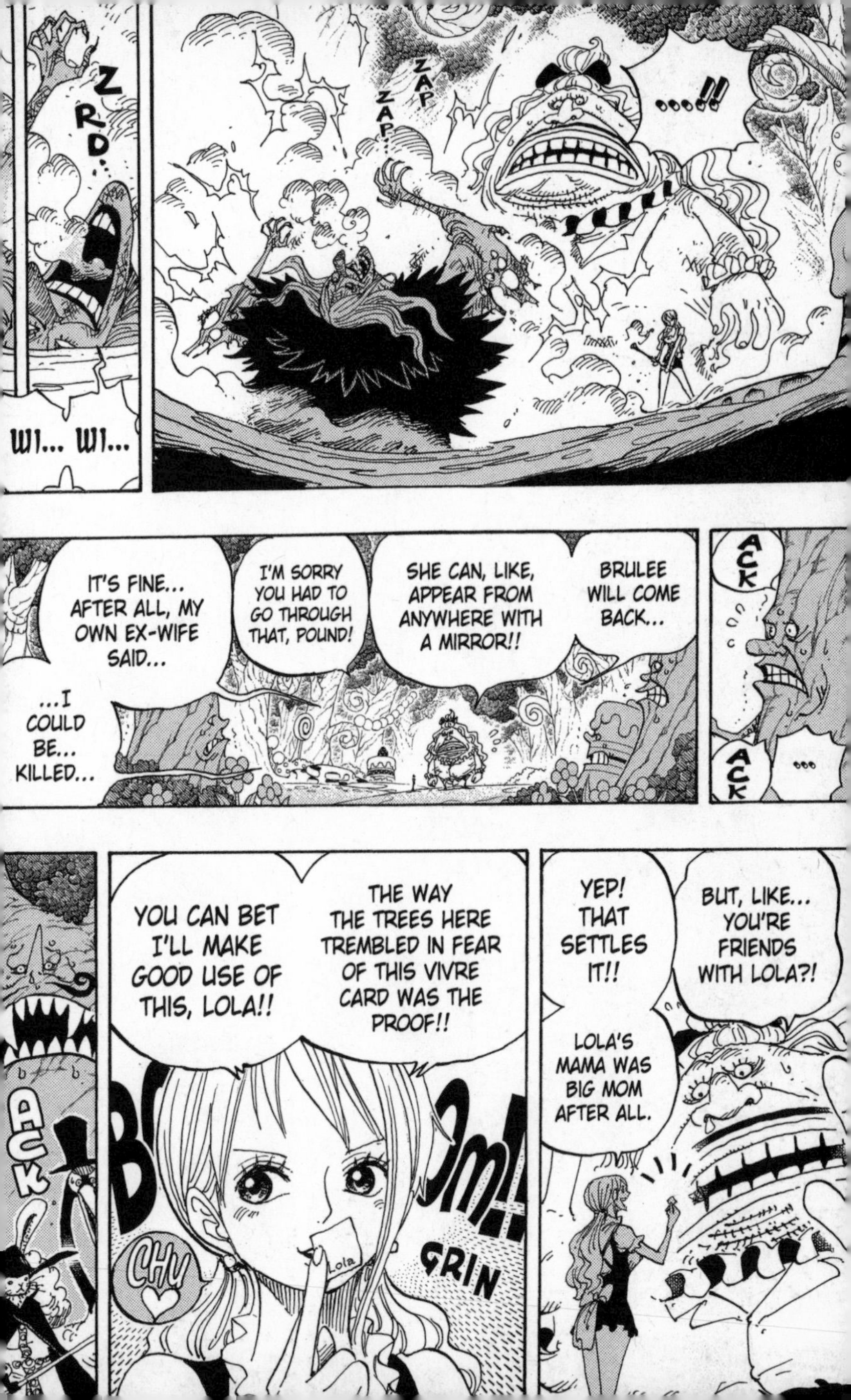

ZAP
ZAP
....!!
ZRD...
WI... WI...
ACK
...
ACK
BRULEE WILL COME BACK...
SHE CAN, LIKE, APPEAR FROM ANYWHERE WITH A MIRROR!!
I'M SORRY YOU HAD TO GO THROUGH THAT, POUND!
IT'S FINE... AFTER ALL, MY OWN EX-WIFE SAID...
...I COULD BE... KILLED...
BUT, LIKE... YOU'RE FRIENDS WITH LOLA?!
YEP! THAT SETTLES IT!!
LOLA'S MAMA WAS BIG MOM AFTER ALL.
THE WAY THE TREES HERE TREMBLED IN FEAR OF THIS VIVRE CARD WAS THE PROOF!!
YOU CAN BET I'LL MAKE GOOD USE OF THIS, LOLA!!
GRIN
CHU
Lola
ACK

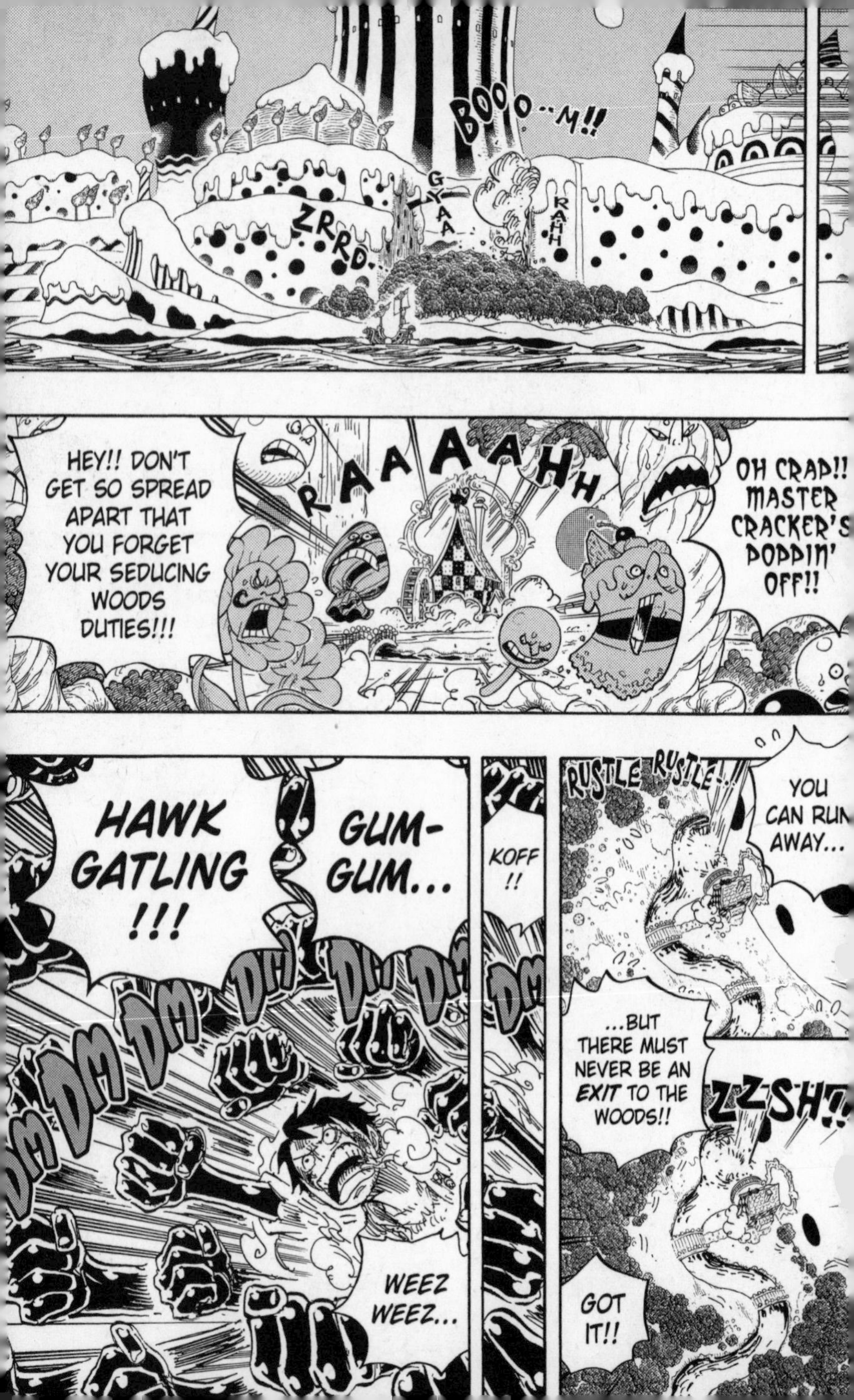
RAHH
BOOO..M!!
GYAA
ZRRRD...
OH CRAP!! MASTER CRACKER'S POPPIN' OFF!!
RAAAAAHH
HEY!! DON'T GET SO SPREAD APART THAT YOU FORGET YOUR SEDUCING WOODS DUTIES!!!
RUSTLE RUSTLE..!!
YOU CAN RUN AWAY...
...BUT THERE MUST NEVER BE AN EXIT TO THE WOODS!!
ZZSH!!
GOT IT!!
KOFF !!
DM
GUM-GUM...
HAWK GATLING !!!
DM DM DM DM DM DM DM DM
WEEZ WEEZ...

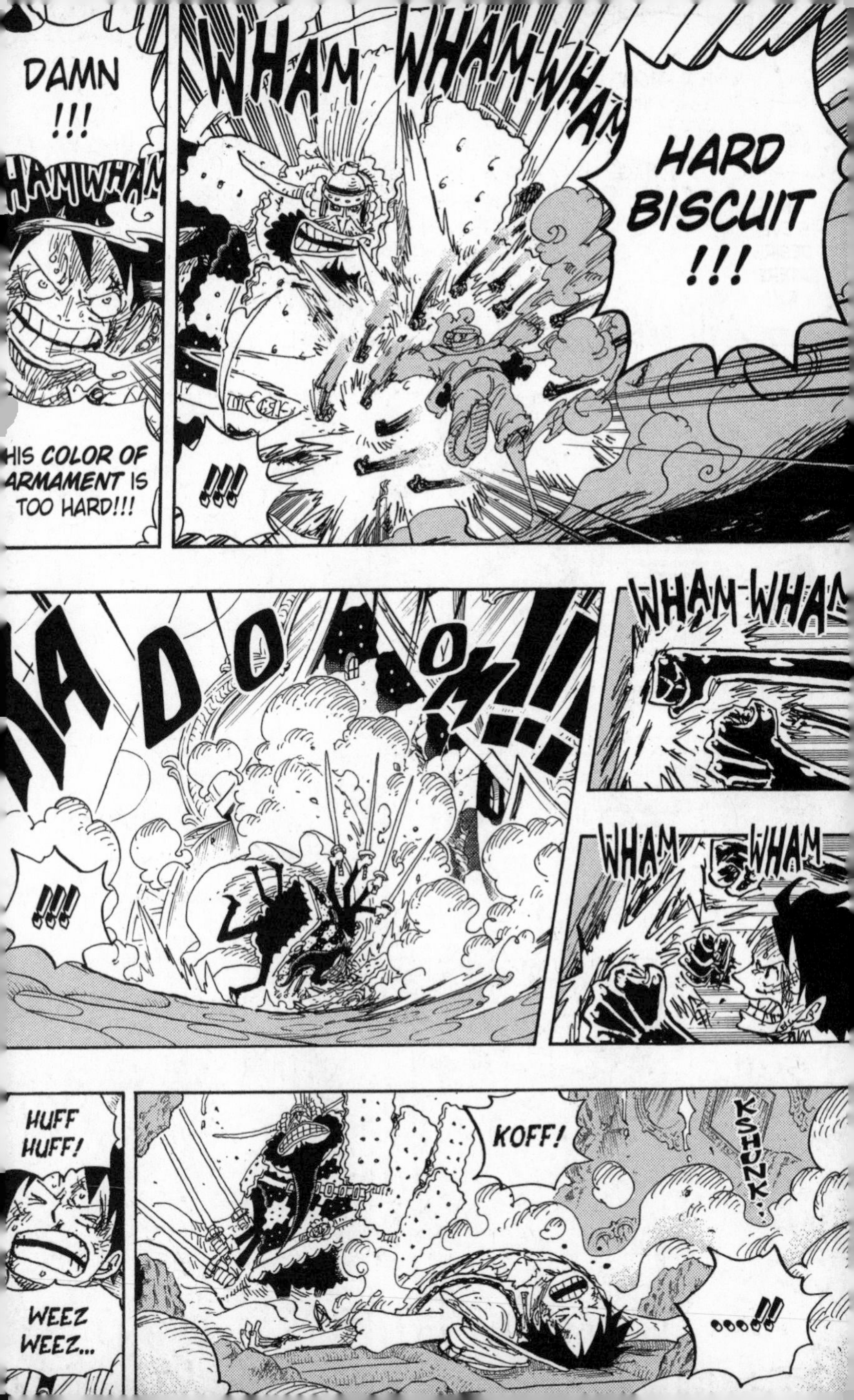
HARD BISCUIT!!!
WHAM WHAM WHAM
!!!
DAMN!!!
HAM WHAM
HIS COLOR OF ARMAMENT IS TOO HARD!!!
WHAM WHAM
WHAM WHAM
ADOOM!!
!!!
KSHUNK...
KOFF!
....!!
HUFF HUFF!
WEEZ WEEZ...

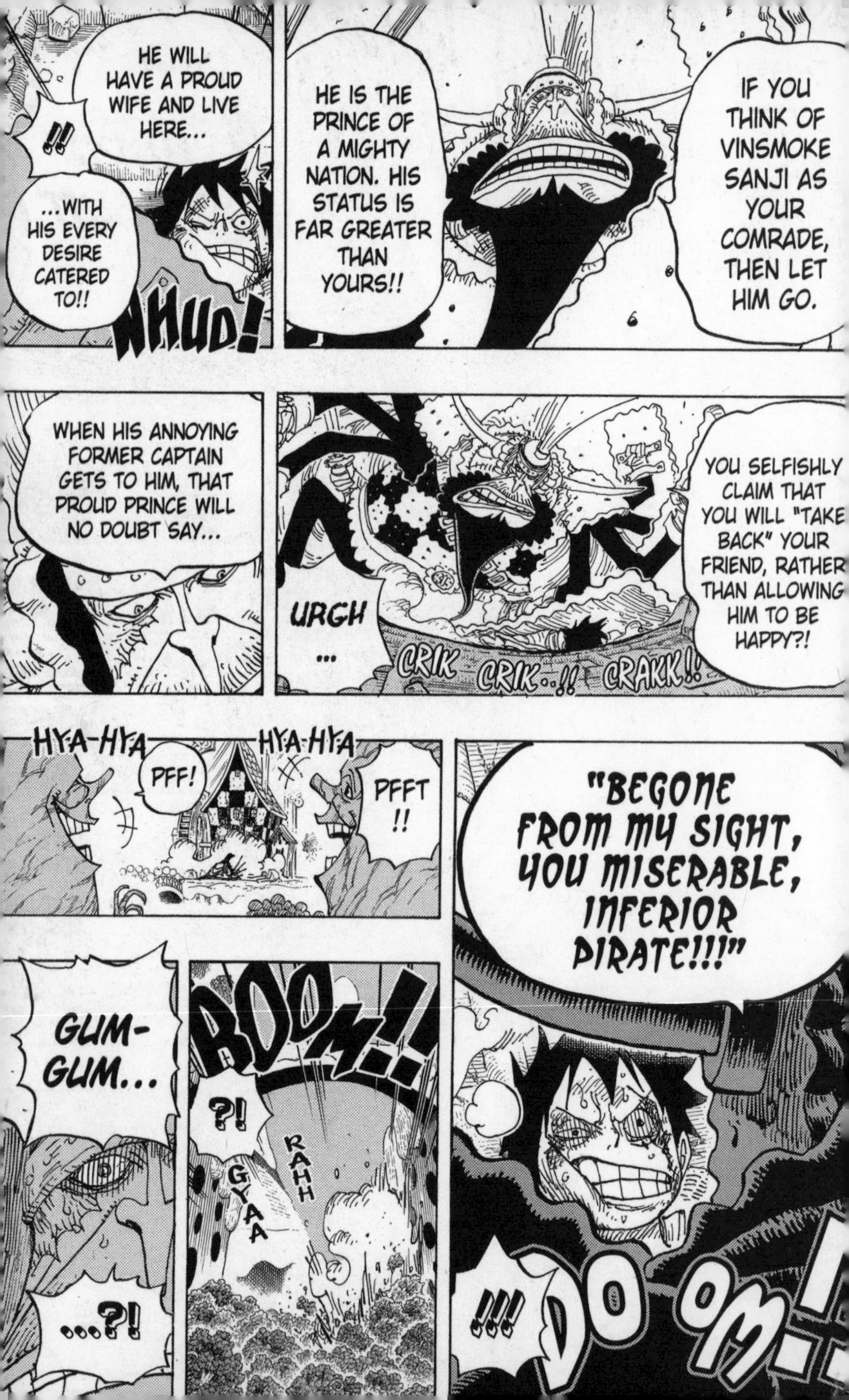
IF YOU THINK OF VINSMOKE SANJI AS YOUR COMRADE, THEN LET HIM GO.
HE IS THE PRINCE OF A MIGHTY NATION. HIS STATUS IS FAR GREATER THAN YOURS!!
HE WILL HAVE A PROUD WIFE AND LIVE HERE...
!!
...WITH HIS EVERY DESIRE CATERED TO!!
WHUD!
YOU SELFISHLY CLAIM THAT YOU WILL "TAKE BACK" YOUR FRIEND, RATHER THAN ALLOWING HIM TO BE HAPPY?!
URGH ...
CRIK CRIK..!! CRAKK!!
WHEN HIS ANNOYING FORMER CAPTAIN GETS TO HIM, THAT PROUD PRINCE WILL NO DOUBT SAY...
"BEGONE FROM MY SIGHT, YOU MISERABLE, INFERIOR PIRATE!!!"
!!!
DOOM!!
HYA-HYA
PFFT !!
HYA-HYA
PFF!
BOOM!!
?!
RAHH
GYAA
GUM-GUM...
...?!

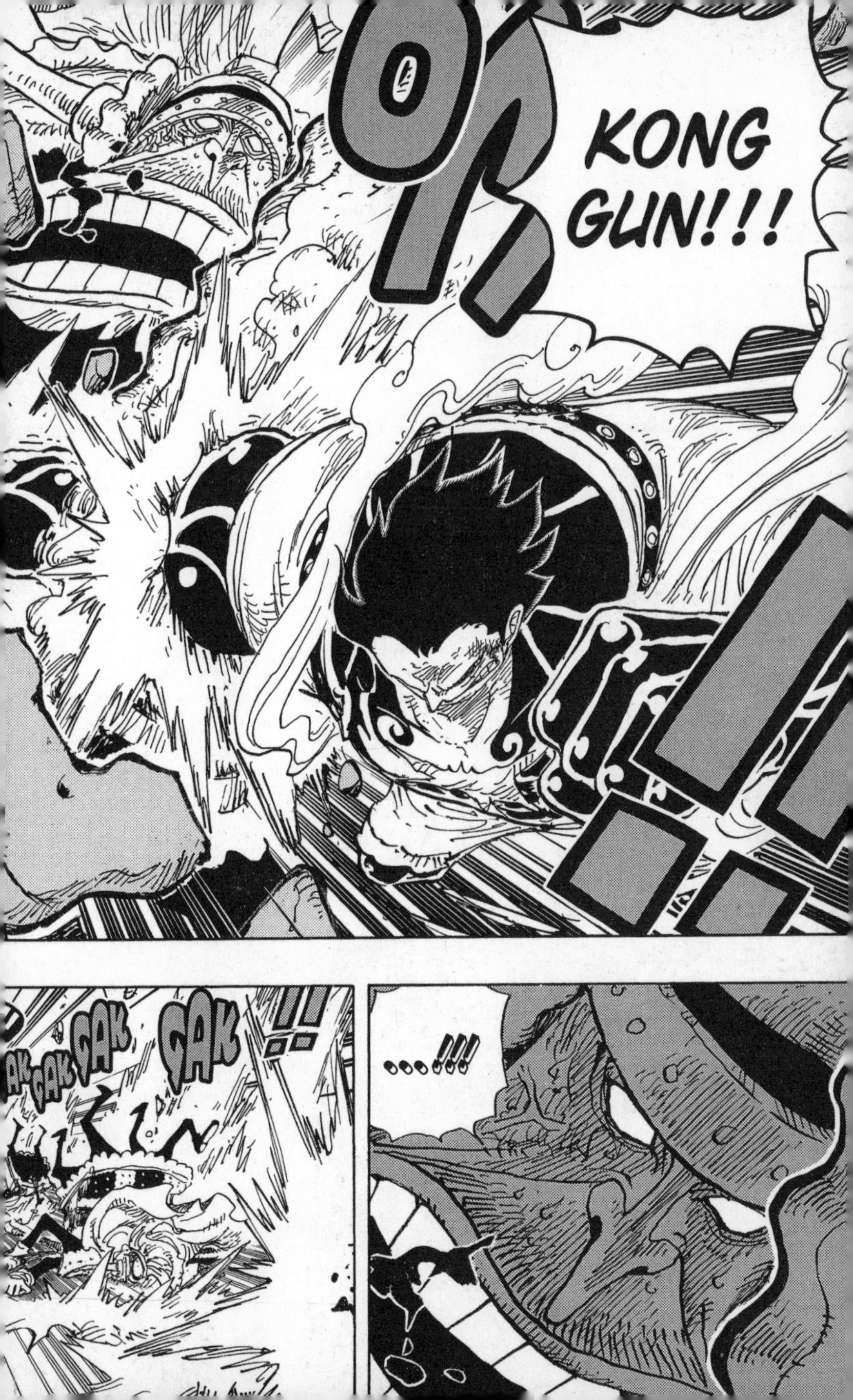
KONG GUN!!!
...!!!
GAK GAK GAK!!
KIN

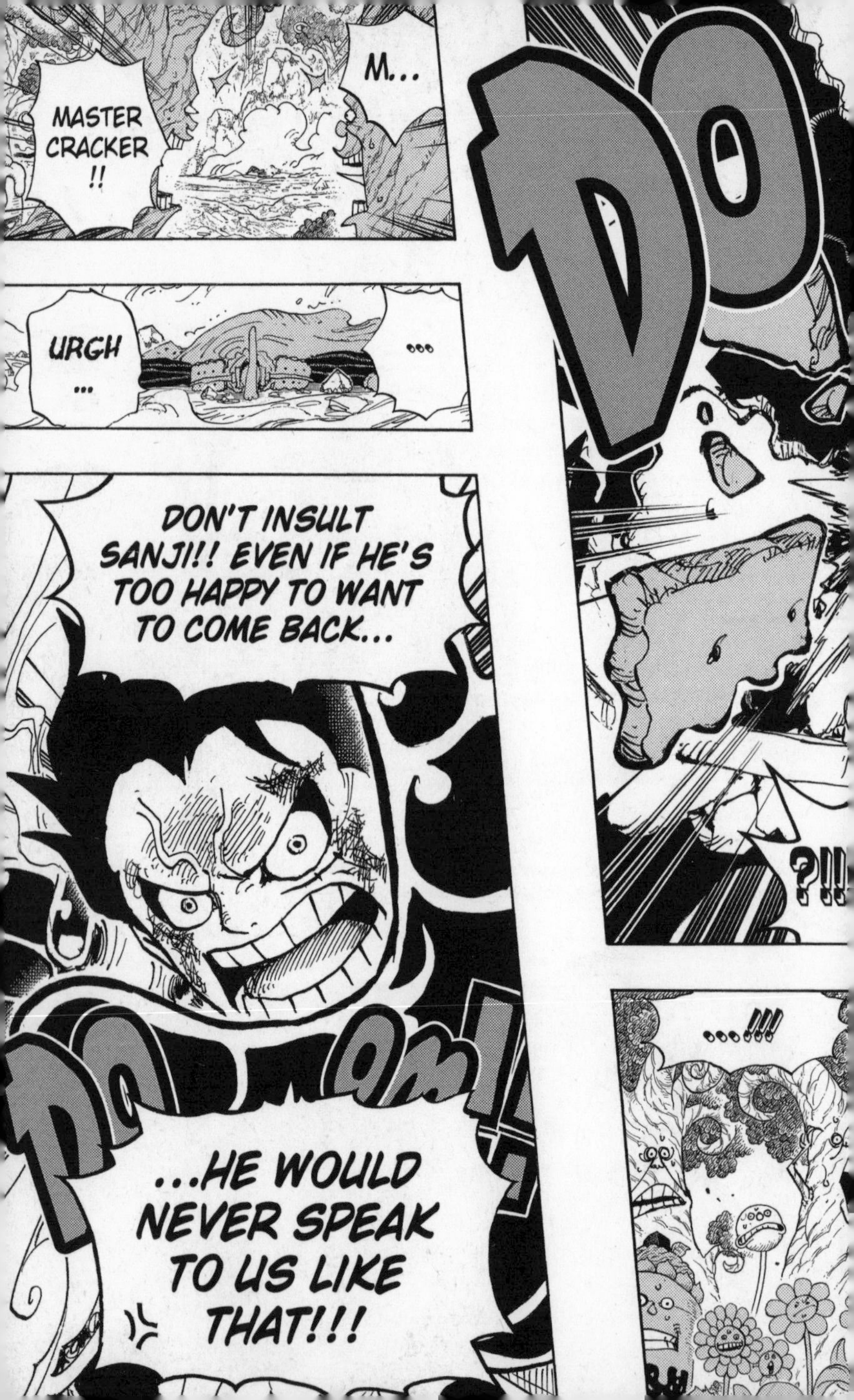
DO
?!!
...!!!
M...
MASTER CRACKER !!
...
URGH ...
DON'T INSULT SANJI!! EVEN IF HE'S TOO HAPPY TO WANT TO COME BACK...
DOOOM!!
...HE WOULD NEVER SPEAK TO US LIKE THAT!!!

SBS Question Corner

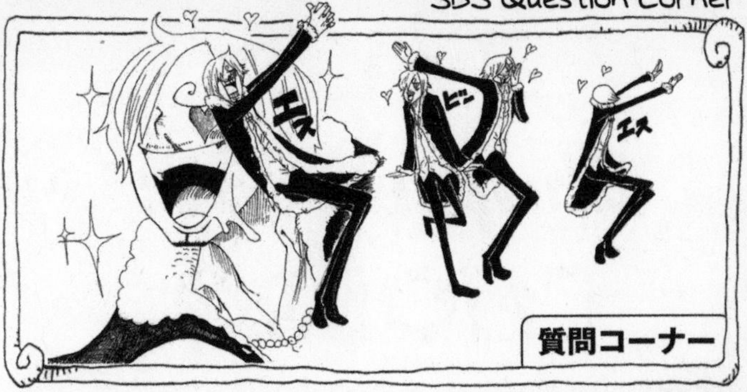
質問コーナー

(Iwashita Family Love, Okinawa)

Q: Odacchi!! In Volume 79, you said we should use whatever logic we could to connect characters to dates, so I did my best!! For Viola, the V is a "B" sound in Japanese (B→13) and o is a zero. 1/30!! January 30th is blank!! I'm a genius!! Hope you like it!!

--Summer Mandarin

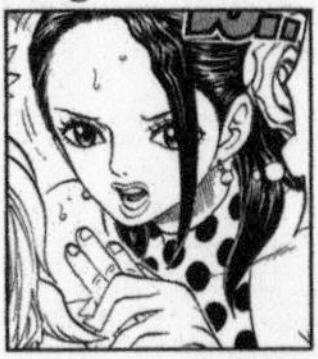

A: Whaaaat?! Okay.

Q: Greetings, Oda Sensei! I'm here to fill in some calendar blanks!
Sai ⇒ 8/13 (Happosui's "eight treasures," 13th chieftain)
Baby 5 ⇒ 5/15 (May + d (maid), d is "10" plus Baby "5")
Chin Jao ⇒ 12/12 (12th chieftain of Happosui)
Boo ⇒ 8/20 ("eight treasures" and bu-u stands for "2-0")
How old is Sai, anyway? What's the age gap with his wife? Depending on the answer, I might need to call the cops…out of jealousy.
--Uhyalicia

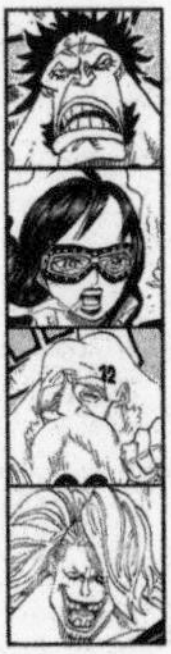

A: Whaaaat?! Okay. Sai's age is... Actually, why don't I tell you the ages of all the people who drank from the son's cups?

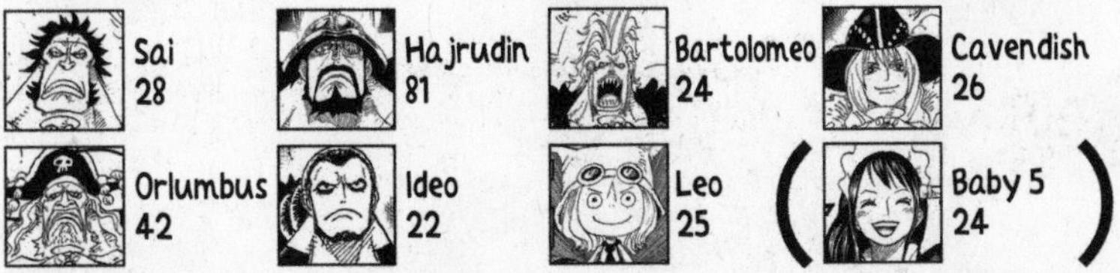
Sai 28
Hajrudin 81
Bartolomeo 24
Cavendish 26
Orlumbus 42
Ideo 22
Leo 25
(Baby 5 24)

Sai's actually quite young. Did he look old to you?

Q: Odacchi! What happens if you rip off a woman's bra like Smoker does? (See Volume 67 SBS.)
Won't know until you try it! Here we go!
P.S. Dear Eiichiro Oda, they arrested me. Why?

--Chagero Shimizu Fan

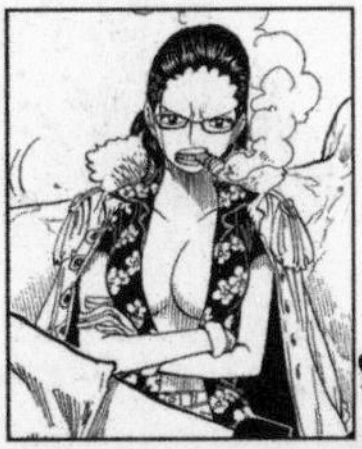

A: That's all! No more SBS! See you next volume!!

Chapter 838: CHOBRO

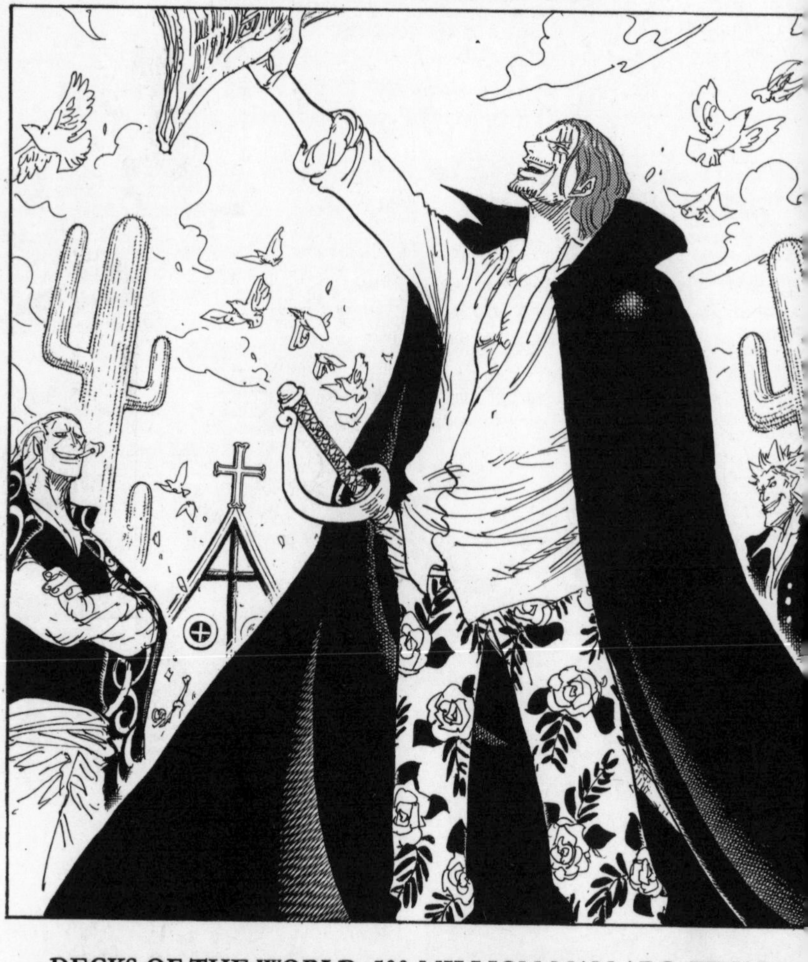

DECKS OF THE WORLD, 500-MILLION-MAN ARC, FINAL VOLUME: "A WEDDING AT A CERTAIN RUINED ISLAND"

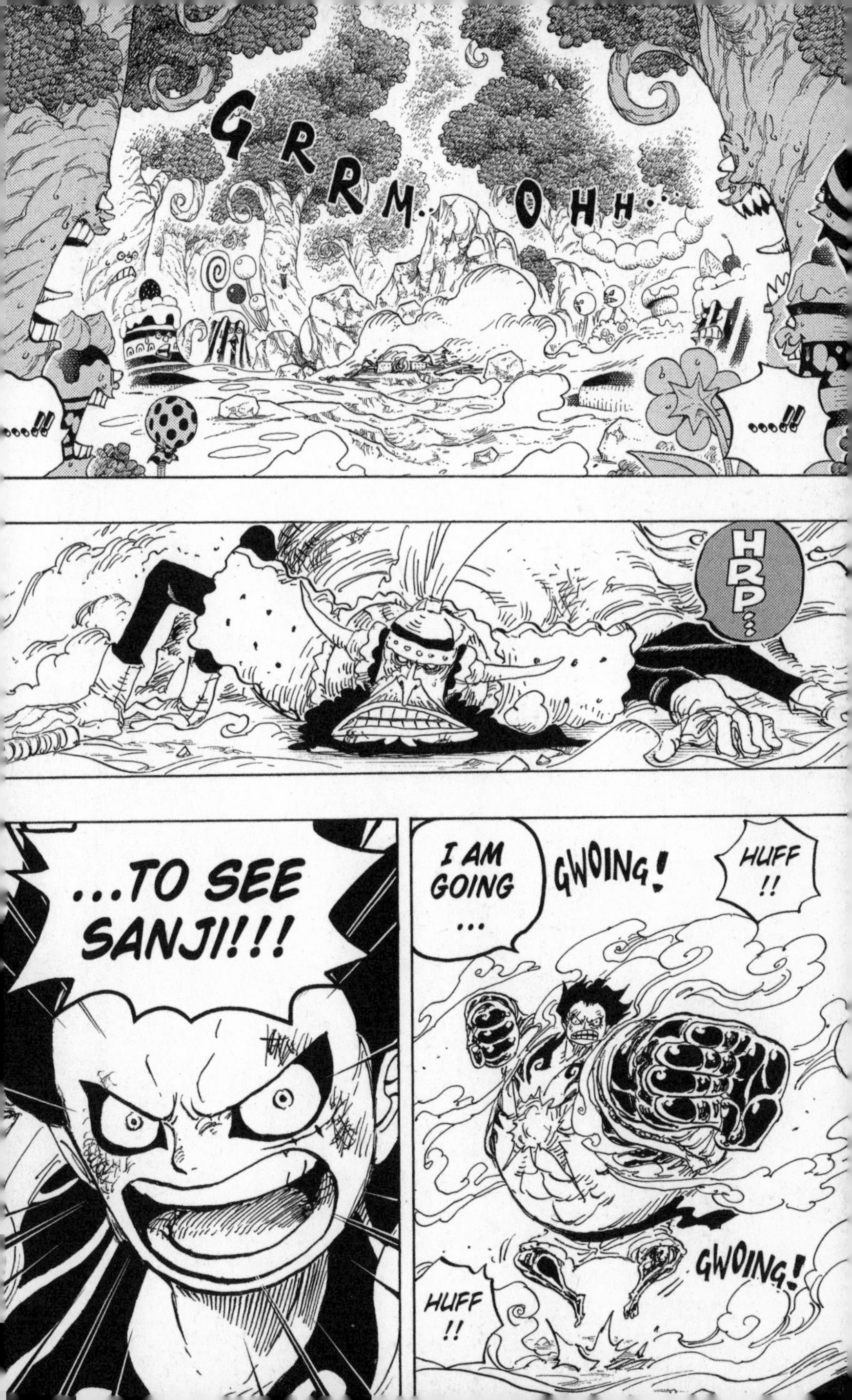
GRRM..OHH...
....!!
....!!
HRP...
HUFF !!
GWOING!
I AM GOING ...
GWOING!
HUFF !!
...TO SEE SANJI!!!

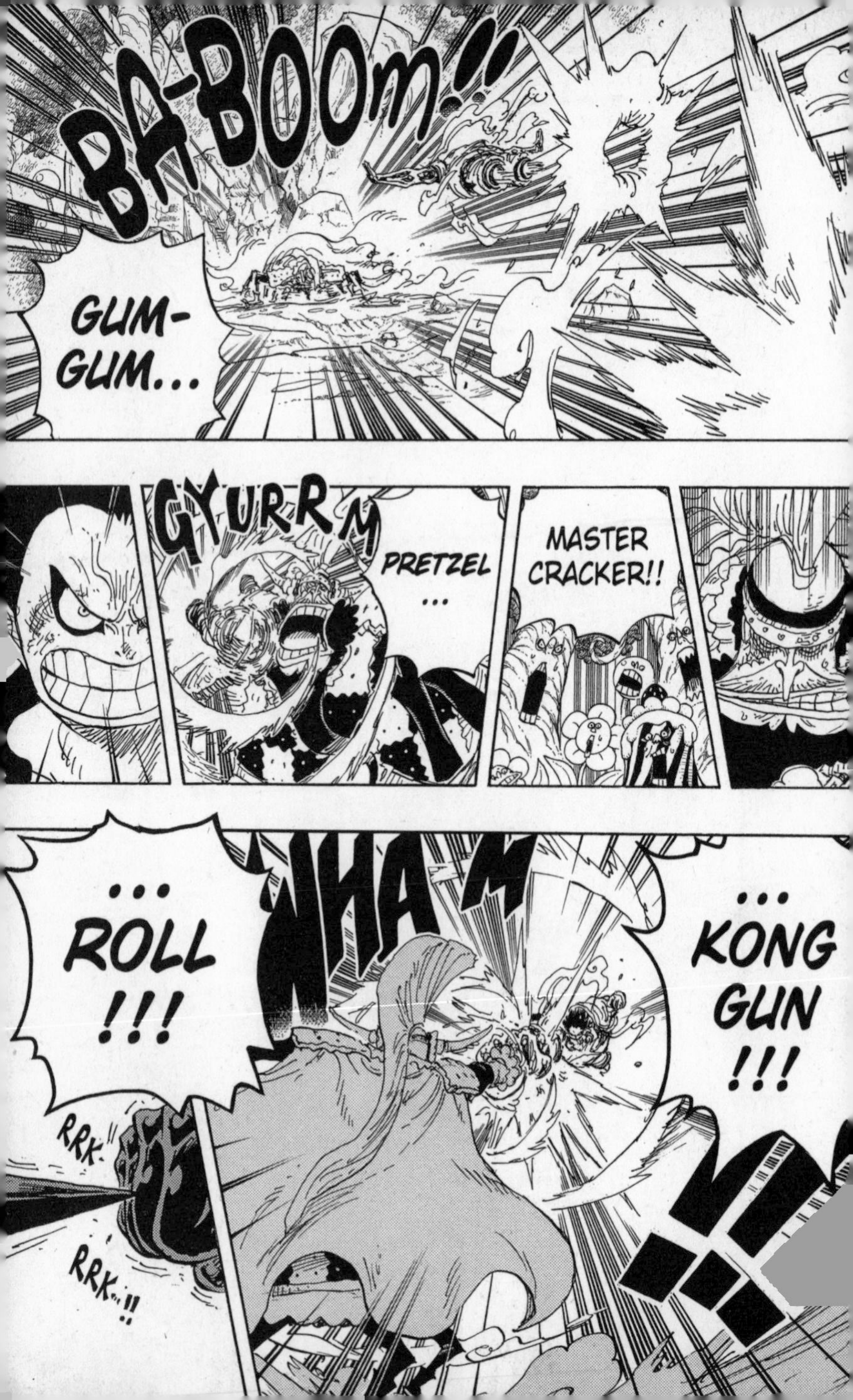
BA-BOOM!!
GUM-GUM...
MASTER CRACKER!!
PRETZEL ...
GYURRM
... KONG GUN !!!
WHAM
... ROLL !!!
RRK
RRK...!!

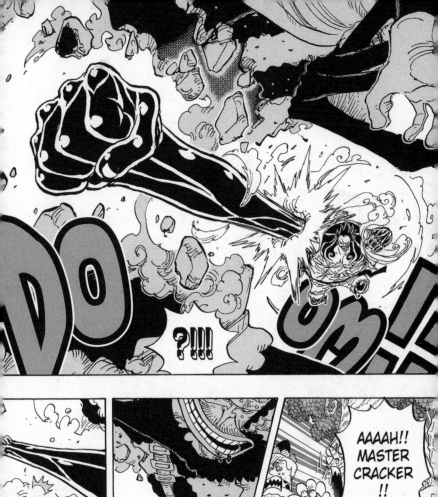

?!!!!

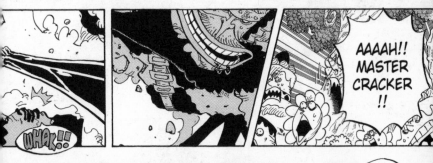

AAAAH!!
MASTER
CRACKER
!!

WHA!!

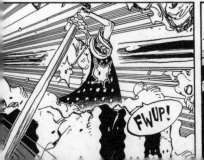

HRP

FWUP!

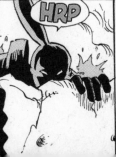

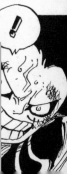

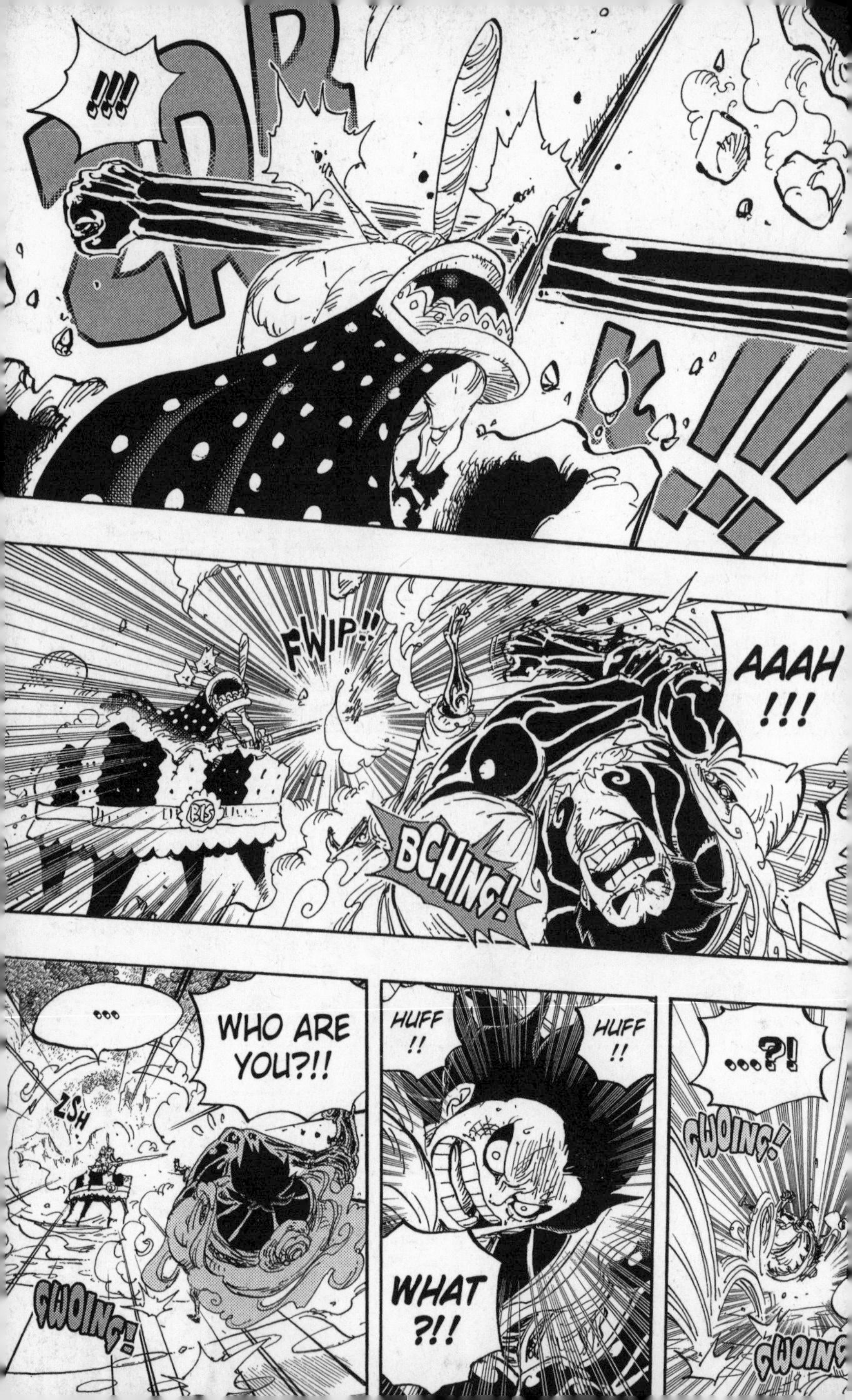
!!!
AAAH !!!
FWIP!!
BCHING!
...?!
GWOING!
GWOING
HUFF !!
HUFF !!
WHAT ?!!
...
WHO ARE YOU?!!
ZSH
GWOING!

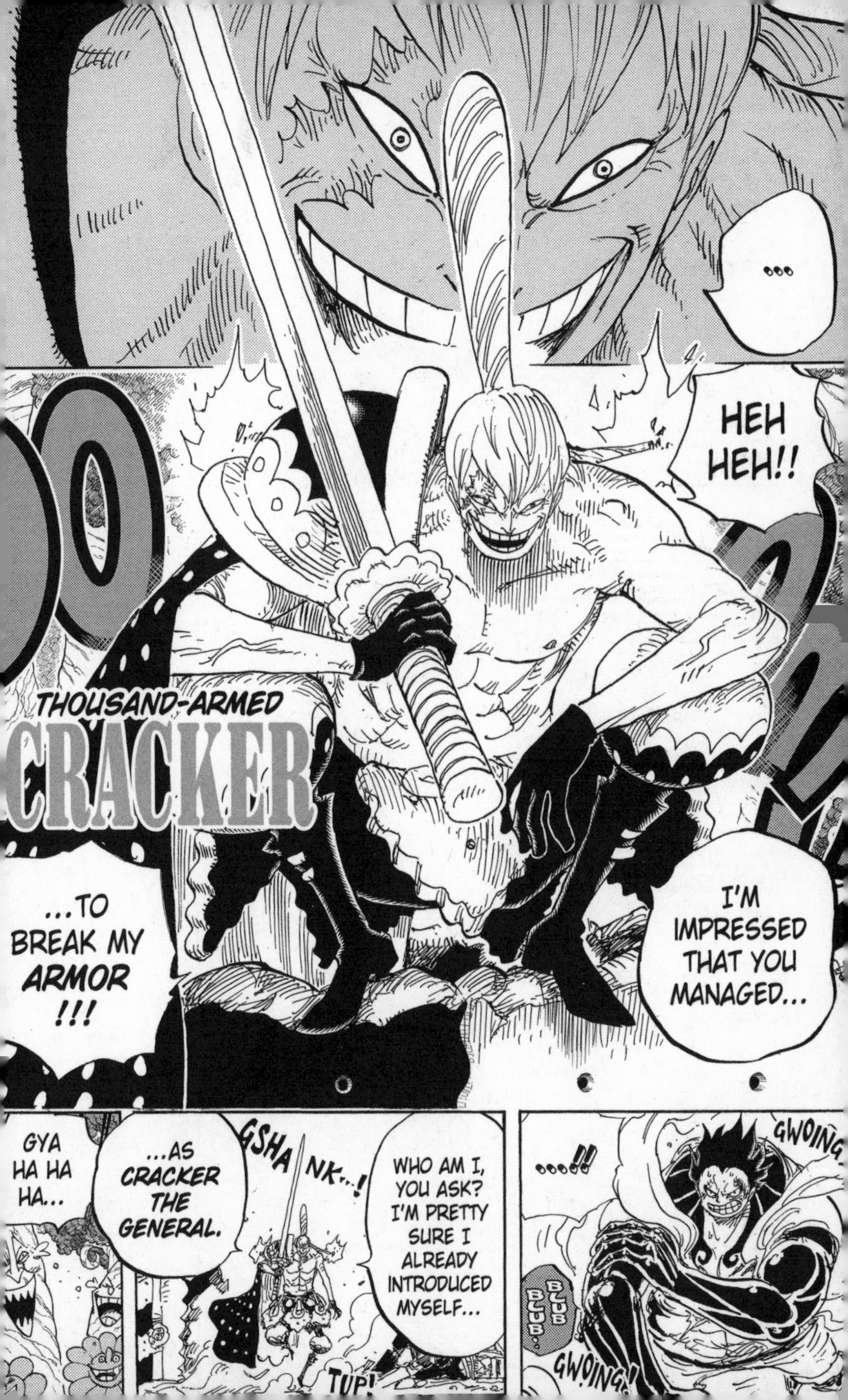
...
HEH HEH!!
I'M IMPRESSED THAT YOU MANAGED...
...TO BREAK MY ARMOR!!!
THOUSAND-ARMED
CRACKER
GWOING
...!!
BLUB BLUB
GWOING!
GSHANK..!
WHO AM I, YOU ASK? I'M PRETTY SURE I ALREADY INTRODUCED MYSELF...
...AS CRACKER THE GENERAL.
TUP!
GYA HA HA HA...

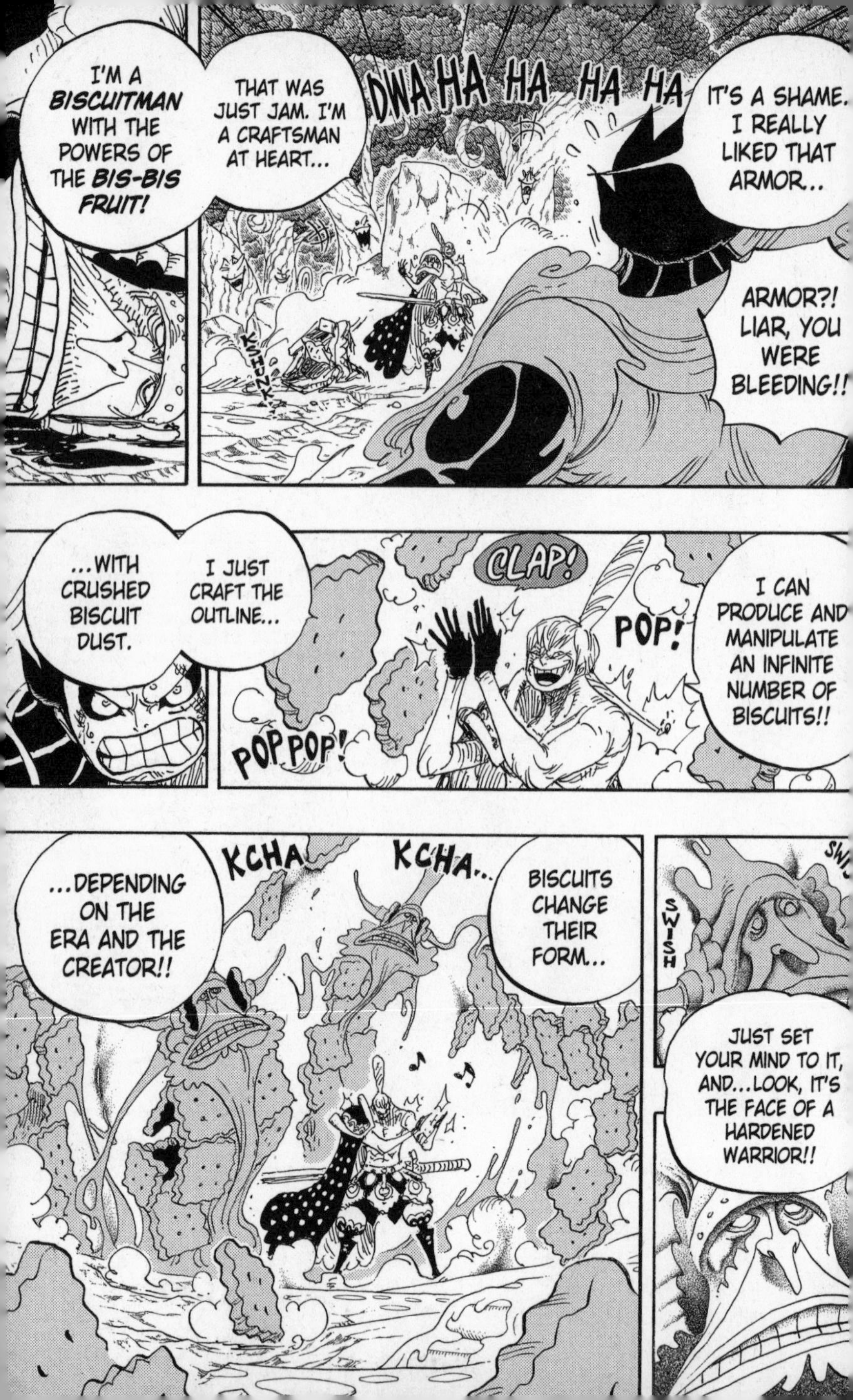
DWA HA HA HA HA
IT'S A SHAME. I REALLY LIKED THAT ARMOR...
ARMOR?! LIAR, YOU WERE BLEEDING!!
THAT WAS JUST JAM. I'M A CRAFTSMAN AT HEART...
KSHUNK
I'M A BISCUITMAN WITH THE POWERS OF THE BIS-BIS FRUIT!
I CAN PRODUCE AND MANIPULATE AN INFINITE NUMBER OF BISCUITS!!
CLAP!
POP!
POP POP!
I JUST CRAFT THE OUTLINE...
...WITH CRUSHED BISCUIT DUST.
SWISH
JUST SET YOUR MIND TO IT, AND...LOOK, IT'S THE FACE OF A HARDENED WARRIOR!!
BISCUITS CHANGE THEIR FORM...
KCHA KCHA...
...DEPENDING ON THE ERA AND THE CREATOR!!

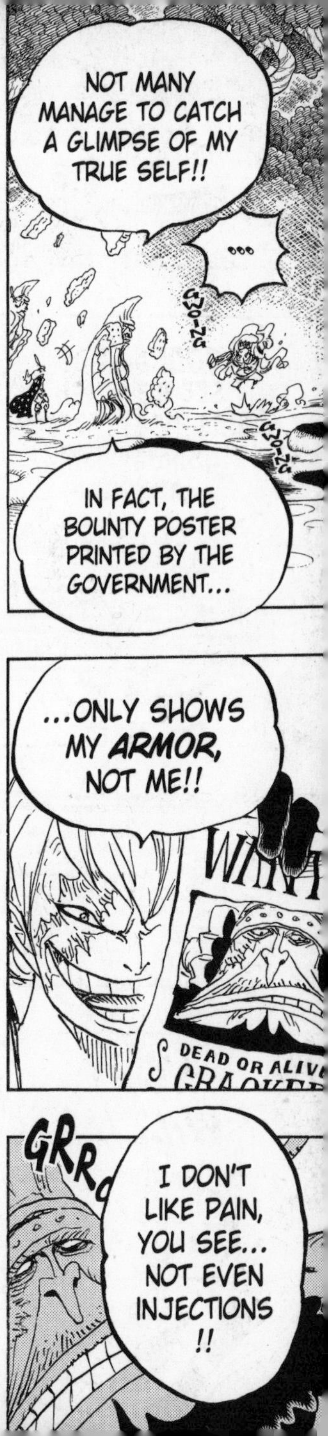
NOT MANY MANAGE TO CATCH A GLIMPSE OF MY TRUE SELF!!
...
GWO-NG
GWO-NG
IN FACT, THE BOUNTY POSTER PRINTED BY THE GOVERNMENT...
...ONLY SHOWS MY ARMOR, NOT ME!!
DEAD OR ALIV
GRR
I DON'T LIKE PAIN, YOU SEE... NOT EVEN INJECTIONS!!
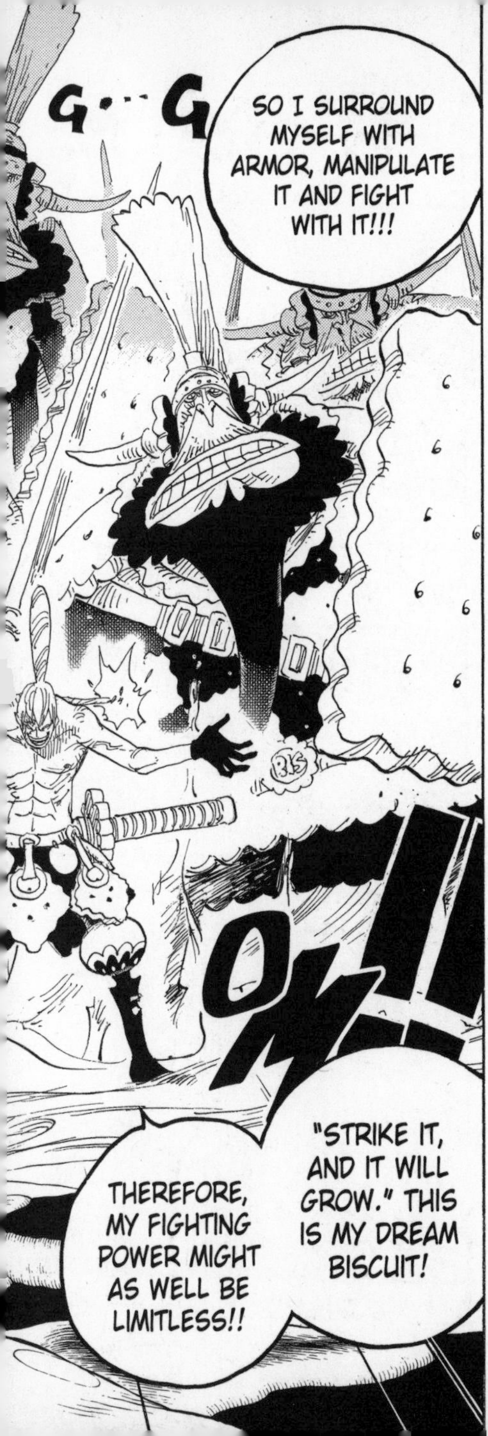
G...G
SO I SURROUND MYSELF WITH ARMOR, MANIPULATE IT AND FIGHT WITH IT!!!
"STRIKE IT, AND IT WILL GROW." THIS IS MY DREAM BISCUIT!
THEREFORE, MY FIGHTING POWER MIGHT AS WELL BE LIMITLESS!!

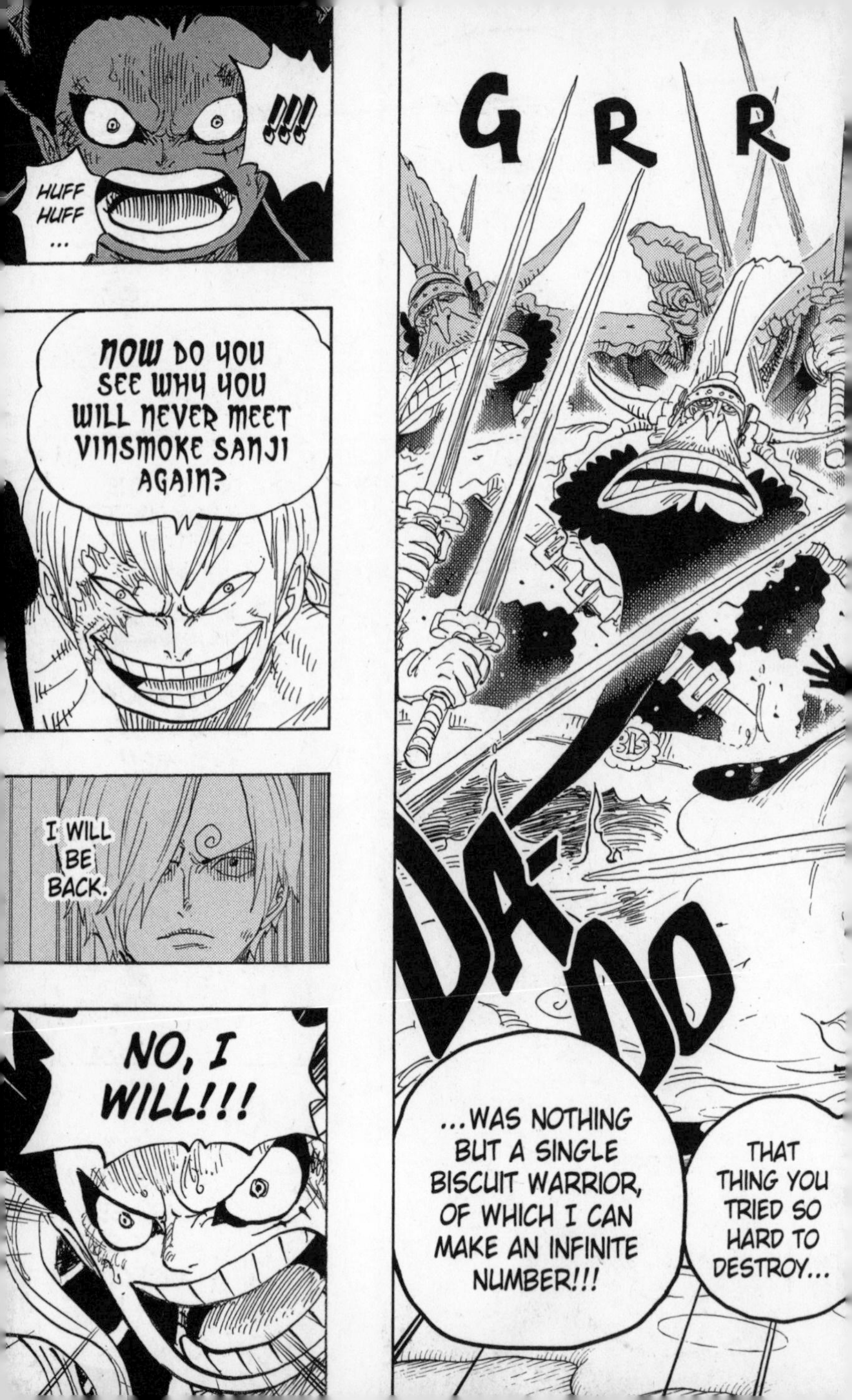
GRR
DA-DO
THAT THING YOU TRIED SO HARD TO DESTROY...
...WAS NOTHING BUT A SINGLE BISCUIT WARRIOR, OF WHICH I CAN MAKE AN INFINITE NUMBER!!!
!!!
HUFF HUFF ...
NOW DO YOU SEE WHY YOU WILL NEVER MEET VINSMOKE SANJI AGAIN?
I WILL BE BACK.
NO, I WILL!!!

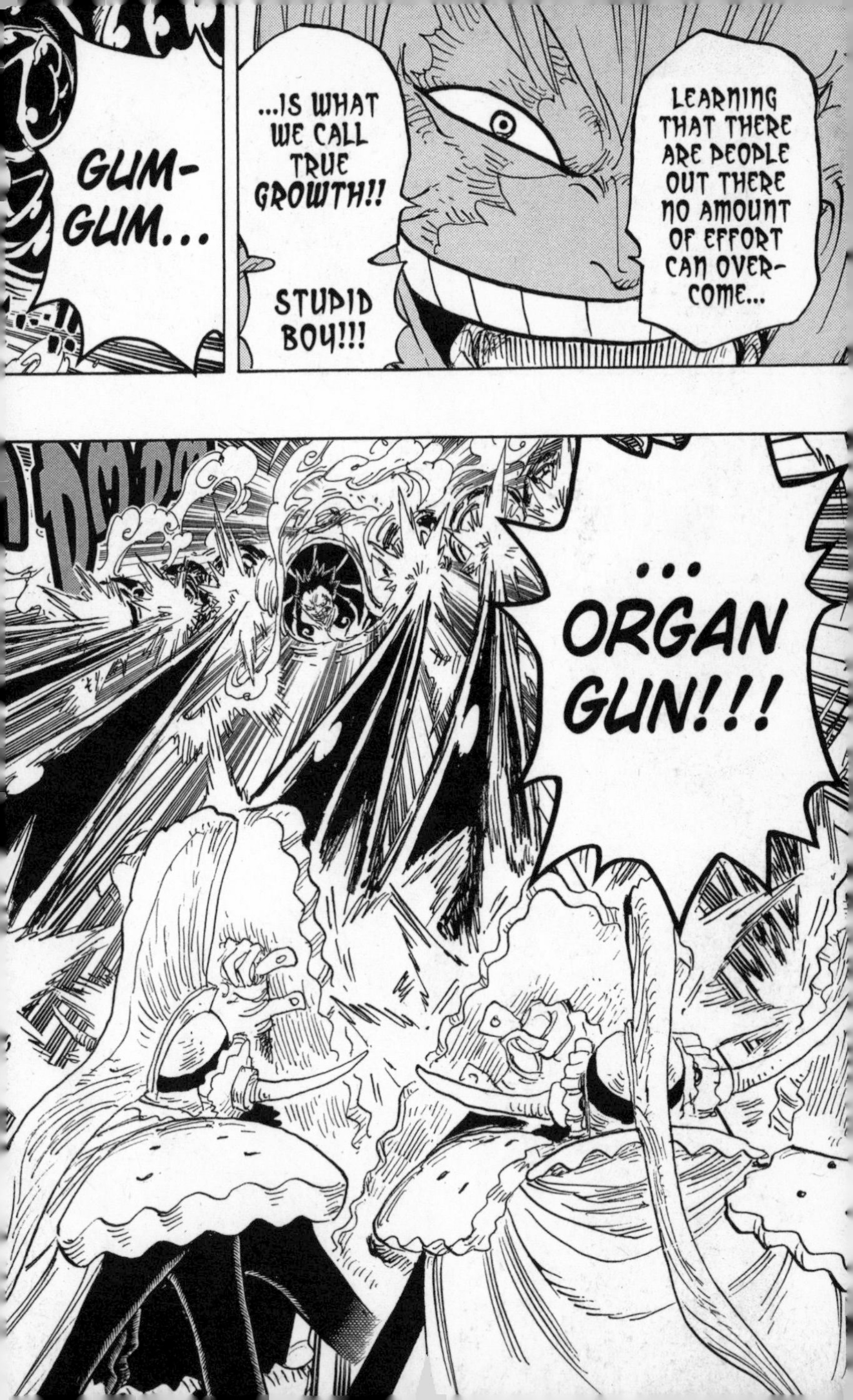
LEARNING THAT THERE ARE PEOPLE OUT THERE NO AMOUNT OF EFFORT CAN OVER-COME...
...IS WHAT WE CALL TRUE GROWTH!!
STUPID BOY!!!
GUM-GUM...
...ORGAN GUN!!!

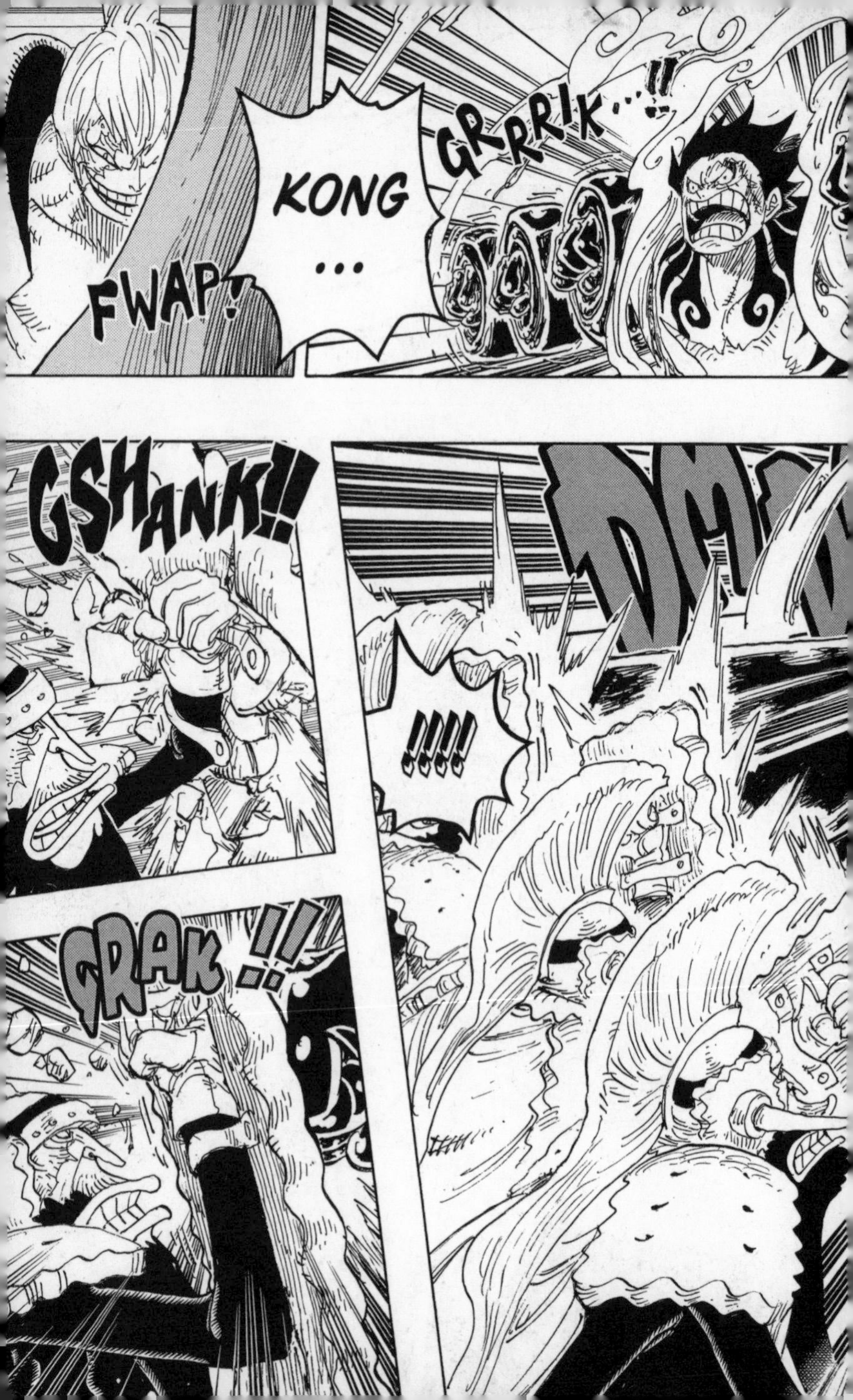
GRRRIK...!!
KONG
...
FWAP!
!!!!
GSHANK!!
GRAK!!

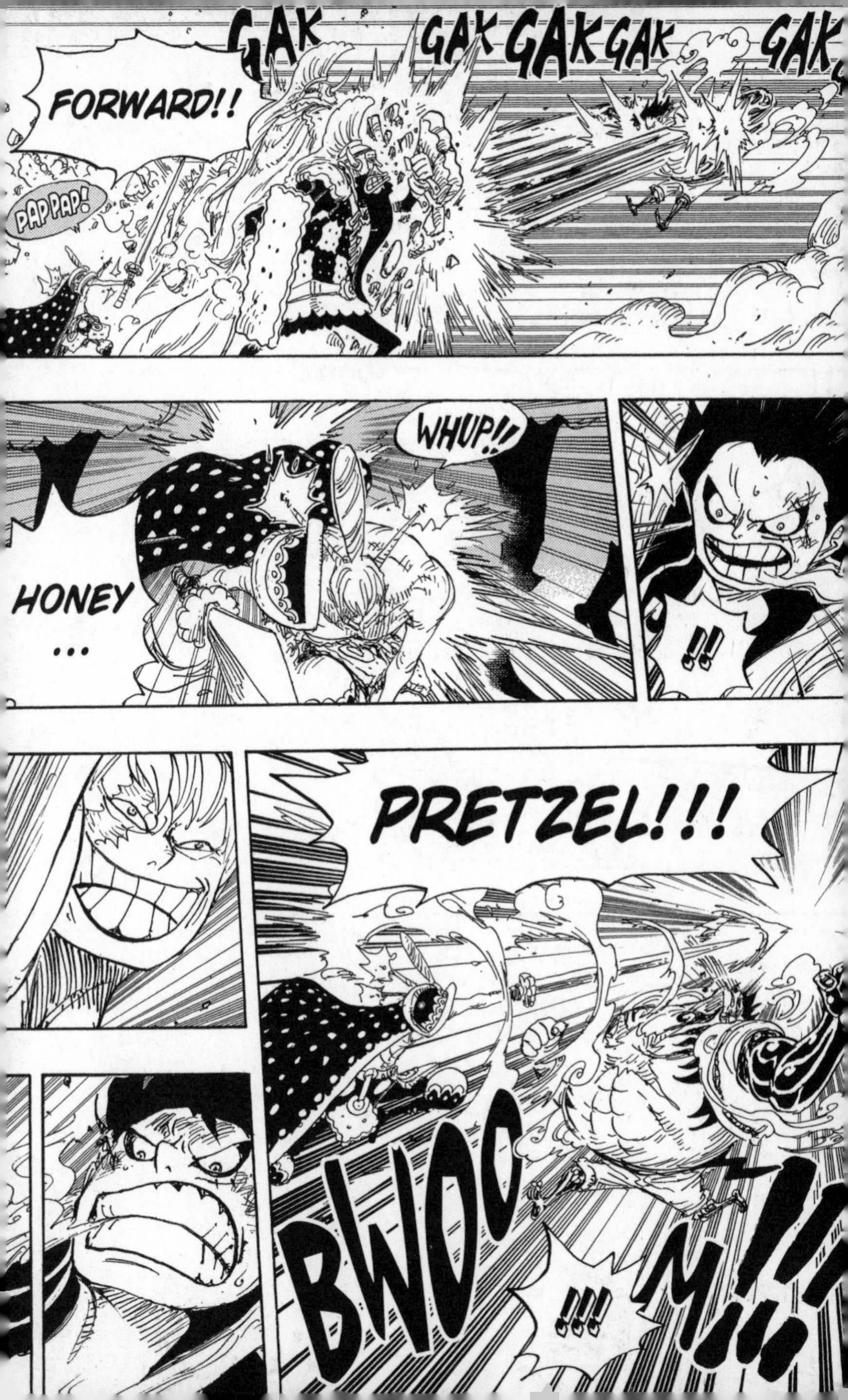
GAK
GAK
GAK
GAK
GAK
FORWARD!!
PAP PAP!
!!
WHUP!!
HONEY ...
PRETZEL!!!
BWOOM!!!
!!!

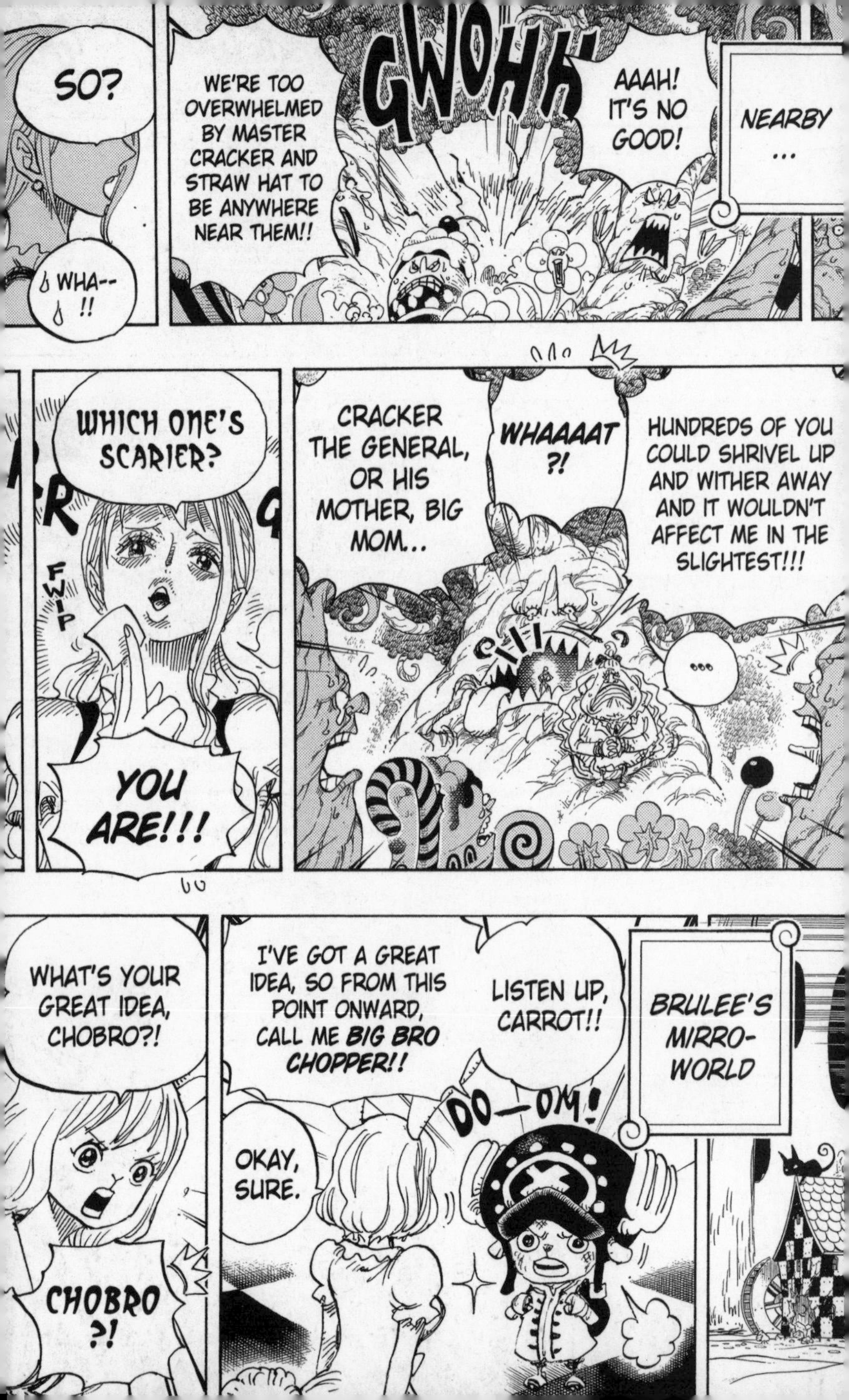
NEARBY ...
AAAH! IT'S NO GOOD!
GWOHH
WE'RE TOO OVERWHELMED BY MASTER CRACKER AND STRAW HAT TO BE ANYWHERE NEAR THEM!!
SO?
WHA-- !!
HUNDREDS OF YOU COULD SHRIVEL UP AND WITHER AWAY AND IT WOULDN'T AFFECT ME IN THE SLIGHTEST!!!
WHAAAAT ?!
CRACKER THE GENERAL, OR HIS MOTHER, BIG MOM...
...
WHICH ONE'S SCARIER?
FWIP
YOU ARE!!!
BRULEE'S MIRRO-WORLD
LISTEN UP, CARROT!!
I'VE GOT A GREAT IDEA, SO FROM THIS POINT ONWARD, CALL ME *BIG BRO CHOPPER*!!
DO—OM!
OKAY, SURE.
WHAT'S YOUR GREAT IDEA, CHOBRO?!
CHOBRO ?!

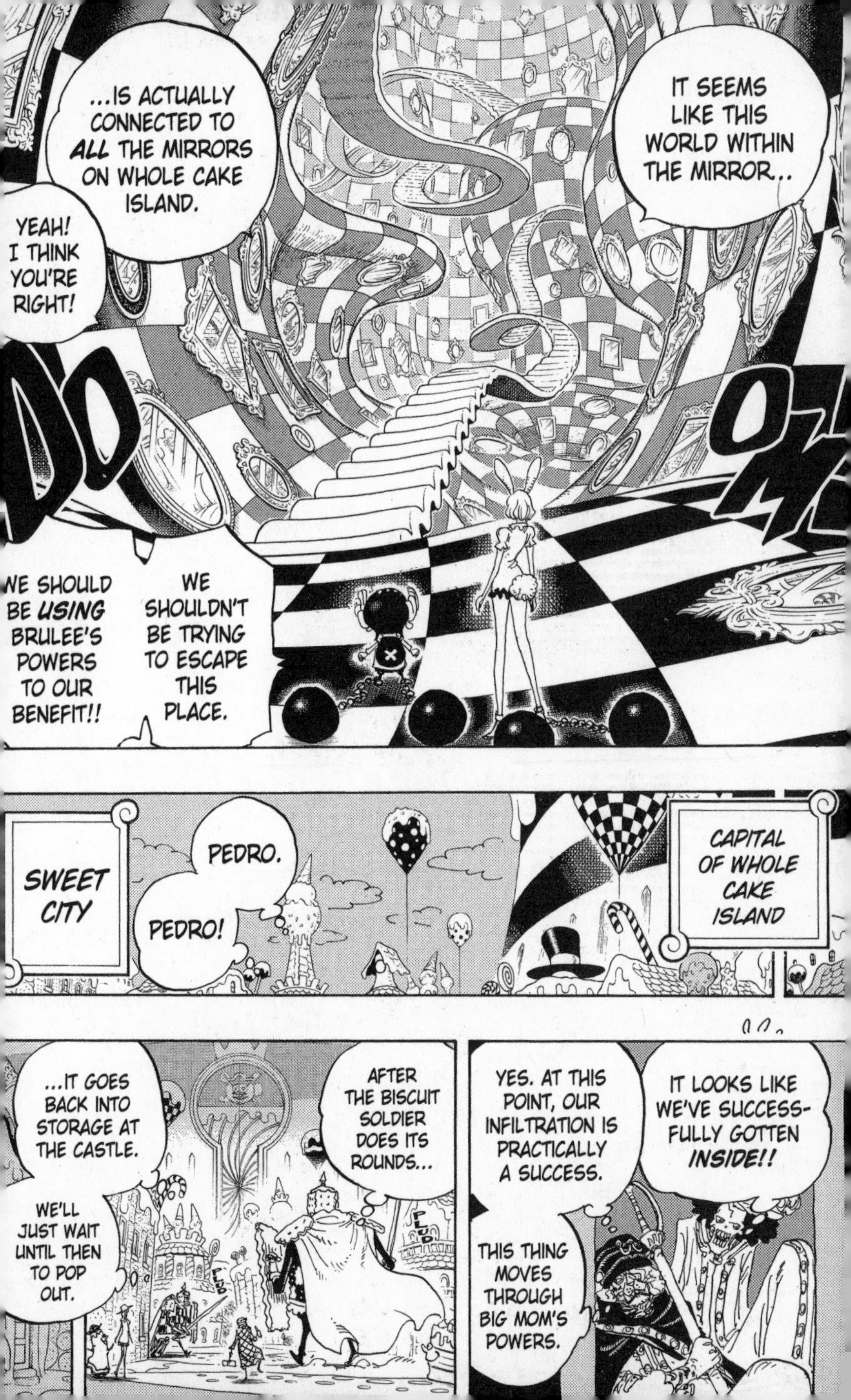
IT SEEMS LIKE THIS WORLD WITHIN THE MIRROR...
...IS ACTUALLY CONNECTED TO ALL THE MIRRORS ON WHOLE CAKE ISLAND.
YEAH! I THINK YOU'RE RIGHT!
WE SHOULDN'T BE TRYING TO ESCAPE THIS PLACE.
WE SHOULD BE USING BRULEE'S POWERS TO OUR BENEFIT!!
CAPITAL OF WHOLE CAKE ISLAND
PEDRO.
PEDRO!
SWEET CITY
IT LOOKS LIKE WE'VE SUCCESSFULLY GOTTEN INSIDE!!
YES. AT THIS POINT, OUR INFILTRATION IS PRACTICALLY A SUCCESS.
THIS THING MOVES THROUGH BIG MOM'S POWERS.
AFTER THE BISCUIT SOLDIER DOES ITS ROUNDS...
...IT GOES BACK INTO STORAGE AT THE CASTLE.
WE'LL JUST WAIT UNTIL THEN TO POP OUT.

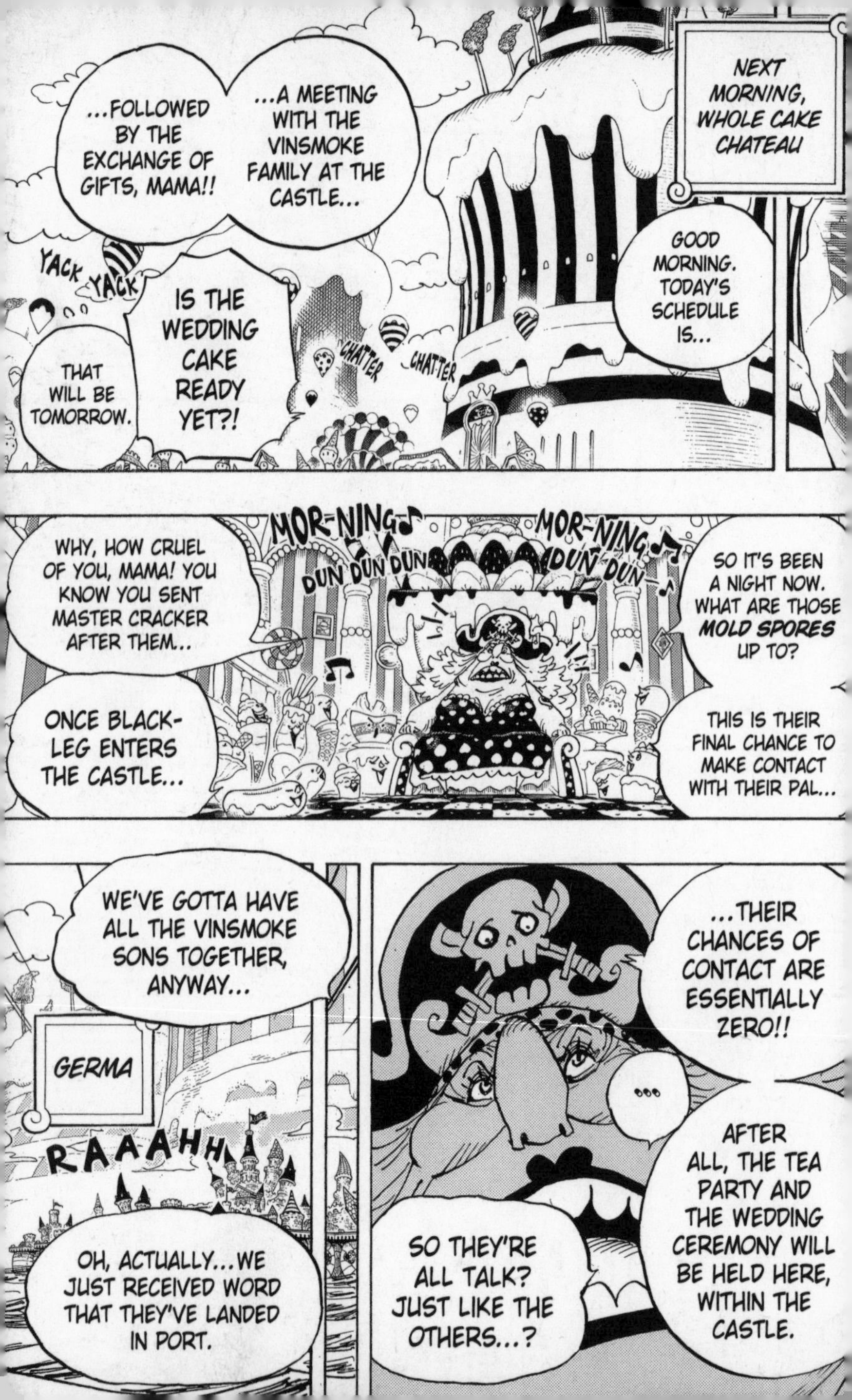
NEXT MORNING, WHOLE CAKE CHATEAU
GOOD MORNING. TODAY'S SCHEDULE IS...
...A MEETING WITH THE VINSMOKE FAMILY AT THE CASTLE...
...FOLLOWED BY THE EXCHANGE OF GIFTS, MAMA!!
CHATTER
CHATTER
IS THE WEDDING CAKE READY YET?!
YACK YACK
THAT WILL BE TOMORROW.
MOR-NING♪
DUN DUN
MOR-NING♪
DUN DUN DUN
SO IT'S BEEN A NIGHT NOW. WHAT ARE THOSE MOLD SPORES UP TO?
THIS IS THEIR FINAL CHANCE TO MAKE CONTACT WITH THEIR PAL...
WHY, HOW CRUEL OF YOU, MAMA! YOU KNOW YOU SENT MASTER CRACKER AFTER THEM...
ONCE BLACK-LEG ENTERS THE CASTLE...
...THEIR CHANCES OF CONTACT ARE ESSENTIALLY ZERO!!
AFTER ALL, THE TEA PARTY AND THE WEDDING CEREMONY WILL BE HELD HERE, WITHIN THE CASTLE.
...
SO THEY'RE ALL TALK? JUST LIKE THE OTHERS...?
WE'VE GOTTA HAVE ALL THE VINSMOKE SONS TOGETHER, ANYWAY...
GERMA
RAAAHH
OH, ACTUALLY...WE JUST RECEIVED WORD THAT THEY'VE LANDED IN PORT.

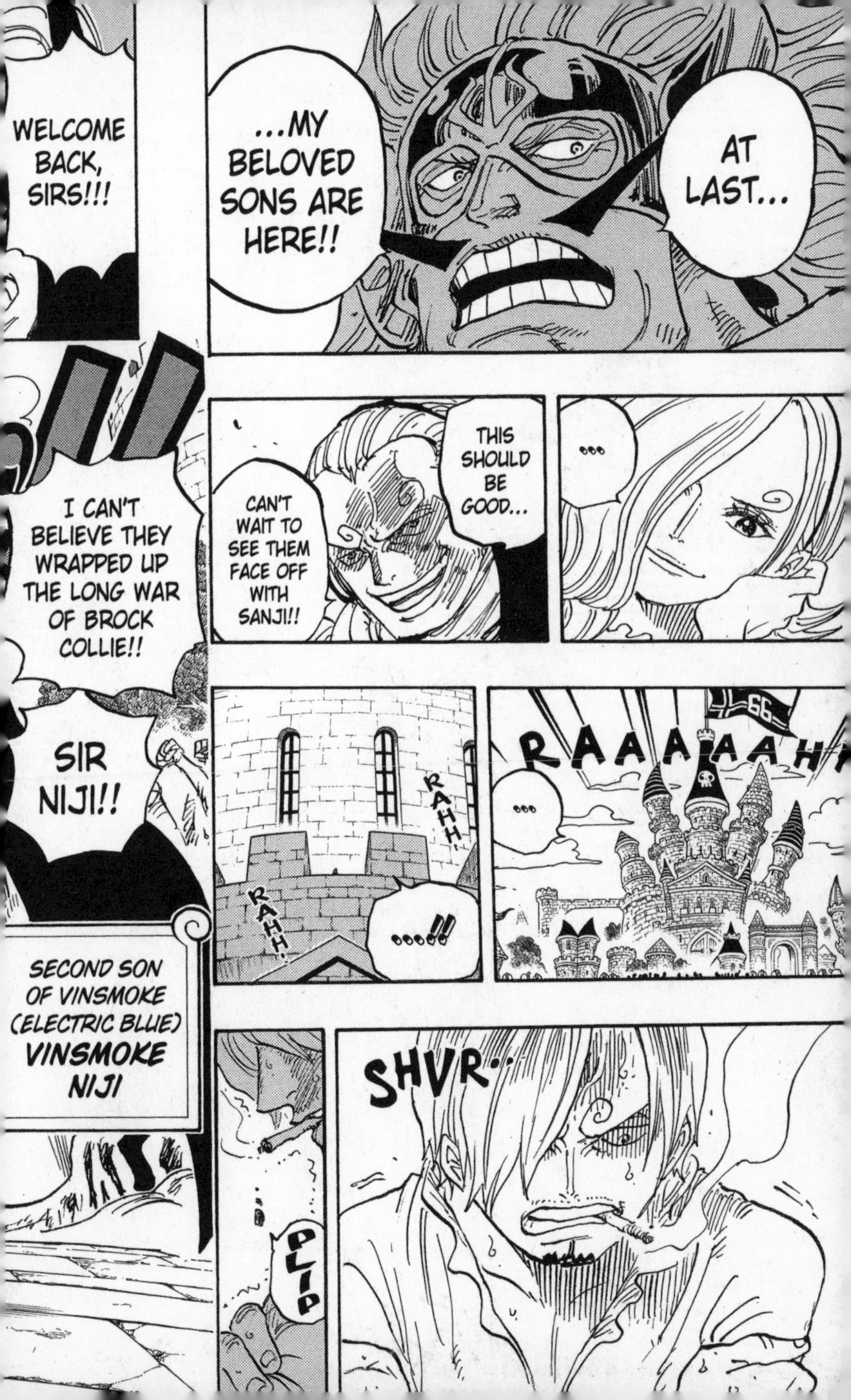
AT LAST...
...MY BELOVED SONS ARE HERE!!
WELCOME BACK, SIRS!!!
...
THIS SHOULD BE GOOD...
CAN'T WAIT TO SEE THEM FACE OFF WITH SANJI!!
RAAAAAAH
...
RAHH
RAHH
....!!
I CAN'T BELIEVE THEY WRAPPED UP THE LONG WAR OF BROCK COLLIE!!
SIR NIJI!!
SECOND SON OF VINSMOKE (ELECTRIC BLUE) VINSMOKE NIJI
SHVR..
...
PLIP

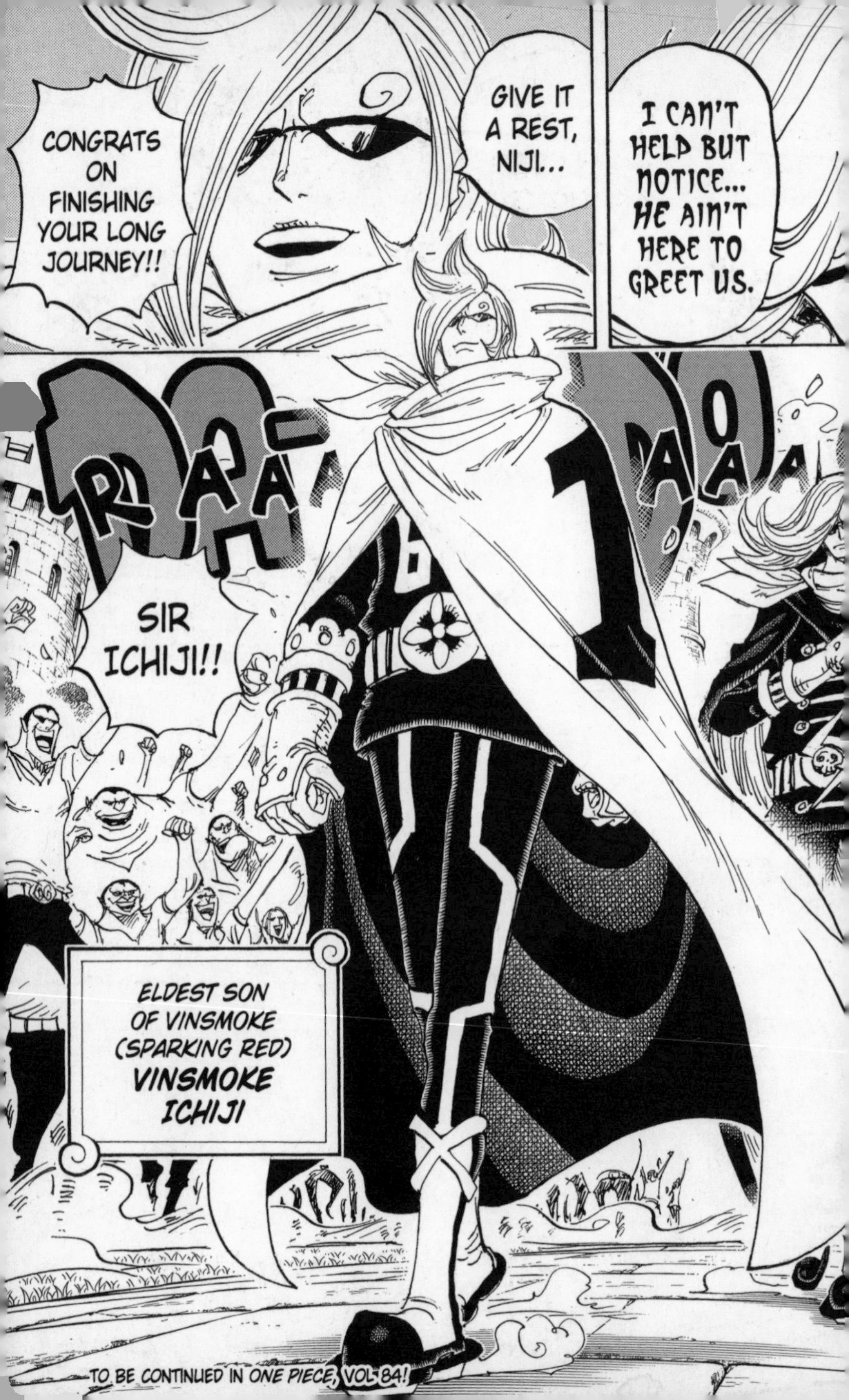
I CAN'T HELP BUT NOTICE... HE AIN'T HERE TO GREET US.
GIVE IT A REST, NIJI...
CONGRATS ON FINISHING YOUR LONG JOURNEY!!
DOOAAAA
ROOAAAAA
SIR ICHIJI!!
ELDEST SON OF VINSMOKE (SPARKING RED) VINSMOKE ICHIJI
TO BE CONTINUED IN ONE PIECE, VOL. 84!

COMING NEXT VOLUME:

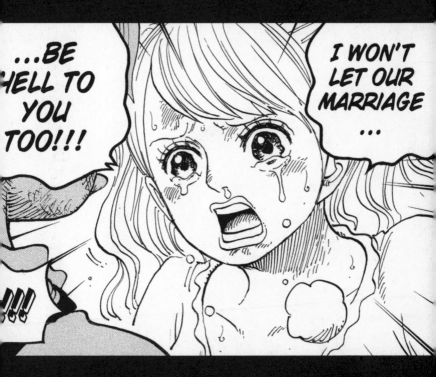

I WON'T LET OUR MARRIAGE ...
...BE HELL TO YOU TOO!!!

Sanji is finally reunited with his family, but unfortunately for him, the Vinsmokes are truly despicable! Luffy and the other Straw Hat members on Whole Cake Island are intent on saving Sanji, but there's a whole lot of sweets standing in their way!

ON SALE NOVEMBER 2017!